Gary Schwartz has been studying and writing about Dutch art for well over half a century. He is the author of several books on Rembrandt, of which *Rembrandt's Universe* was published by Thames & Hudson in 2006. He has also written highly regarded books on Jheronimus Bosch, Pieter Saenredam and Johannes Vermeer, in addition to more than six hundred articles, essays and columns in the press, scholarly journals and proceedings, museum catalogues, and his website, the Schwartzlist. Schwartz has been distinguished with fellowships of the Getty Center and the Netherlands Institute for Advanced Studies, and is the bearer of the Prince Bernhard Cultuurfonds Award for the Humanities.

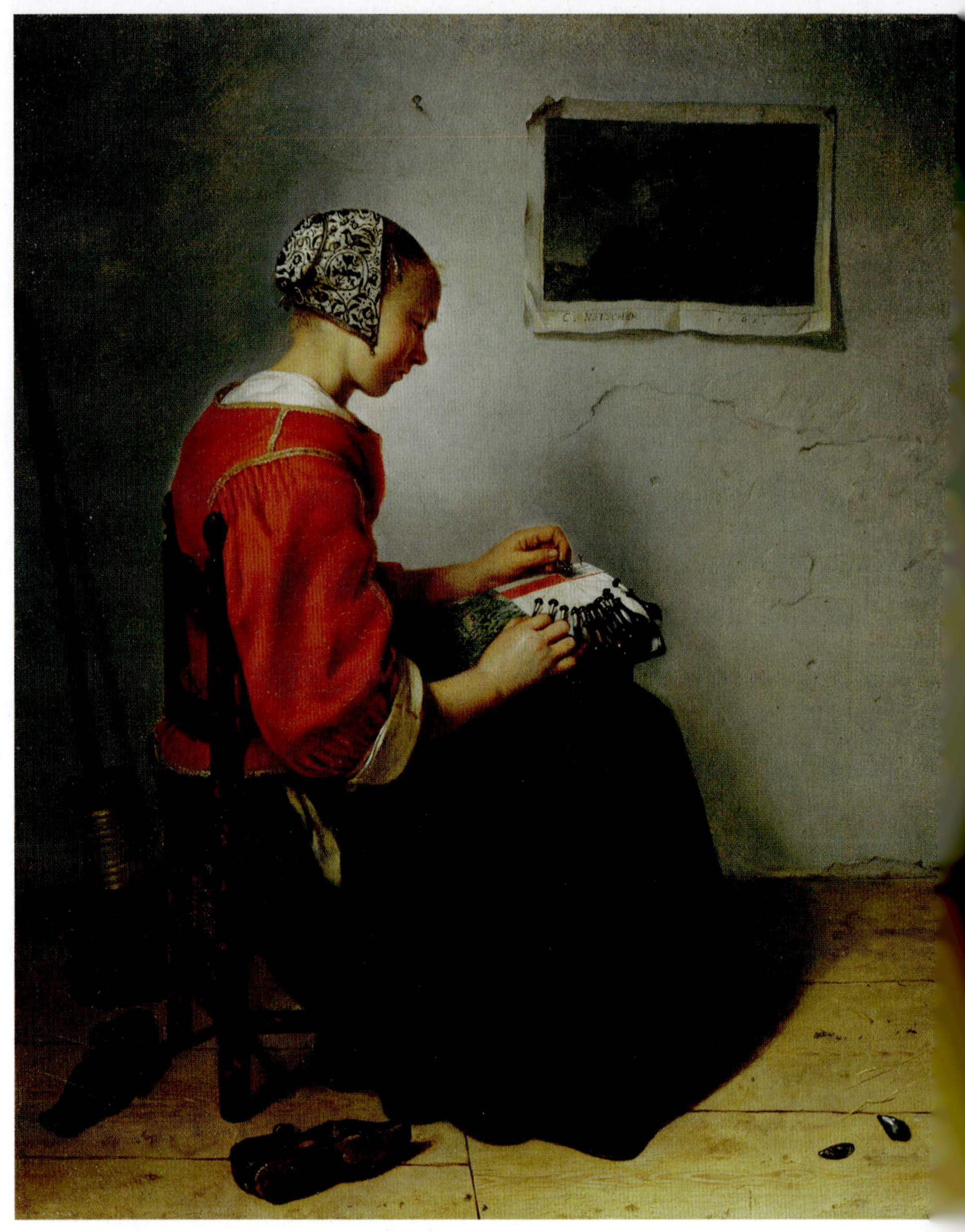

1 Caspar Netscher, *The Lace-maker*, 1662

World of Art

Dutch Painting
Gary Schwartz

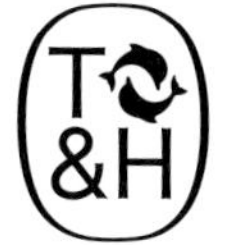
T&H

To the memory of Albert Blankert

The author wishes to express his gratitude to
the Johannes Vermeer Foundation for its support
in the research and writing of this volume.

First published in the United Kingdom in 2026 by
Thames & Hudson Ltd, 6–24 Britannia Street,
London WC1X 9JD

First published in the United States of America in 2026 by
Thames & Hudson Inc., 500 Fifth Avenue, New York,
New York 10110

Art direction and series design by Kummer & Herrman
Layout by Adam Hay Studio

EU Authorized Representative: Interart S.A.R.L.
19 rue Charles Auray, 93500 Pantin, Paris, France
productsafety@thameshudson.co.uk
interart.fr

A CIP catalogue record for this book is available from
the British Library

Library of Congress Control Number 2024950024

ISBN 978-0-500-29774-2
01

Printed and bound in China through Asia Pacific
Offset Ltd

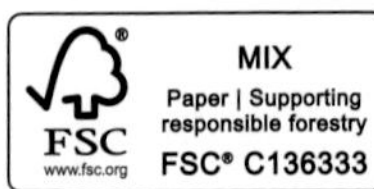

Contents

6　Preface

Chapter 1
8　**Making an Art World**

Chapter 2
44　**Patronage and the Market**

Chapter 3
70　**The City Environments**

Chapter 4
93　**The Female Brush**

Chapter 5
99　**Families and Children in Paintings**

Chapter 6
108　**Dutch Painters Abroad**

Chapter 7
123　**The Grand Traditions**

Chapter 8
142　**Genres and Subgenres**

Chapter 9
243　**Afterword on Attribution**

248　References
258　List of Illustrations
264　Index

Preface

The paintings created in the Dutch Republic in the seventeenth century constitute one of the defining schools of Western art. The image that is conjured up by that phrase is exemplified by superbly crafted genre paintings of domestic interiors; the lives of women and children, peasants and workmen; landscapes under high, cloudy skies reaching as far as the eye can see; streets and markets in cities of legendary cleanliness; portraits of proud burghers, their boards and civic-guard companies; still lifes of flowers and modest meals; pious Protestant church services. The look of the art is accompanied by a certain image of the Dutch state and society. In a revolt that shocked and impressed the rest of Europe, the seven northern provinces of the Netherlands, which from 1482 to 1581 had been part of the Habsburg Empire, had liberated themselves in a war that lasted eighty years, from 1568 to 1648, and built a self-governing republic guided by a commitment to Calvinism and down-to-earth business interests. The image is set off against the aristocratic and Catholic art and society of the Southern Netherlands, which continued to be governed by the Spanish Habsburgs.

In later centuries, the link between the history of the Netherlands and its art resonated deeply, for different reasons. In the early nineteenth century, the German philosopher, Georg Wilhelm Friedrich Hegel, assigned to Dutch genre painting a crucial place not only in European art history, but also in the evolution of humanity. Hegel argued that this style could only have emerged in a nation that had freed itself from religious and political subjugation, thereby reflecting and actually contributing to the liberation of humankind. In 1941, during the German occupation of his country, the director of The Hague's Gemeentemuseum, Gerhardus Knuttel, wrote movingly about the innate honesty of Dutch art. He saw in it an 'inborn awareness that it is not outward display but the acceptance of the things of this world in their true guise that is the most pious approach, leading to total honesty in representation, even to the point of asceticism.' Art that 'idealizes form or appearance, to show things prettier than they are', is 'alien to the Dutch spirit', even when it is made by Dutch artists.

The climate in which I studied Dutch art – in American universities during the 1950s and 60s, and in the Netherlands from 1965 onwards – felt quite different. Knuttel's belief that Dutch artists were uniquely endowed by their national character with 'total honesty in representation' no longer rang true to me. I was committed to the view that artworks were not expressions of inherent national traits but products of cultures in constant flux. The further I went, the more aware I became that Dutch paintings exist within overlapping local, national, pan-Netherlandish and European contexts, and that their meanings evolve not only as objects of philosophical reflection and nationalist attachment, but also as objects of delight, study and investment. Dutch painting – or should I say all art? – resists the attempt to enclose it in strict frameworks or divide it into mutually exclusive categories. In keeping with that view, this book features a broad range of Dutch painting traditions. In this I was inspired by my late friend and colleague, Albert Blankert (1940–2022). The inclusive approach that I share with Blankert leaves room for special appreciation of the qualities cherished by Hegel and Knuttel, though not as a uniquely Dutch, superior system of values.

As the reader will see, this book is more about the subjects that painters thought fit to depict, their interaction with the world around them, and the posterity of their creations than in their techniques and styles. I have set out to tell the most engaging and instructive things that I have found out about Dutch painting. Conciseness is called for, but certain biographies, iconographies, historical backgrounds, provenances and study in scholarship are given more extensive treatment than others.

Chapter 1
Making an Art World

Painters of the Seventeen Provinces

One of the distinctions in Dutch art that has probably been overdrawn is that between the art of the Northern and Southern Netherlands. It was not until the nineteenth century, as the countries of Europe were seized with nationalistic sentiments, that writers on the art of the Low Countries began to see essential differences between Dutch and Belgian or Flemish art. No one in the seventeenth century thought in such terms. This even extended to the shape of the countries themselves. For centuries after north and south became politically divided, maps of the Low Countries continued to show them as the Seventeen Provinces, with no boundary indicated between the Spanish Netherlands in the south (Flanders for short) and the Republic of the Seven United Netherlands in the north (Holland). In the map illustrated opposite, the identity of the Low Countries is evoked in vignettes of the cities of the north (right) and south (left), peopled by burghers in the upper margin and peasants in the lower, flanking the coats of arms of all seventeen provinces.

While this book is devoted to the art of the northern provinces only, we will see that a good number of the artists represented were themselves born in the south and brought the fruits of their training to the north. Specialities in seascape and landscape, still life and merry companies were imports. The continental border of the Alps was also readily passed by Dutch painters, some of whom participated fully in the studios and patronage powerhouses of Italy.

Another sense in which our picture of what is typically Dutch is skewed has to do with chronology. The domestic interior did not come into its own until after 1650. A telling example is found

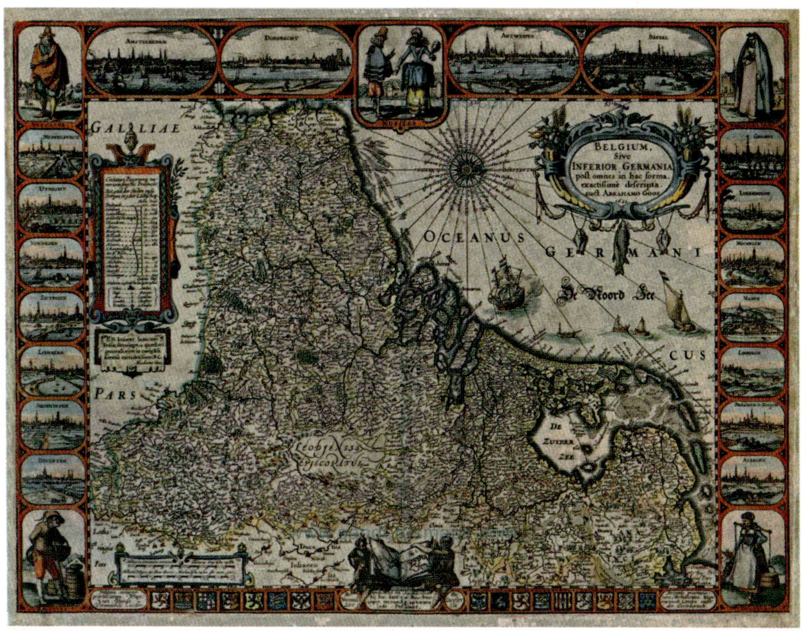

2 Abraham Goos, map of the seventeen provinces of Southern and Northern Netherlands, with north to the right, Amsterdam 1621

in the paintings of Pieter de Hooch. While the Eighty Years' War was still in progress, he painted soldiers enjoying drinks in the courtyards and salons of his own city, Delft, served by housemaids who sometimes drank with them. These paintings are far less well known than the mothers and children of which he made a popular speciality after the mid-century. In this book, space is made for as much of the full panoply of Dutch painting as can be offered, including work by little-known masters and less popular periods. As a result, fewer familiar masterpieces are illustrated and discussed than one might expect. In defence of this choice, let it be said that illustrations of the main paintings of Rembrandt, Vermeer and Frans Hals are easily found elsewhere. The reader is invited to become acquainted with the impressively wide range of subjects and styles created by what was the largest school of painters in the Europe of its time.

Migration from South to North

In the course of the sixteenth century, when Europe was shaken to its core by the Reformation, the group most directly affected, after people of the church, were artists, the artists of the Netherlands above all. For followers of the Protestant

reformers, one aspect of Catholicism to which they most
strongly objected was the devotion paid by worshippers to
statues and paintings of religious persons and themes. In their
eyes, Madonnas and images of Jesus and the saints in churches
were a pernicious form of idolatry that kept believers from
fulfilling true faith in God. In 1566, adherents of one of the
stricter Protestant churches, Calvinism, gave violent expression
to their rejection of images by smashing them in an outbreak of
iconoclastic fury. This affected artists in more ways than one.
The work they had delivered to churches was destroyed, they lost
the patronage of the religious establishment, and the subjects
they were trained to paint had been cancelled.

In the Northern Netherlands, Calvinism became the official
religion of the government, but in Flanders, Catholics regained
the upper hand and persecuted Protestants. Artists who had
gone over to Protestantism were forced to flee their country.
Economic circumstances played a role as well. In 1589, the Dutch
closed the mouth of the Scheldt River, cutting off the city of
Antwerp, the financial heart of the country, from the sea, with
devastating effects on the livelihoods of Flemings. Most of these
refugees, some of whom were Catholic, ended up in the cities of
the newly founded Dutch Republic, where they enriched cultural
and artistic life beyond measure. Mutual ties between artists on
either side of the border did not depend on emigration alone.
Border crossings went on throughout the seventeenth century,
and writings on Netherlandish art drew no distinction, until the
mid-nineteenth century, between Dutch and Flemish artists.

Two of the most important of these immigrants were Karel
van Mander and David Vinckboons. At the age of thirty-five, in
1583, van Mander settled in Haarlem, where he participated in
the formation of an informal academy for teaching and thinking
about art and portraying nude models. In 1602, towards the
end of his life, he painted a Bible story that reflects on his
own Protestant faith, in the Mennonite church. It shows the
Israelites in the desert in the time when their leader Moses was
on Mount Sinai, receiving the law from the Lord. In his absence,
they reverted to idol worship, casting a statue of a golden calf
that they worshipped as a god. Coming from Karel van Mander,
this can be read as a denunciation of Catholic practice. But van
Mander was also appalled by iconoclasm.

David Vinckboons was ten years old when in 1586 his family
fled Flanders for the Dutch Republic. First they sought refuge in
Middelburg, the closest city across the border, but in 1591 they
moved to Amsterdam, where David lived for the rest of his life.
His painting of a somewhat raucous country fair is in the spirit
of the great Antwerp master Pieter Bruegel (1526–69), whose

4

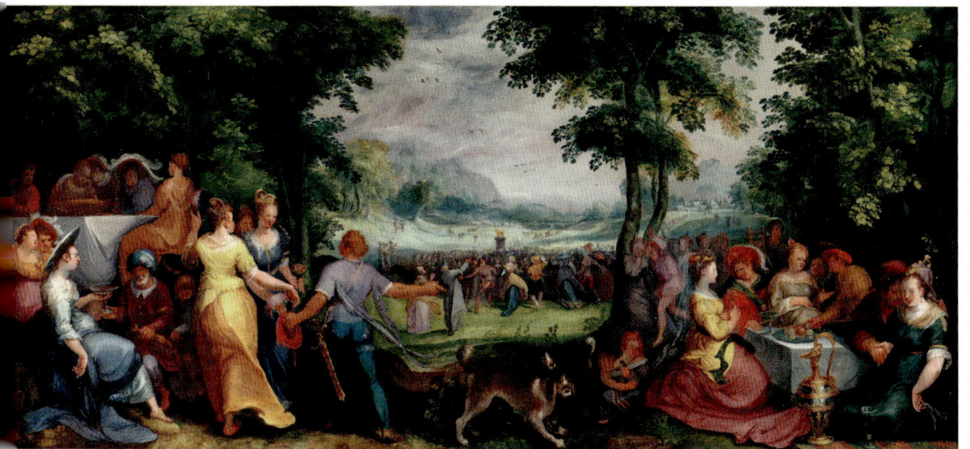

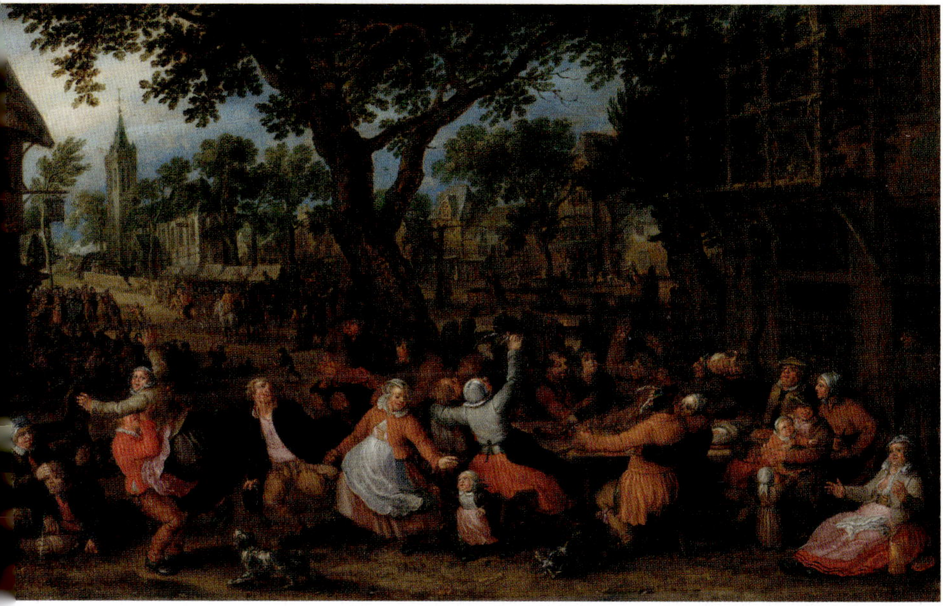

3 TOP Karel van Mander, *Dance Around the Golden Calf*, 1602
4 ABOVE David Vinckboons, *A Country Fair*, 1629

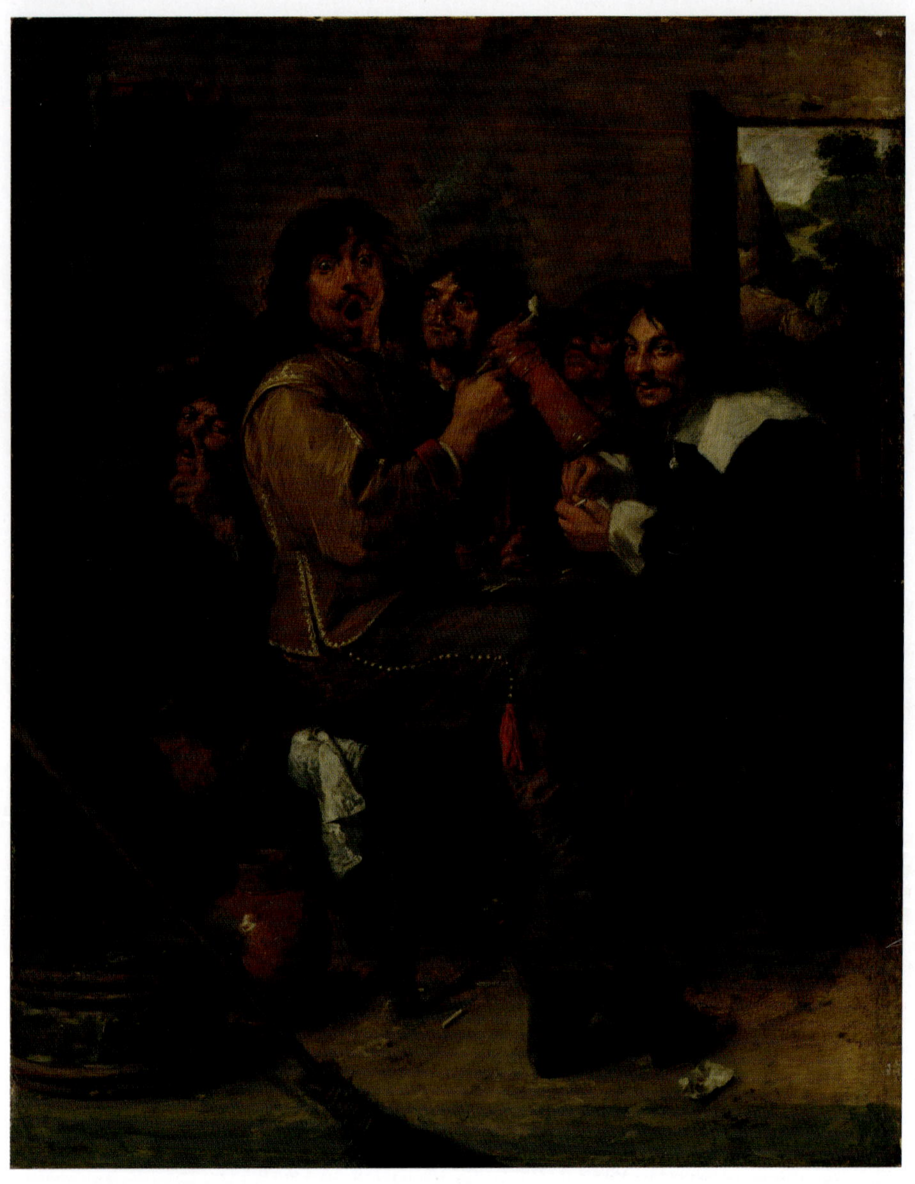

5 Adriaen Brouwer, *Self-portrait Among Artist Friends, known as 'The Smokers'*, c. 1636

inspiration, through prints as well as paintings, was inescapable for all Netherlandish artists. One feature apparent in these compositions is the extensiveness of detail. Viewers of the time would have relished going through the scenes, paying leisurely attention to the action and to how it was depicted, in lively discussion with others, especially the owners. A biography of Karel van Mander from 1617 devotes attention to his *Dance Around the Golden Calf*, telling us that the brightly coloured women in the foreground are Moabite strumpets who are being lured by the men – Israelites who have had too much to drink.

The children of both these immigrant artists, who came from cultivated backgrounds, pursued careers in the arts. Those of van Mander became painters, while Vinckboons became the founder of what has been called the family 'art factory', with one son becoming a painter, another a famous architect and three cartographer-engravers.

South to north migration was not the only way in which Flemish and Dutch artists became close colleagues. A number of artists worked on both sides of the border, even during the Eighty Years' War. Prominent among them was Adriaen Brouwer. A native of the Flemish city of Oudenaarde, brought up in Gouda, in the province of Holland, he was a prominent figure in both Haarlem in the north and Antwerp in the south. He left us delightful pictorial evidence of a key moment in the mid-1630s when two Dutch painters (Jan Davidsz de Heem and Jan Lievens) and three Flemish colleagues (Brouwer, Joos van Craesbeeck and Jan Cossiers) got together for a drink and a smoke. This constellation has a wealth of associations. In 1635 de Heem and Lievens, having moved to Antwerp from the north, were registered in its guild of St Luke for artists. Brouwer himself was admitted that year to the chamber of rhetoric De Violieren, a literary adjunct to the St Luke guild. In 1662 the cataloguer of the collection to which the painting belonged noted (in Latin): 'Brouwer shows himself with his drinking companions amidst the pestiferous stench of tobacco.' The unpretentiousness of the scene, the willingness of the friends to let down their hair and own up to their self-indulgence was appreciated and admired from the start. Brouwer's work was collected by the far-from-unpretentious master Peter Paul Rubens (1577–1640), who regretted that the decorum expected of him prevented him depicting emotions so directly.

Shaping a Canon, Setting Terms: Karel van Mander

Karel van Mander's significance for the history of Dutch painting goes far further than his production as a painter. The man was a phenomenon. As a lifelong participant in the artistic-literary rhetorical societies to which the cultural elite of Dutch cities belonged, he wrote and directed the moralizing entertainments that they staged. His religious poetry was published and republished after his death. Mainly, however, he was the author of the most influential book on art ever written in Dutch, *Het Schilder-boeck, The Book of the Painter*.

The publication has six parts. It opens with the fourteen chapters of *Foundation of the Noble, Liberal Art of Painting*, directed at 'youths avid to learn'. In strictly rhymed and metrical eight-line stanzas, the *Foundation* covers more than six hundred theoretical, practical and ethical issues for the young painter to learn about. The stanzas are numbered. The shortest, with fourteen stanzas, is 'On the Sorting and Arrangement of Pigments', the longest, with eighty-eight, is 'On the Composition and Invention of Histories' – that is, narrative subjects. Nothing like the *Foundation* was available to young artists who did not read Dutch.

Following are three sections with biographies of the 'Renowned, Illustrious Painters' of classical antiquity, Italy and the Netherlands. As with Vasari's *Lives of the Artists*, parts of which van Mander translated in the *Schilder-boeck*, the lives of the 'Netherlandish and German Painters' established a canon of excellence for early Netherlandish painting and provided a pedigree for their followers to be proud of. A leitmotiv of the lives is the admiration bestowed on painters by rulers and other powerful patrons, and how richly they were rewarded for their work. This was a prodding hint to governments and art lovers of his own time, urging them to live up to the standards of their forebears. In a time and place when traditional patronage from church and court had fallen away, this message was especially vital.

The last two sections of *The Book of the Painter* provide references to the mythological subjects with which painters could show off their mastery of the allusions that were most highly prized by sophisticated buyers. First comes a prose digest of the fifteen books of Ovid's long poem, *Metamorphoses*, the source of nearly all the stories about ancient gods that found their way into art. It is followed by five short 'books' on the 'Depiction of Figures', an abbreviated lexicon of emblematic motifs. The mere existence of *The Book of the Painter*, in all its richness, gave fledgling Netherlandish artists an advantage enjoyed by none of their European peers.

Becoming a Painter: The Studio

In the prologue to the *Foundation of the Noble, Liberal Art of Painting*, Karel van Mander sketches the way Dutch youngsters might become painters. Their desire to make art would surface early, when they filled their notebooks with drawings of figures, ships and animals instead of their school lessons, impressing their parents with their inborn talent. All well and good, van Mander says, but he emphasizes the difficulty of becoming a *good* artist. He writes verse after verse warning such children and their parents not to take it for granted they would become masters of the art, when only one in a hundred makes the grade. He was exaggerating. For one thing, more than one in a hundred painters, perhaps even a majority, trained their children in the art, without many of them falling out of the boat.

Dutch schools did not offer art education. The only place to acquire the necessary training was the studio of an established master, first as a paying pupil, then, given the ability, as an assistant who was paid for his work. Master painters had to be members of a city guild, which laid down certain rules about administrative matters, such as the number of pupils a master could take on (usually no more than three), the duration of tutelage (two to four years), and the conditions governing the way an apprentice left his master's studio. Pupils would learn about materials and techniques, copy compositions by their masters and others, and receive instruction in the use of colour, composition, perspective and iconography. The first style they would learn would be that of the master, and it would be a matter of pride if they could channel it well enough for a visiting client to take a student's work for the master's. Children started on this training in the early to mid-teens. Those who stuck with it were ready to become registered masters by the age of twenty. They would then have to join a guild, possibly submit a masterwork, and start paying dues.

While contemporary depictions of painters' workshops cannot be taken at face value, they nonetheless reveal something about how artists saw themselves. Three examples take us from a low- to middle- to a high-class painter. In a rather scruffy space, the floor littered with trash, where Adriaen van Ostade's artist is at work, a young apprentice is grinding pigments and an older one is preparing a palette. Why he should be doing that while the painter must already have a palette in hand tells us something interesting. The pigments with which painters worked had such different properties that separate, small palettes were used, each with mutually compatible materials. A notch up from Adriaen van Ostade's painter's studio is that in a bourgeois interior by Jan Miense Molenaer. The well-dressed painter and his models are taking a breather from work on a fun-filled genre scene of a

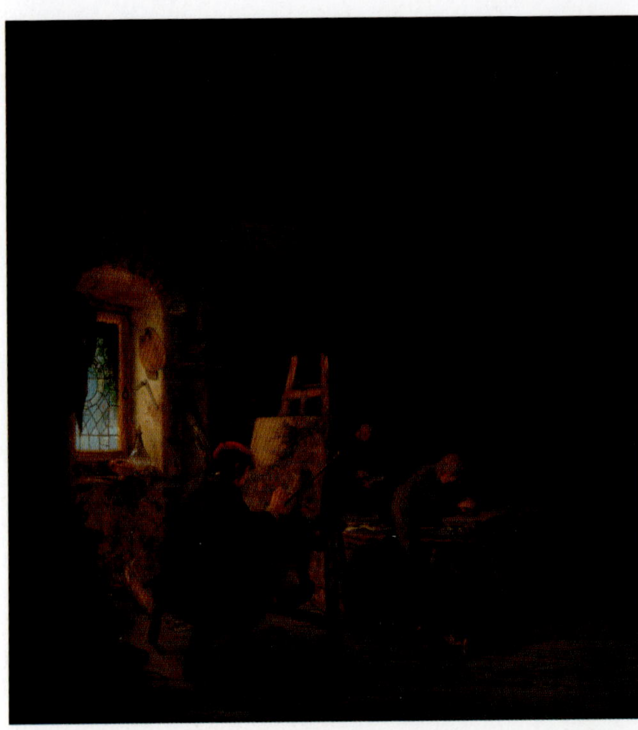

6 LEFT Adriaen van
Ostade, *A Modest
Painter's Studio*,
c. 1647–50
7 BELOW Jan Miense
Molenaer, *The Painter's
Workshop*, 1631
8 OPPOSITE Michael
Sweerts, *An Artist's
Studio*, 1652

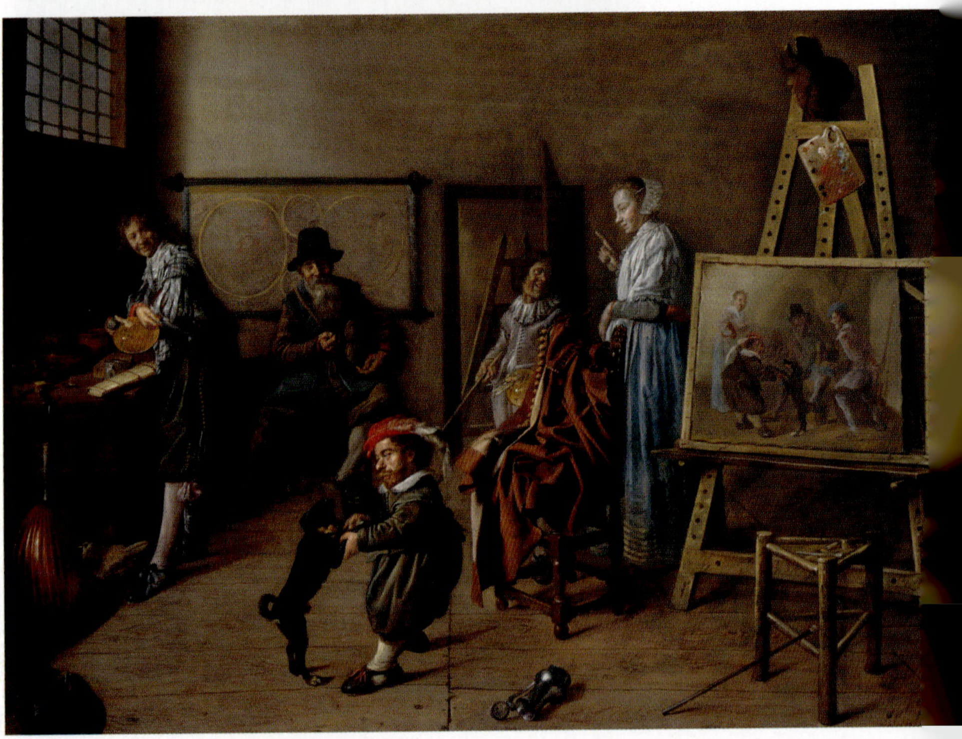

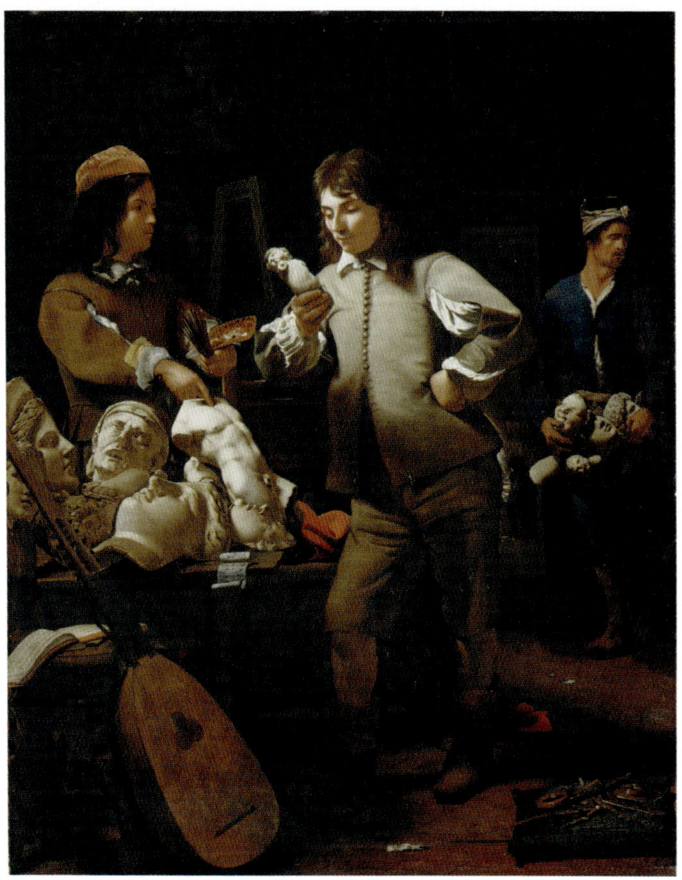

dwarf dancing with a dog to the music of a hurdy-gurdy. The subject is infectious: during their break the old man is grinding his instrument for real and the dwarf is playing with the dog.

The easel of both painters is of a standard model. Van Ostade's painter is working on a wooden panel and Molenaer's on a stretched canvas, which cost more. The rectangular palette hanging from the latter's easel has pigments that look like red lake, lead white and perhaps an umber. Attributes attesting to education are absent in the van Ostade, and in the Molenaer are limited to a world map on the wall and a lute on the floor. The step up to Michael Sweerts's atelier is high indeed. In a painting inscribed *Michael Sweerts | fecit | Roma | A.D. 1652*, a painter is pointing out to his visitor that the small fragment he is holding, a limbless Cupid, belongs, together with the torso on the chest, to a dismembered cast after a bronze sculpture of Apollo and

Cupid by the Flemish sculptor, François Duquesnoy (1597–1643). Other sculptures in the studio have been identified as casts or copies of Hellenistic and Roman antiquities, some owned by Sweerts's patron, the papal nephew Camillo Pamphili. Sweerts belonged to the inner circle of artists and antiquaries in Rome and lived up to their level of cultural sophistication, a status he lends to his painter. The lute on the ground demands musicianship. Using the tools on the cushion in the right foreground calls for technical knowhow, and the books on a shelf in the background attest to a degree of learning. The painter may look like a craftsman, but Sweerts gives him the attributes of an educated intellectual, a figure to whom patricians on the grand tour, which his visitor looks like, can turn for instruction.

Because he has never become famous, Michael Sweerts's superb art has remained available for discovery by aesthetically sensitive non-art historians. At exhibitions, visitors can find themselves suddenly captivated by one of his paintings.

	1601–10	1611–20	1621–30	1631–40	1641–50	1651–60	1661–70	Total
Northern Netherlands	140	150	190	140	90	75	40	825
Italy	110	95	85	90	75	105	100	660
France	55	65	55	70	65	75	30	415
Germany	30	25	45	40	35	55	50	280
Other	25	25	40	20	35	55	60	260
Southern Netherlands	45	60	50	40	15	25	20	255
Great Britain	15	25	20	25	35	25	20	165
Spain	25	25	20	25	20	15	10	140
Total	445	470	505	450	370	430	330	3,000

Table 1 3,000 artists from the main schools of European art, tabulated decade for decade by year of birth. The sample, from the Getty Union List of Artist Names, is only a fraction of the total and may not be optimally representative, but the ratios may be taken to be reliably indicative.

The population of the Dutch Republic in the seventeenth century averaged about two million, some 2.6 percent of the seventy-five million people in Europe. The representation of Dutch artists, mainly painters, among all the artists of Europe was no less than 27.5 percent. A lot more Dutch parents were sending their children to learn to be painters than van Mander, protective of the quality of their creations, would have liked. The skyline of the European populace of professional artists shows how exceptional the Northern Netherlands was (Table 1). The seventeenth century is sometimes called the Age of Patronage. But the Barberini, Borghese and Chigi popes and princes, the Bourbon kings of France, the late Medici in Florence, William and Mary in Restoration England made do with about the same number of artists throughout the century. In the Dutch Republic, where such patronage was minimal, the numbers shifted wildly. After a rise of 35 percent in the artist population between roughly 1620 and 1650, over the next forty years the number of Dutch painters declined by some 80 percent. The most important factors in this unique development were surely the economy and the division of wealth. Until 1650, the Dutch were the dominant economy in Europe and the leading colonial power; they lost this status following three sea wars with Britain (1652–54; 1665–67; 1672–74) and an invasion on land by France, Münster and Cologne in 1672. The considerable wealth that remained was evermore concentrated in the hands of oligarchs who chose increasingly to decorate their interiors with murals and gold leather rather than easel paintings. The downturn in fortune did not have an immediately negative effect on Dutch painting. In the 1650s, a vast cohort of highly trained painters, facing a shrinking market, found themselves in competition with each other. This induced them to do their very best, upping their production in painting existing genres, and diversifying into specialities to which they could attach their names.

* * *

The study of the volume of artistic production was revolutionized in the 1980s when economic historians turned their attention to it. While art historians had tended to assume that not many more paintings had been made than the 650,000 registered in the RKD (Netherlands Institute for Art History), the economic historians Ad van der Woude and Jan de Vries shattered that naive notion and argued persuasively that the real number was at least ten times as high, and probably higher, with shockingly high rates of loss. This subverted a lot of received ideas, and is still being digested.

The immense productivity and rivalry between good masters was all to the benefit of posterity, but the situation was devastating for painters. Rembrandt went into bankruptcy in Amsterdam in 1656, Frans Hals had to apply to the township of Haarlem for welfare in 1662, and Johannes Vermeer died in Delft in 1675 – 'of a frenzy', as his widow told the court, since he was unable to sell either his own paintings or those of artists he dealt in. Painting in the Netherlands never regained its

leading position as a European school, and it is no wonder that
the period when it did have that status was looked upon as a
Golden Age. (The use of that term is now criticized, and will be
avoided here, as being insensitive to the widespread poverty in
the country, including the misery of painters themselves, and
the considerable extent to which wealth in the Netherlands
was amassed through colonial dominance, the enslavement
of Africans and Asians, and profits from the slave trade.)

Materials and Manufacture

Making a professional picture is a manufacturing as well as an
intellectual and creative process. Much as writers on art like
Karel van Mander emphasize the latter, classifying painting
among the liberal arts, it also belongs to the mechanical
arts. The materials and techniques involved are written up in
manuals that also describe how to make furniture, weapons
and hand tools.

Nearly all the paintings in this book are easel paintings
on panels (the preferred wood was Baltic oak) or canvas.
Both materials were widely available in the shipbuilding
Netherlands. The surface of the support would be smoothed
over with a ground layer, a composite that would usually
contain lead white, sourced mainly from England. As has
recently been discovered, the makeup of the lead changed
during periods when the Netherlands was at war with England,
allowing for more refined datings of some paintings. A
smaller number of paintings were made on copper and even
fewer behind glass. The composition would be laid down in a
monochrome medium, called underpainting or dead-colouring.
This would be done in a cheap substance like raw umber,
a mining product with a mixture of metals and oxides. The
coloured pigments for the painting itself were mainly metallic
oxides, with some organic materials such as lakes. They would
be bound together by a medium like linseed oil. To give a
painting a bright finish, it would be covered with varnish.

Over the past half-century, the field of conservation science
has been taken more and more seriously by museums.
Art historians have been challenged by initiatives such as the
Rembrandt Research Project to pay closer attention to the
physical properties of artworks. Examination techniques
are steadily improving, making art historians take account of
facts that do not always accord with their expectations. The
assignment of authorship by personal connoisseurship faces
increasing criticism. Collaboration between scholars and
scientists can lead to new, more evidence-based insights into
the creation of historical art.

Study in archives, libraries and labs is enriching our understanding of what took place in artists' studios. Anna Tummers, in her book *The Eye of the Connoisseur*, has shown that the buyers of Dutch paintings in the seventeenth century entertained fairly relaxed and graduated standards of quality and evaluation. That is hard to reconcile with the present-day aggrandisement of paintings as unquestioned original creations by a venerated master, which command astronomically higher prices than paintings seen as workshop productions, no matter what their quality. Moreover, Dutch theorists, including those who were artists themselves, espoused a principle that they regarded as indispensable to good art. The word they used was *houding*, which referred to harmony between all the elements of a painting – light and colour as well as the evocation of space and the scale of figures, as discussed by Paul Taylor in his article 'The Concept of Houding in Dutch Art theory'. This realization sharpens our own eye for what went into a Dutch painting.

* * *

Once a painter had learned the craft, there were more ways to employ it than making easel paintings. The mansions of wealthy patrons were increasingly decorated with wall and ceiling paintings, demanding the acquisition of sophisticated techniques for the way space and light were treated. Painters were called upon to paint memorial escutcheons in churches, family trees and coats of arms. These would not be signed, and few have been attributed to a specific master. But as we know from a letter of Pieter Saenredam, one of the most refined artists of the century, he did not think himself too superior to paint, for the prince of Orange, a family tree of the Hohenzollern electors of Brandenburg to whom he was related. Saenredam might have thought it beneath him to paint signboards for shops and taverns, but other painters did not. Painters would also work on other artistic creations that are not covered in this book, such as tapestries, damasks, manuscript illumination and stained-glass windows. The conventional designation 'Dutch painting' is too contained a concept for all the ways that Dutch painters exercised their talents.

One of those applications of artistic skill was miniature portraiture, which was practised not by specialists, but by a small number of painters alongside their more standard production. One charming example is a pair of miniatures by Gerrit Lundens. These unassuming portraits, dated 1650 and identified by inscription as depicting a fifty-year-old woman

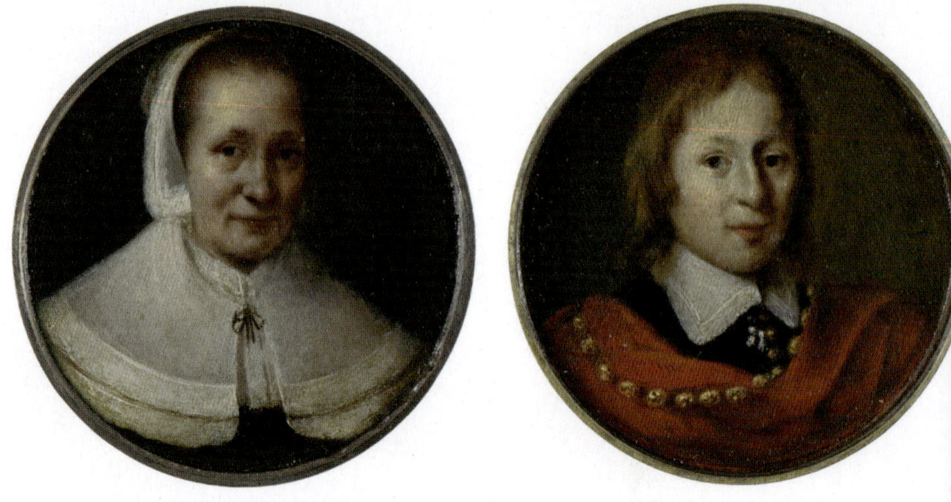

9, 10 Gerrit Lundens, *Miniature Portraits of a Fifty-year-old Woman and a Fifteen-year-old Boy*, 1650

and a fifteen-year-old boy, are painted on the inside surfaces of two different medals that were sliced in half and fitted to click together. The woman's portrait is inserted into a hollowed-out silver medal commemorating the victory of the States Army over the Spanish in Nieuwpoort, Flanders, in July 1600. The year is included in the image. By using a medal dated 1600 in the year 1650 to paint a woman who turned fifty that year, the artist is celebrating her jubilee year. The boy's portrait is inserted into a *riksdaler*, a Swedish coin with an image of King Gustav II Adolf (1594–1632). The two portraits, joined in one, are the most intimate paintings imaginable, accessible only to the owner.

Like many Dutch artists of modest talent and insufficient patronage, Gerrit Lundens cobbled together a living with any kind of work he could get. Painting peasant life, seductions, portraits – and a famous copy after Rembrandt's *Night Watch* – was only one of his livelihoods. He also ran an inn and sold wine. None of this saved him from going bankrupt in 1671, with nearly nothing to his name.

Drawings, Prints, Paintings

At the same time, Dutch painting cannot be distinguished unequivocally from other kinds of art. Paintings often share their composition with preparatory drawings and prints that are published with credit to the painter as 'inventor'. The overlap of media could go very far. The remarkable Hercules Segers was said by his contemporaries to print paintings,

11

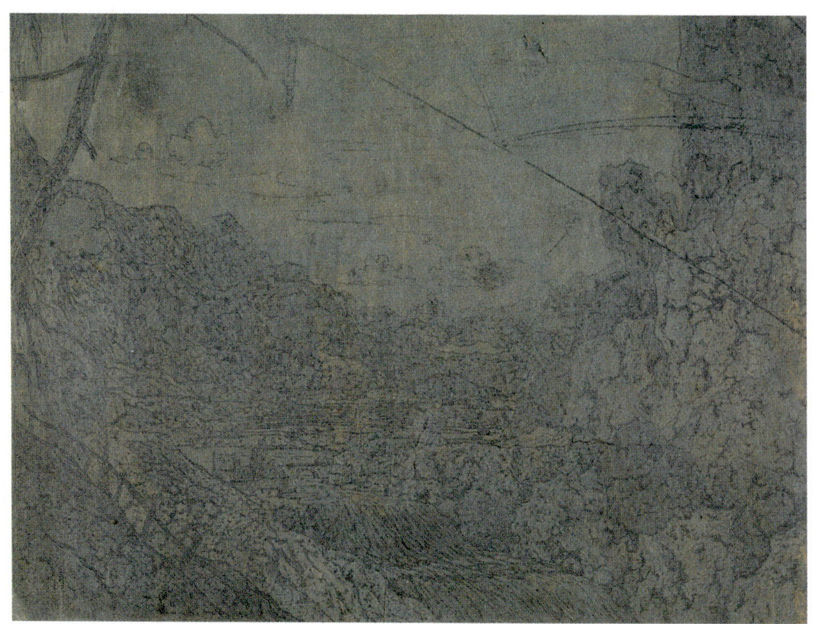

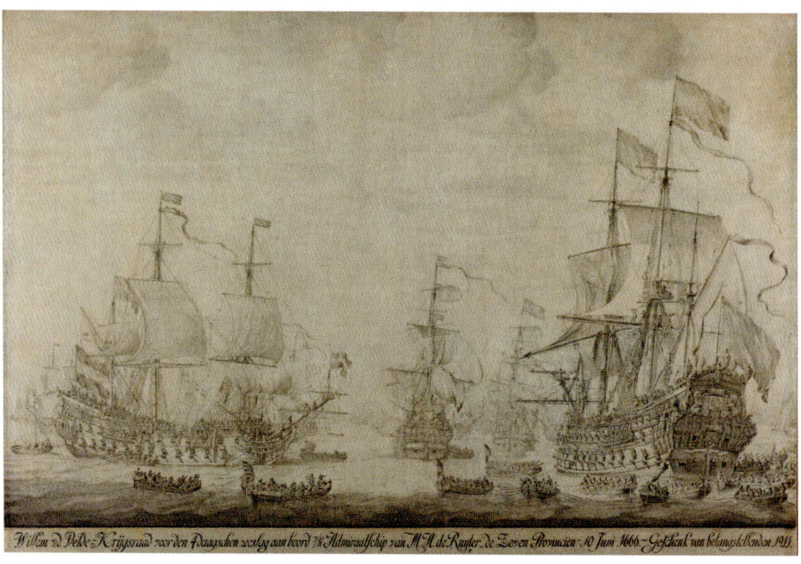

11 TOP Hercules Segers, *Landscape with a Waterfall, First Version*, c. 1627
12 ABOVE Willem van de Velde the Elder, *Council of War Aboard 'The Seven Provinces', the Flagship of Michiel Adriaensz de Ruyter, 10 June 1666, Preceding the Four Days' Battle: Episode from the Second Anglo-Dutch War, 1666–93*

while there are paintings by Willem van de Velde the Elder that look like prints. The careers of the two could not have been more different. Segers struggled, unsuccessfully, to keep body and soul together in an Amsterdam attic, while van de Velde and his son were provided by King Charles II with studios in the Queen's House in Greenwich, London, now part of the National Maritime Museum. Before Segers and van de Velde, Hendrick Goltzius ushered in the seventeenth century with a mixed-media work that defies any notion – mainly a twentieth-century notion, be it said – that works of art should obey the mandates of their medium. These three men were exceptional personalities. By far the largest number of Dutch painters were conventional craftworkers who were content to practise what they had been taught.

The Europeanness of Dutch Art
Another of the distinguishing features of Dutch painting that calls for qualification is its 'Dutchness'. The artists of the Netherlands participated fully in European artistic and cultural

13 Gabriël Metsu, *Portrait of the Family of Jan Jacobsz Hinlopen and Leonora Huydecoper*, 1663

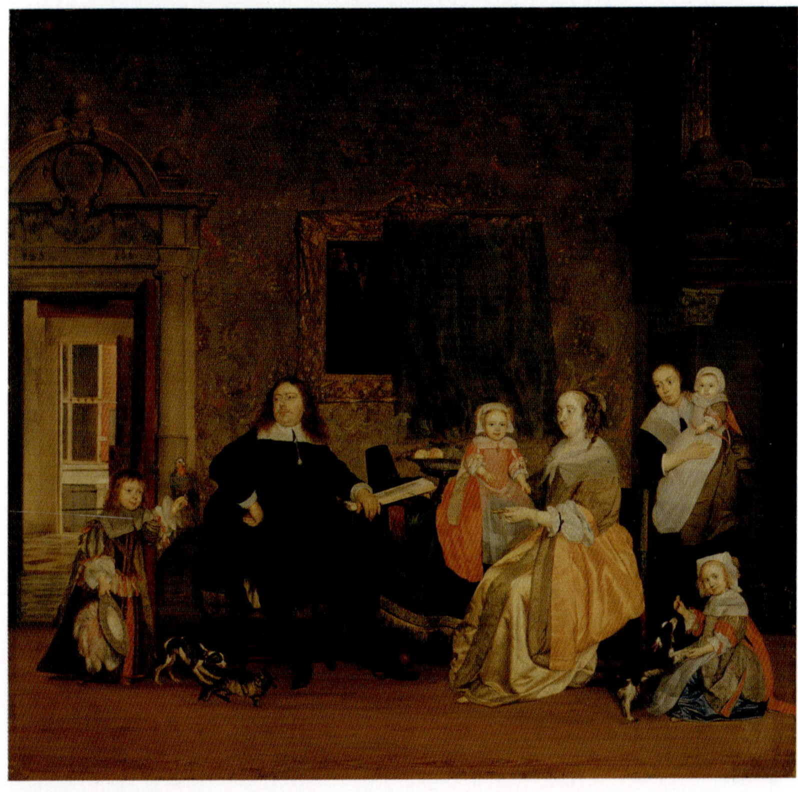

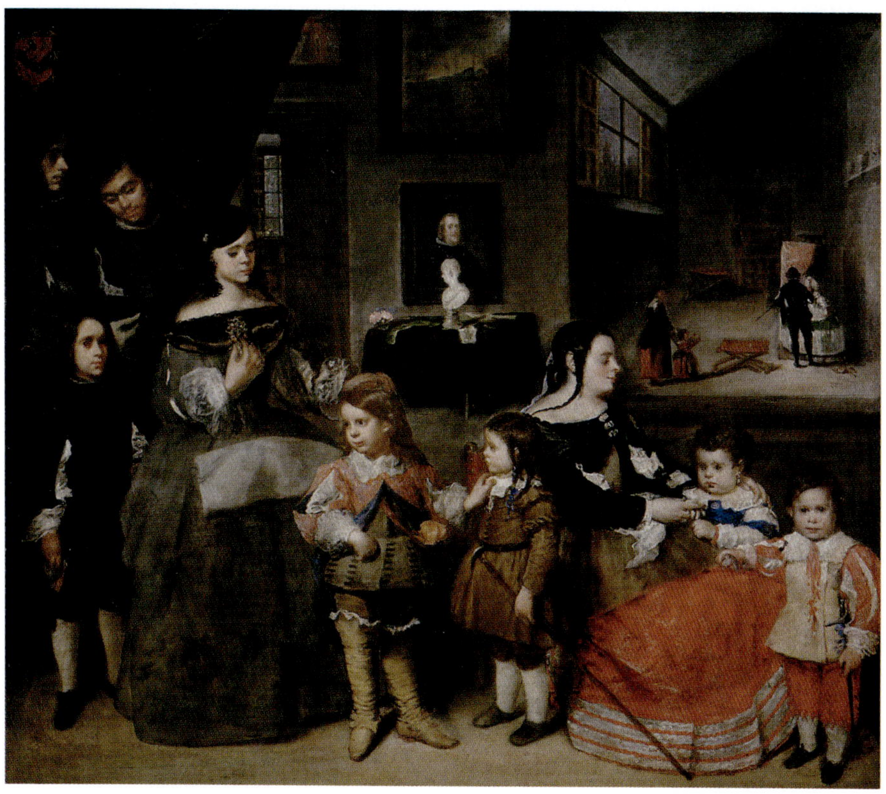

14 Juan Bautista Martinez del Mazo, *Family of the Artist, c. 1664–65*

13   developments. A 'typically Dutch' painting such as Gabriël
      Metsu's group portrait of a distinguished Amsterdam family,
      for example, has a close equivalent in a portrait of his own
14   family by the Madrid painter, Juan Bautista Martinez del Mazo
      (a son-in-law of Velázquez). This puts the Metsu at one remove
      from Velázquez's immortal masterpiece *Las Meninas*, a portrait
      of the Spanish Infanta and her entourage that inspired Mazo.
      This example is more typical than exceptional. In every branch
      of painting but one, we find canvases that have seriously been
      assigned to artists from other countries and schools. (For the
      exception, civic guard group portraits, see pp. 36, 38, 153–56.)

      The permeability of the boundary between Dutch art and
      that of other schools is reflected in the mobility of Dutch artists
      around Europe and their acceptance wherever they went. This
      phenomenon was written up in an influential book of 1942 by
      the eminent art historian Horst Gerson. His work was expanded
      on by the RKD, who noted that no fewer than 838 Dutch and

Flemish artists worked in Britain, for example. In countries
with few artists of their own, as in most of north and east
Europe, Netherlandish artists produced the bulk of the work,
setting a model for what then became the national school.
This was as true in printmaking, sculpture and architecture
as in painting.

Frames and Contexts

Most Dutch paintings were portable, made for the open market
or for portrait sitters and their families. However, some major
works were made for specific locations or provided with custom
frames that became part of a very specific meaning. Two
examples shown here were made for the most famous men in
the country.

Had you asked an art-world insider in the Netherlands in
1650 who was the most prominent painter in the Republic, the
answer would have been Jacques (Jacob) Jordaens (1593–1678).
This Flemish master had been brought from Antwerp to The
Hague to paint the main scene in the most glamorous ensemble
of the time. It was a room in a small country palace dedicated
to the memory of Frederik Hendrik, the prince of Orange and
as 'stadholder' (deputy in charge) the most important official in
the country. The title originally referred to the person exercising
power for the Habsburg ruler of the Netherlands, but after the
country overthrew that rule, the title was maintained for the
commander-in-chief of the armed forces.

The palace, Huis ten Bosch (House in the Woods), was first
intended as a retreat for Frederik Hendrik and his wife Amalia
van Solms. When Frederik Hendrik died unexpectedly in 1647,
Amalia revised her plans for the estate, to adorn it with
paintings glorifying her late husband, in a centralized space
called the Oranjezaal, the Hall of [the House of] Orange. With
the end of the Eighty Years' War in 1648, it became possible
to bring artists from the Southern Netherlands to the north,
and the organizers of the Oranjezaal did just that. They
commissioned six painters from the south (labeled Brabanders,
from the cities of Brabant) and six from the north (Hollanders)
to paint more than fifty narrative and mainly allegorical
evocations of the life and death of the hero, filled out with
emblematic and decorative vignettes. The crowning scene,
The Apotheosis of Frederik Hendrik, was given to Jordaens. A few
years later, Jordaens, a Protestant, was brought back north to
work in the even more prestigious town hall of Amsterdam.

Before the Oranjezaal was completed, the House of Orange
was thrown out of high position, while Admiral Michiel de
Ruyter, the most celebrated Dutch naval commander, was on

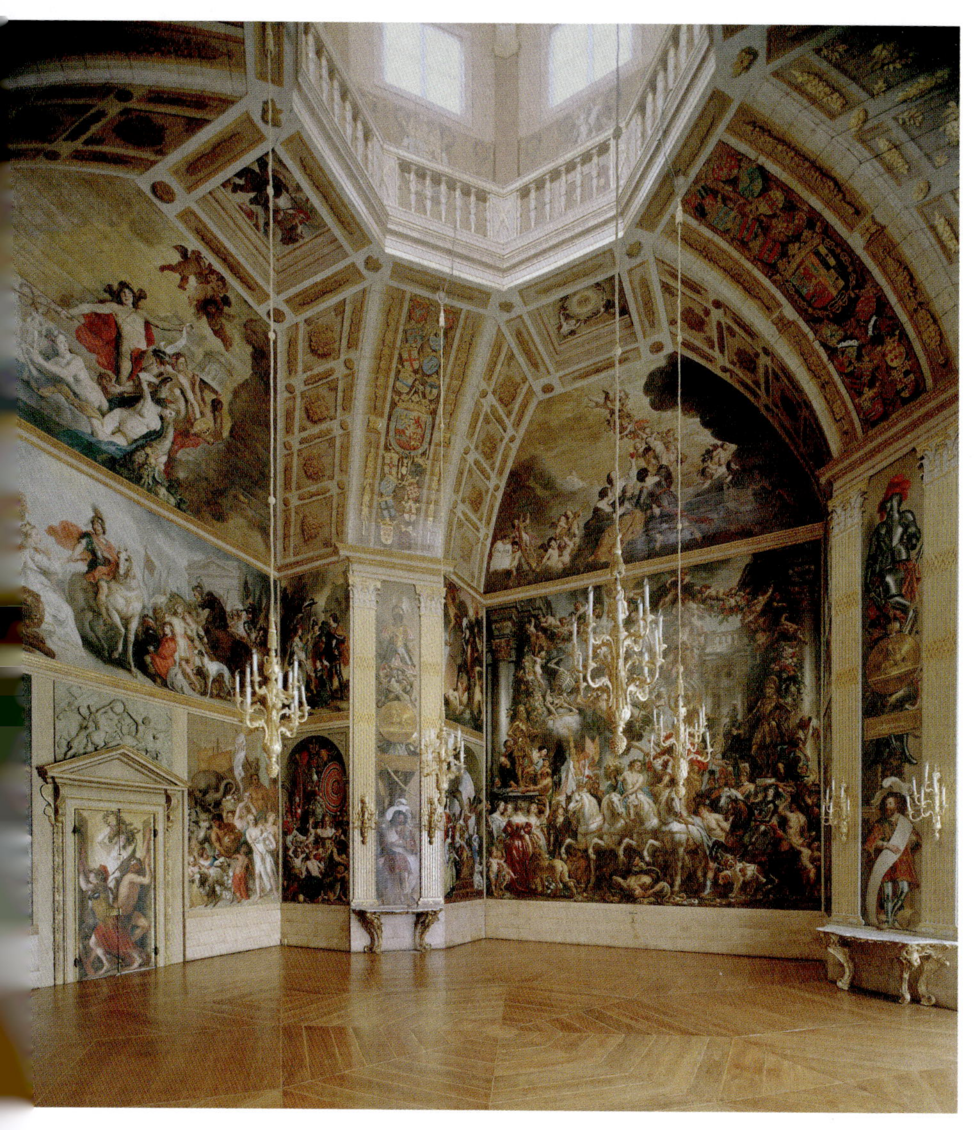

15 The Hague, Huis ten Bosch, the Oranjezaal, 1645–52

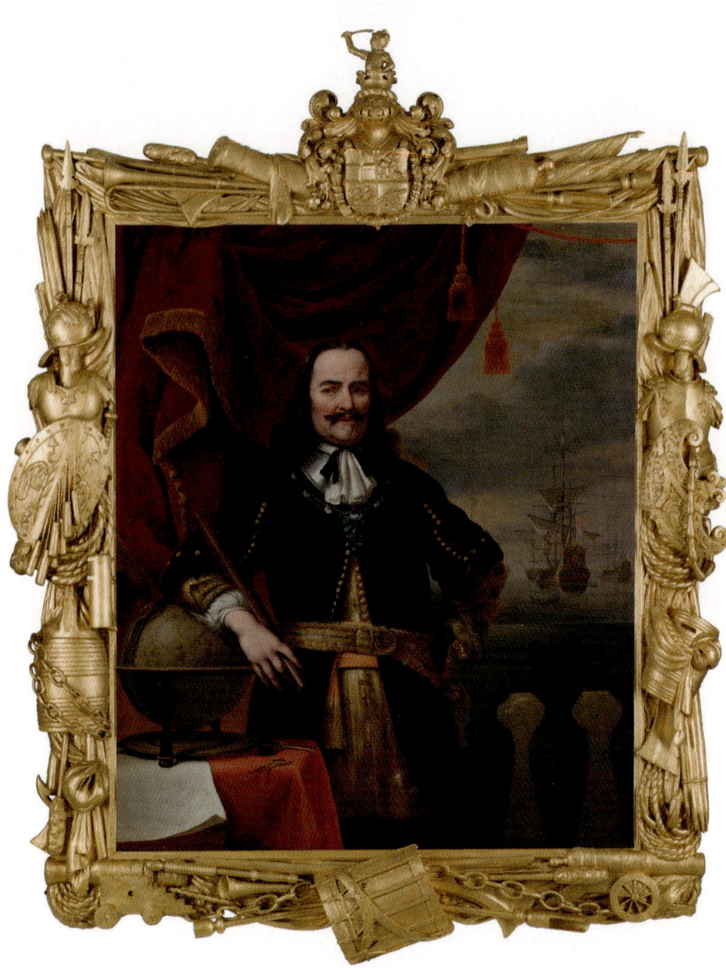

16 Ferdinand
Bol, *Michiel de
Ruyter*, 1667

his way to an unassailable position as a national hero. He had
risen from modest parentage to victorious leadership of the
Dutch fleet. His portrait in the Mauritshuis is one of six
identical versions he commissioned from Rembrandt's pupil,
Ferdinand Bol in 1667. They were made to be presented to the
six headquarters of the five Admiralties for which, the year
before, de Ruyter had led the legendary raid on the British fleet
at Chatham, in the Medway. The gilded trophy frame is a
display of military arms and attributes, topped by de Ruyter's
coat of arms. The frame is the beginning of the wider context
in which the painting should be seen.

Because buildings such as the Oranjezaal and the
Admiralties were tourist attractions, the paintings they held

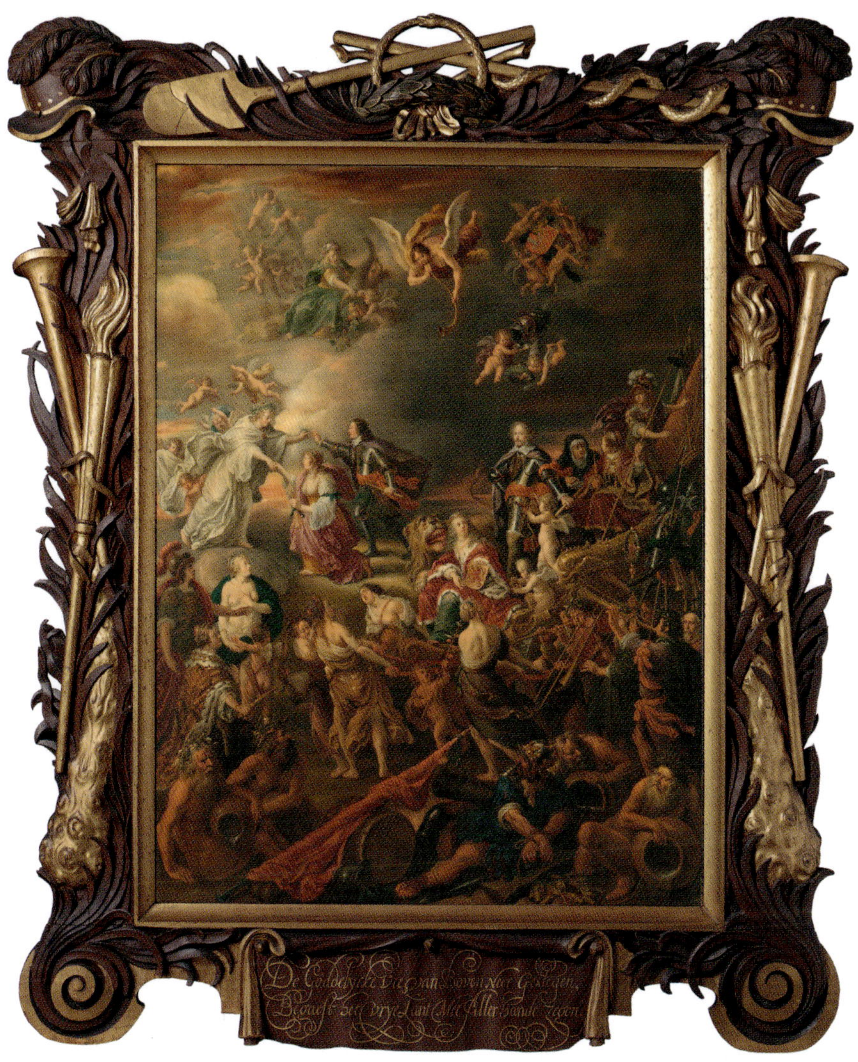

17 Adriaen van Nieulandt, *Allegory of the Peace under Stadholder Willem II*, 1650

were more accessible for viewing than privately owned easel paintings, and had a larger impact on the public – Dutch and visiting foreigners – than their number would indicate.

Modes

In 1650, two years after the Treaty of Münster ended the Eighty Years' War, Adriaen van Nieulandt filled a canvas with personifications, gods, national icons, emblematic figures, symbolic representations of Dutch rivers and more, to celebrate the success of the House of Orange in bringing peace to the nation. (This was a somewhat dubious proposal, since Stadholders Frederik Hendrik, on the right, and his son Willem II, receiving an olive branch from Divine Peace, on the left, would have liked the war to go on.) The sources for imagery of this kind were to be found in handbooks like that of Karel van Mander. It was a coded or visual language, but to make sure the message got across, an inscription or caption would often be added. This one, in the decoration surrounding the original frame, reads: 'Divine Peace, descended from on high, / Bestows abundant blessings on a nation free.'

The same thought – peace at the close of the Eighty Years' War – is expressed in Rembrandt's painting of a mill on a bluff. In our eyes the modes of the two paintings could not be more unrelated: van Nieulandt's a panoply of personifications, Rembrandt's an image of how secure and peaceful things had become. The son of a miller whose mills had to stand on a protected fortification invented an image of a proudly exposed mill standing on a bulwark that has been converted from a military to a milling function – swords into ploughshares, as expressed in the Bible. Beneath it, country folk go unworriedly about their tasks. Dutch viewers of the mid-seventeenth century may have reacted to both these evocations of the long-awaited peace with the same contented sigh.

The Diversity of Dutch Art

While the name of Rembrandt, for example, immediately resonates with audiences, there are very many outstanding and ever-popular artworks to be found decade by decade throughout the seventeenth century. The following is a refined selection of these, along with more familiar examples, indicating the great variety of subject and speciality that typifies Dutch painting.

1601–10 Born deaf and mute, which engendered his nickname, The Kampen Mute, Hendrick Avercamp lived at home all his life, except for the years of his training in Amsterdam, when he stayed in the house of his master, Pieter Isaacsz (1568–1625).

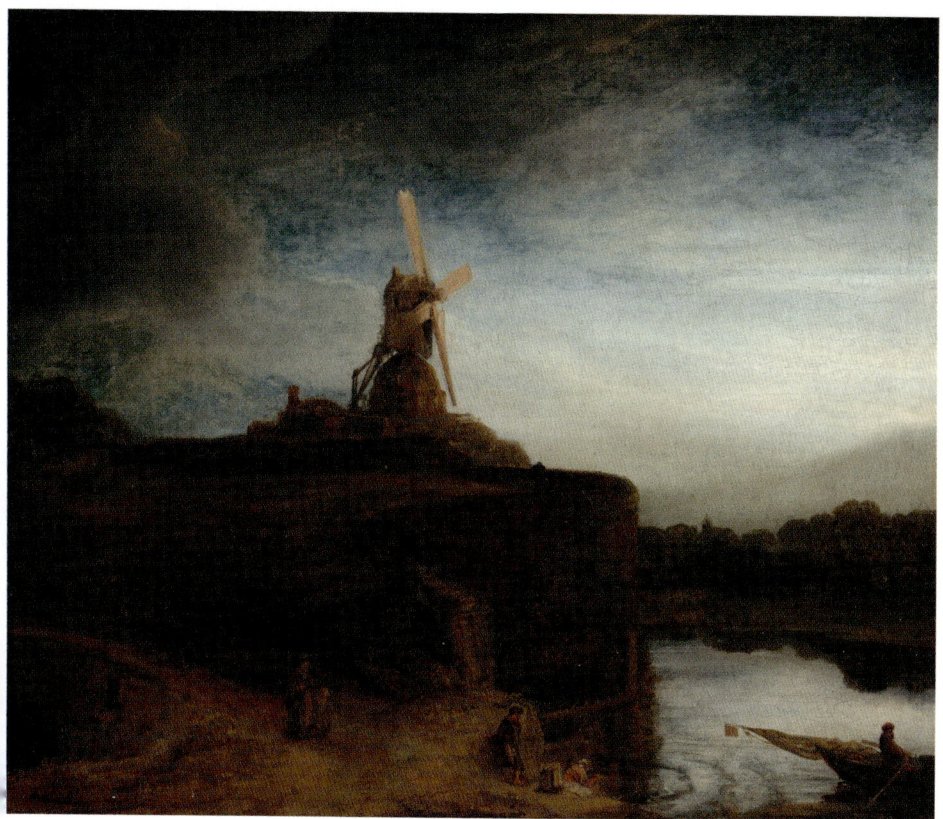

18 Rembrandt van Rijn, *The Mill, c.* 1648

The profession of painter was considered appropriate for those with his kind of disability. Samuel van Hoogstraten, in an outstanding book on the art of painting (1678), quoted a source from Roman antiquity that stated, 'most deaf-mutes have been encouraged to take up painting, just as the blind are usually considered to be most suited to making music or playing musical instruments'. Avercamp surely made the most of the opportunity offered to him by his supportive family. The irresistibly attractive speciality Avercamp chose to cultivate as his own, skaters on the ice, was first painted by Pieter Bruegel. The horizon in Bruegel's composition is very high, as was the practice in the mid-sixteenth century Low Countries. Avercamp lowers it to half-height, a development that was to be followed later in the century with still lower horizons.

1611–20 During a lull in the Eighty Years' War enabled by the Twelve Years' Truce (1609–21), Willem Buytewech cut loose to

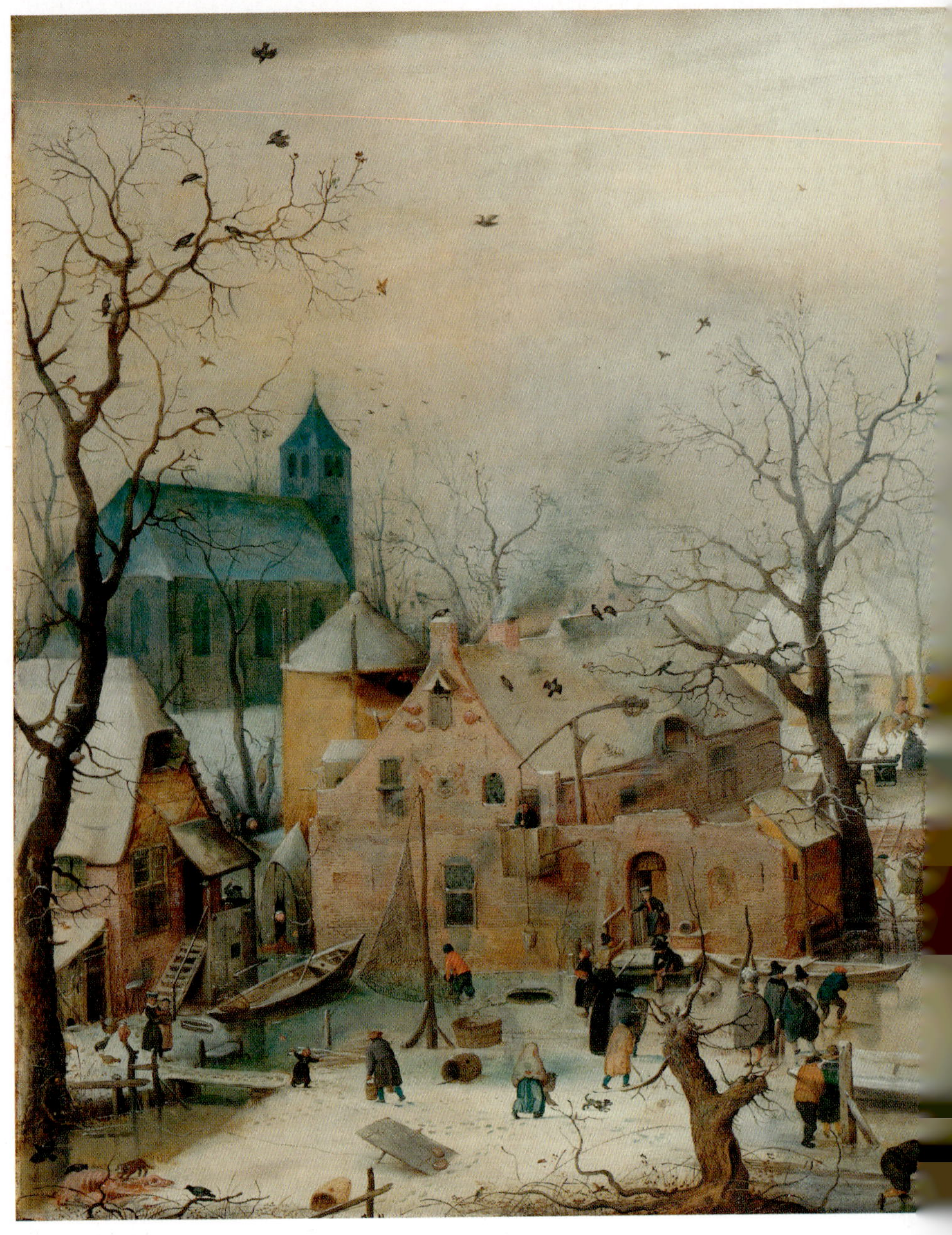

19 Hendrick Avercamp, *Winter Landscape with Ice Skaters*, c. 1608

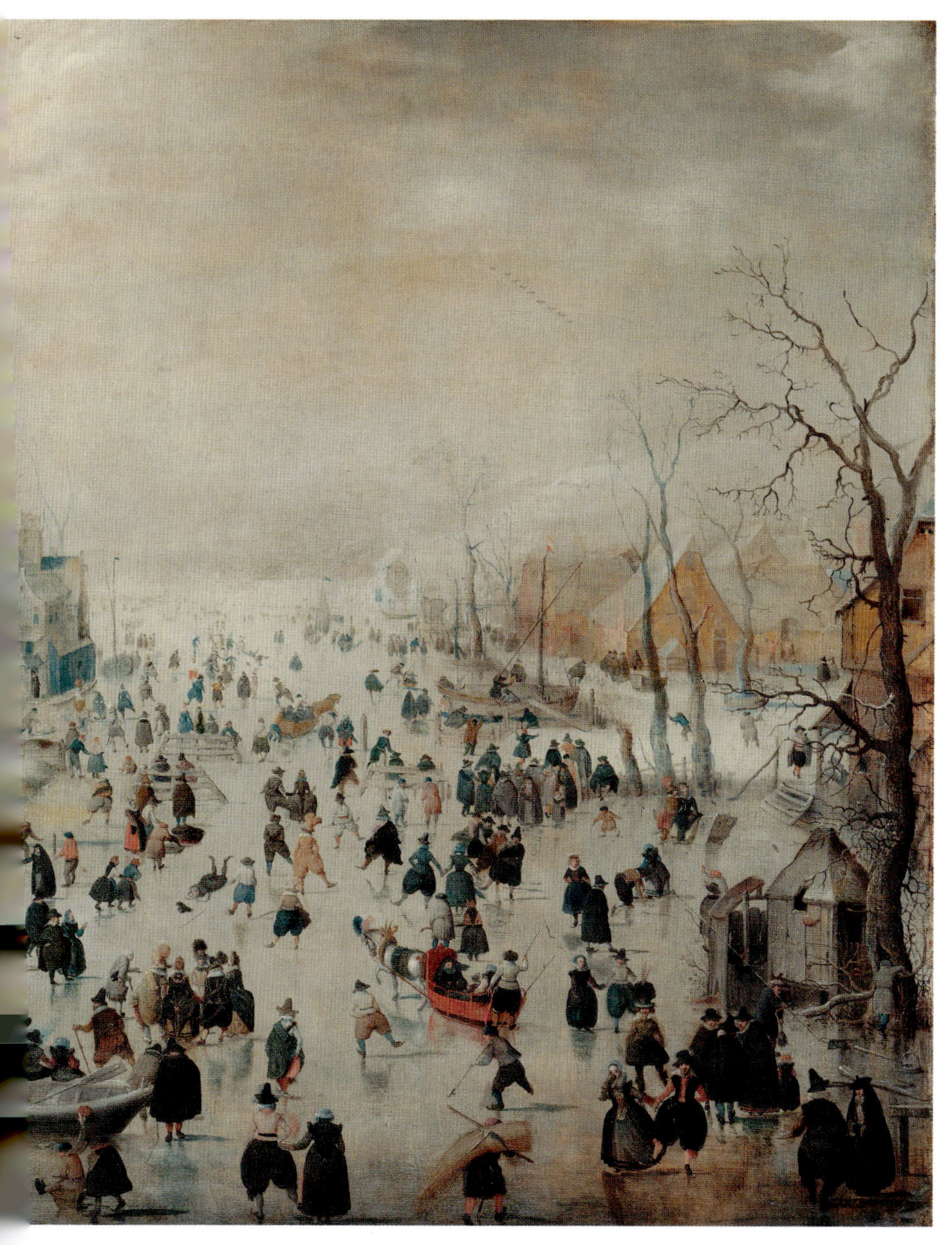

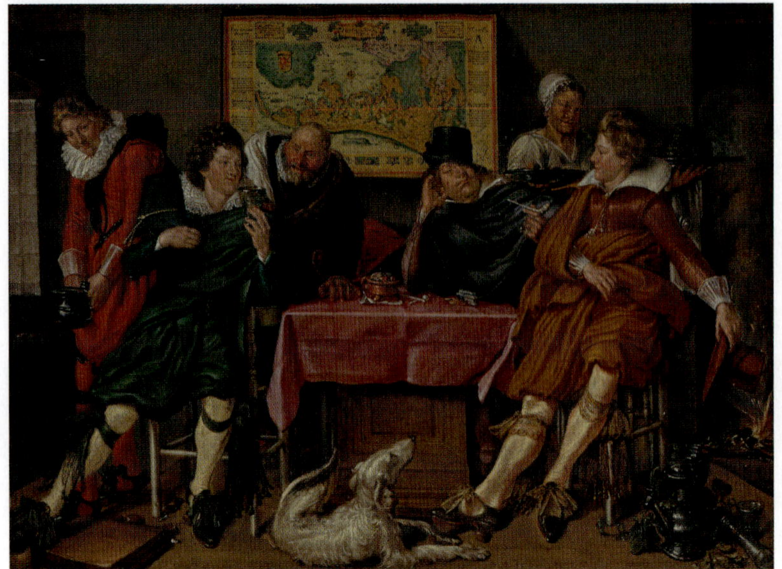

paint a scene of extremely slack behaviour. The smoking and drinking young men at the table are so drunk they cannot sit up straight, and their standing companion at the left is holding a chamber pot into which he will relieve himself in semi-public. They are being served in their dissipation by willing older accomplices. The merrymakers are wealthy young men of leisure, dressed expensively but informally. Paintings of subjects like these were called 'modern' in documents of the time. An ongoing discussion among art historians concerns the question of whether they convey a moral. They do not include obviously condemnatory or admonitory details in these works, such as skulls or smug finger-waggers. The absence of moralizing motifs does not, however, mean that no message is being conveyed. It would seem that the artist deliberately left this question unresolved, allowing viewers to participate in discussions, perhaps debates, about the ethics of the scene.

1621–30 *The Laughing Cavalier* exemplifies two of Frans Hals's exceptional qualities. The liveliness of his sitter engages the viewer at a personal level. And Hals has the ability to create a full visual effect with brushstrokes that are more suggestive than descriptive. This made a powerful impression on nineteenth-century artists who set out to do the same. In 2018, the Haarlem museum that bears his name held an exhibition titled *Frans Hals and the Moderns*, with paintings by Edouard Manet, Max Liebermann and Vincent van Gogh, who saw in

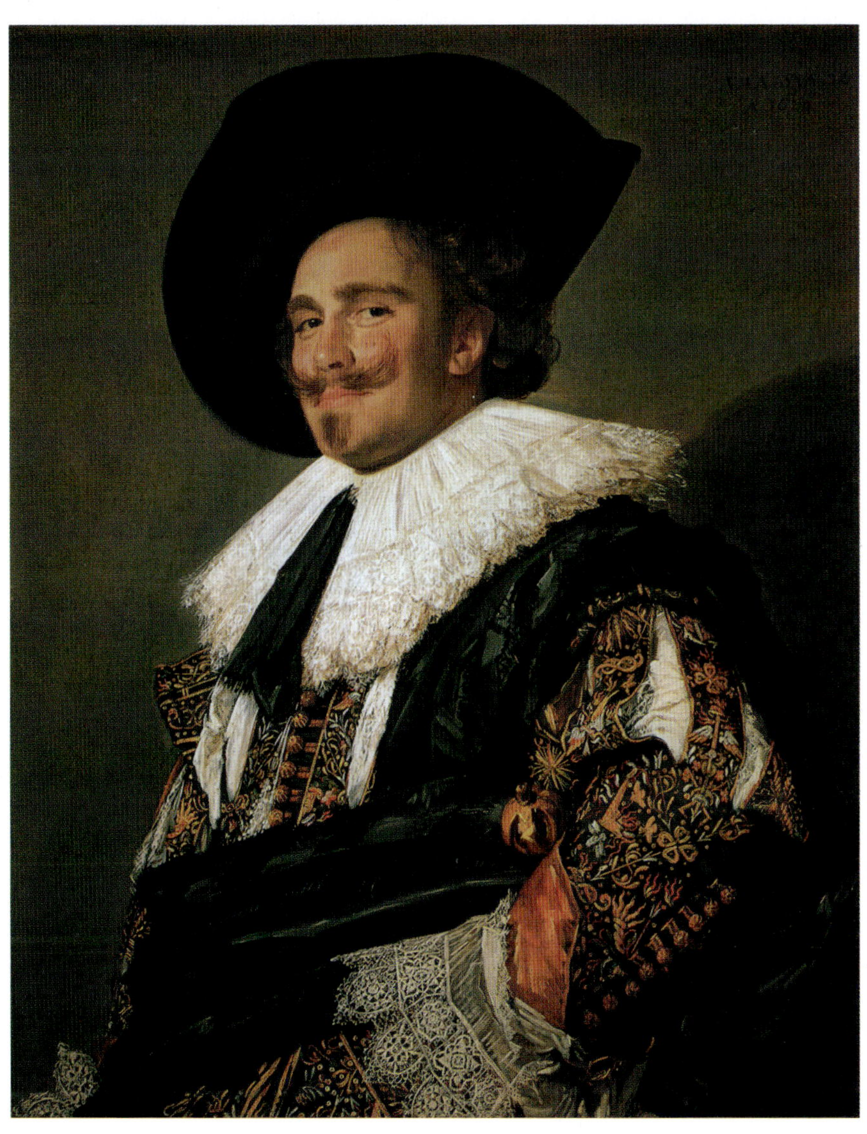

20 OPPOSITE Willem Buytewech, *Merry Company*, c. 1617 20
21 ABOVE Frans Hals, *Portrait of a Man, known as 'The Laughing Cavalier'*, 1624

Frans Hals a forerunner of Impressionism. But there is more
to this portrait than what immediately meets the eye. The
sitter's sleeve, which will have cost more than the painting,
is embroidered with bees, referring to the sting of Cupid's
arrows; flames that burn the heart; and lovers' knots. Most
specific is Mercury's cap and wand, an emblem for 'Fortune,
Companion of Manly Effort'. The sitter is asking us to admire
him both for his macho bravura and his helpless dedication
to the love of his life.

1631–40 Constantijn Huygens (1596–1687) was one of the most
remarkable personalities of the European seventeenth century.
He produced a constant stream of writings, mainly poetry, in
Latin, Dutch, French, Italian and English, composed music,
corresponded with scholars, scientists and philosophers, and
– for our purposes, paramount – engaged with artists and
architects. He did this out of personal interest, but also as a
courtier for the House of Orange. Most famously in that role,
it was he who launched the career of the young Rembrandt.
Huygens was a dedicated family man, the father of the even
more famous mathematician, natural philosopher and
astronomer Christiaan Huygens. Jacob van Campen, architect
and painter, shared with Huygens a passionate interest in
classical architecture. He helped Huygens and his wife Suzanne
build a stately home in The Hague. That he painted Suzanne,
whom Constantijn called Sterre (Star), looking at us over
Constantijn's shoulder lends a touch of familiarity to the
double portrait. The early death of Sterre two years later was
a blow from which Constantijn never recovered.

1641–50 Amsterdam had three civic guard branches, named
after the weapons they bore: the Crossbowmen, Handbowmen
and Kloveniers. (The *kloven* was a musket.) In the 1630s,
the Kloveniers built a new meeting hall. Each of the seven
companies was asked for a group portrait of its officers. The
largest was painted by the young Bartholomeus van der Helst,
the preferred portraitist for the powerful family of the captain
of this company. A striking but often overlooked detail is the
young Black boy front centre. He may have been a company
mascot, like the little girl in Rembrandt's *Night Watch*, which
hung in the same hall. The group portraits in the hall invited
comparison by visitors with an interest in art. Samuel van
Hoogstraten wrote that, next to Rembrandt's *Night Watch*,
'in the judgement of some, all the other paintings in the
Kloveniers hall look like playing cards'. This assessment was
not shared by the public. Bartholomeus van der Helst's more
colourful group was more popular than the *Night Watch* until
well into the nineteenth century.

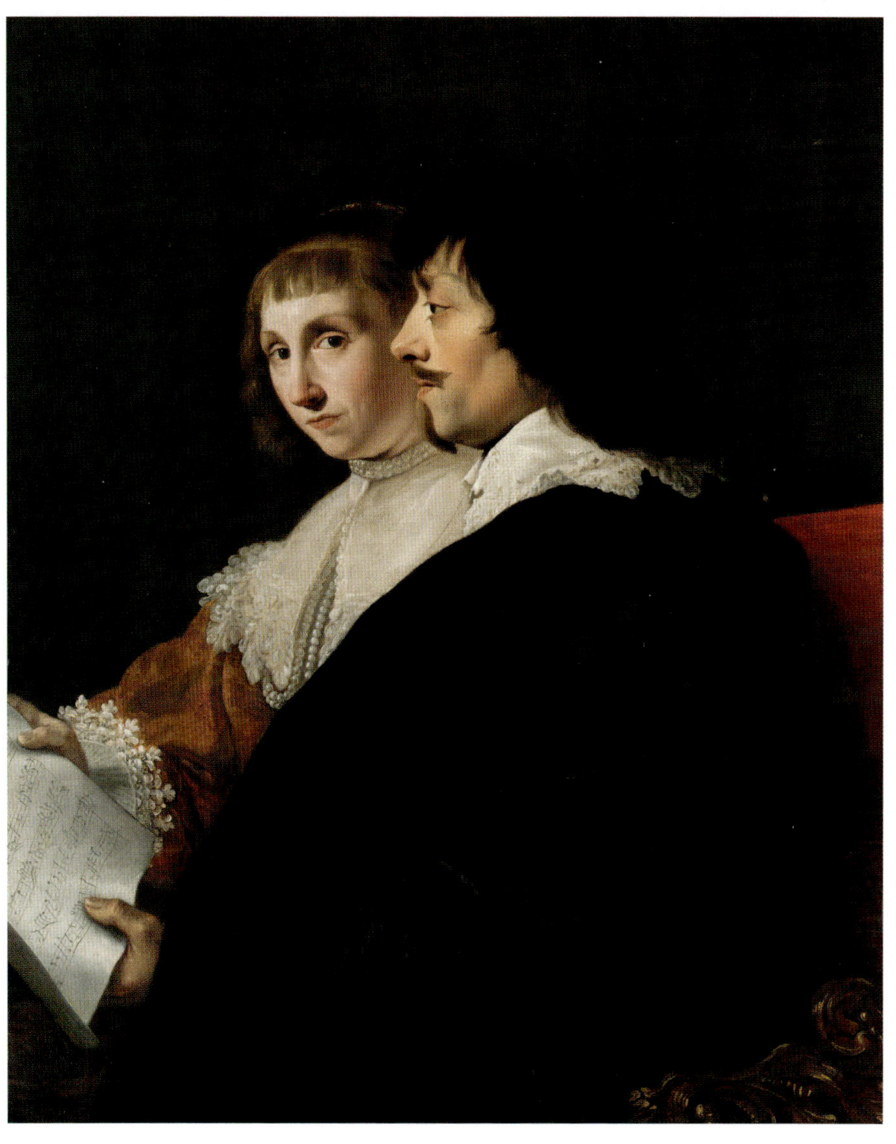

22 Jacob van Campen, *Double Portrait of Constantijn Huygens and Suzanne van Baerle*, c. 1635

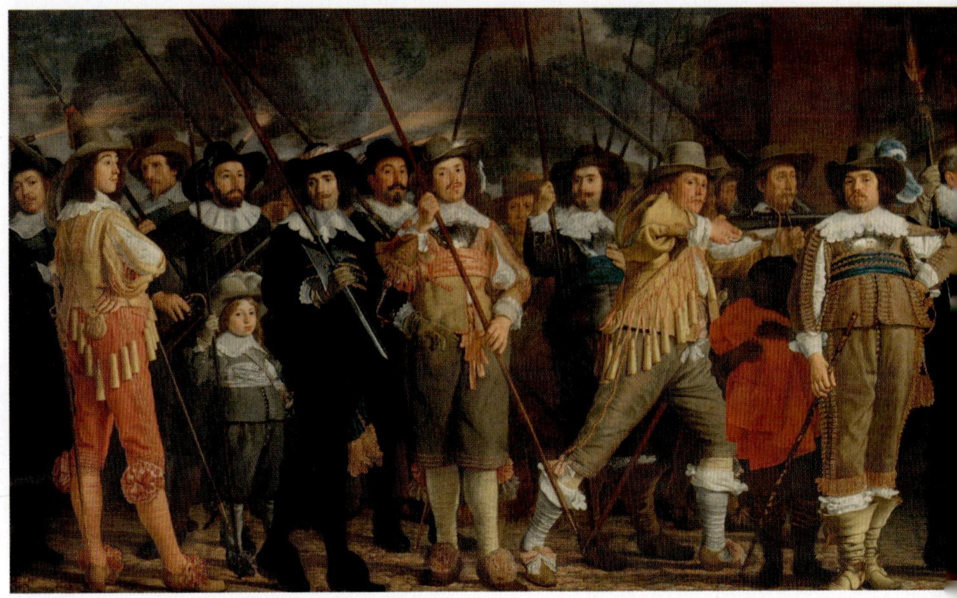

24   **1651–60** *The Goldfinch* is a tribute to the daring imagination and painterly finesse of Carel Fabritius. The first publication on it, in 1859, lovingly calls this modest painting '*un petit morceau de rien*', a little nothing. The bird chained to the box in which it would be put to bed at night has symbolic meanings of all kinds, none of which seem to apply to *this* goldfinch. The painting comes with a story of another kind. Signed and dated *C. FABRITIUS 1654*, it links itself to the early death of its maker. On 12 October 1654, the artist was painting a portrait when a nearby gunpowder storage vault exploded, levelling part of the city and killing hundreds, among them Fabritius, then aged thirty-two years, and his sitter.

Although the term *trompe l'oeil*, deceiving the eye, does not appear in print until 1800, it would have been understood entirely by Dutch artists and art owners of the seventeenth century. Countless still lifes, animal paintings and other genres, hung in the right way, lent themselves to pleasant deception, to the sudden awareness that something you took for real life was actually a painting.

25   **1661–70** The thoughts on the Rembrandt painting called *The Jewish Bride* in the first catalogue of his paintings, by the art dealer John Smith in 1836, could have been written by any of its admirers today:

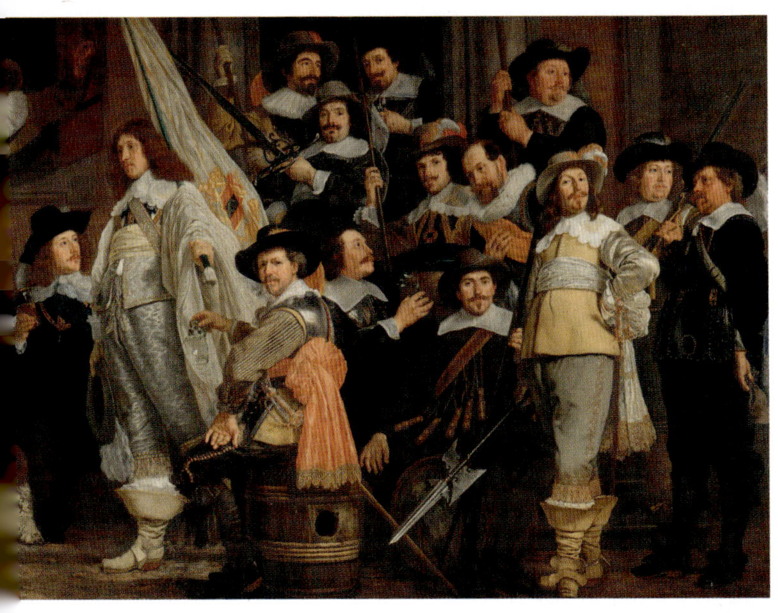

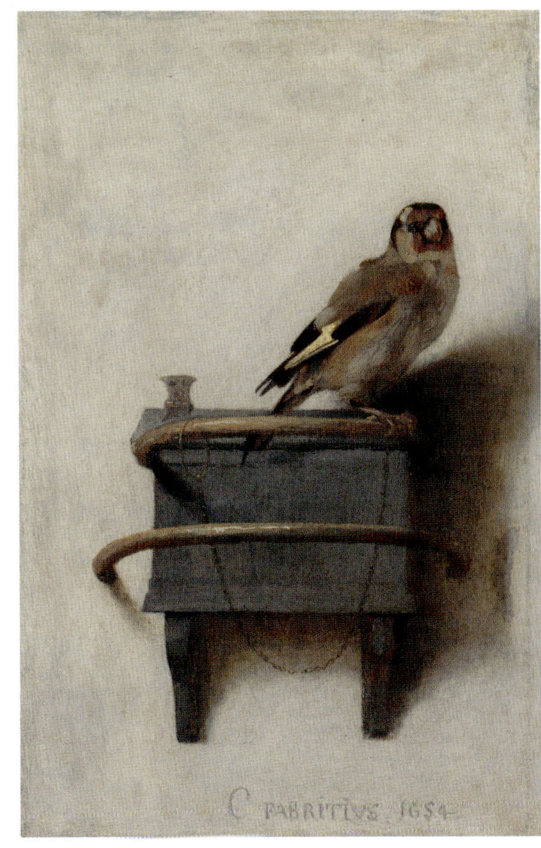

23 ABOVE Bartholomeus van der Helst, *Militia Company of District VIII under the Command of Captain Roelof Bicker*, c. 1640–43
24 RIGHT Carel Fabritius, *The Goldfinch*, 1654

The picture is painted with astonishing freedom and mastery of hand, and with a prodigality of colour and brilliancy of hues, rarely exceeded by the master. In its execution may be discovered the application of the colour with the palette knife, the thumb, the dry stick, and the broad spreading brush. He has seldom produced anything finer in portraiture...

Uncertainties attend the subject. Are the figures portraits? Are they Jewish or not? Ambiguities of this kind occur frequently in Rembrandt's work. He plays with the expectations of the viewer, withholding conclusive evidence while enticing us into forming an opinion. Is the painting a *portrait historié*, with a couple acting like biblical personages, a Bible painting of Isaac and Rebecca, or a poetic riff on the theme of connubial love. The issue will probably never be decided, which is probably the way Rembrandt would have liked it.

1671–80 As with some other important genres, the painting of seascapes, ship portraits and battles at sea were first brought into the mainstream in mid-sixteenth-century Antwerp by the great Pieter Bruegel. But it was the Hollanders Willem van de Velde the Elder (the son of a skipper) and the Younger who practised these subjects most intensely, creating standards that were not surpassed for two centuries. So highly desired was their art that they were able to work for both of the two warring nations across the North Sea – the Netherlands and Great Britain.

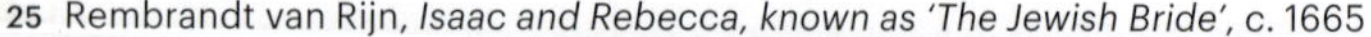

25 Rembrandt van Rijn, *Isaac and Rebecca, known as 'The Jewish Bride'*, c. 1665

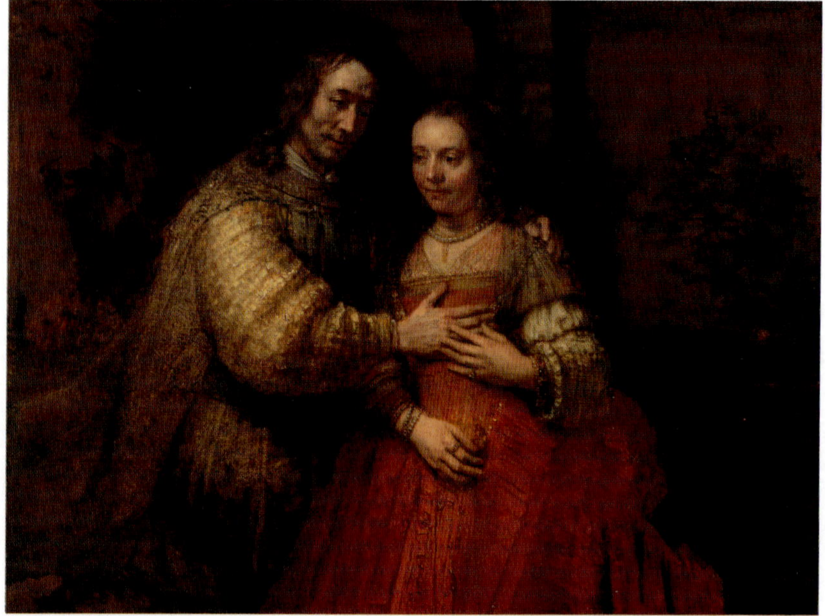

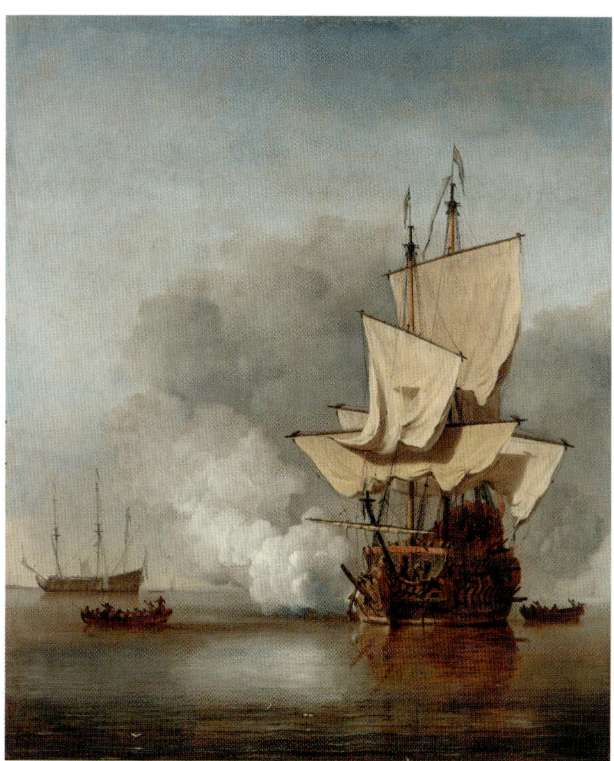

26 Willem van de Velde the Younger, *The Cannon Shot*, c. 1668

To an even greater degree than flower painting, for which botanical knowledge is an asset, the painting of vessels at sea demands expertise. No artist who was not totally familiar with the build, sails, rigging and armaments of a warship could have painted an image as accurate as *The Cannon Shot*. What the artist saw from his perch in a small, bobbing boat, was a roiling, constantly changing scene. In the studio, with the help of ship's models, he evoked that dynamism in a static image.

1681–90 *The Avenue at Middelharnis* has been laden with some of the most hyperbolic compliments in the literature of art. The art historian Cornelis Hofstede de Groot called it 'one of the most beautiful landscapes ever painted'. All the more remarkable, then, that it occupies an eccentric position in the artist's oeuvre. Orphaned at a young age, Hobbema was apprenticed to the arch-landscapist Jacob van Ruisdael. Nearly all of his production was made in the years 1658–68, at first in heavy debt to Ruisdael but heading off in more personal, lighter directions. In 1668, he took a civil service job as a wine-gauger for the customs office, after which he hardly painted at all. But then, in 1689, somewhat

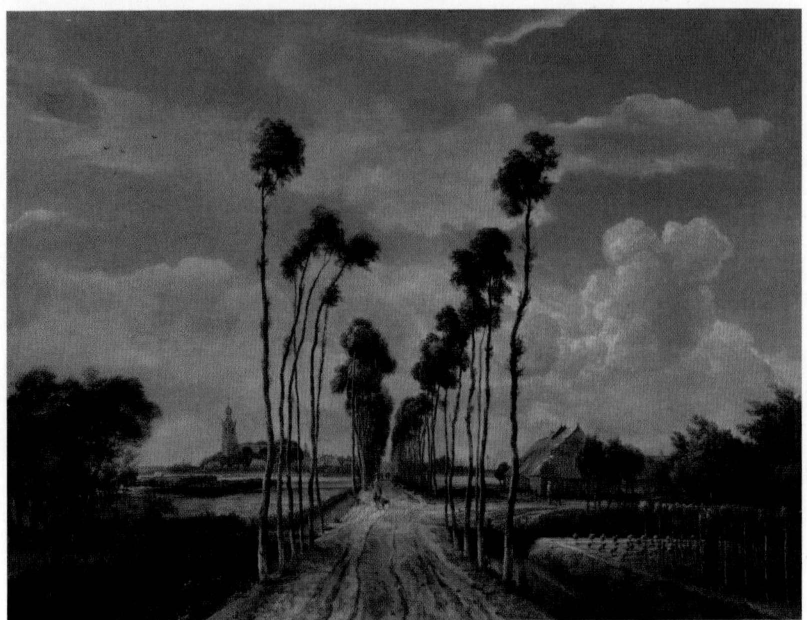

miraculously, came *The Avenue at Middelharnis.* It did not lead
to a revival of Hobbema's career as a painter. He died twenty
years later in poverty.

The view in the painting was recognizable until December
2010, when a big-box store surrounded by a huge parking lot was
opened, ruining the most iconic view in Dutch landscape painting.

1691–1700 If Adriaen van der Werff's *Self-portrait with the
Portrait of his Wife, Margaretha van Rees, and their Daughter Maria*
is not well known, it is because the art of its period has declined in
appreciation and prestige. That is ironic, because van der Werff
was one of the most successful Dutch painters of the seventeenth
century. The style he displays in this painting is perhaps the
most constant of all in Dutch painting, that of the fine brush.
Appropriately, it is coupled to a refined iconography, with subtle,
classicizing allusions. This mode had great drawing power on
foreign courts. In 1697, the Elector Palatine Johann Wilhelm
contracted van der Werff for a salary about twenty times what a
Dutch divine minister or skilled craftsman would earn, to work
for him half the year. The family self-portrait, sometimes with
parents, belongs to a venerable, sympathetic tradition that couples
the artist's skill with his affection for loved ones. Here van der
Werff shows off his status as well with the golden chain and
medal conveyed on him by Johann Wilhelm.

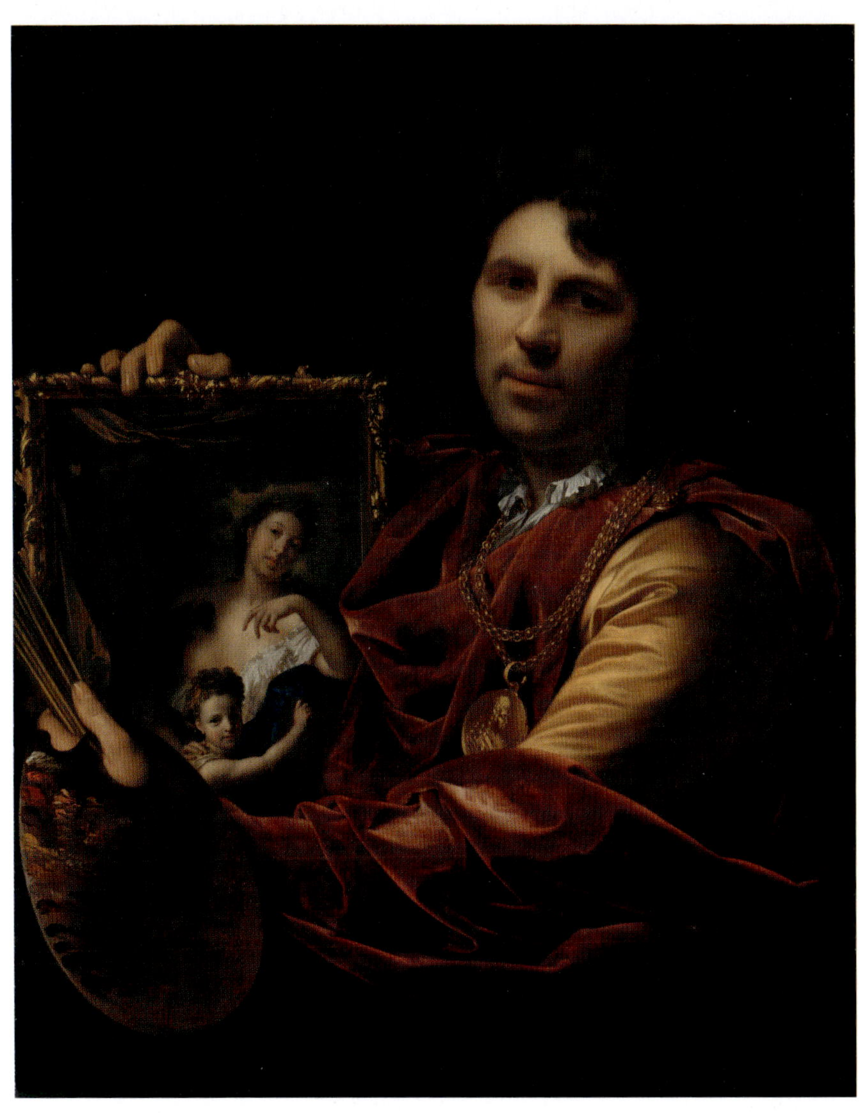

27 OPPOSITE Meindert Hobbema, *The Avenue at Middelharnis*, 1689
20 ABOVE Adriaen van der Werff, *Self-portrait with the Portrait of his Wife, Margaretha van Rees, and their Daughter Maria*, 1699

Chapter 2
Patronage and the Market

In the seventeenth-century Netherlands, patronage was an inescapable, all-pervasive system governing political and professional relations. Opportunities in government and commerce arose through connections. For artists, especially portraitists and specialists in history painting, commissions came mainly from people with whom they had some kind of relation. Family came first, but artists could also manoeuvre themselves into a position of mutual benefit to other people in circles where art was valued. Genteel manners and good contacts were part of the mix. The greatest success in this realm in Amsterdam was achieved by Govert Flinck, who painted the portraits of the mightiest regents and received the best commissions. The market was not the wide-open, anonymous arena of supply and demand postulated by economists. For one thing, most artists were born into families of artists, with existing networks in trade and patronage that a newly trained master would enter. At the top of the chain of patronage, as attained by Flinck and masters such as Gerard Dou, Frans van Mieris and Adriaen van der Werff, artists even gained a measure of leverage over their patrons, who were grateful for anything they produced. At that level, patronage generated market possibilities, with ambitious collectors emulating royal courts and mighty regents. Needless to say, this was not the way most artists worked for a living, if they could earn one at all.

Protestant Churches – Paintings For and Of
When the provinces of the Northern Netherlands rose up against Habsburg rule, many of their grievances (except about taxes) were rather abstract, having to do with historic rights, administrative arrangements, judicial competence and such

matters. Closer to the daily lives of the inhabitants was the fight against the imposition of Catholicism. In concrete terms, this took the form of control over the many hundreds of churches in the country. When a polity joined the rebellion, its Catholic churches were expropriated by the local government and made available for Protestant services. Individuals were free to profess their own religion, but when it came to public practice, the Calvinist denomination enjoyed priority. Calvinist church councils were appointed, which then assumed responsibility for services and church furnishings.

As region after region joined the Revolt, church buildings were stripped of the religious art that gave offence to Protestants. Artists were no longer commissioned to make the kinds of paintings that filled Catholic churches. What was left by way of painted decoration in Protestant churches was modest indeed – escutcheons above burials of distinguished families, panels with the Ten Commandments, Bible stories on organ shutters. Most ambitious were the stained-glass windows of decorative armorial and figurative motifs, which the Calvinists did not think of as idolatrous.

While painting *in* the church was thus suppressed, paintings *of* churches flourished as a genre. Some were fantasy evocations of ecclesiastical spaces. Painting of this kind was initiated by the sixteenth-century Leeuwarden master Hans Vredeman de Vries (1525–1609), with his printed albums of models and instruction in perspective. Around 1630, a major shift took place when the Haarlem artist Pieter Saenredam, began making portraits of existing buildings. Saenredam applied perspective in a basic form, with a single vanishing point and views towards walls parallel with the picture plane. In the 1650s, in Delft, the possibilities were expanded when Gerard Houckgeest, Emanuel de Witte and Hendrick van Vliet mastered the technique of multi-point perspective, allowing for more dynamic and dramatic church interiors. Exteriors became the stock in trade of later painters, such as the Berckheyde brothers in Haarlem and the Amersfoort painter Caspar van Wittel, one of the fathers of the Italian *vedute* – scenic exteriors.

Commissions for the painting of organ shutters were not very lucrative or prestigious, and were usually given to painters lower down the scale than the leading masters. One of these was David Colijns, a versatile artist who amplified his limited talents with clever borrowings from sixteenth-century prints. About 1635, he was chosen to paint the shutters of an organ in an interesting medieval chapel in the middle of Amsterdam: the Nieuwezijds Kapel (Chapel on the New Side [west of the old centre]), which attracted pilgrims for more than one miracle said to have taken place there. The iconography, a favourite for organ shutters, was a story about David, who the Bible says was a musician and author of the Book of Psalms. Colijns's painting shows him entering Jerusalem with the severed head of Goliath, the Philistine giant he had slain (1 Samuel 17:54). It is combined with 1 Samuel 18:6, which tells of an entry by King Saul: '...the women came out from all the towns of Israel to meet King Saul with singing and dancing, with joyful songs and with timbrels and lyres.' The songs they sing, to Saul's distress, are in honour of David, who was destined to become the next king. Besides the musical theme, what made the story fitting for a church is that David's lineage led to the birth of Jesus Christ.

The Zuiderkerk (South Church; 1603–11) was the first Protestant church built in Amsterdam after the Alteration, in which the Catholic city government was replaced with a Protestant one. This church was adorned with sixteen large, figurative stained-glass windows and two rose windows. The origin and fate of the windows are tied in with confessional contention. The city government that furthered construction of the Zuiderkerk was led by moderate Calvinists, known as Remonstrants (or Arminians), who were more tolerant towards adherents of other kinds of Christianity than the Counter-Remonstrants who opposed them. The commissions were extended not by the city or the church but by Amsterdam guilds. The goldsmith's guild did not have to look far for a painter. The highly skilled Pieter Lastman (1583–1633) happened to be the brother of the guild dean, Zeger Lastman, and lived across the street from the church. (Both were Catholics.) The rare subject for the window was suggested by the interests of the guild. A painting of King Cyrus returning to the Jews '5,400 objects of gold and silver' (Ezra 1:9–10) that Nebuchadnezzar had taken from them allowed for foregrounding the kind of lavish objects in precious metals that were the pride of the guild members. The interests of the church and the city were also served. Cyrus's grand gesture was intended to stock the Second Temple, the building of which he was sponsoring, just as the township was now building the first Protestant church in Amsterdam. That the Dutch identified themselves with the persecuted Israelites of the Old Testament made the subject all the more appropriate.

After 1650 the complexion of the city government changed, and the strict, Counter-Remonstrant Calvinists came into power. Probably to spite the Remonstrants, in 1658 they removed the stained-glass windows from the Zuiderkerk. It was at that point that a faithful representation of Pieter Lastman's window was painted by (the Remonstrant) Thomas de Keyser,

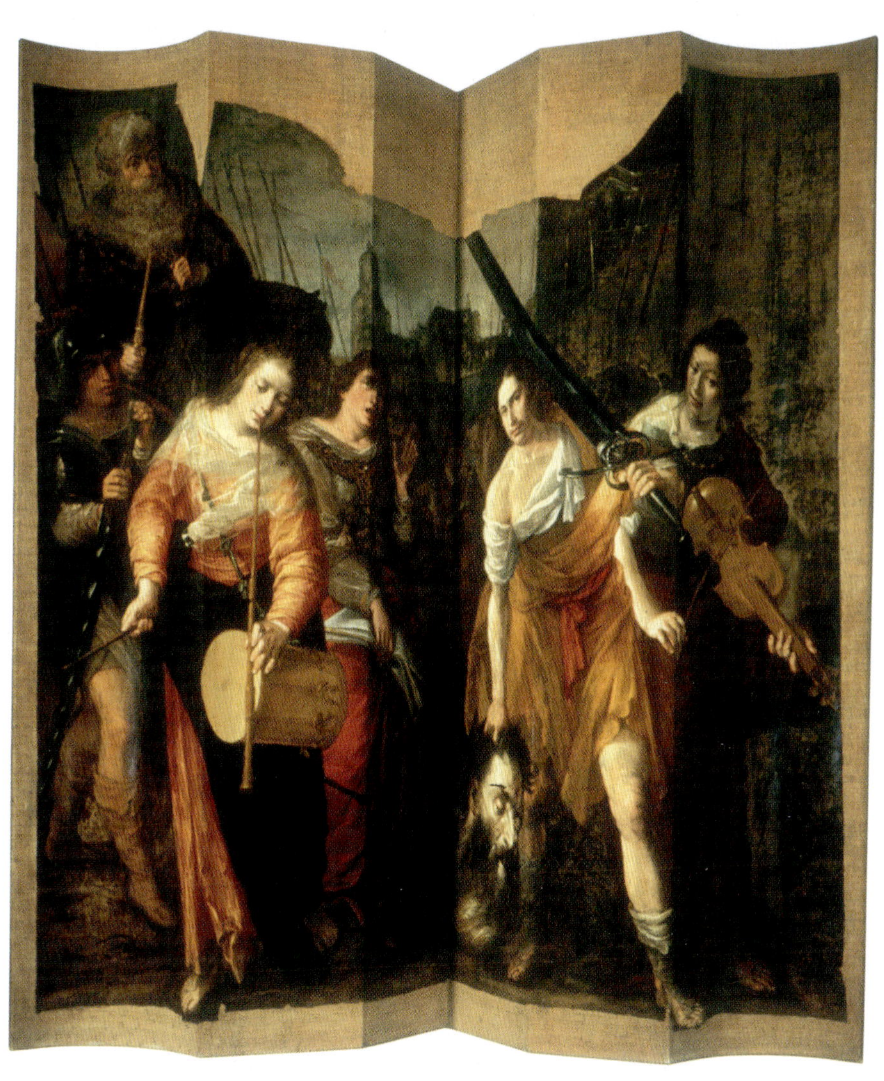

29 David Colijns, *Organ Shutters with Depiction of David with the Head of Goliath,*
c. 1635–40

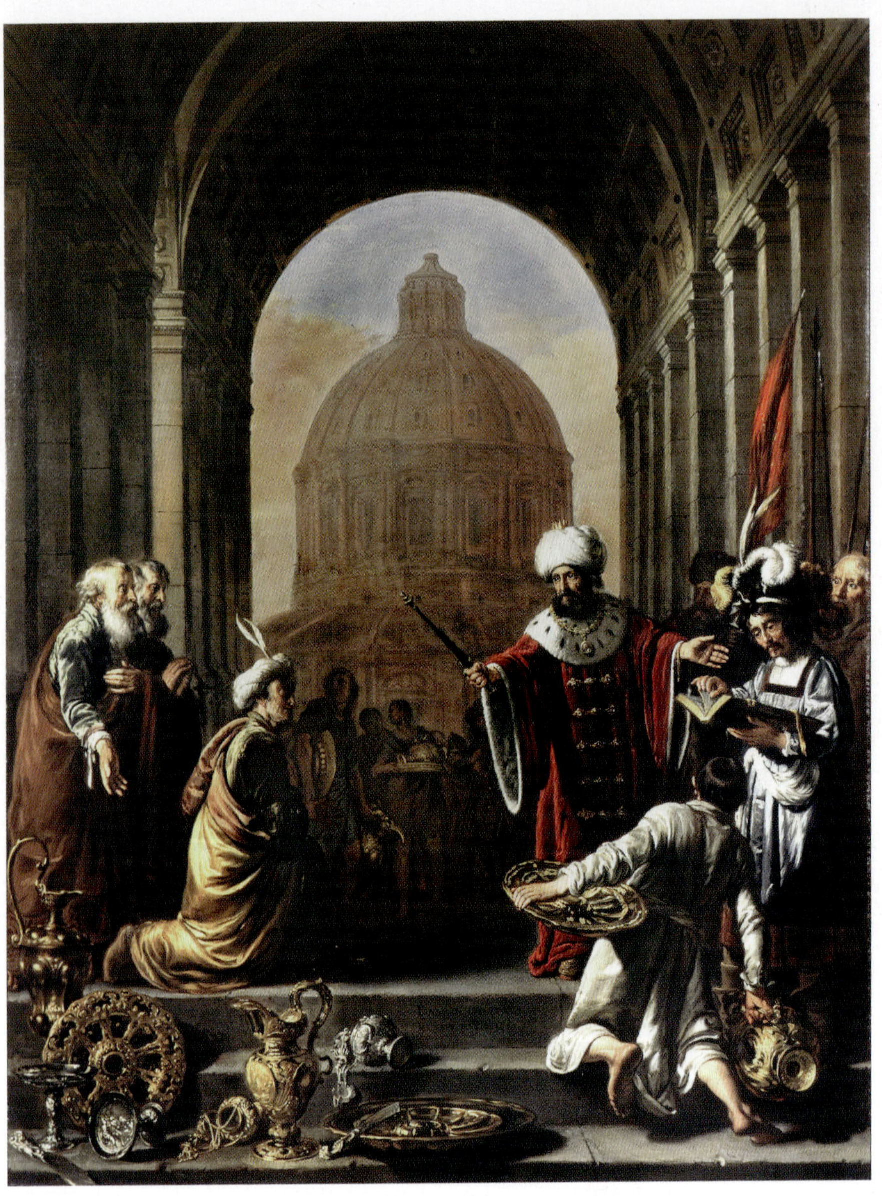

30 ABOVE Thomas de Keyser, after a lost stained-glass window of 1611 in the Zuiderkerk, Amsterdam, by Pieter Lastman, *Cyrus Restores the Treasures of the Temple*, 1660
31 OPPOSITE Pieter Saenredam, *Interior of the Sint Odulphuskerk (Church of St Odolphus), Assendelft*, 1649

a son of the architect of the Zuiderkerk, Hendrick de Keyser (1565–1621). The criss-cross of professional, confessional and family ties both in the window and the painting are an illustration of patronage in operation.

Like Thomas de Keyser's painting, Pieter Saenredam's *Interior of the Sint Odulphuskerk* embodies a wealth of associations. The artist was born in a house not a hundred metres from the church. His father, the esteemed engraver Jan Saenredam (1565–1607), an elder in the church council, is buried there, under a tombstone whose lettering, in the right foreground, is piously rendered by Pieter. The family tomb is also marked as the last resting place of the town sheriff, Pieter de Jonge, and his son Gerard de Jonge, an attorney. Pieter de Jonge had taken on parental responsibility for his young namesake after the early death of Jan Saenredam. Although the minister on the pulpit is not a portrait, members of the clan will have thought of the two Saenredam-de Jonge relatives who served in that function. This is one of four paintings that Saenredam made of the church of his youth.

Saenredam was impressively conscientious, preparing full-size construction drawings after sketches on site for all of his carefully composed paintings. Also exceptional was his practice of dating his drawings and paintings to the day, allowing his biographers to follow his career with greater exactitude than any other Dutch painter of the century. His light touch, delicate use of colour and evident respect for the churches he depicted give his work a distinct look. Architectural painting was so

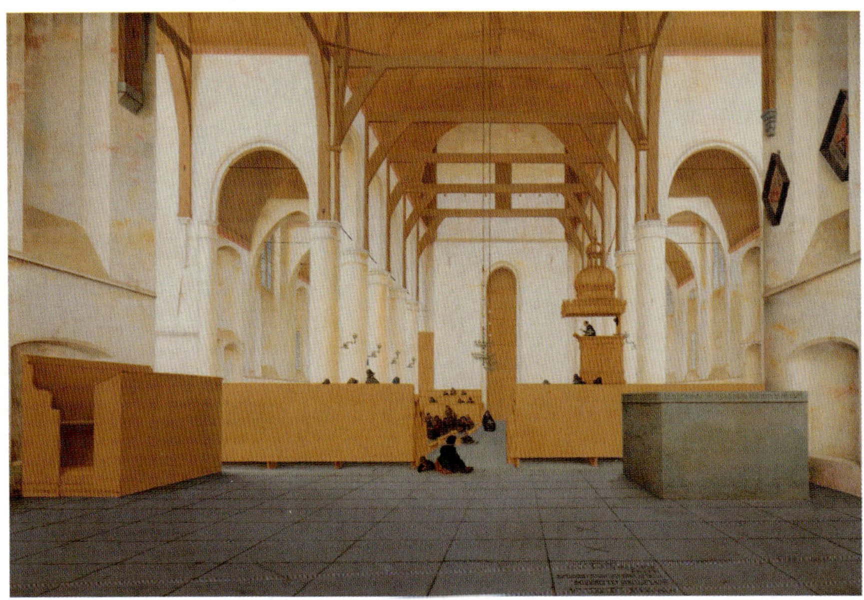

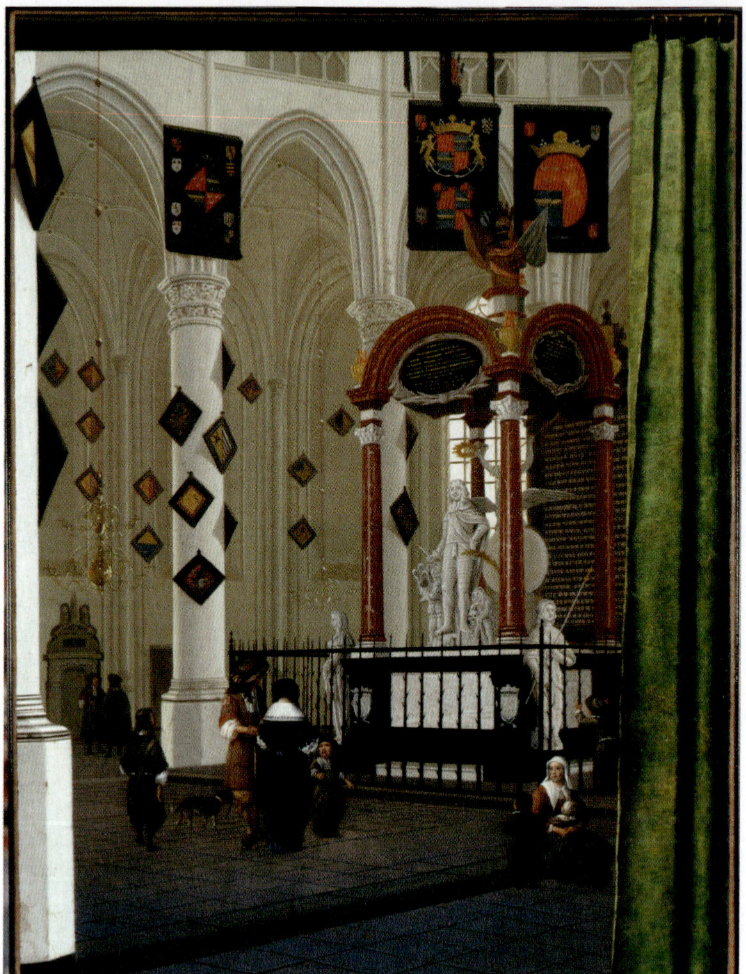

demanding and time-consuming that it was considered a recipe for impoverishing yourself and failing to provide for your family. For Saenredam this was not an issue; his inheritance from his father of shares in the Dutch East India Company was large enough for him not to have to sell his art to pay the rent.

On Sundays and holidays, the pious Dutch went to church, to pray and be preached to. The rest of the time the church was open for sightseeing, special events and recitals. For locals it was a place to socialize, protected from the elements. A major function for the sightseer was to gaze at the monumental tombs of high officials, especially naval heroes. More Dutch church

interiors show this kind of informal goings-on than sermons or
ecclesiastical ceremonies. Hendrick van Vliet's painting of the
Great Church in The Hague, with its dogs, woman with baby, and
men chatting is typical of the genre. The monument being
admired by a dignified-looking family, dedicated to Admiral
Jacob van Wassenaer Obdam, is one of the most exceptional in
the country. Only one other funerary monument is under a
baldachin – an ornamental, free-standing structure. That is the
tomb of William of Orange in the Nieuwe Kerk (New Church) in
Delft. Entirely unique is that van Wassenaer Obdam is not lying
at rest but standing, in an action pose. This form was chosen
because the admiral was not buried here. He had been blown up
on his ship in the Battle of Lowestoft on 13 June 1665. What we
see is not a tomb but a cenotaph. It was commissioned by the
States-General and placed in the Great Church in The Hague,
dedicated to the admiral's name saint, on the spot in the middle
of the choir where previously the main altar had stood.

Hendrick van Vliet modelled his compositions on those of
his Delft colleague, Gerard Houckgeest. His oblique view of the
cenotaph owes much to paintings by Houckgeest of the tomb
of William of Orange. To streamline the laborious process of
painting architecture, he made use of standardized details that
could be cut and pasted, as it were. In a not uncommon form of
trompe l'oeil, a green curtain has been drawn across a rod, as if
to reveal the monument and the long inscription behind it.

Catholic Places of Worship

It is not entirely wrong to call the Dutch Republic a Protestant
country. Its founding story features the rejection of Catholicism,
and the Reformed Church, although not a state religion as
such, was privileged over other faiths. (This strict Protestant
denomination has since the mid-nineteenth century been
called Calvinism. The foremost other Protestant churches in
the Netherlands, standing in various degrees of tension to
Calvinism, were the Anabaptists or Mennonites, Lutherans,
and Remonstrants or Arminians.) Office-holders were not at
first required to be Calvinists, but in practice they all were.
That is the official side of things. The makeup of the population
offers a different picture. The Catholic church was a unity,
while Protestants were divided among various denominations.
Another consideration is that the offspring of Catholic parents
all remained Catholic, while full membership of a Reformed
congregation was contingent on strenuous conditions that were
not always met. As a result, Dutch Catholics outnumbered the
adherents of any individual Protestant sect throughout the
century. There were cities and regions where everyone

was Catholic. While holding the mass was not prohibited,
the public display of Catholicism was forbidden, whether in
church-building, processions or ostentatious gatherings. The
solution found by the Catholic clergy, which operated in low
key as a mission directed from the Spanish Netherlands,
was to convert private dwellings into church spaces. For large
congregations, which could run into the high hundreds,
adjoining properties would be united behind the façades.
There was no restriction on the furnishing of these concealed
churches, and it goes without saying that they would be
adorned with religious paintings. Nearly all were given in
commission to Catholic artists.

The cities of the Netherlands with the most active Catholic
communities were the former bishoprics Utrecht, Haarlem and
Den Bosch (formally 's-Hertogenbosch). For all of these cities,
the foremost Dutch Catholic artist of his time, Abraham
Bloemaert, produced outstanding work. Although he never went
to Italy or spent time in the Southern Netherlands, Bloemaert
was steeped in the art of Caravaggio and Rubens, making
elements of their styles and idiom his own. His *Supper at
Emmaus* is based on a print after a painting by Rubens, which
is itself indebted to Caravaggio for the lighting, the proximity of
the half-length figures, and the emotional power of the scene.

33 Abraham Bloemaert, *The Supper at Emmaus*, 1622

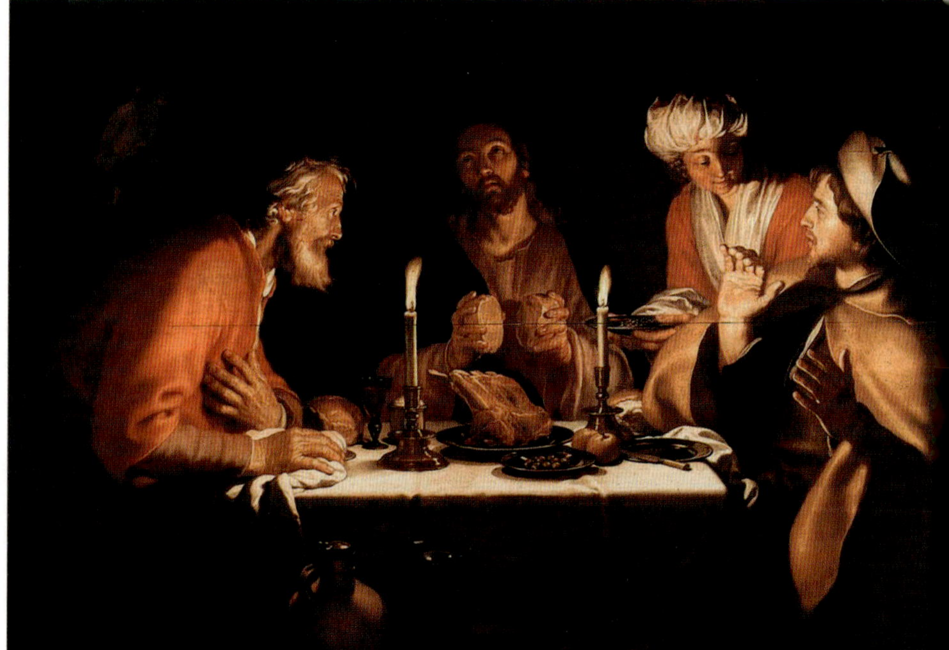

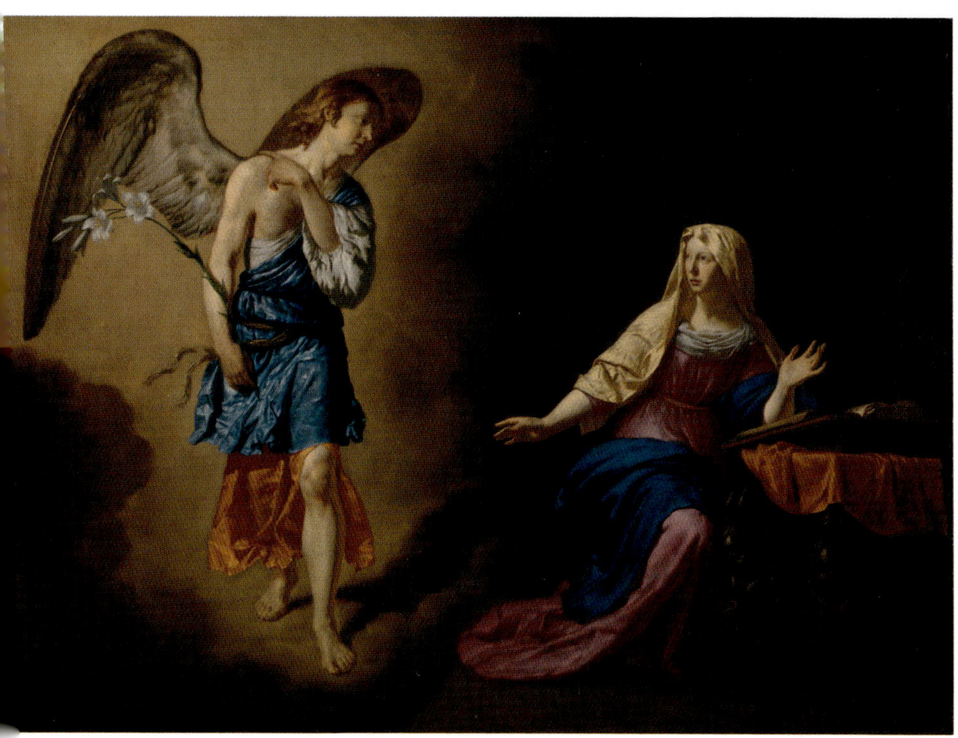

34 Adriaen van de Velde, *The Annunciation to the Virgin*, 1667

Bloemaert was a highly effective personality. He was one of
the founders of the painters' guild of Utrecht, where he lived for
the last half-century of his life. He gave direction and guidance
to younger painters of the city, including his own sons, most of
whom did visit Italy.

Catholics were not always born, but sometimes made.
Adriaen van de Velde, the highly gifted and versatile son of
Willem van de Velde the Elder and brother of the Younger, took
a Catholic bride at the age of twenty-one, with whom he had
five children who were baptized as Catholics. This made him a
likely recipient of commissions for Catholic church art. His
Annunciation, with its large format and iconography that for
Protestants verged on idolatry, has all the appearance of having
been painted for a hidden church, though we do not know
which one. Another painter of van de Velde's generation who
was born Reformed and married into a Catholic family was
Johannes Vermeer. He too received a church commission,
for an allegory of faith, uncharacteristically full of symbols and
emblematic references. While van de Velde's *Annunciation* has

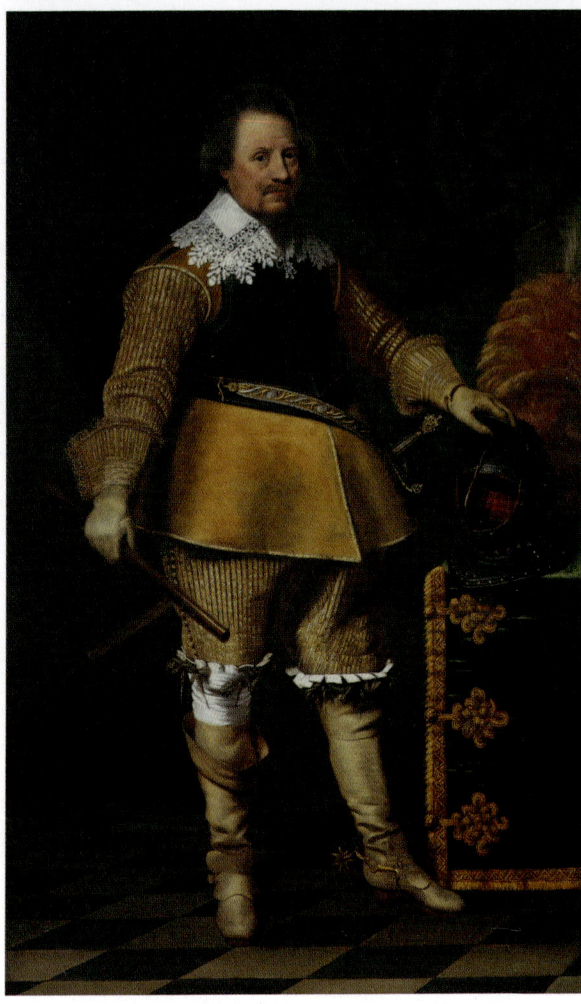

35 Wybrand de Geest,
*Ernst Casimir, Count of
Nassau-Dietz,* 1631

always enjoyed high repute, Vermeer's allegory, from a few years
later, has often been criticised by art historians who cannot
forgive him for having painted something so off-profile.

The Court

Along with the decline of church commissions, posterity has
commiserated with Dutch artists for the waning of royal and
aristocratic patronage. This too calls for qualification. The
Netherlands retained a number of aristocratic courts, even if
they were not rulers over a realm, and they did dispense artistic
patronage. Foremost was the House of Orange-Nassau, whose

leaders served as stadholders of Holland, Zeeland and Utrecht. The head of the family was Willem van Oranje (anglicized to William of Orange, 1533–84), commonly known as William the Silent. He was succeeded by his sons Maurits (1567–1625) and Frederik Hendrik (1584–1647), then by Frederik Hendrik's son Willem II (1626–50) and grandson Willem III (1650–1702). The House of Orange had royal aspirations that found promise in the marriages of Willem II and Willem III with Stuart princesses, and fulfilment in 1689, when Willem III, with his wife Mary Stuart (1662–94), became king and queen of England, Scotland and Ireland.

The most glamorous court in the country for several years had no formal status at all. In 1622 a nephew of Stadholder Maurits, Friedrich V, Elector Palatine of the Rhine (1596–1632), showed up at the door, with a household of 223 persons. He had been driven out of Prague in 1620, following a reign of one year and four days as king of Bohemia. With him was his wife Elizabeth Stuart (1596–1662), the daughter of King James I and elder sister of Charles I. The States-General saw itself obliged, with contributions from the English crown and the House of Orange, to offer rich, though steadily declining hospitality to the couple known as the Winter King and Winter Queen, in mocking reference to their year in Prague. Their house in The Hague and palace in the town of Rhenen, in Utrecht province, became show-off in-country models for how European royalty lived, to the admiration of some and distaste of others.

Cousins of the Orange-Nassaus, the counts of Nassau-Dietz, served as stadholders of the northern provinces Friesland, Groningen and Drenthe. They held court in the Frisian city of Leeuwarden. The Frisian stadholders were more in the field than at home, and did little to further cultural life in their provinces. They did, however, frequently engage the foremost artist in Leeuwarden, Wybrand de Geest, to paint their portraits. The portrait of Ernst Casimir in the Dutch royal collection has been documented in the family since 1633. The imposing, life-size, standing format had been reserved in the sixteenth century for emperors and kings. Among the artists who first employed it was the Utrecht portraitist to the Habsburgs, Antonio Moro (Anthonis Mor; 1516/21–1576/77). Soon it became standard for paintings of military leaders. Close attention was paid to the accuracy of details, especially with regard to weapons and signs of distinction.

As the granddaughter of a sister of William of Orange, Amalia van Solms (1602–75), born into German nobility, was a not-too-distant relation of Frederik Hendrik, whom she married in 1625. She was eminently suited to the prominent

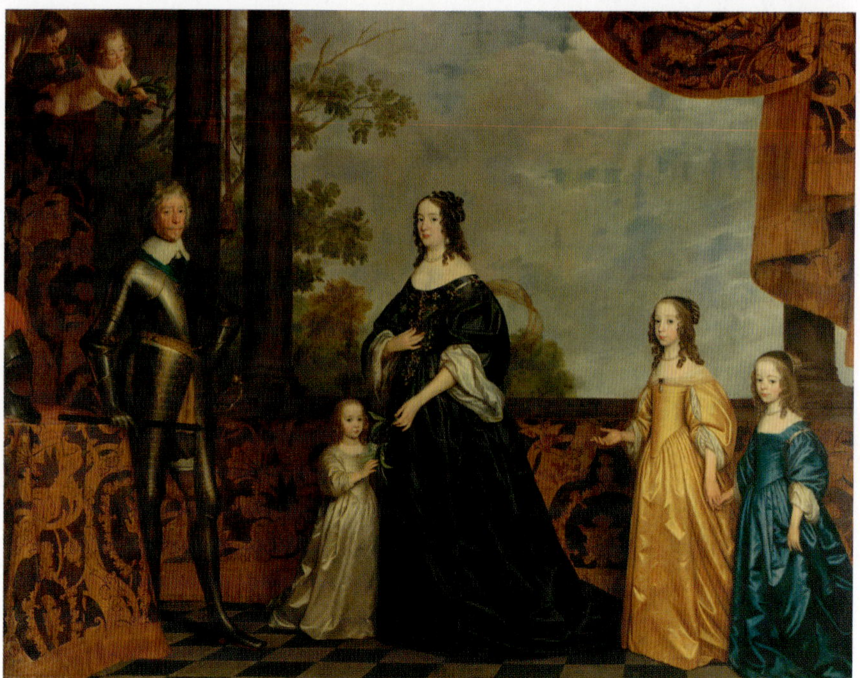

36 Gerard van Honthorst, *Portrait of Frederik Hendrik, Prince of Orange, his Wife Amalia van Solms and their Three Youngest Daughters Albertina Agnes, Henrietta Catharina and Maria, c.* 1647

position she came to play, as a formidable guardian of family interests. In a highly formal family portrait by Gerard van Honthorst, Frederik Hendrik is shown in two major roles – as a warrior and as the progenitor of a clan. This was not his idea. The painting was ordered by Amalia for Huis ten Bosch, hoping to share it with Frederik Hendrik. However, he died before they could move in, whereupon she dedicated the decoration of the main hall, the Oranjezaal, to his glory and memory (see pp. 26–27). The daughters of Frederik Hendrik and Amalia van Solms were married off to German princes, whose courts they coloured orange – Oranienburg near Berlin, Oranienstein and Oranienhof in the Rhineland, Oranienbaum near Dessau. The collections assembled in these palaces were outposts of the Dutch art scene in Germany.

The most personal of all Orange portraits was painted by Godfried Schalcken, one of the best-known and most admired painters of his time. As a child he moved from the village near Breda where he was born to Dordrecht, where his father became head of the Latin school. There Godfried learned painting from

Rembrandt's most innovative and learned pupil, Samuel van Hoogstraten. He was the leading painter in Dordrecht in the 1670s and 80s, which he built on to establish a splendid career in The Hague and London, enjoying high patronage wherever he went. Schalcken cultivated a particular, highly conspicuous speciality: lighting by candlelight. In his portrait of the Dutch stadholder who became King William III of England, he was able to put this effect to double use. It is striking in itself as lighting for a royal portrait, calling for closer, quieter contemplation of the man than the usual, pushy presentation of monarchs. And sophisticated viewers will also have perceived a certain symbolic association between a burning candle and the likeness of a ruler and other prominent persons. The caption to an image of a candle in several emblem books – *Aliis inserviendo consumor* – has been translated as 'I am consumed in the service of others', which would here refer, appropriately or not, to William.

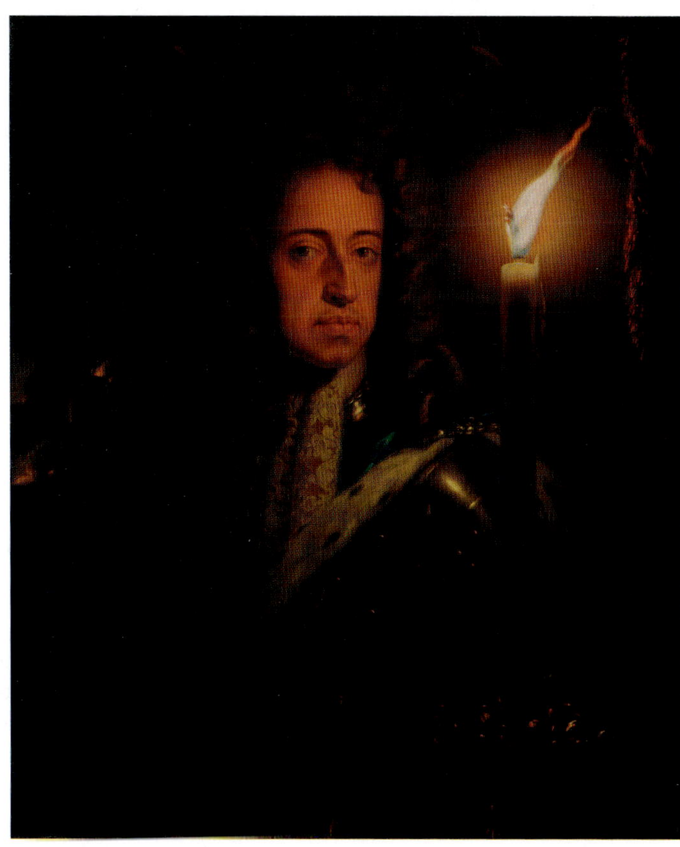

37 Godefridus (Godfried) Schalcken, *Candlelit Portrait of Stadholder-King William III*, c. 1692–97

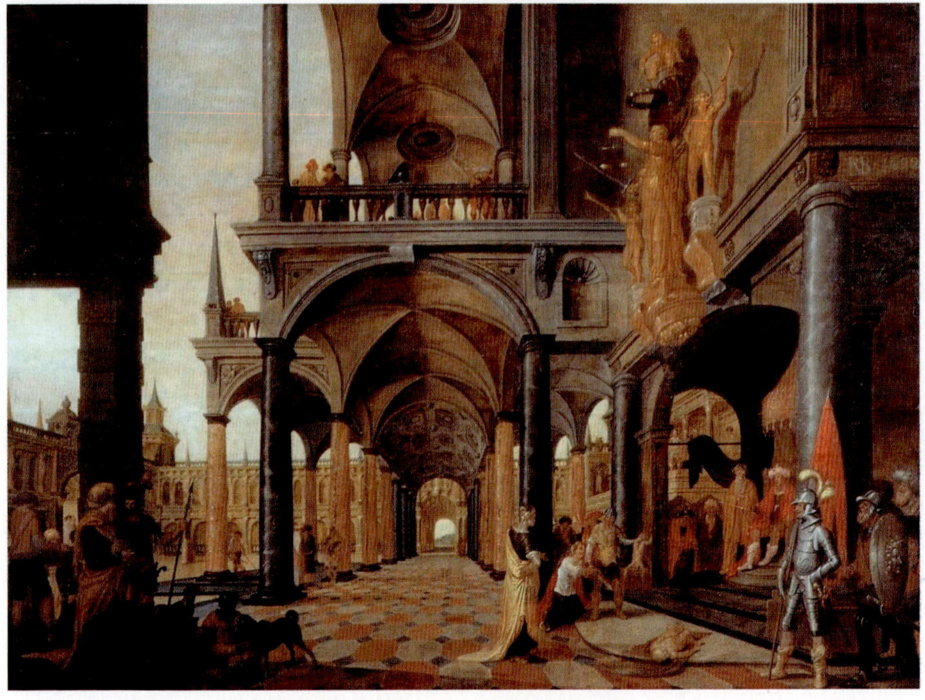

38 Pieter van Bronckhorst, *The Judgement of Solomon*, 1622

City Governments

There may not be a municipality in Europe, from the Middle Ages on, that did not wish to back up its authority with images of courts and governments from the Bible and classical antiquity. Or to show to its own magistrates models of good or bad behaviour, as exhortation or admonition. Netherlandish townships, richly endowed as they were with professional artists, gladly embraced this practice. A theme that lent itself, in courts of law, to encourage just judgement, was the story from the Hebrew Bible about how King Solomon, as judge, resolved a difficult conflict (1 Kings 3:16–28). Two prostitutes who lived in the same house came to Solomon with a baby who had been born to one of them. Both had delivered boys at the same time, and one had died on the third night after the birth. One woman accused the other of swapping her dead baby for her own live infant, which the other denied. Solomon considered, then ordered the surviving baby to be cut in half and shared between the two. One of the women cried out in protest, begging the king not to kill the baby, but to give it to her rival, and Solomon concluded that she must be the mother

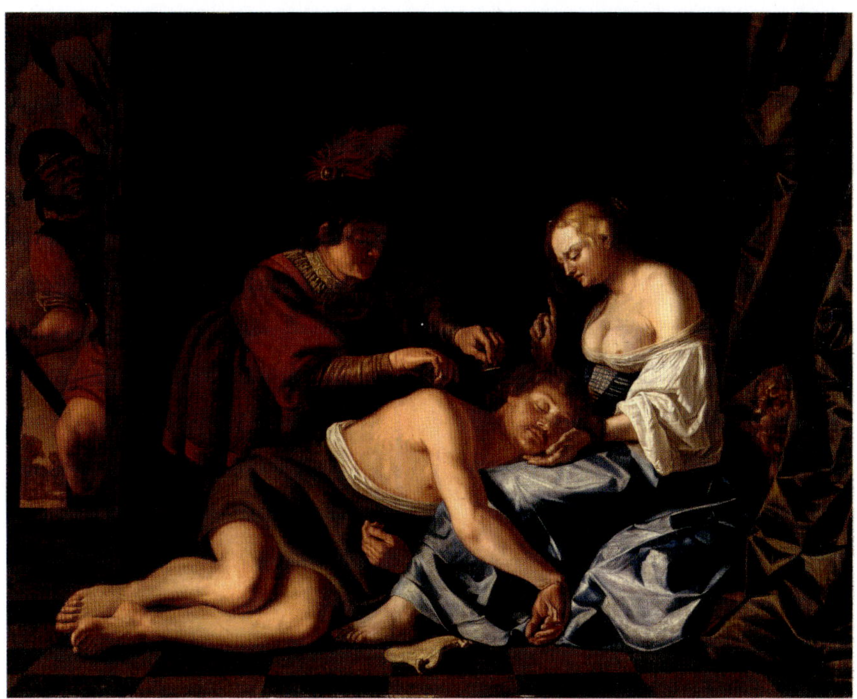

39 Christiaen van Couwenbergh, *The Capture of Samson*, 1630

and judged in her favour. In 1622, the township of Delft ordered
a painting of the subject for its courtroom. They commissioned
it from a local artist, Pieter van Bronckhorst, one of the
founders of the painters' guild. The architectural setting in
which he placed the scene, intended to evoke the Temple of
Solomon, is inspired by the perspective models of Hans
Vredeman de Vries (see p. 45).

The admonitions to town councils, in their meeting halls,
could be political as well as moral. That seems to be the motive
behind the purchase in 1632 by the Dordrecht government,
for seventy-five guilders, of a painting of Samson asleep, to be
hung in its meeting hall. The greatest issue before the council
in that year, as before every other important ruling body in
the country, was whether or not to accept a peace offer being
dangled by the Spanish Netherlands. Hanging this painting
in front of the council reflects on that debate. Samson had
allowed himself to be lulled into complacency by an enemy
person – his own wife, Delilah – and to have fallen asleep in
her lap, dropping the jawbone with which he had killed a
thousand Philistines. She brought in her countrymen, one

of whom robbed Samson of his strength by cutting his hair, after which he was dragged off in chains (Judges 16). The Dordrecht councillors who voted to buy and hang a painting of this subject would have been suspicious of the peace offer.

Christiaen van Couwenbergh, who was married to the daughter of a burgomaster of Delft, was to become one of the favourite painters of Stadholder Frederik Hendrik. He had two specialities: paintings of weapons and erotic genre scenes. *The Capture of Samson* brings together van Couwenbergh's twin interests of sex and violence. He based his composition on a well-known print by the Dutch engraver Jacob Matham, after a composition by Peter Paul Rubens.

The biggest artistic patronage project of the Dutch seventeenth century was the design, construction and furnishing of the town hall of Amsterdam. Planning began in 1639, the commission to the architect Jacob van Campen was extended in 1648, the sculptures were carved by the Fleming, Artus Quellinus, from 1651 to 1665, and the paintings began to be made in 1655 but were never completed. The most prestigious commission of all was for the burgomasters' chamber: two enormous paintings extolling the integrity of incorruptible, lion-hearted Roman consuls. Ferdinand Bol painted Gaius Fabricius Luscinus being tempted and taunted to no effect by an enemy commander, King Pyrrhus of Epirus. On the facing wall was placed Govert Flinck's painting of Marcus Curius Dentatus, in another confrontation with an enemy. During a war against the Samnites, Marcus was approached by an enemy delegation bringing precious gifts, an inducement to end the fighting. Plutarch tells how they found him boiling turnips for his dinner, and as he turned down their offer, he quipped that someone who can be satisfied with a vegetable stew has no need for gold. These subjects had never been painted before, and would have been incomprehensible without the explanatory verses by Joost van den Vondel that were mounted beneath them.

Civic Bodies

Dutch government and civil society were interwoven through and through. Few social services were provided by government itself. Instead, civic bodies were chartered to exercise charitable, financial and even military functions. Few burghers, male or female, would not have served on the boards or in the wards of a charity, a hospital, a lepers' colony, a penal institution, a guild, a civic guard company. These bodies also hired stewards and aides, nurses and attendants, so that they accounted for a good proportion of the economy. Many of them predated the

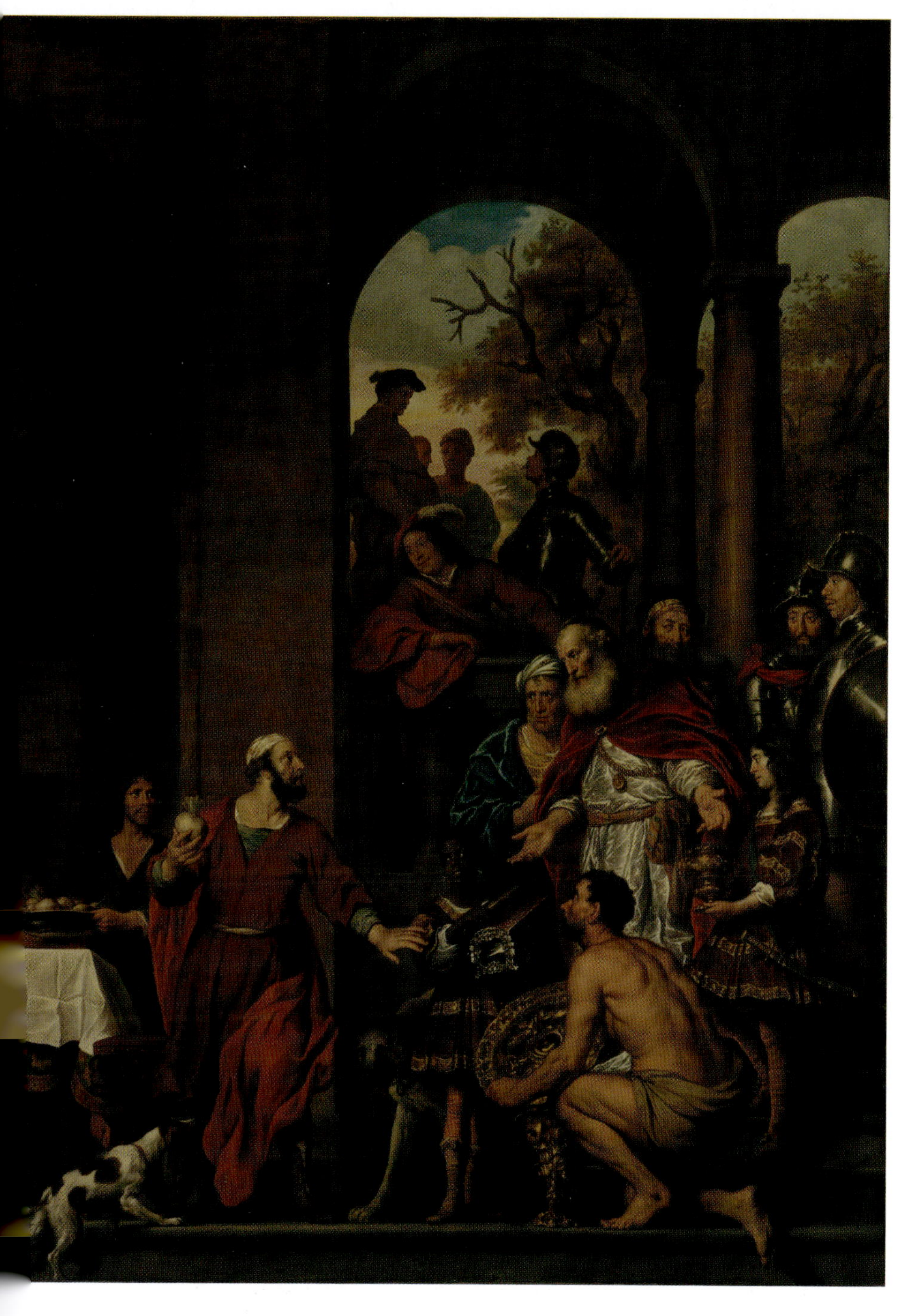

40 Govert Flinck, *The Roman Consul Marcus Curius Dentatus Refusing the Gifts of the Samnites*, 1656

Republic, and cultivated a measure of institutional pride that often found expression in paint. One such institution, immortalized in a painting by Jan Victors (see also p. 129), was an orphanage founded in 1657 for the care of girls and boys whose parents had been members of the Reformed Church but had not been *poorters* (registered citizens) of Amsterdam. The creation of this particular institution was not straightforward. The burgomasters resisted the establishment of a religiously restricted facility for a function that was otherwise seen as the responsibility of the city. It was only after an outbreak of the plague in 1655 and the feeling that it was a punishment for sin that the city relented, and allowed the town architect, Daniël Stalpaert, to build the monumental orphanage.

The painting of the mess hall has the appearance of truth to life, perhaps even with likenesses of some girls. The sobriety of the facility is not immediately visible, but looking closely, we see that the porridge being dished up from the huge pan on the floor goes into metal bowls from which more than one girl eats. Thin beer is tapped from a keg into mugs that on the right go around the table for the older girls, and on the left is served by caretakers to the little girls, one gulp at a time. The meal is accompanied by a Bible reading. The painting is one of a pair, each commissioned by six of the twelve deaconesses who ran the orphanage for the Reformed Church Council that year. Their names are inscribed on the lower right, with an indication of who was married or widowed.

41 Jan Victors, *Dining Hall of the Reformed Diaconate Girls' Orphanage*, 1659–60

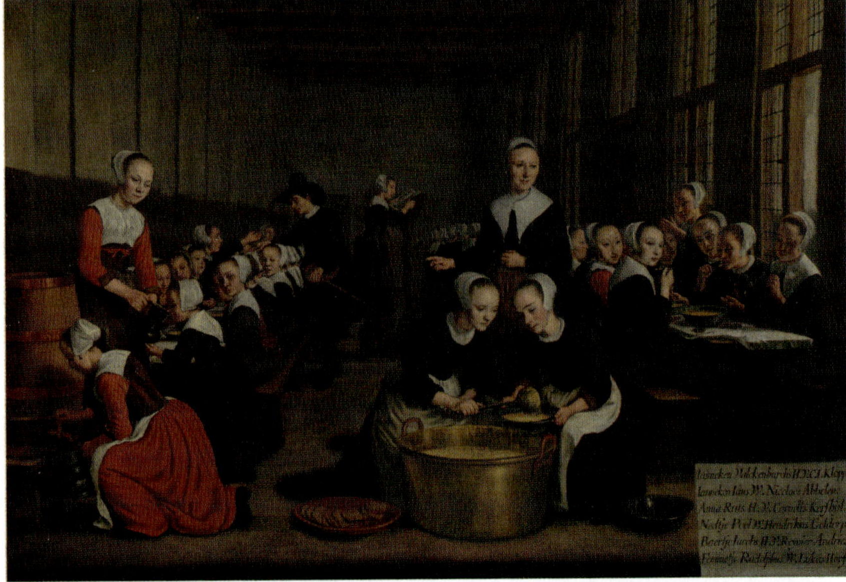

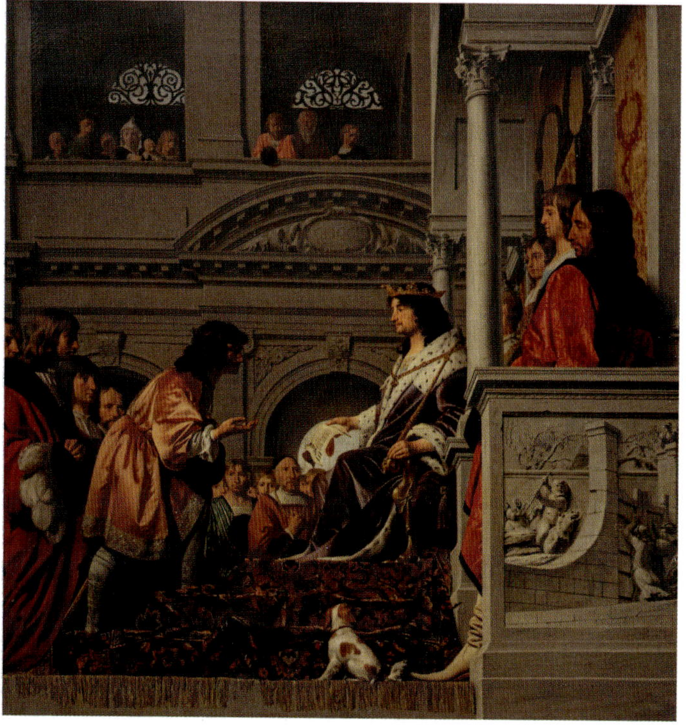

42 Caesar van Everdingen and Pieter Post, *Count Willem II Granting its Charter to the Rijnland Water Board*, 1655

One of the proudest civic institutions in the Netherlands was the Rijnland Water Board (*hoogheemraadschap*), which was responsible for the management of surface water in part of the province of Holland. The body still exists as one of the oldest corporate entities in the world. In 1655, it inaugurated new quarters and ordered a painting commemorating its founding in 1255. That was the year the board was licensed by Count Willem II of Holland and Zeeland, who was also bearer of the title King of Germany and Rome. The figures were painted by Caesar van Everdingen, while the architecture was done by the designer of the new building, Pieter Post (1608–69). Though Post well knew what thirteenth-century Dutch throne rooms looked like – built from brick, with pointed vaults – he provided Willem with a marble hall in classical form. This was in line with the Rome-inspired style that Post's friend and collaborator Jacob van Campen brought to the town hall of Amsterdam. It went with an open disdain for medieval architecture, which Constantijn Huygens, in a eulogy for van Campen in 1657, was to characterize as 'curly Gothic foolery'. Appropriating ancient Rome as a forebear, Amsterdam called its government and citizenry by the Latin acronym,

S.P.Q.A., for The Senate and People of Amsterdam. Classicism was seen to confer greater authority than medieval styles. Style can have its own meaning.

Private Patrons

In the Netherlands there were relatively few major collectors of paintings by living artists. This situation worsened as collectors gravitated to artists of the past. A change in the style of interior decoration contributed to this, as the walls in wealthy households began to be covered in gilt leather or murals, which were not suitable for hanging easel paintings. For top-notch players such as Frans van Mieris, commissions from abroad became more important. Lower down the scale, such windfalls were not to be expected, and the number of painters who could support themselves through their art plummeted.

Until fairly recently, Johannes Vermeer was thought to have sold his paintings on the open market. Only in 1989, when the American economist John Michael Montias published his years-long research on the artist, was it noticed that a good half of his production, brought to auction in Amsterdam in 1696, derived from a single collection in Delft, that of Pieter Claesz van Ruijven (1624–74), whom he called 'Vermeer's only true patron'. It has recently been argued convincingly that Vermeer's real collector in the van Ruijven household was not Pieter but his wife Maria Simonsdr de Knuijt (1623–81). Johannes grew up a few doors from her family home, and she took the extraordinary step of leaving him a bequest of five hundred guilders, double a median year income. The paintings owned by the van Ruijven-de Knuijt couple came from the period after 1656, when Vermeer stopped painting narratives in favour of genre subjects. One of the earliest was the painting in the Rijksmuseum known as *The Milkmaid*, but more properly called *A Kitchen Maid Making Bread Pudding*. Knowing that Vermeer's paintings were commissioned by a woman casts a new light on the large part of the oeuvre dedicated to the life of women. It also reminds us that the purchase of household furnishings, including paintings, were mainly the domain of the woman of the house. This turn in the history of Vermeer's paintings emphasizes the role of the patron – in this case the female patron – nearly as a crucial facilitator of his oeuvre.

The highest class of collectors were rulers who could dispense public funds for private purchases. One such was Archduke Leopold Wilhelm, governor of the Habsburg Netherlands, who was seduced by the paintings of Frans van Mieris. Arnold Houbraken's biographical sketch of van Mieris is instructive about how such a predilection could come into being. It is the

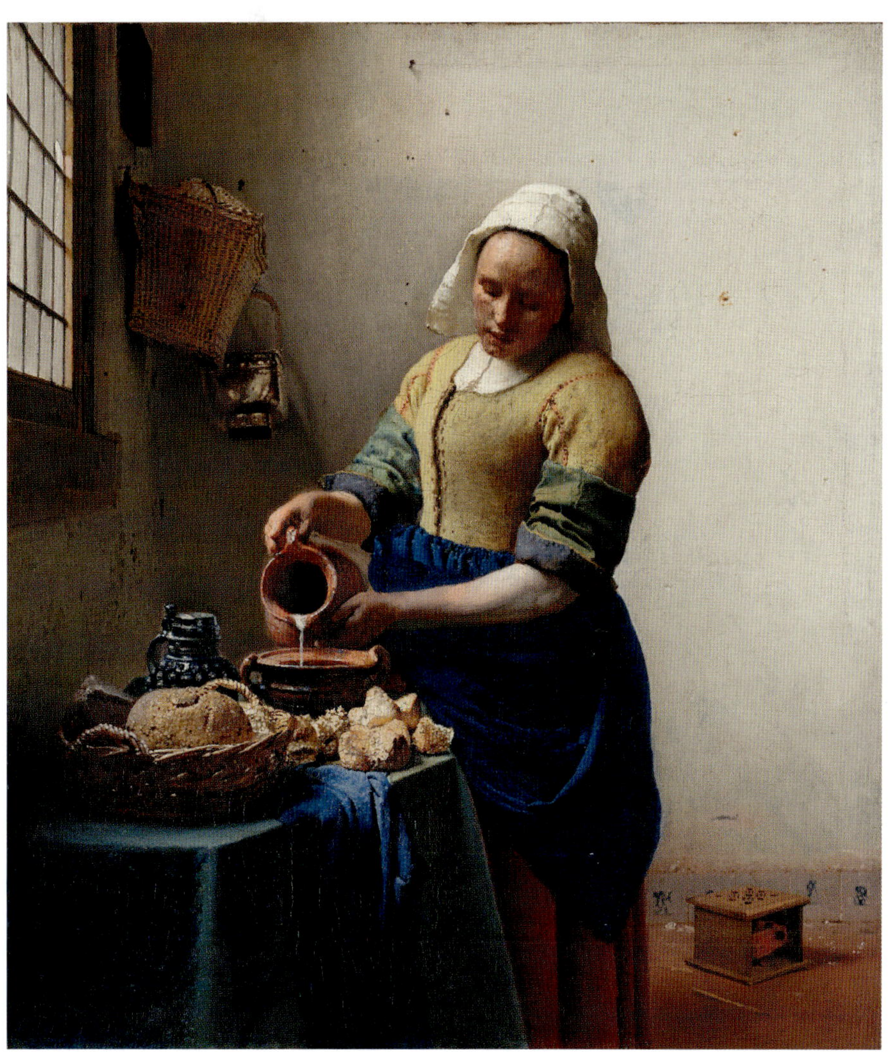

43 Johannes Vermeer, *A Kitchen Maid Making Bread Pudding, called 'The Milkmaid'*, c. 1658/59

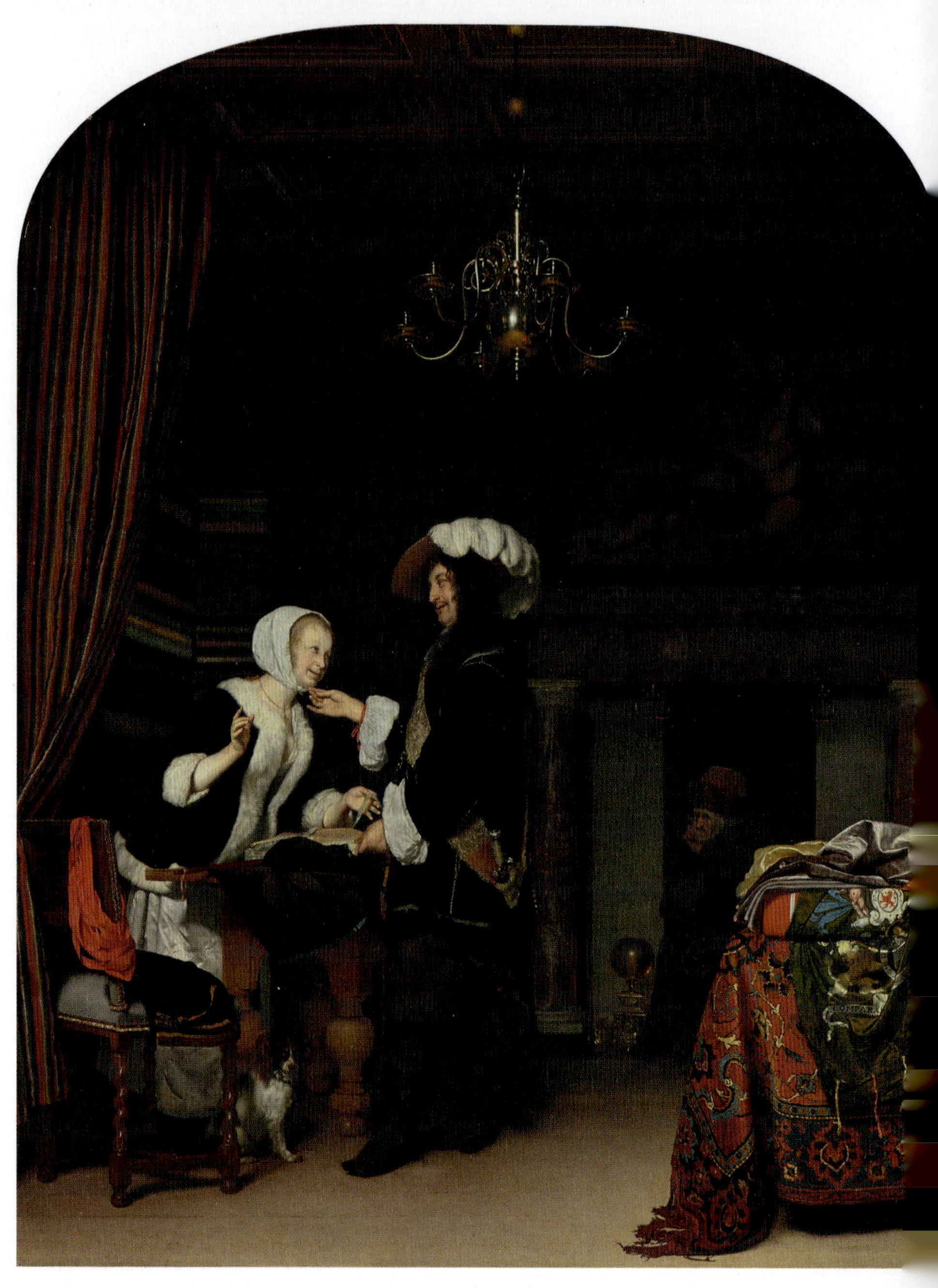

44 Frans van Mieris, *An Officer in a Fabric Shop*, 1660

story behind van Mieris's *Officer in a Fabric Shop*. From the start, he tells us, van Mieris's brushwork drew admirers and patrons, including the Leiden professor Franciscus de le Boë Sylvius. Sylvius often requested priority in acquiring all his work, or at least getting the right of first refusal, an encouraging gesture for a young artist. Through Sylvius, van Mieris got the opportunity to make a painting for Archduke Leopold Wilhelm. It showed a beautiful woman in a silk store alongside a cavalier distracted by her charm. The Archduke was so impressed that he paid a thousand guilders and offered him a position at the Vienna court with an annual bonus of 2,500 guilders, which he declined, citing his wife's disinclination as an excuse.

Whether or not the details of the transaction are accurate, Leopold Wilhelm's acquisition is still one of the proud displays of the Kunsthistorisches Museum in Vienna, which came out of the Habsburg holdings. Van Mieris's fine style, which he learned from Gerard Dou, was highly regarded and richly rewarded. Another archduke, Cosimo III de' Medici, was an even more devoted fan. He bought and ordered about ten paintings from van Mieris, which share space in the Uffizi today with other paintings in the mode known as *Feinmalerei* – precision painting, highly detailed pictures painted with the finest of brushes. Sad to say, despite his high earnings, van Mieris lived in constant debt and even penury. Commentators blamed it on his disorderliness and alcoholism.

The Market

The classic image of the Dutch painter is of a craftworker-retailer who produced at his own risk and sold his work to customers in his shop. It comes as a shock, then, to read the findings of Michael Montias, who did more archive research than anyone on the economics of Dutch painting. Of all the many kinds of transactions he found in the records, not a single one referred to a purchase by an individual buyer directly from a painter. This implies that, aside from direct patronage, there would have been a middleman involved in the sale of paintings. Indeed, in all the art centres of the country we encounter entrepreneurs buying and selling art. Unfortunately, no firm records have been preserved. Our information about dealers' activities must be reconstructed from traces of individual transactions. Hendrick Uylenburgh (1587–1661), one of the major Amsterdam dealers from the 1620s on, is recorded as having been active in an extremely broad range of art-related activities, from selling his own paintings to publishing etchings by others to cleaning and varnishing paintings. Young artists lived in with Uylenburgh at various times. Among them were the high-fliers Rembrandt and Govert

Flinck. Uylenburgh maintained excellent contacts with the city authorities, whereby he brought in commissions for his artist clients.

Business of this kind extended over the borders to wherever the Dutch traded, which was more or less everywhere. Resident or visiting agents would work local markets for what they were worth. Art was often among their wares. One famous example is the way Rembrandt received commissions from Don Antonio Ruffo, a major collector in Sicily. His *Aristotle with a Bust of Homer* (the subject is disputed – Ruffo himself thought it may have been the medieval philosopher Albertus Magnus) was commissioned through a friend of Ruffo's who traded with a wealthy Amsterdam merchant. Subsequent orders went through two commercial Dutch agents and the Italian consul in Amsterdam. Networking and connections were everything.

Inventories of shopkeepers often contain stocks of paintings, usually more than one per master. This was typical of frame makers, painters' supply stores and bookshops. There are also regular indications of commerce in art at taverns, breweries and bakeries. From the point of view of the public, these selling points had the lowest threshold. On occasion, town governments, orphan chambers, courts of justice, civic institutions, guilds and charities would maintain showrooms or hold art auctions, while raffles regularly offered works of art as prizes. Further downmarket were open-air sales at fairs and *kermises* (festivals), pushcarts in the marketplace and peddlers of second-hand goods. Under the right circumstances, such as having an art-loving baker or butcher, barter could be an attractive option for an artist. Yet, with all these possibilities, painters were often stuck with their creations. An inventory of Rembrandt's goods drawn up in 1656 in connection with his bankruptcy (the result of poor judgment, soured relations with those in high places and bad luck) included more than sixty paintings by himself. More Dutch painters died in poverty than prosperity.

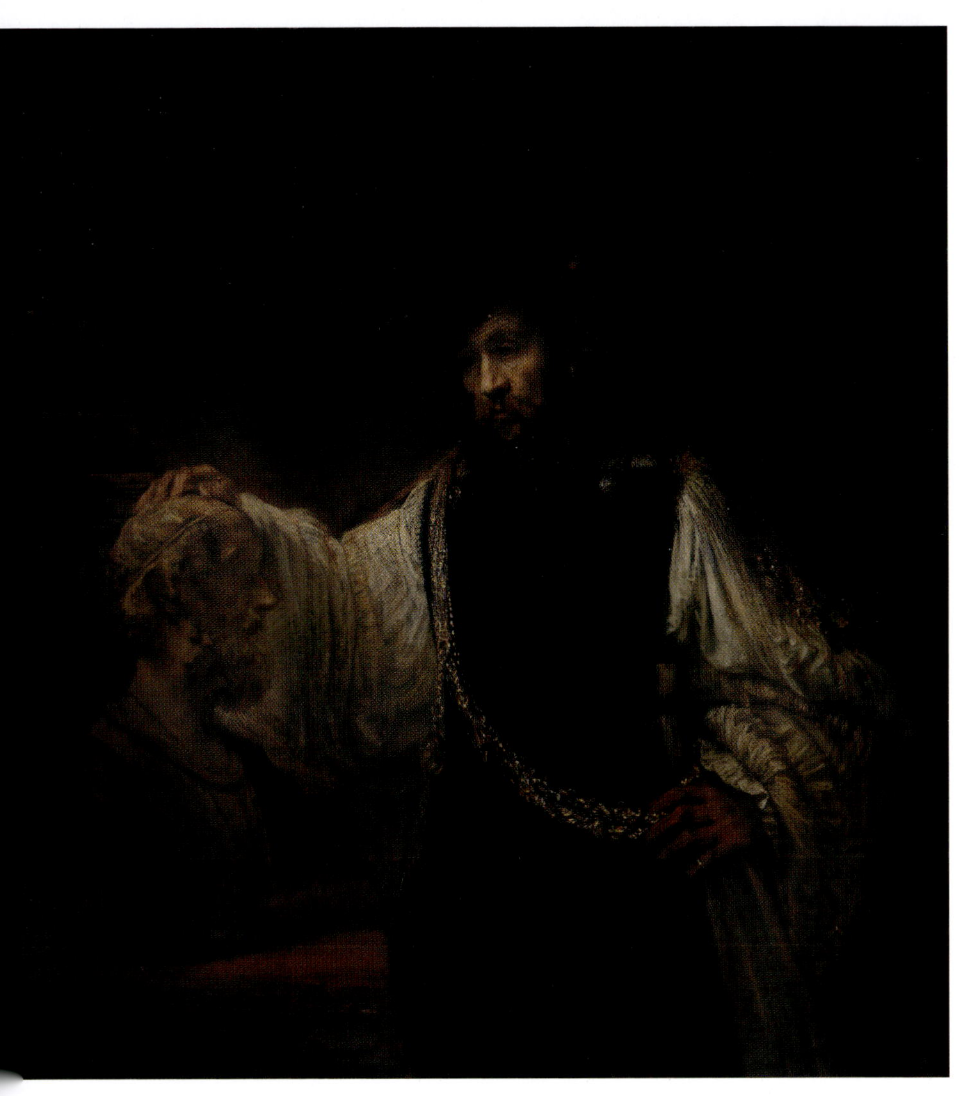

45 Rembrandt van Rijn, *Aristotle with a Bust of Homer*, 1653

Chapter 3
The City Environments

If there is one factor above all others that explains why the
Netherlands produced so many more painters than other
European countries, it would be urbanization. Painting is a
profession for city kids, and for centuries more kids were born
in cities in the Low Countries than anywhere else. In 1600, the
average for Europe was under 10 percent, for the Dutch Republic
more than 50 percent, and for the county of Holland 65. Only
the north of Italy and the Southern Netherlands – important
centres of art production themselves – came anywhere close.
The expansion of the cities, with an increasingly affluent
populace, brought with it a growth in the number of households
calling for decoration. To become a painter was, for the
first half of the seventeenth century, a responsible career
choice. Each of the cities that became a major source for art
production had roots in the Middle Ages and hallmarks of
local pride, in geography, history or tradition, that citizens
were sure distinguished them from everyone else in the world.
Untrue as this was, the factors could play into the way art was
commissioned and made. City chauvinism was strong and
visitors to the country relished the palpable differences between
one town and the next. As discussed by Elisabeth de Bièvre in
her book on Dutch art and urban cultures, the stereotypes were
not airtight. Rembrandt could be a typical Leiden painter and
Emanuel de Witte a typical Delft painter until each of them
moved to Amsterdam and became a typical Amsterdamer.

Dordrecht

In writings and ceremonies in which the cities of Holland
are ranked hierarchically, precedence is always given to, or
taken by, Dordrecht. This privilege derives from its having
been the first to be granted city rights, by Count Willem I in

the year 1220. It was here that, in 1572, the first assembly of
the States-General was held after the renunciation of Spanish
rule. In the seventeenth century the city gave its name to
the ecclesiastical Synod of Dordt (1618–19) at which the strict
Calvinists discredited the more moderate Remonstrants,
leading to the execution (decried as judicial murder) of the
Grand Pensionary Johan van Oldenbarnevelt on 13 May 1619.

For its size, about 12,000 inhabitants in 1650, Dordrecht
produced more excellent artists than anywhere else. Staying
put and serving the locals were four members of the Cuyp
family, Godfried Schalcken and Arnold Houbraken. Better
known are those who moved to Amsterdam and became pupils
of Rembrandt: Ferdinand Bol, Samuel van Hoogstraten,
Nicolaes Maes and Arent de Gelder. The connection between
Rembrandt and the artistic society of Dordrecht may be related
to Rembrandt's longest-standing friendship, with the sombre
Calvinist poet Jeremias de Decker (Dordrecht 1609–1666
Amsterdam). The friendship between the two is exemplary for
the relationship between the visual and verbal arts. In a poem
on Rembrandt's *Christ Appearing to Mary Magdalene*, de Decker
praised Rembrandt's ability to give life to the Bible text. Samuel
van Hoogstraten and his pupil, Arnold Houbraken, wrote two
eminently important books on their art. Hoogstraten, who also
wrote for the theatre, paraphrased the Roman poet Horace in a
somewhat commonplace thought that became a leitmotiv in
writings on art throughout the century: 'The pen has long been
family of the brush, as if it were painting with speech; just as
painting is taken for silent poetry.'

While it may not strike the eye immediately, a famous
genre painting by Nicolaes Maes takes its terms from classical
antiquity, and links word to image. *The Eavesdropper* holds her
finger to her lips, as if to say, 'If only you would be quiet, you
would be able to hear what is going on in this painting.' This
refers to the words of love being spoken to the young lady below
by the officer, who has left his outer clothing and sword on a
chair beneath a map of the world. Above the eavesdropper's
head is a bust of Juno, Roman goddess of marriage and the
household. Of all the ways of reading this intriguing painting,
one of them lies in the homely wisdom that young people are
drawn to each other by erotic passion, only to become confined
in a bourgeois marriage. Nicolaes Maes was born into a well-off
family and enjoyed the privileges of expensive training and
travel abroad before his career firmed up and he began earning
good money on his own, mainly painting portraits in Dordrecht
and Amsterdam.

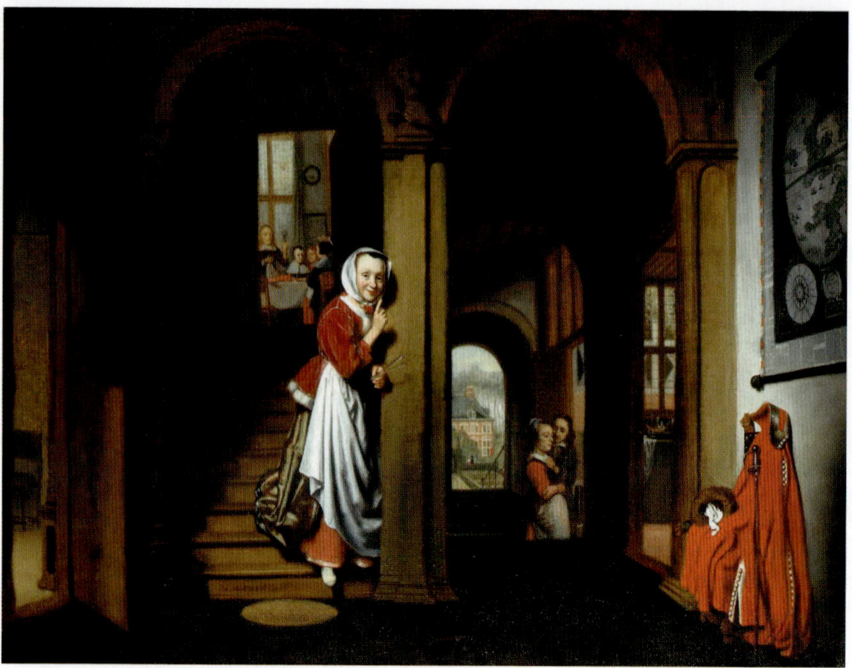

46 Nicolaes Maes, *The Eavesdropper*, 1657

Amsterdam

Until deep into the seventeenth century, the government and bureaucracy of Amsterdam had their premises in a collection of late medieval buildings on Dam Square. The name is descriptive; it was here that the first dam was built on the Amstel River, creating a public space for purposes of all kinds. In addition to the town hall, there stood a weighing hall, a stock exchange and the Nieuwe Kerk (New Church). That government housing was inadequate had been apparent for long, but there was also a kind of pride attached to the legacy site. This is apparent from the fortunes of Pieter Saenredam's depiction of the old town hall. He first drew it, in the words of his characteristically exact inscription, 'on 15, 16, 17, 18, 19, 20 July 1641'. The painting was not made until sixteen years later, in 1657. In 1658 it was bought by the burgomasters. Out of attachment to their past, they ordered it to be hung in their own meeting hall in the new town hall, the true power centre not only of Amsterdam but of the Republic itself.

The replacement of the old town hall was designed by Jacob van Campen, who was a close friend and collaborator of Saenredam's. It has been argued that Saenredam made his drawing of 1641 as an aid to van Campen, who at that time was beginning to formulate

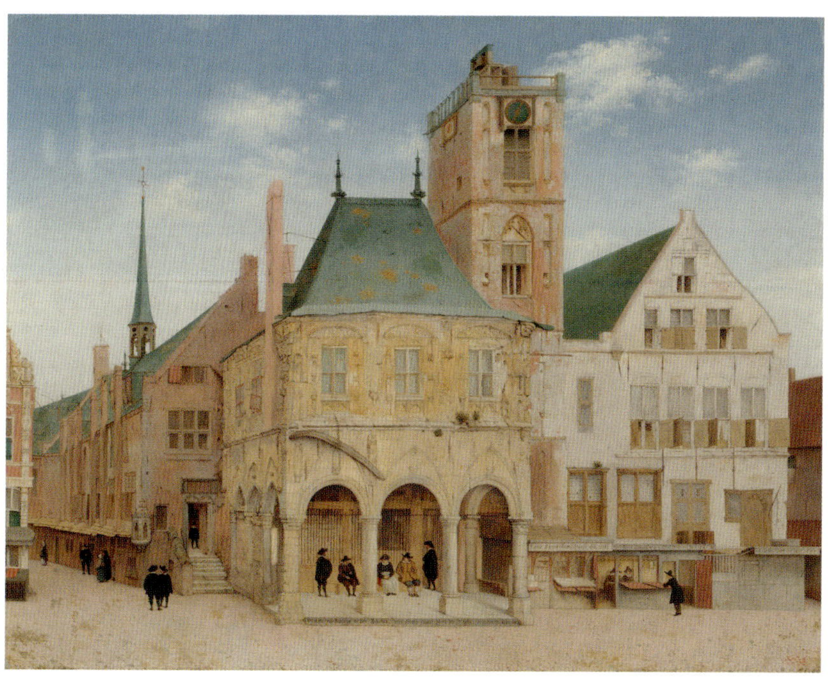

47 Pieter Saenredam, *The Old Town Hall of Amsterdam*, 1657

his ideas for a new town hall. His classical building is immensely
larger than the old premises, and was immediately praised in
book-length poetic encomiums as the Eighth Wonder of the World.
There were of course critics; some considered it too expensive,
others an impious challenge, in the height of its cupola, to the
neighbouring Nieuwe Kerk. Among its defenders was Constantijn
Huygens, who was a patron of both van Campen and Saenredam.
He wrote a congratulatory poem to the burgomasters, saying
that it was God himself who placed them where they now were.
In the 1660s, the burgomasters had the poem carved in black
marble, to hang opposite Saenredam's painting. Both hung in
their original locations until 1808, when the building was turned
into a royal palace.

In 1607, the Amsterdam city government decided that it needed
an imposing home for the legions of traders who came to their
city from all over the world. They sent the town architect
Hendrick de Keyser to London to see how he could vie with the
Royal Exchange that had been opened by Queen Elizabeth I in
1571. De Keyser's building, like the London Exchange and its
model in Antwerp (1531), was an open-air rectangular enclosure
within covered galleries on all sides. Each of the forty-two pillars

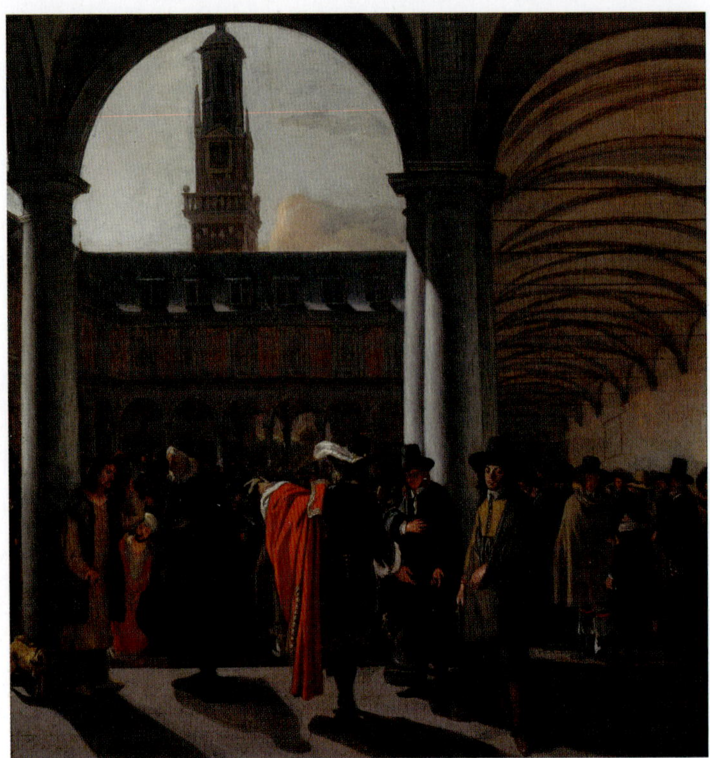

48 Emanuel
de Witte,
*Courtyard of
the Exchange
in Amsterdam,*
1653

was numbered, and traders could apply for a fixed position at
one of them. Most of the trade was in produce, manufactured
goods, valuables and imports, but traffic in bonds, shares and
futures was steadily increasing. The exchange was open only for
one hour a day, from noon, leading to the kind of crowd scene
that Emanuel de Witte shows us in his painting of the building.

Emanuel de Witte was one of the foremost painters of
architecture in the Netherlands. He had his training and
early years as a master in Delft, where from the later 1640s on,
he cultivated the speciality of the church interior. In this he
was joined by two contemporaries, Gerard Houckgeest and
Hendrick van Vliet, so that Delft and its churches, alongside
Pieter Saenredam's church portraits in Haarlem and Utrecht,
became synonymous with architectural painting. In 1650, de
Witte moved to Amsterdam, where he started painting outdoor
markets, soon to return to church interiors. Of these, 130 survive,
divided between church portraits and what has been called the
realistic imaginary church (compare fig. 114). His painting of
the Exchange precedes these. It is the only motif in de Witte's

work that he painted only once, feeding the supposition that it was a commission. The human element is prominent in this painting, above the institutional and the architectural. One feature that recurs in Amsterdam street scenes is the presence of foreigners – exemplified here in the figures in oriental dress on the left. In life, humanity was not de Witte's strong point. He was constantly at odds with his environment. Arnold Houbraken's downbeat report on him, which ends with his suicide in an Amsterdam canal, is accepted as reliable.

The painting that exemplifies Amsterdam pride in the mid-seventeenth century is a city view by the German-born Johannes Lingelbach. (Note that more artists represented in this book died in Amsterdam than were born there.) It's all here. In the right background appear the masts of ships on the Damrak, bringing in goods from the ports of the world. On the facing shore, the backs of the houses on the Warmoesstraat show where the wealthiest merchants lived, with storage of their wares on the upper floors. Across the Damrak sacks are being brought into one of the houses. Beside a loading winch are small market stalls. In the middle is the weighing hall, where officials controlled the quality and weight of goods being brought into the city and levied customs fees. In the left background stands the Nieuwe Kerk, where the Reformed regents prayed. The throng in the square is an encyclopedic compendium of all the mercantile, hawking, cart-pushing and socializing activities a Hollywood director might later put into a big-city crowd scene, complete with a

49 Johannes Lingelbach, *Dam Square in Amsterdam, with the New Town Hall under Construction*, 1656

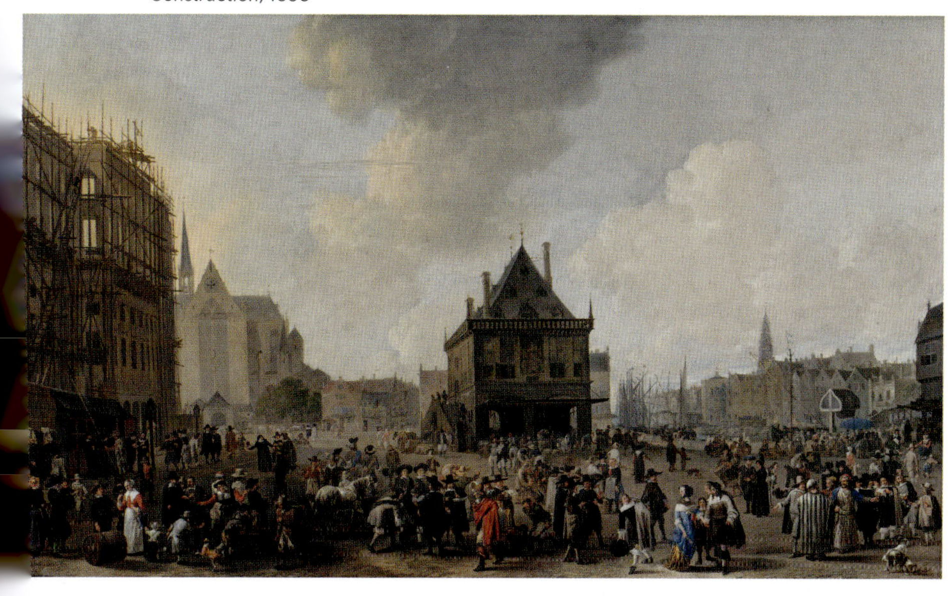

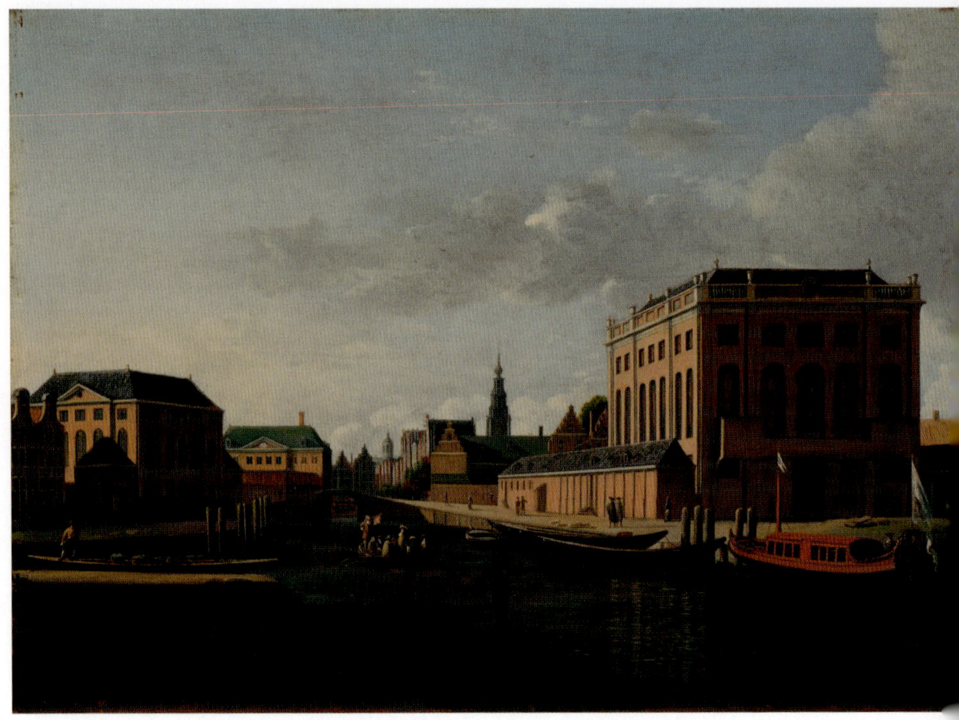

50 Gerrit Berckheyde, *The Two Synagogues in Amsterdam*, c. 1680–85

drummer, stray and pet dogs, and a number of 'easterlings' to show how cosmopolitan Amsterdam was. The painting is from the historical holdings of the city, suggesting that it was made on commission by the town government.

To the left the new town hall is under construction. At its foot is a remnant of the old situation we know from the Saenredam – the exchange booth, whose operations had to go on even in the midst of building activities. Next to it, at the very left, two men are studying a list chalked on the wall. You would not know it from the buoyant mood of the crowd, but they are pointing out the names of the latest victims of the bubonic plague that was killing thousands of Dutch people that year. Above the door to their right we read '896 deaths'. Not until a deadlier outbreak ten years later did the city take steps to counter the spread of the disease, by quarantining seamen coming ashore from ports where the plague raged.

Another source of Amsterdam pride was its reputation for confessional tolerance in a Europe ravaged by religious warfare. The Jewish communities formed one of the city's most prominent immigrant populations. Their acceptance by the city went in stages. The first refugees from the Iberian peninsula fled there in the 1590s and were admitted as Catholics, which they had had to pretend to be in Spain and Portugal. Soon enough in the seventeenth century, a more realistic policy was adopted; the Sephardim from southern Europe and the Ashkenazim from central Europe were allowed to practise their religion under certain restrictions. At first, these included the stipulation that places of worship should not be recognizable from the street. By 1639, this had been relaxed to the point that the Sephardim were allowed to put an impressive façade on their synagogue. In 1642, it received a historical, ground-breaking visit from Stadholder Frederik Hendrik; Henrietta Maria, queen consort of Charles I of England; and her daughter Mary, who was married to the stadholder's son. About 1670, both communities built monumental synagogues, with the city providing the services of the town architect to supervise their design and construction. Between them, they were a beacon for Jewish religious and communal life, and a highlighting of Amsterdam's tolerance. The synagogues were a tourist attraction from the start, and a thankful motif for artists, including a view of both buildings by Gerrit Berckheyde who, with his older brother Job, was the foremost painter of townscapes in Holland.

Delft

Art in seventeenth-century Delft started off in the portrait factory of Michiel van Mierevelt (1566–1641) and his engraver son-in-law Willem Jacobsz Delff (1580–1638). Michiel's paintings of Prince Maurits, the first of which was a commission, and other dignitaries, were so highly desired that he produced them en masse, making use of templates and stencils to replicate not only the figures but even the faces of his sitters. Michiel's portraits of public figures would be published in engravings by Willem, adding to the revenues. The relation with the House of Orange was not coincidental. From 1572 to 1584, Delft was home to Willem van Oranje – William of Orange, the Father of His Country, also called William the Silent. He lived in a house since called the Prinsenhof, Court of the Prince, now the home of the Delft museum of art and history. After he was murdered there in 1584 and buried in the Nieuwe Kerk, where a spectacular tomb monument by Hendrick de Keyser was completed in 1623, Delft became a pilgrimage site for his admirers. For the painters of Delft, this provided a rich motif. The tomb was depicted by all three architectural painters named above – Gerard Houckgeest, Emanuel de Witte and Hendrick van Vliet – and several others. Something of the geometry of their work,

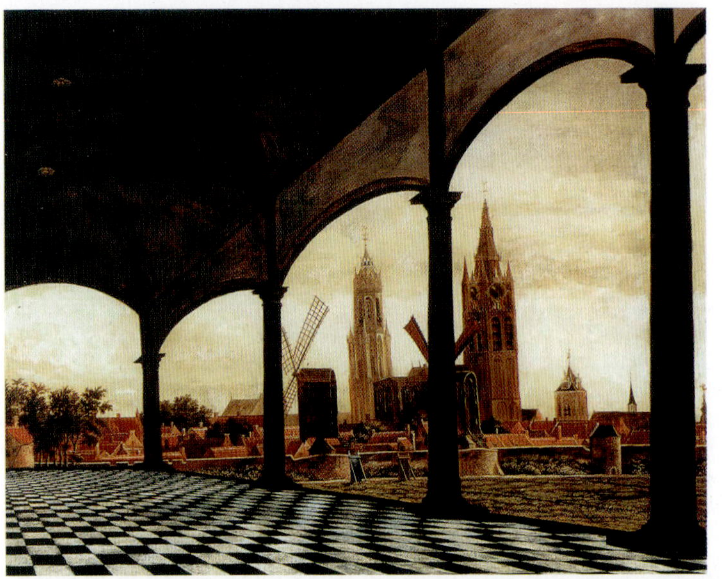

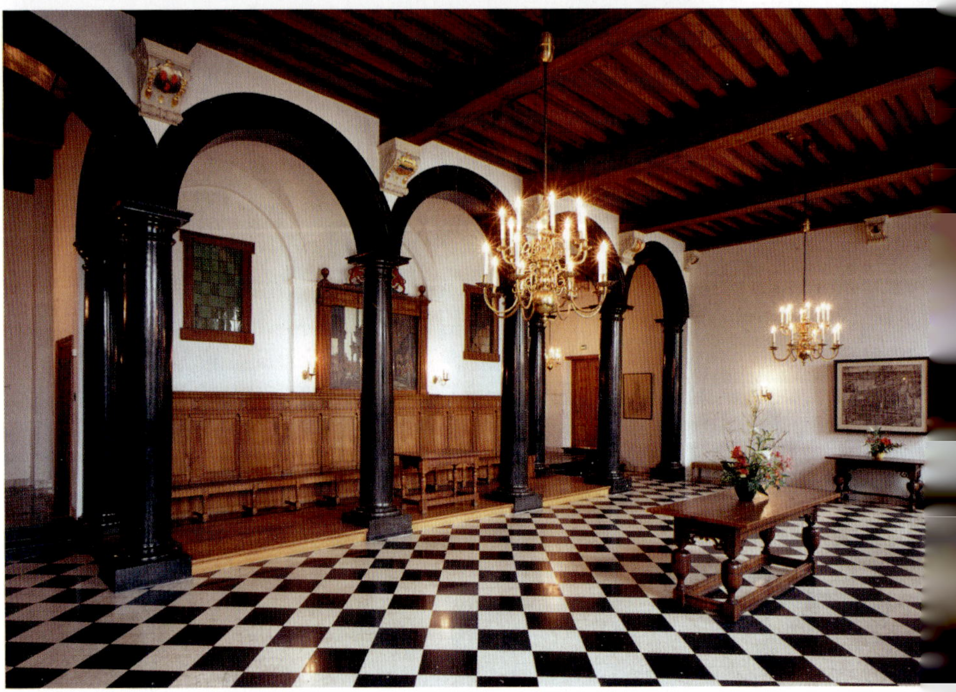

51 TOP Daniël Vosmaer, *View of Delft*, 1663
52 ABOVE Gallery above the tribunal chamber, town hall of Delft

their interest in perspective and optical effects fused with a new image of the Delft School. Such characteristics were seen in other genres of painting in Delft, such as Johannes Vermeer's exteriors and interiors, the courtyards and households of Pieter de Hooch, and the town views of Carel Fabritius and Daniël Vosmaer.

The daring view of the Nieuwe Kerk in Delft from a music shop that Carel Fabritius painted in 1652 was reiterated in 1663 by Daniël Vosmaer, in apparent tribute to his late colleague. Here the eye-catching vantage point is a gallery whose classical elements contrast with the medieval forms of the church towers it frames. It was long assumed that the loggia sprang from the fantasy of the artist. However, a clever curator of the Prinsenhof pointed out that the Delft town hall has a gallery with architectural elements identical to Vosmaer's loggia, while the vaulting corresponds to the baldachin above the tomb of William of Orange in the Nieuwe Kerk. This insight tells us that Vosmaer's painting is a deliberate melange of authentic Delft motifs and warns us against accepting received opinion uncritically.

Haarlem

Haarlem claims a special place as a centre for Dutch painting, thanks to Karel van Mander. The first Dutch painters whose lives he described – Albert van Ouwater, Geertgen tot Sint Jans and Dieric Bouts – were born and trained there, giving it the deserved reputation of having brought forth 'very good, or the best painters in the entire Netherlands'. At the end of the century, it was van Mander himself, with Cornelis Cornelisz van Haarlem and Hendrick Goltzius, who took the lead in providing the craft of painting with a theoretical underpinning, institutionalized in an Academy which obtained permission to employ nude models. The particular excellence that distinguished Haarlem, noted in writings on the city, was its natural setting on the Spaarne River, in the bosom of fields and forests, dunes and beaches that made for delightful outings. In 1611, this reputation was bolstered with the trend-setting publication of eleven etchings of *Plaisante Plaetsen*, pleasant country locations in the environs of Haarlem. In Dutch painting, it is fair to say that no better landscapes and townscapes were made than in Haarlem.

If church towers are the defining features in the skylines of Dutch towns and cities, that of the Bavokerk in Haarlem takes the main prize. No artist pictured that radiant, nearly mystical view as brilliantly as Jacob van Ruisdael. Such was the impact of his several panoramas of Haarlem that they became a concept.

Inventories of the time call them *Haarlempjes*, little Haarlems. Everything else in the painting – the smaller towers on the horizon, human activity in the foreground bleaching fields, the very clouds in the sky – pay homage to the church tower, the scale of which, in a bit of artistic cheating, is considerably enlarged. A pious viewer of a *Haarlempje* will have seen rising to the sky the house where he would go to hear the word of God.

The location of the Bavokerk within the city was every bit as spectacular as its appearance from the surroundings. Called the Grote Kerk (Great Church), it stood on the Grote Markt (Great Market Square). On the square lie small market halls that now serve cultural functions. The earmark city views of Haarlem, including several by the Berckheyde brothers, showed the Grote Markt. The signature church interiors were made

53 Jacob van Ruisdael, *View of Haarlem from the Northwest, with Bleaching Fields in the Foreground*, c. 1670–75

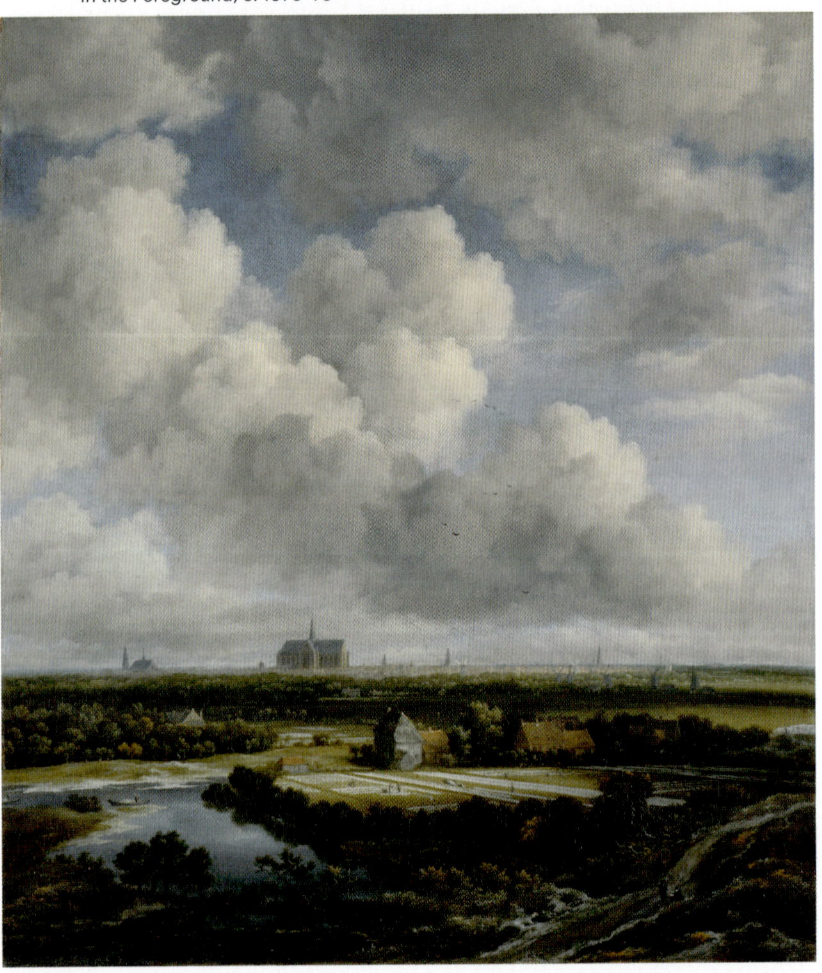

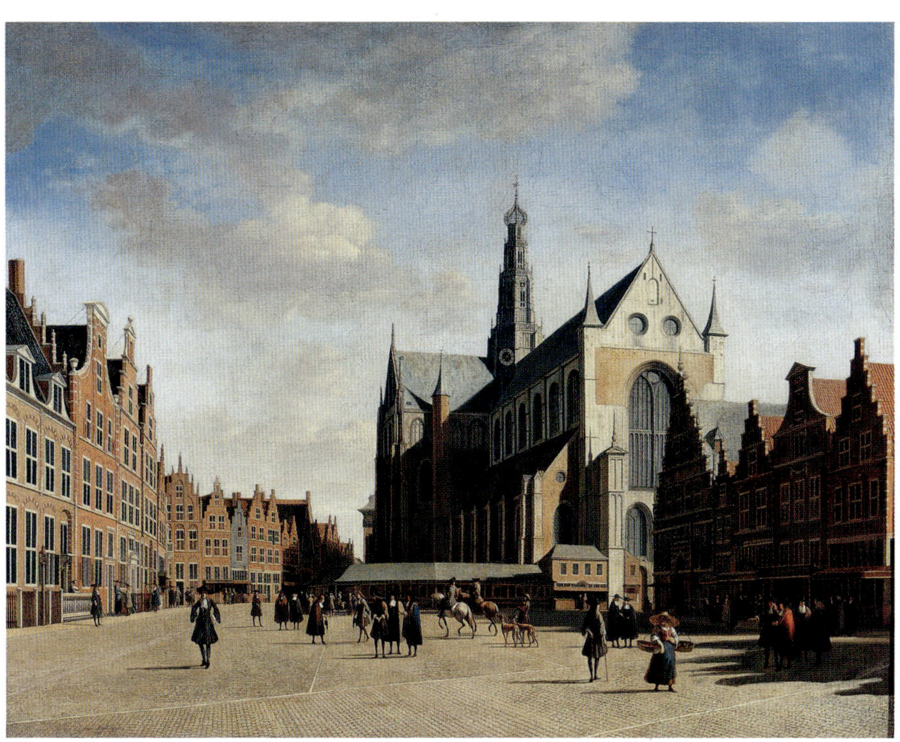

54 Gerrit Berckheyde, *The Great Square and Bavokerk in Haarlem*, 1696

inside the Bavokerk. In the masterful hands of Pieter
Saenredam, paintings of the Bavokerk virtually defined the
genre of the church interior from 1630 to 1650, when it was
joined by the Nieuwe Kerk in Delft. On the other end of the
Grote Markt stands the town hall (1370) and the adjacent
Prinsenhof, the Prince's Court, which was a showplace for art.
In 1590, the township commissioned three major history
paintings and one contemporary one for the adornment of the
building, an expropriated Dominican monastery (1290), where
two paintings by Maarten van Heemskerck already hung.
Haarlem distinguished itself in this way as the city providing
the most highly esteemed hospitality for the stadholder. The
building was later to house the municipal museum, before it
moved to the old men's home and was dubbed the Frans Hals
Museum. What these circumstances amount to is that the
museification of Haarlem had already begun by 1600 and has
been in steady progress since, a harbinger of a development
that is overtaking all the city centres of Europe.

The Hague

The Hague enjoyed two main distinctions. It was home to
the physical premises from which the Netherlands had been
ruled since the thirteenth century – and still is, as the oldest
functioning parliamentary complex in Europe. The main
bodies of government, the States of the provinces and the
States-General in which they joined, met here. And it was the
residence of the princes of Orange and their families, the
leading political and military personalities in the country.
These elements are on prominent display in a painting by
Paulus van Hillegaert. The main motif is a show-off cavalcade
of leading personages from the House of Orange. Their formal
relationship to the States-General was that of appointed
officials, mainly as commanders-in-chief of the States Army.
That is not, however, how they saw themselves. Although the
stadholderate was never occupied by any other than Orange-
Nassaus, it did not become their final right by inheritance
until the mid-eighteenth century. In the constellation of the
painting, the lead is taken by the highest-ranking persons:
Friedrich V of the Palatinate, the king-for-a-year of Bohemia,
and his royal wife, Elizabeth Stuart. Identifiable in their train
are stadholders Maurits, his half-brother Frederik Hendrik
and cousin Willem Lodewijk.

The guiding thought of the painting is the status of the
House, which can be deduced from the fact that two of the
riders were no longer alive: William of Orange himself, and
his deceased oldest son Philip Willem, who had lived in
Spanish capture and remained a Catholic. A mercenary leader
in the service of the States, Christian of Braunschweig, is
recognizable, but the identity of the others is uncertain. The
painting is confected from different sources, the cavalcade
from one print and the buildings from another, while several
of the equestrians and their mounts were traced over from
existing templates. This is one of the Dutch paintings most
obviously catering to special interests and furthest removed
from being 'art for art's sake'.

Leiden

Leiden was a 'town and gown' place. It was the foremost centre
of the textile industry, not only in the country but in all of
Europe. Given the variety and unrivalled quality of woollens
made there, Leiden cloth was the paragon of its kind. This
position was attained through a selective immigration policy,
as Leiden absorbed the best entrepreneurs, craftsmen
and workers among the refugees fleeing to the Northern
Netherlands in the last quarter of the sixteenth century.

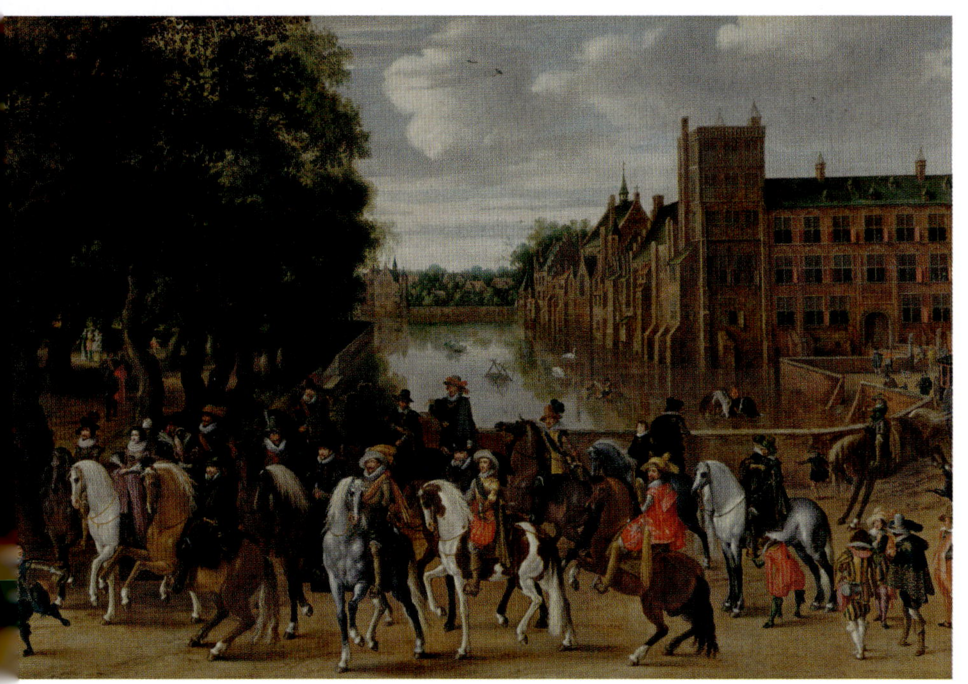

55 Paulus van Hillegaert, *The Princes of Orange and their Families on Horseback, Riding Out from the Buitenhof, The Hague*, c. 1621–22

The innovations brought by the immigrants led the town to advertise their wares as the New Drapery. The main products, heavy baize and its lighter variant serge, set the standard for cloth quality everywhere. But there were several other varieties of textile, each with its own workshop and supervising body. The industry gave employ not only to Dutch and Flemish workers but also to thousands from Germany. It must be said that the prosperity this brought with it was not equally shared. Poor working conditions, including child labour, were an enduring source of misery.

At the start of this development, Leiden enjoyed another demographic windfall. On 2 January 1575, the valuable right to found a university was granted to the city. As with the textile industry, this was fed by the Revolt. According to chroniclers, Leiden was being compensated for the losses it incurred in the Spanish siege, which had been broken on 3 October 1574. The importance of this licence can hardly be overstated. Until that time, the foremost university in the Low Countries, where the leaders of church and state were educated, lay in Louvain, in the Spanish Netherlands. When the hostilities made it impossible not only for the Dutch, but for Protestants from all over Europe, to study there, Leiden University became the place to go, not only for theology and law, but also medicine, natural history, the classics and oriental languages. The city became the academic and publishing capital of Protestant Europe, adding more thousands of faculty, students and high-class professionals to the population.

Personal genius also played a role. The Dutch artist of the greatest renown in the sixteenth century was Lucas van Leyden (Leiden 1494–1533 Leiden). The spread of his highly coveted prints throughout Europe carried with it the name of his city. Rembrandt was known as a Leidener, although he moved at a young age to Amsterdam. Of the artists who stayed in the city, Gerard Dou and Frans van Mieris made the Leiden School famous for the kind of fine painting that strongly appealed to German and Italian courts (see p. 67). In the second edition of the authoritative *Description of the City of Leiden* by its burgomaster, Jan Jansz Orlers, twenty-eight pages are dedicated to 'The Famous Painters that were Born in this City Leiden'.

Isaac Claesz van Swanenburg belongs to a special, fascinating group: artists who occupied high political appointment, from which they give themselves commissions. Among them are two of the greatest European artists of the preceding centuries: the Italian Piero della Francesca, town councillor in Borgo San Sepolcro (*Christ Resurrected, c.* 1458); and the German Albrecht Altdorfer, Outer Council member of Regensburg, Bavaria (*The Town Synagogue on the Eve of its Demolition, Ordered by the Council*, 1519). Isaac Claesz, as councillor, magistrate and burgomaster of Leiden, not only received the best painting commissions from the municipality, but also supplied designs for the new town hall. That these artists were all masters of technique and perspective was surely a major factor in their success. Isaac Claesz's painting of a stage in wool production is one of seven large panels ordered by the township in 1594 for the governors' chamber of the recently constructed Serge Hall. Two of them are allegories, and the others depictions of the actual work. The series is exceptional for its thoroughness and shows just how seriously Leiden took the art of painting as an adjunct to its hard-core industry.

A follow-up commission was given to Abraham van den Tempel in 1650 for three magnificent allegories in up-to-date classical style and with reference to the success of the Revolt. One shows the Leiden Maiden being crowned by Minerva. The goddess of wisdom stands for the university, paying tribute to its domicile. She is accompanied by Mercury, bringing the business sense that an industry needs, and Justice, to be provided and enforced by the city. The second painting shows the woeful effects of warfare, as Mars, the god of war, drives off the Cloth Industry, along with

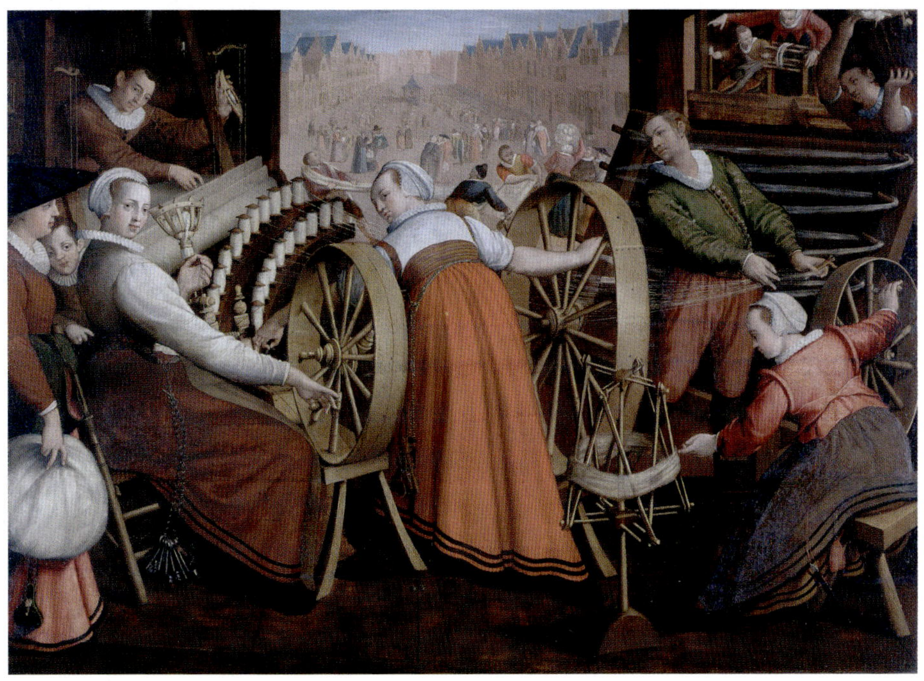

56 Isaac Claesz van Swanenburg, *Spinning, Shearing the Warp and Weaving Wool,* c. 1607

Minerva and Mercury. The third allegory depicts the peacetime reception accorded to Cloth Industry by the Leiden Maiden, again with her divine protectors.

Van den Tempel was particularly gifted in what the Dutch call *stofuitdrukking,* capturing the singular properties of different materials, especially textiles. The satiny finish of the thin woollen garments depicted is achieved by 'fulling' the cloth. This was the most expensive variety of textile, and as the painting shows, it took dyes brilliantly. Van den Tempel was the son of a leading Leeuwarden artist, Lambert Jacobsz. After his father's death in 1636, he continued his training in Amsterdam, under one of his father's best pupils, Jacob Backer, and in emulation of the polished portrait style of Bartholomeus van der Helst. In 1646 he moved to Leiden, giving his profession as *laeckendrapier,* cloth dealer, when he married a year later. In 1653, at the age of thirty, he matriculated as 'a famous painter' into Leiden University to study mathematics. It is assumed that he followed not the Latin courses of the academic curriculum, but those given in Dutch for 'the unlearned, such as bricklayers, carpenters and the like' in a church across the canal from van den Tempel's house. The

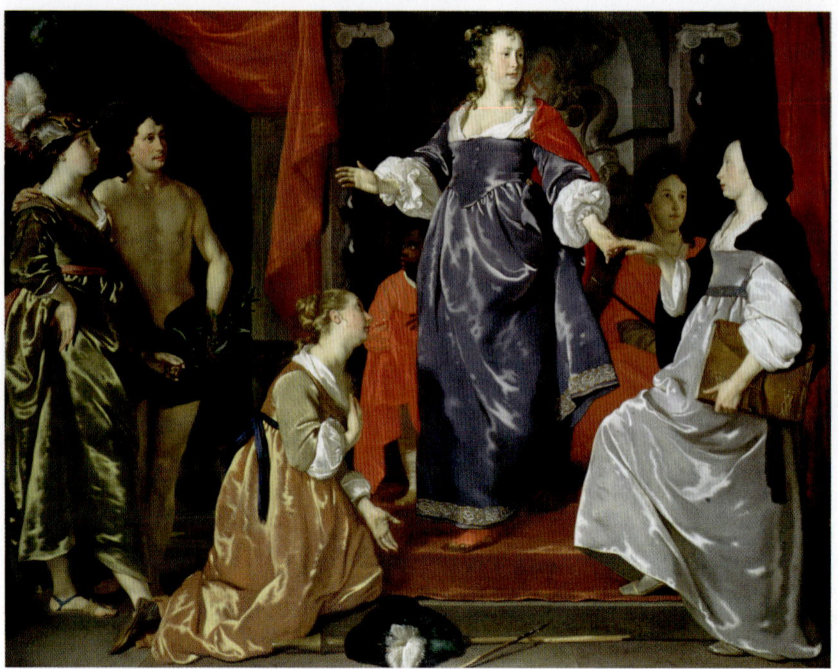

lecturer was Professor Franciscus van Schooten, brother of the painter Joris van Schooten, another beneficiary of municipal patronage. As in the civic guard portrait by Bartholomeus van der Helst, which he certainly knew, van den Tempel too painted a small Black boy into the composition, behind the skirts of the Leiden Maiden. He is gazing up wide-eyed at Minerva and Mercury on the left. None of the writings on the painting mention him, and his role in the scene remains obscure.

Pictures of university life, aside from student revelry, are so rare that the same painting by Hendrick van der Burch is always illustrated. Coming out of the handsome stone gate of the Academy Building are the two university beadles, with their rods of office, followed by the degree recipient, in a flat cap, flanked by two professors in high hats, presumably the one who supervised the dissertation and the rector who put the bull into the hands of the successful candidate. The building with the red tile roof on the right was the shop of the university printers, the Elseviers. Not many painters went to university. Famously, Rembrandt was inscribed in the rolls of Leiden University. It was long assumed that this was merely a matter of form, because all pupils of his Leiden Latin school were matriculated upon graduation. It was worth doing so for the privileges attached to the status of student.

They did not have to pay tax on beer and wine, and were exempted from service in the civic guard. It was even doubted whether Rembrandt ever attended classes. Recently, however, Leiden University archivist Mart van Duijn discovered that he was registered for a second year, leaving no doubt that he did at least one full year of academic study. The importance of the university for young artists went further than the opportunity to study. It was a resource for knowledge, especially of the ancients and of oriental languages, while bringing to the city a population of cultivated individuals, some of whom collected or commissioned art. For example, the Utrecht patrician Johannes Wtenbogaert, who as a law student in Leiden lodged with a relative of Rembrandt's, later became his patron and protector.

Utrecht

From the year 695 to 1580, Utrecht was the seat of the largest diocese in the Low Countries, presided over by a bishop (from 1559 on an archbishop) who was also a prince-bishop, with secular as well as religious authority. The Revolt did not entirely

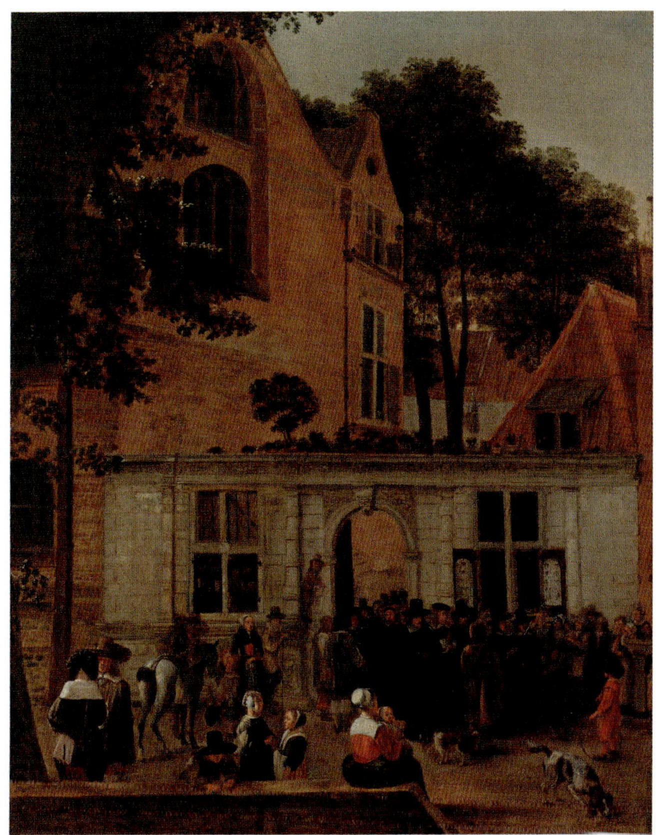

57 OPPOSITE Abraham van den Tempel, *The Leiden Maiden Receives the Broadcloth Industry*, 1651
58 RIGHT Hendrick van der Burch, *The Conferring of a Degree at Leiden University*, c. 1650

undo these powers. Although all ecclesiastical properties were expropriated by the new Republic, one Catholic institution managed to retain its holdings and prerogatives. These were the canons' chapters attached to five Utrecht churches. The canons were not ordained monks, and were allowed to continue running their institutions if they agreed to call themselves Protestants. In this way sizeable fortunes in land remained in the hands of bodies formed increasingly by aristocrats and patricians who took little pain to disguise their sympathy for Catholicism. Their taste in art tended towards mythology and pastoral scenes, with their literary associations and sublimated eroticism. They shared this predilection with courtiers and principals of the House of Orange, some of whom bought their way into the wealthy chapters, and of the Winter King and Queen, whose palace lay in Utrecht province. Into the 1630s, when Amsterdam artists began to butt into the field, the production of pastorals and portraits with pastoral themes was a Utrecht monopoly.

Utrecht artists enjoyed other Catholic connections that affected their careers and choice of specialities. After the church hierarchy was disbanded in the Revolt, the Mother Church was allowed to establish, in Utrecht, an apostolic vicariate for the protection of Catholic interests in the Republic. The artistic needs of Catholic places of worship were filled in the first place by artists from that city. The route to Rome was also more heavily travelled by Utrecht artists than those from the cities of Holland, the province of the other six centres in this chapter. They brought back with them a taste for the less sublimated eroticism of Venetian courtesan paintings and for Caravaggesque sensuousness.

The Utrecht artist at the forefront of the fashion for paintings of shepherds and shepherdesses was Paulus Moreelse. He enhanced the attractiveness of the genre by conflating it with portraiture. The first known instance of this is his portrait of two little girls who have not yet been identified, but who undoubtedly had the good fortune to be born to wealthy parents from the Utrecht elite. That the animal in their care is not a sheep but a goat, which is usually a symbol of licentiousness, has been played off against the floral symbolism in the painting as a signal of moral tension. The goat stands for the temptations of the flesh that the girls will later face, while the white lily that they hold is a token of their youthful innocence. Maybe.

Moreelse, who practised architecture as well as painting, is another artist who occupied political office and, as a member of the Utrecht town council, used it to bring in major commissions. In 1636 he designed a city gate and a year later

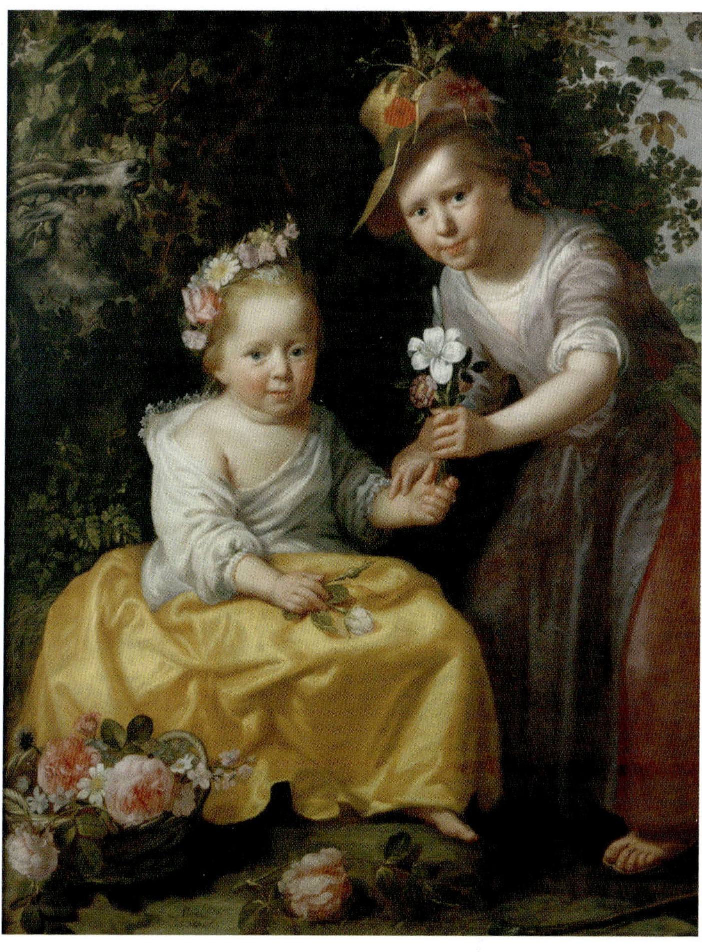

59 Paulus Moreelse, *Pastoral Portrait of Two Little Girls*, 1622

the city meat market. He owed his lifelong appointment to the council to his reactionary politics. In the turbulent 1610s, with tensions between Remonstrants and Counter-Remonstrants running high and lives at stake, Moreelse, together with Joachim Wtewael and his family (see pp. 124–6), lent his support to the Counter-Remonstrant faction, to the point of participating in a coup in 1618. This was the side favoured by the stadholder, Prince Maurits, who installed his local allies in prime positions.

Not all Caravaggist paintings made by Utrecht masters were salacious. Hendrick ter Brugghen, the only one of the group who may actually have met Caravaggio in Rome before the Italian master fled the city in 1606, used Caravaggesque devices

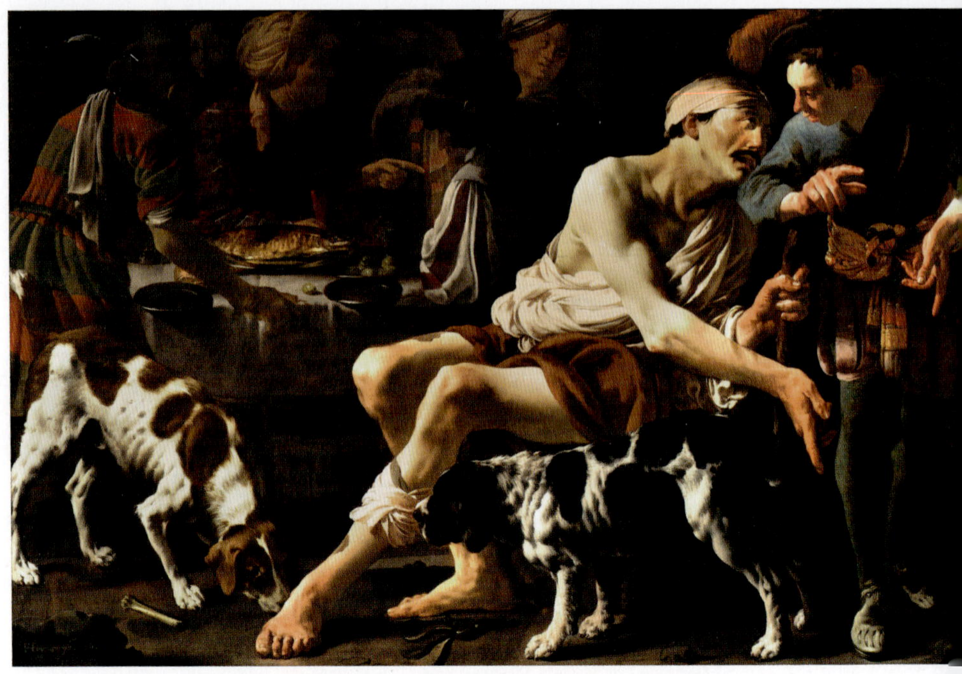

60 Hendrick ter Brugghen, *Lazarus and the Rich Man*, 1625

to convey moral messages, as in *Lazarus and the Rich Man*. The strong light-and-dark division and the theatrically intense contact between the main figures, pushing out of the picture plane, were surely inspired by Caravaggio. Specific motifs in the painting are however derived from sixteenth-century print cycles, a source to which Dutch painters often turned.

There was a rich man who was dressed in purple and fine linen and lived in luxury every day. At his gate was laid a beggar named Lazarus, covered with sores and longing to eat what fell from the rich man's table. Even the dogs came and licked his sores. (Luke 16:19–21)

Ter Brugghen lays it on even thicker by showing one of the rich man's servants sending Lazarus away, denying him even the crumbs from the rich man's table. What every Christian viewer of the painting knew is that the ultimate victim in this parable is the rich man. After both men died, Lazarus is taken into the arms of the patriarch Abraham in heaven, while the rich man is tormented in hell. His plea to Abraham to allow Lazarus to 'dip the tip of his finger in water and cool my tongue' is refused

by Abraham. The immense wealth that flooded to the Dutch
upper classes brought with it, at least to some sensitive souls,
the discomfiting feeling that they might end up in hell. Their
way of dealing with this was to perform acts of charity. A
painting such as this large, expensive canvas, by a top artist of
the time, would have been paid for by a private, wealthy patron
to be presented to a charitable institution. Because the Bible
makes a point of Lazarus's sores, there is a certain logic in
thinking that the recipient organization was a leper asylum.

Hendrick ter Brugghen was another of the artists born into
a distinguished milieu. His father held high administrative
posts in Utrecht and The Hague. There is every reason
to assume that he attended a Latin school before being
apprenticed to Abraham Bloemaert.

An Inland City: Zwolle

Today's Kingdom of the Netherlands and its predecessor,
the Republic of the Seven United Provinces, are often called
Holland, which may be taken as an affront by the inhabitants
of the other, currently eleven and formerly six provinces.
Many artists featured here are from the province of Holland,
now divided into North and South Holland. In a gesture of
redress, also included is a provincial painting of great charm
by the Zwolle artist Hendrick ten Oever. This is a pastoral of
another kind.

Ten Oever shows not shepherds and shepherdesses from
Virgil's *Eclogues*, but a bunch of city folk skinny-dipping in
farmland waters. Only an artist who lived in the provinces
would have come up with the idea of taking this as a subject,
and ten Oever painted it more than once. (But it must be
said that he also painted three children in the Moreelse
mode.) Incidental records tell us that he dealt in painting
supplies, was a member of the church council, and that
Stadholder Willem III blocked his appointment to the post
of alderman because of his supposed anti-Orangism. It may
not reflect his own opinions, but it took a certain daring to
paint the portrait of highly controversial Zwolle bookseller,
Barend Hakvoort, who was accused of being an atheist and
whose books were later banned.

The artistic background and identity of Hendrick ten Oever
are attached to two amorphous personalities. In biographical
entries he is said to have been trained by the female artist Eva
van Marle. This would have made him unique among Dutch
artists of his time. However, recent evidence explored by Saskia
Zwiers indicates that the woman named Eva van Marle was not
a painter at all. There is a male candidate for the painter who

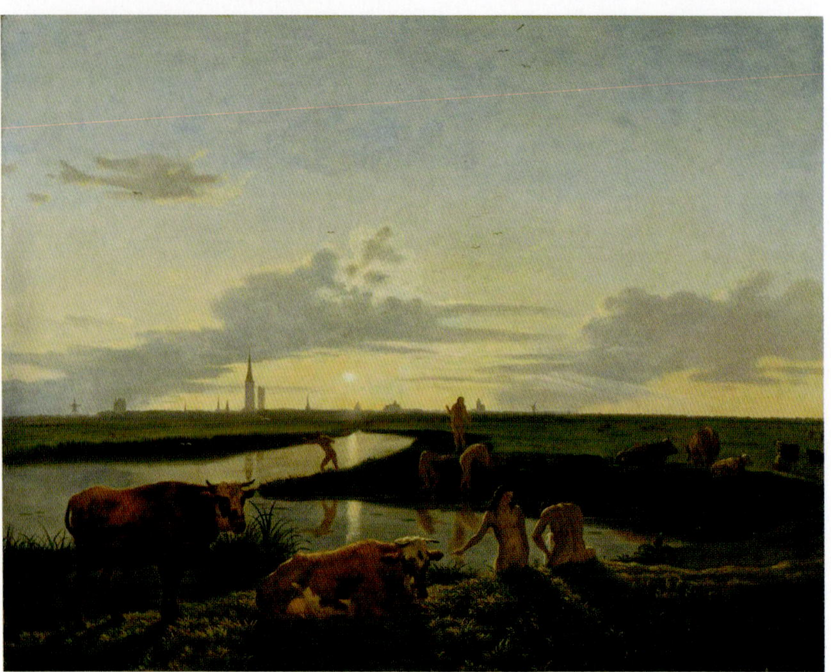

61 Hendrick ten Oever, *Landscape Outside Zwolle with Cows and Bathers*, 1675

signed with the monogram EM: Evert Meertman. Hendrick's touch was attractive enough to inspire imitation, in the case of one unidentified master so closely that he has been dubbed the Pseudo-ten Oever.

Chapter 4
The Female Brush

In 1718, Arnold Houbraken published the first of the three
volumes of his compendious lives of painters from the
Netherlands, with biographical sketches of all the important
painters who lived after the time of Karel van Mander and
were not in *The Book of the Painter.* Although it did not include
many female artists, he gave his book the title *Great Theatre
of Netherlandish Painters and Paintresses.* This was a big step
up from van Mander, who mentioned only two from the
Netherlands: Marguerite van Eyck, the sister of Jan and Hubert;
and Anna Smijters, a miniaturist whose 'astonishing neatness
and precision with paint and brush' made a great impression
on van Mander. Since we know of more women artists from
before 1604, we can only say that van Mander took no pains
to find out who they were. Houbraken did make some effort,
and mentions seventeen Dutch and Flemish women painters,
miniaturists, textile and glass artists post-van Mander, and
some who should have been in van Mander's book, such as
Catharina van Hemessen. By Houbraken's time, it had become
a theme in writings on art to single out women, often with
the remark they were as good as or better than their male
colleagues. In an article on the women artists in Houbraken,
Margarita Russell made this enlightening observation:

*With few exceptions, all belonged to artists' families; usually
they were daughters, sisters, or wives of well-established painters.
This was almost a prerequisite of their success. Indeed, the
painter-father of Adriana Spilberg realized that his daughter's
talent would be stunted in a conventional marriage and insisted
that she marry a painter; she followed his advice twice.*

The exceptions were women such as Aleida Greve and Anna Maria van Schurman, who felt too constrained by society's constructs and set off on their own, choosing not to marry. The general rule, however, was that women artists worked in family ateliers. Sometimes, their work was incorporated into the oeuvres of the men in their family. It seems quite possible, though not to all, that after her marriage to Jan Miense Molenaer, Judith Leyster continued to paint, but that her production was sold as his work, which commanded a higher price. Given Molenaer's chronic shortage of cash, it would seem unlikely that, as received scholarly wisdom has it, Leyster never painted after their marriage.

* * *

Collated below are the women painters from the Northern (and Southern) Netherlands featured in the *Great Theatre*, with dates, specialities, and volume and page references to the first edition:

Anna Francisca de Bruyns (1604/05–1656),
portraits, 1:163
Diana Glauber (1650–1721),
portraits, histories, 3:220
Margaretha van Godewijk (1627–77),
glass painter, needlework, 1:316–17
Maria de Grebber (1602–80),
portraits, 2:122–23
Johanna Koerten (1650–1715),
portraits on glass and paper, 3:230
Maria Sibylla Merian (1647–1717),
portraits, still life, 3:220–24
Maria van Oosterwijck (1630–93),
flowers, 2:214–18
Catharina Oostfries (1636–1708),
glass painter, 2:209
Geertje Pieters (also Geertgen Wyntges; 1636–1712),
flowers, 2: 216
Miss Rozee (1632–82),
embroiderer in silk, 2:262–63
Rachel Ruysch (1664–1750),
still life, flowers, 3:278
Anna Maria van Schurman (1607–78),
calligrapher, painter, sculptor, printmaker, 1:313–16
Adriana Spilberg (1656–97),
portraits, 3:45–46, 173

Anna van Thielen (also Anna Maria van Thielen; 1642–after 1664),
flowers, 2:52; 3:105–06
Francisca Catharina van Thielen (1645–81),
flowers, 2:52; 3:105–06
Maria Theresia van Thielen (1640–1706),
flowers, 2:52; 3:105–06
Alida Withoos (1662–1730),
landscape, still life, flowers, 2:188

Houbraken, too, is seriously incomplete. Among those missing,
skipping over his own daughter Antonina, are Gesina ter Borch,
Justina van Dyck, Margaretha de Heer, Clara Peeters, Susanna
van Steenwijck-Gaspoel, a number of van Veen women, Anna
Roemers and Maria Tesselschade Visscher, Michaelina Wautier,
Maria Withoos, Aleida Wolfsen, Henriëtta Wolters-van Pee and
Margaretha Wulfraet. More names were added by Houbraken's
successor biographers, Jacob Campo Weyerman (1729) and Johan
van Gool (1750–51), both of whom followed Houbraken's example
by including *schilderessen* (paintresses), in the titles of their
books. Their German colleague, Joachim von Sandrart, had gone
further in 1686, with an outright call for paying more respect
to women in the arts. Pieter Groenendijk's 2008 biographical
lexicon of Netherlandish artists from *c.* 1350 to *c.* 1720, lists
140 women, most of them from the Dutch seventeenth century.

In the twentieth century a vanguard of women art historians
brought the spirit of feminism into their studies and changed
the field. The impulse has never let up, with new books and
exhibitions on women artists coming out all the time. For
Dutch and Flemish artists, the major effort was an exhibition
of 1999–2000 in Antwerp and Arnhem, curated by Katlijne van
der Stighelen and Mirjam Wester. The enigmatic title, *Elck zijn
waerom*, was taken from the motto of Maria Tesselschade
Visscher: 'To each his why' – everyone has reasons of their own.
The catalogue bears the dedication: 'In memory of the countless
artistic women who have disappeared, faceless and nameless, in
the crevices of time.' The time is soon to come, it may be hoped,
when bringing women artists into the canon and to art-historical
attention has reached the point where it will no longer be
necessary to single them out for special compensatory attention.
To help this process along, the paintings by women artists
included in this volume are illustrated in the sections to which
they belong by subject. They are Gesina ter Borch, Judith Leyster,
Maria van Oosterwijck and Rachel Ruysch.

One exception is made for the most idiosyncratic painting
in the book, by a woman who herself created a feminine
environment for her art. Aleida Greve, born into a family of

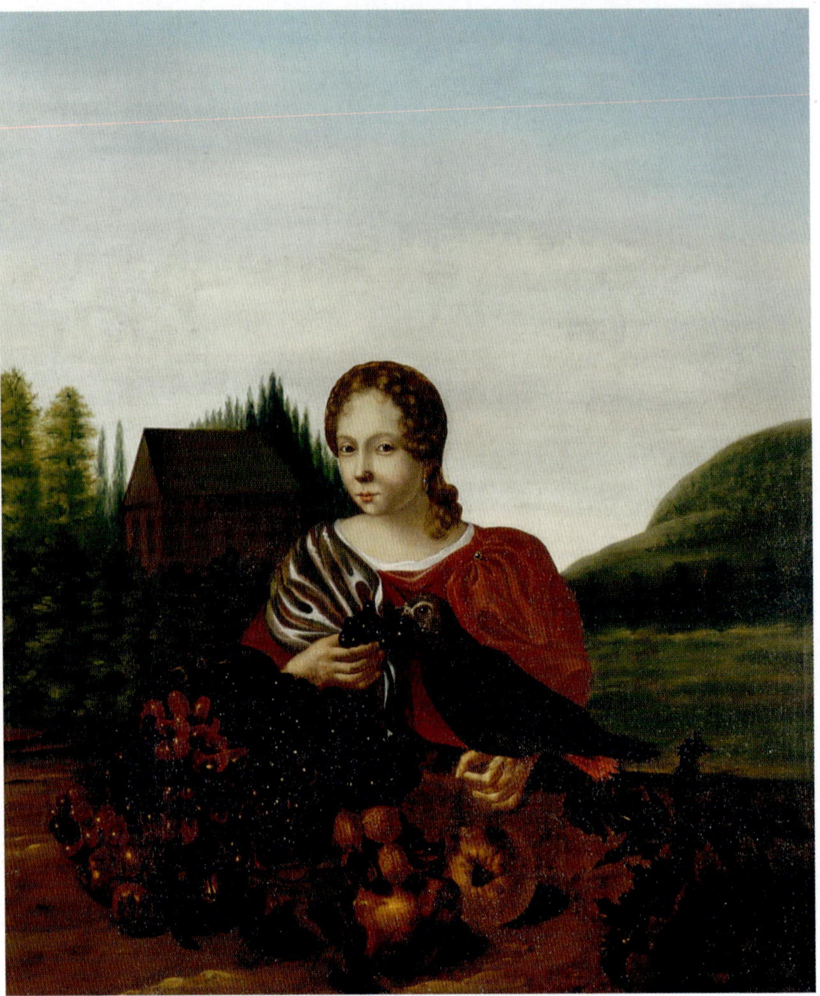

62 Aleida Greve, *Self-portrait in a Landscape*, 1686

Zwolle magistrates, and remaining unwed, put together a
small family coterie of women painters. In 1686, when she was
sixteen years old, she, her half-sister and two cousins made
four large-scale paintings pertaining to their personalities
as women artists. Two of them painted strong, self-assured
women, Cleopatra and Diana; those by the other two look like
self-portraits. Aleida Greve's shows a girl silhouetted against
a landscape with a lonely house in a copse, feeding grapes to
a bird that has been identified as a *grijze roodstaartpapegaai*
(grey parrot), popular as a pet.

When later in life she bought a house that had belonged to
a predecessor painter who was a namesake, Aleida Wolfsen
(1648–92), Greve furnished it with these paintings and six more
by her club. Upon her death, she bequeathed the house to a
family trust, to serve as housing for unmarried older women
and widows who belonged to the Reformed Church, a function
it has been fulfilling since her death. In 1987 the ground floor of
the Vrouwenhuis (Women's House) was converted to a museum,
which can be visited only by appointment. Because the trust
has honoured Aleida's testamentary stipulation that the salon
remain unchanged, the ten paintings by women artists still
hang where she put them. With a bit of exaggeration, we can
call Aleida Greve's Vrouwenhuis unique in the world as a
250-year-old institution dedicated to women's art.

A portrait of a female artist whose own work has never
been identified was painted by Gerrit van Honthorst, who, we
assume, trained her. He immortalizes her in the act of making

63 Gerrit van Honthorst, *Margaretha Maria de Roodere with her Mother Maria
van der Putten and the Portrait of her Father Gerard de Roodere*, 1652

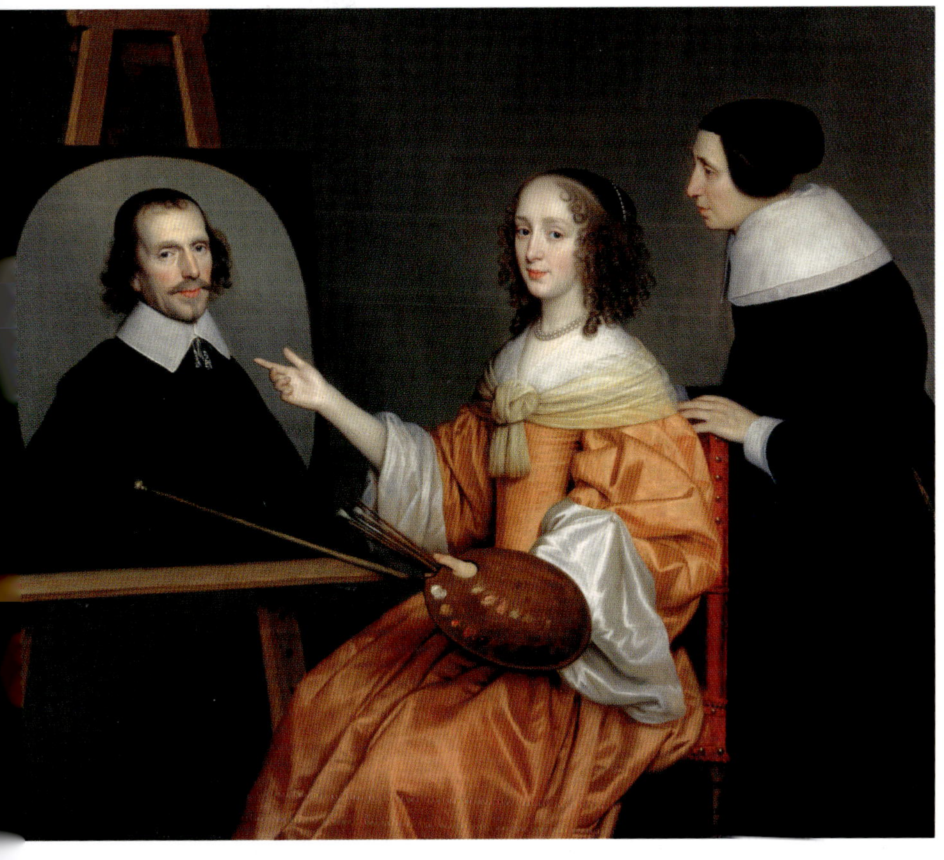

a skilful portrait of her father. Without this portrayal, we would have no evidence of Maria's artistic talent. This is the case for many women artists whose work either hasn't survived, is limited to one or two pieces, or has been absorbed into the works of better-known male artists. Honthorst also painted at least seven portraits of another of his female pupils, Louise Hollandine van de Palts (1622–1709), daughter of Friedrich V. Most of her surviving works are family portraits. Honthorst's connections to the court, including his paintings for Frederik Hendrik's family, align this body of work with European court art, far removed from the world of the bourgeois painter-shopkeeper.

Chapter 5
Families and Children in Paintings

In the early 1990s, the Dutch government funded a research project called *Dutch Culture in European Context*. The objective was to firm up the position of Dutch culture in the ongoing process of European integration. The form chosen was to focus on the key years 1650, 1800, 1900 and 1950. The 1650 team built a database of 1,823 European paintings from 1625 to 1675 in eight major museums, aiming to analyze where Dutch painting differed from or aligned with European trends. One surprising find concerned the depiction of women and children. Contrary to the common image of Dutch paintings showing mothers and children, we found a higher representation of women and children in portraiture from France and Spain than in the Netherlands. Although Dutch artists painted more secular scenes than those in Catholic countries, they trailed France and Italy in portraying women and children in genre painting. Thus, there is no claim for Dutch exceptionalism when presenting the paintings below.

An all-time favourite from early in the century is a painting of a woman with a child by Frans Hals. Until 1975, the identities of the sitters were unknown. There was debate over whether the woman was the child's mother or a nursemaid, and whether the child was a boy or girl. In that year, the Amsterdam archivist Bas Dudok van Heel resolved these questions. Archivists like him have provided invaluable information for understanding Dutch art. Dudok van Heel discovered an entry in the estate inventory of Pieter de Graeff (1638–1709) that listed 'a nursemaid with a small child by Frans Hals'. He traced this back to the period when the Amsterdam regent Pieter Jansz Hooft and his wife, Geertruid Overlander van Purmerland, were living in Haarlem with their two-year-old daughter, Catharina – later Pieter de Graeff's mother. This identification connects the painting to Dutch political and

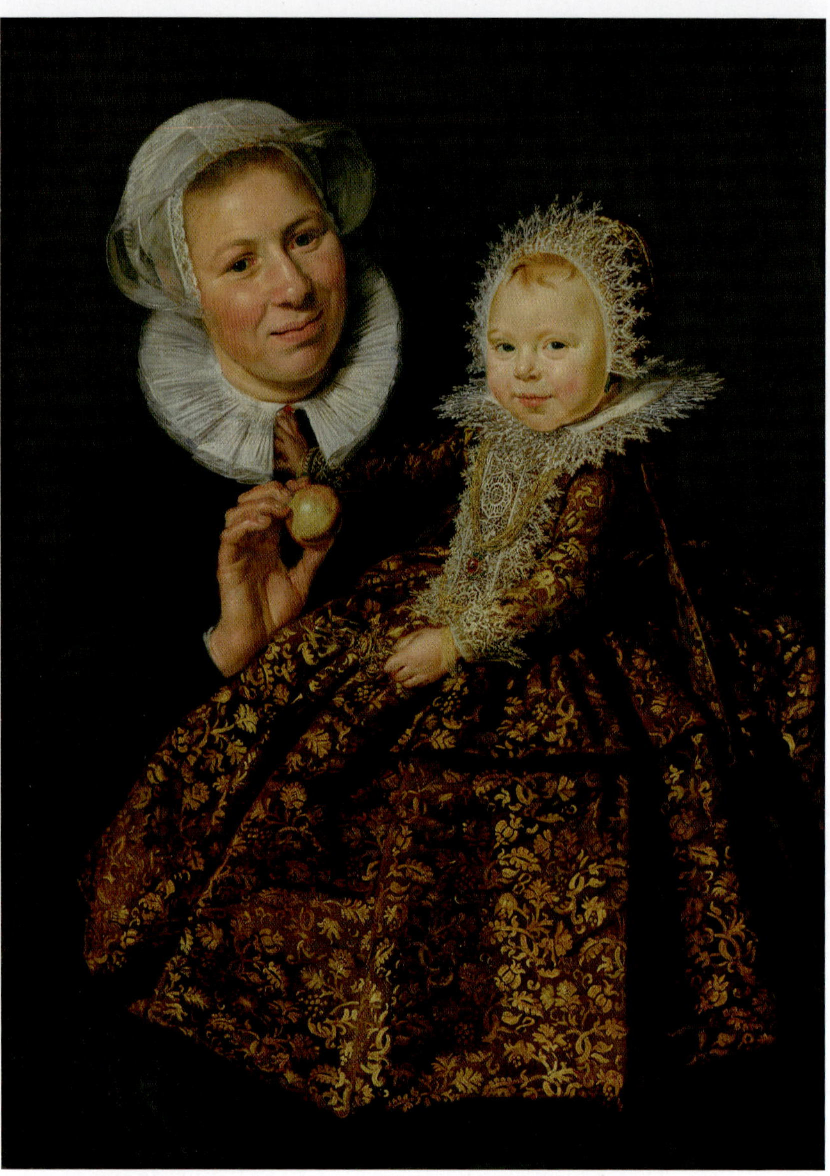

64 ABOVE Frans Hals, *Catharina Hooft and Nurserymaid*, c. 1620
65 OPPOSITE Jan Miense Molenaer, *Self-portrait with Family*, c. 1635–36

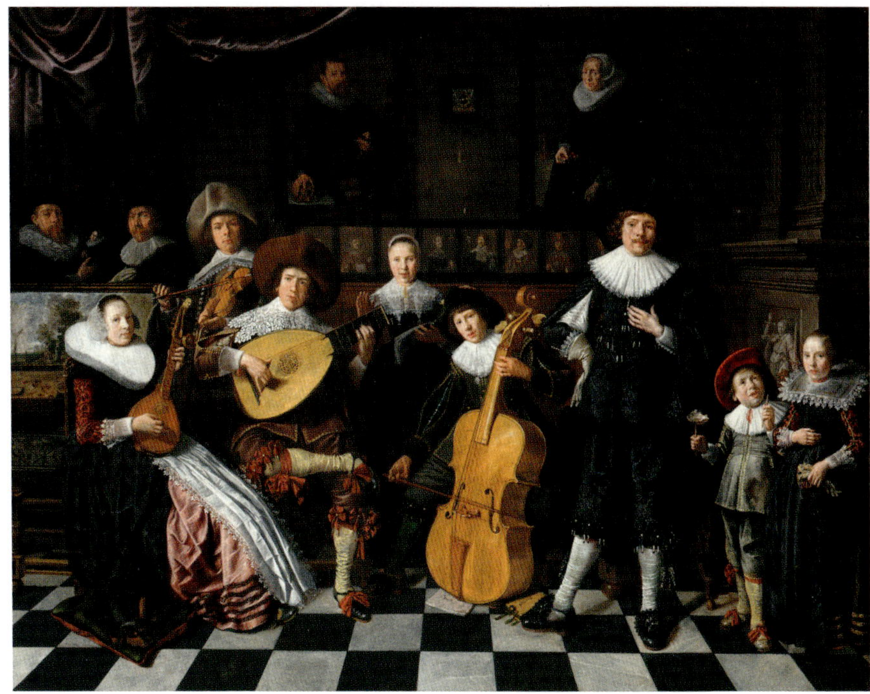

social elites. At eighteen, Catharina married Cornelis de Graeff, head of a powerful Amsterdam regent family, which was often at odds with the Calvinists. The painting remained in the de Graeff family for over two centuries, until it was sold in 1872 to the German entrepreneur and major collector, Barthold Suermondt. Two years later, when his financial position wavered, he sold his paintings to the Kaiser-Friedrich Museum in Berlin, now the Gemäldegalerie (Painting Gallery) of the Berlin State Museums, part of the Prussian Cultural Heritage Foundation.

This work challenges the image of Hals as solely a painter with a free, loose style. His depiction of Catharina's dress and lace could not be more highly detailed. Simultaneously, Hals's renowned ability to capture the personality of his subjects shines through. The nursemaid's warmth and good humour are particularly striking, making her perhaps the most beautifully portrayed servant in Dutch painting, a testament to Hals's sensitivity towards women and children in his work.

Another painting that has gained in charm and interest through the identification of formerly anonymous sitters is a family group by Jan Miense Molenaer in the Frans Hals Museum. In 2002, research by Dennis Weller showed that this captivating painting

65

is probably a self-portrait of the artist, the man with his hand on his heart, with his family. In short order those identifications were filled out to recognize four brothers and three sisters, four of them playing a string instrument and one singing. A half-brother holds a small portrait of his mother. The large pendant portraits on the wall show the father of them all and his second wife. The eight small portraits below them are surely relatives as well. They have coats of arms that remain to be identified. The tradition of creating family portraits like this, often featuring the painter at the easel and deceased relatives brought back to life, has deep roots in both the Northern and Southern Netherlands. Before the identification was made, a study of the painting's iconography by Eddy de Jongh noted that the siblings making music symbolize family harmony, while reminders of life's fragility are woven throughout. The boy blowing a bubble – nervously waiting for it to burst – symbolizes the inevitability of death. A clock between the parents ticks away time, and the father's portrait includes a skull, a *memento mori*. Additionally, the relief of Justice behind the children hints at divine justice and the Last Judgment. The curtain in the upper left adds another layer, suggesting the scene is staged for the viewer, with the curtain ready to fall, a metaphor for life's end. This moment arrived for father Molenaer in 1636, probably around the time the family portrait was completed. Jan Miense Molenaer's own life was far from harmonious. He was frequently embroiled in conflicts, accused of dishonest business practices, and faced legal charges for fighting and abusive language. It is to be hoped that he treated his wife, the painter Judith Leyster, better than he did others.

An instructive comparison to Jan Miense Molenaer's family group is another by Jan Steen. During the long time that Molenaer's painting was not seen as a self-portrait with family, Steen's was thought to be just that. This supposition was triggered by the self-portrait that it does contain: the man in the high hat on the right. There is even good reason to think that the woman having her elegant wine glass refilled is a depiction of Steen's wife, Grietje van Goyen, who stood him as model in a fair number of paintings. This easily led to the assumption that the Steens lived a dissolute life, and were unashamed to raise their children the same way. The notion even entered the Dutch language, with a 'Jan Steen household' defined in a standard repertory of sayings as 'a chaotic household, lacking rule and tidiness; essentially, a household where things are as disordered as in that of Jan Steen'. Current opinion sees these works less as portraits than as genre paintings, lighthearted scenes in which the Steen family

66

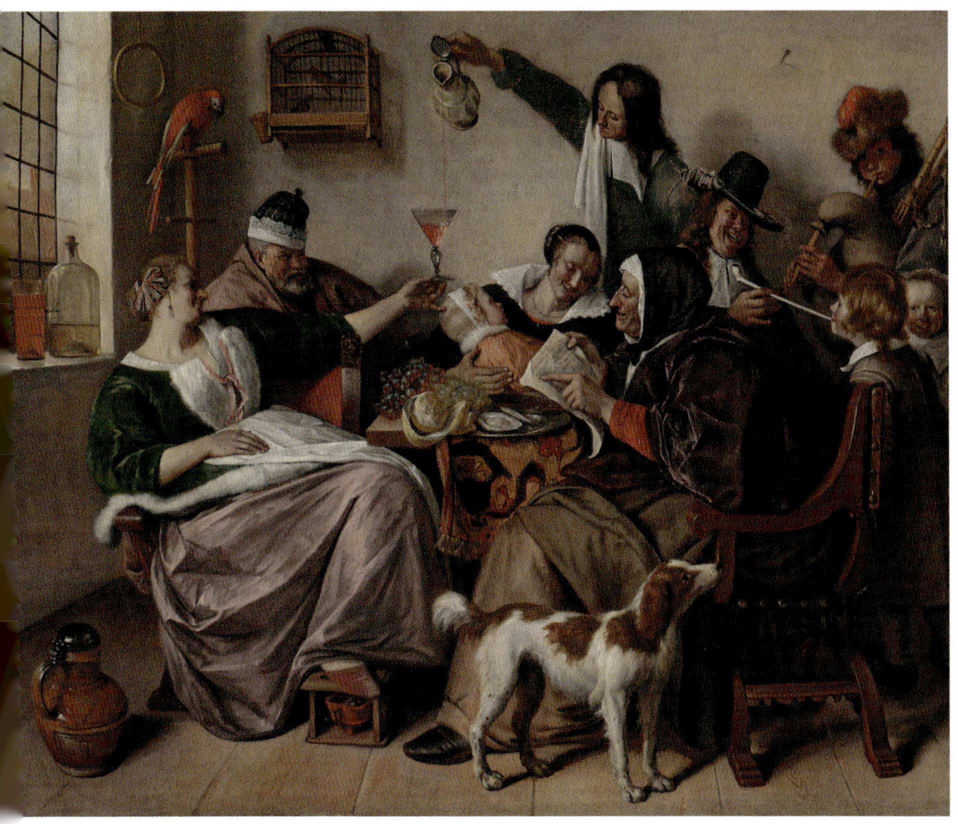

66 Jan Steen, *As the Old Sing, so Pipe the Young*, c. 1663

pokes fun at itself. The inspiration for this type of composition can be traced to Pieter Bruegel's depictions of Flemish proverbs. The proverb in this painting is written on the sheet of paper from which the old woman seems to be reading or singing:

What elders sing, children will pipe too. That has long proven true. What I sing to you now, follow me in playing on a pipe, from the time you're one until you're a hundred.

The 'one-year-old' refers to the baby in the mother's lap at the centre of the painting, whose baptism is being celebrated. We know this because of the slanted special-occasion cap worn by the man on the left, a style reserved for the father of a baptized child. Rather than showing children literally following the example of their elders, Steen gives things a punning twist. The child 'pipes' not on a musical instrument, but on a tobacco

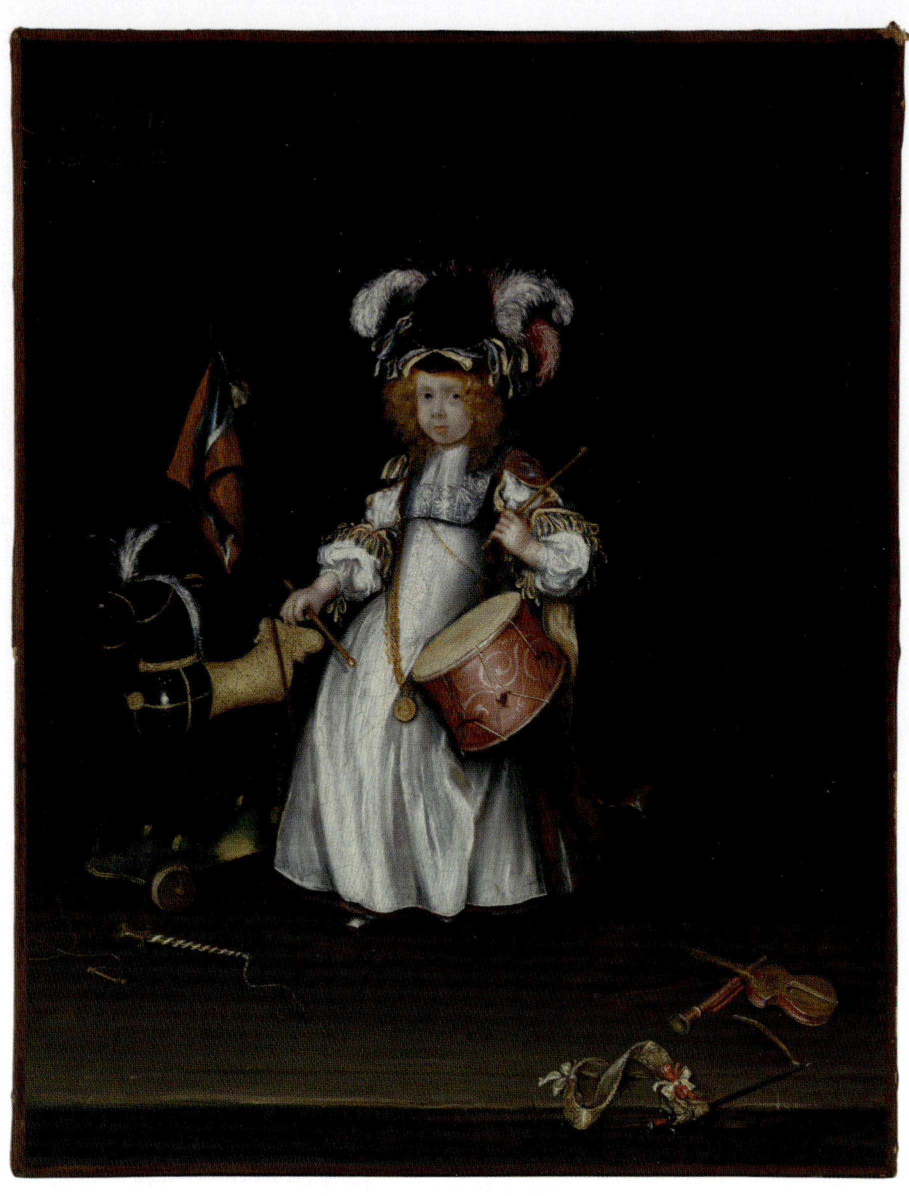

67 Gesina ter Borch, *Memorial Portrait of Moses ter Borch as a Two-year-old in 1647*, 1667

pipe handed to him by his father. Steen doesn't dictate how we should interpret these interactions. Some see him as mocking humanity's flaws, others detect a moral warning to parents to set a better example. It has been suggested by Simon Schama that Steen managed both to celebrate and satirize family life. Steen's connection to literary and theatrical traditions, such as the moral comedies staged by chambers of rhetoric, further supports this ambiguity. These plays, much like Steen's paintings, offered complex situations for viewers to reflect on. One of Steen's great gifts is his ability to engage emotions. It is hard to look at a painting like this, in which everyone is smiling, without breaking into a smile yourself and joining in the fun of the occasion.

A particularly touching portrait of a child family member was painted in 1667 by Gesina ter Borch. She was born into a family devoted to art and each other. For two centuries before her birth, it enjoyed prominence in Zwolle. Her father, Gerard, initially pursued a career as a painter but was forced by circumstances to shift to a stable township post previously held by his father. Despite this, he continued drawing and trained three of his sons, a nephew and two daughters, including Gesina. The only one to achieve significant professional recognition was Gesina's half-brother, Gerard II. The ter Borch family had a tradition of preserving their artworks and personal mementos, often featuring one another. Gerard began this practice by saving and annotating his drawings, including those from his youthful studies in Italy, as well as his children's early works. After his death in 1661, Gesina took over the care of this collection, known today as 'The Ter Borch Studio Estate', which includes loose sheets, notebooks and scrapbooks. Fortunately, the Rijksmuseum acquired nearly the entire collection in 1886.

Gesina never married and spent her entire life in the family home. Her portrait depicts her brother Moses, born when she was fourteen and with whom she had a close bond. His death at the age of twenty during the Second Anglo-Dutch War, at the failed siege of Landguard Fort, devastated her. In 2023, a portrait of Moses long believed to be by Gerard II was identified as Gesina's only known painting. Despite being fully signed, it was misattributed for years. Annotations give the age of the sitter as two years, and 1647 as the date of the painting, when he was that age. With good evidence, the painting is now dated twenty years later, to 1667 – heartrending evidence of Gesina's undying grief.

The involvement of women in the Dutch art world was not limited to painting, collecting or giving commissions. Agnes (or

Agneta) Block collaborated with artists on the documentation and study of nature. Born in Emmerich, Germany, to a Dutch textile dealer, she moved to Amsterdam as a child after the death of her parents. Raised by her uncle, David Rutgers, and his wife, Susanna de Flines, Agnes grew up in a prosperous Mennonite family involved in the wool and silk fabric trade. Her father, uncle and both her husbands were wealthy merchants. Mennonites, a Protestant sect, faced restrictions on joining guilds and Calvinist networks, so a career in trade provided an accessible outlet for social ambition. As did culture. The Rutgers family were close friends of the poet Joost van den Vondel (1587–1679), who admired Agnes and encouraged her passion for the natural world. In 1670, the year her first husband died, Agnes fulfilled a long-held ambition by purchasing a country estate on the Vecht River, in a region known as 'Mennonite Heaven' due to its popularity among wealthy Mennonites. Here, she established a botanical garden featuring a heated greenhouse and aviary, which gained acclaim across Europe. Her garden was not only testament to her interest in collecting plants and animals, but also served as a spiritual retreat at a time when nature was considered a reflection of God's presence.

In a family portrait by Jan Weenix, Agnes is depicted amidst some of the tropical plants she cultivated, including a Brazilian pineapple – she was reputedly the first in the Netherlands to grow a fruit-bearing one – and a bulbous cactus from Curaçao. She holds a bird, one of the fifty-two in her aviary. Agnes documented her collection through hundreds of drawings and watercolours created by various artists, explaining, 'When I have an exotic or unknown plant, I have a drawing made of it from life, so that when they die I have a memento on paper.' The painting features not only plants and animals but also books and sculptures, reflecting the intellectual pursuits that Agnes and her second husband, Sybrand de Flines, shared with their guests. That the painting offers a view in her actual garden is exceptional. Most green background motifs are inventions of the artist.

Agnes was often referred to as Flora Batava, the Dutch goddess of flowers, indicating her reputation for botanical cultivation. She had no children, leading to speculation about the identity of the two young girls in the Weenix portrait. They may be Catharina and Petronella, daughters of Agnes's niece, Agneta de Neufville, who would have been the right age around 1694. Jan Weenix was an apt choice for the commission, given his expertise in painting still lifes and animals. He came from a long line of painters, including his father, Jan Baptist Weenix,

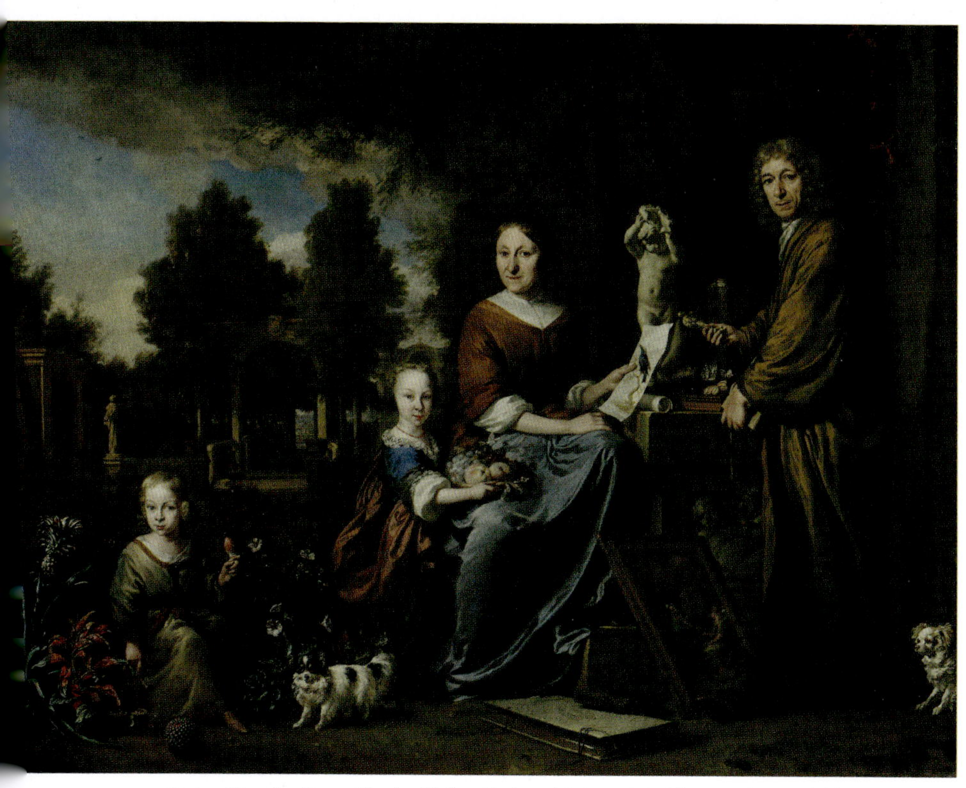

68 Jan Weenix, *Agnes Block with her Husband Sybrand de Flines and Two Children in the Garden at her Estate, the Vijverberg in Loenen aan de Vecht*, c. 1694

and his maternal grandfather, Gillis Claesz de Hondecoeter, who specialized in similar subjects. This artistic legacy spanned multiple generations, illustrating a common pattern among artistic families in Europe.

Chapter 6
Dutch Painters Abroad

In the seventeenth century, the Netherlands exported not only artworks but also highly skilled artists. Many Dutch painters sought opportunities abroad, moving independently to more lucrative markets. There were strong factors attracting them to foreign courts. The British and Danish courts, in particular, relied heavily on Dutch talent from the sixteenth century onwards. As art historian Horst Gerson noted, 'One cannot speak of the influence of Dutch art on the indigenous painting of the Scandinavian countries [or England], because artistic production was almost entirely in the hands of foreigners', who were mainly from the Low Countries. Dutch artists also made significant contributions across Central Europe, from Germany and the Baltic States to Poland and the Habsburg Empire. Their influence did not extend beyond the divide that separated Catholic and Protestant regions from Eastern Orthodox areas. Further east, the Muslim courts of Persia and India were quite receptive to European art, which lent sophistication to their culture and greased the wheels of political and mercantile relations. Between 1605 and 1656, during the peak of the Safavid dynasty, ten Dutch artists are recorded as working in Isfahan for Shah 'Abbas the Great and his successors. None of these works, with the possible exception of some murals in the Forty Columns Pavilion in Isfahan, have come down to us.

Drawing on a wealth of biographical studies and original research, the University of Amsterdam built ECARTICO, a database for information about Dutch and Flemish painters of the seventeenth century. This allows searches for a number of variables, including places of activity. Here are the figures for the main three destinations, in the category 'Painters (artistic status confirmed)':

	Rome	Paris	London
1600–20	123	66	11
1621–40	208	113	45
1641–60	186	121	42
1661–80	141	99	69
1681–1700	93	51	74
Total	751	450	241

Table 2 Number of Dutch and Flemish painters active in Rome, Paris and London from 1600 to 1700. Source: ECARTICO

These are serious numbers, speaking of the greater international mobility of Dutch and Flemish painters elsewhere in Europe than was displayed by artists from other schools. The rise and fall in Rome and Paris follow roughly the same curve, rising until mid-century and declining thereafter. The growth in numbers in London after 1660 has to do with the alliance of the House of Orange with the Stuarts, culminating in Willem III's kingship, as William III of England, in 1689 and the resulting patronage of Dutch painters by him and his court.

Italy

For Dutch artists, Italy held great significance. This is especially true of Rome, which offered the authentic remains of classical art and architecture they had studied in school and in studios. With Greece under Ottoman rule and largely inaccessible (there were just two recorded visits by Dutch artists in the entire century), Rome became the primary destination for those seeking inspiration from ancient antiquities. Venice and Florence attracted far fewer artists, roughly one-tenth as many. Admittedly, none of the Dutch seventeenth-century artists in Italy vied with Maarten van Heemskerck, who created hundreds of drawings during his time in Rome from 1532 to 1537. Pieter Saenredam, who later on owned many of these, used them to paint Roman townscapes without ever leaving Haarlem. It must also be admitted that most Dutch artists who came to Italy did so for more down-to-earth reasons, such as making money and having fun while doing it, than to study Roman art.

Their professional success was phenomenal. For the past forty years, the Netherlands Art History Institute in Florence has been inventorying and cataloguing the Dutch and Flemish paintings in the museums of Italy, most having been made there. They have tallied a total of more than 10,000. Since there are more paintings in private hands and in the trade than in museums, we can raise this estimate to about 25,000. Those are surviving works. Given the high rate of loss detected by economic historians, that figure should be multiplied by a hefty factor. Italian painting of the seventeenth century, we can say, was made in considerable measure by Dutch artists. They were taken up not because of their national identity (they and the Flemings were indiscriminately called *fiamminghi*) but the quality of their work. Their art often blended seamlessly with that of Italian masters whose studios they entered or of local pupils and peers who adopted styles and subjects they introduced.

In their training at home, Dutch painters had become acquainted, through prints, with the work of the Italian masters, Michelangelo and Raphael. Once in Rome, they were exposed to, and some were captivated by the powerful new art of Caravaggio. The influences went both ways. Though from the Southern rather than Northern Netherlands, the *fiammingo* Paul Bril (1553/54–1626) brought an approach to landscape so pervasive that it helped shape one of the greatest landscape painters of the century, Claude Lorrain (*c.* 1600–82). Impressively, Bril was esteemed so highly that in 1621 he was made director of the Accademia di San Luca, the artists' academy in Rome. Not that the Accademia was the preferred gathering spot for Netherlandish artists in Rome. By 1620, they began congregating in taverns near their residences in the parish of Santa Maria del Popolo, where they formed a group known as the Bentvueghels, or Birds of a Feather. They created initiation rituals, adopted nicknames and formed a fraternal network. Compared to collegial get-togethers in the Netherlands, at events like guild meetings and the funerals they were obliged to attend, in Rome bachelor Dutch painters could live a Bohemian lifestyle.

No painting better exemplifies the sophisticated Dutch artist in Rome than a stunning *Liberation of St Peter* by Gerrit van Honthorst. He painted it for Count Vincenzo Giustiniani (1564–1637), who had made a study tour of the Netherlands and liked to house visiting Dutchmen, such as van Honthorst, in his palace. Giustiniani had been the protector, patron and benefactor of Caravaggio, several of whose paintings he owned. Honthorst's composition is clearly based, by way of tribute, on Caravaggio's *Calling of St Matthew*, made for the church of San Luigi dei Francesi across the street from the Palazzo Giustiniani. Attentive visitors who made the connection would have delighted Vincenzo. The angel's commanding gesture imitates the extended arm of Caravaggio's Christ pointing out St Matthew. The head of Christ is painted against a dark background in the Caravaggio; the angel's is silhouetted against the light in the Honthorst. But the angle of the

69

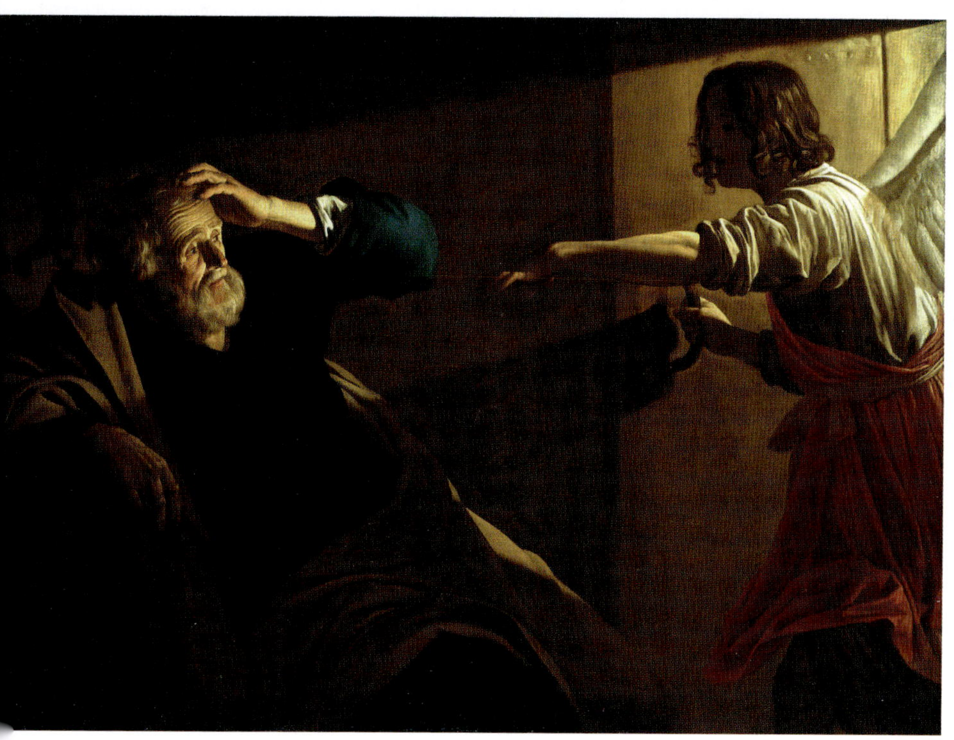

69 Gerrit van Honthorst, *The Liberation of St Peter*, c. 1616–18

shadow above both is the same. Giustiniani could tell visitors proudly that this homage to Caravaggio was painted by an artist from Utrecht.

Just as the Antwerper Paul Bril initiated a school of landscape painting that, starting in Rome, set the tone throughout Europe, the Haarlem artist Pieter van Laer did the same for street scenes of daily, often unruly life. Moreover, van Laer gave his name to this subgenre. His appearance gained him the nickname *Bamboccio*, big baby. Painters whose styles owed a debt to him were dubbed *bamboccianti*. Van Laer's choice of subjects had a deliberately subversive effect on the received idea that history painting, with its grandiose themes, deserved higher esteem than everyday portrayals of real people. He and his Dutch and Italian followers did not think of their art as trivial. They included classical settings and poses from antique sculpture, as if to say that the ancients, too, were people like us. He even extends this message into sacred realms in his painting of two Flagellants – members of a Christian confraternity who mortified the flesh in penitence and in

70

imitation of Christ's suffering. His daring was repudiated by some outraged critics, but van Laer enjoyed appreciation from the same high circles as Honthorst.

Caspar van Wittel is one of the few Dutch painters who stayed in Italy all his life and became a fixture in Italian art. Van Wittel looked at his motifs keenly and sincerely, often taking angles of vision that departed from more standard picture-postcard views. His paintings were in high demand, and he was not always quick enough to deliver orders. A surviving letter to a patron is surely typical of more that he wrote. On 11 March 1707 he excused himself to François de Jaucourt, Marquis d'Ausson, a Protestant French aristocrat living in the Netherlands, for delay in fulfilling an order, pleading that his paintings 'take time and a lot of patience to make, mainly because you work with the love and diligence this genre of paintings demands'. Van Wittel was a living link between earlier Dutch, German and Italian townscape painters and the eighteenth-century Italian painters of what came to be known simply as *vedute*, views – of which Canaletto (Giovanni Antonio Canal) was the leading exponent. A van Wittel painting in this vein juxtaposes the proud dome of St Peter's with Castel Sant' Angelo, built in the mid-second century by Emperor Hadrian as a mausoleum for himself. In van Wittel's time it was a papal residence that doubled as a prison and place of execution.

71

70 Pieter van Laer, *The Flagellants*, c. 1635

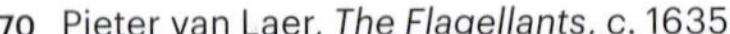

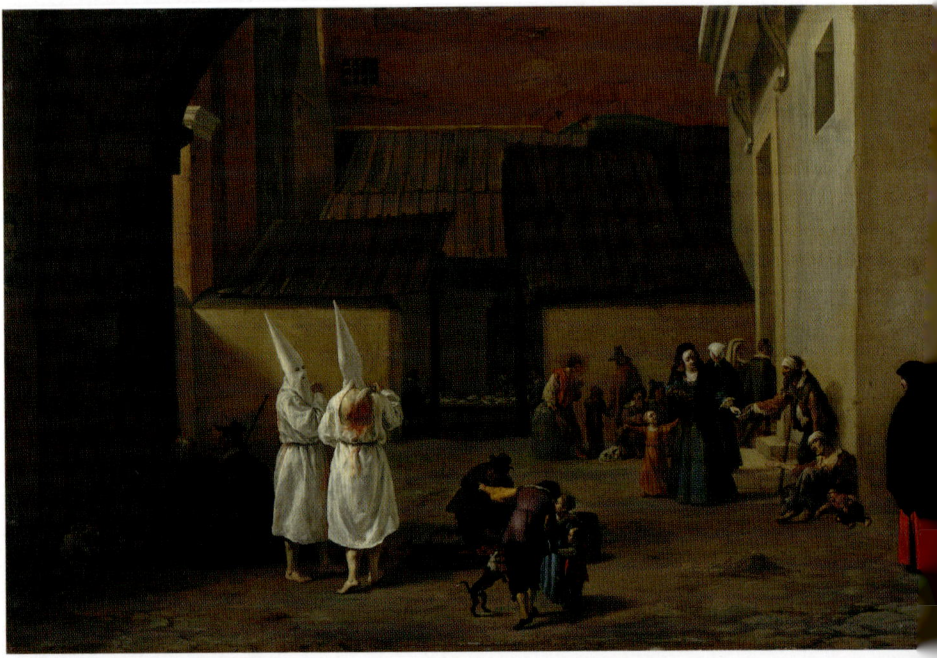

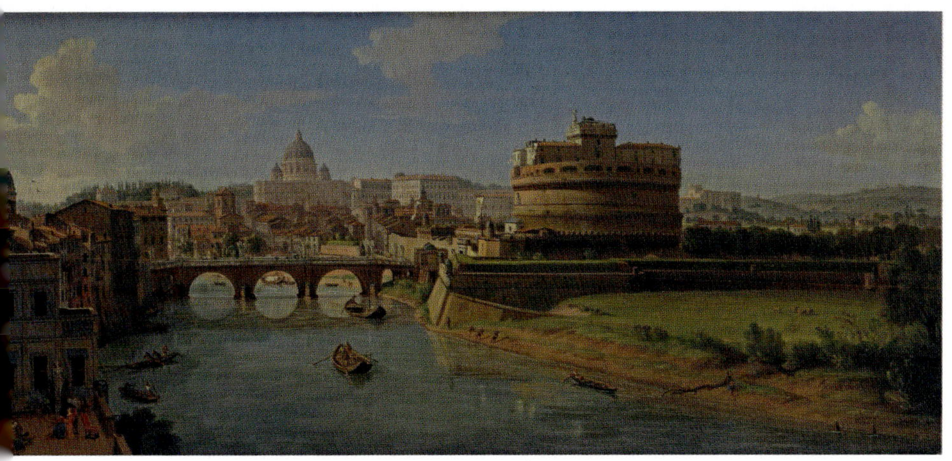

71 Caspar van Wittel, *View of Castel Sant'Angelo in Rome,* late seventeenth century

Scandinavia

The Scandinavian countries further from the Netherlands than
Denmark were not a favoured destination for Dutch painters.
An impressive exception was the Alkmaar painter, Allart van
Everdingen, who in his early twenties took ship to Norway.
There and on the Swedish coast he made drawings of the very
un-Dutch terrain. Back in the Netherlands, first in Alkmaar
and after 1652 in Amsterdam, he developed his drawings into
paintings of Norwegian scenery, becoming the owner of an
attractive motif. The look was so compelling that his master in
Amsterdam, Jacob van Ruisdael, dug into Allard's bag of tricks
for Dutch and German landscapes of his own. Allard was the
logical candidate for a handsome commission from one of the
richest families in the Netherlands. These were the brothers
Louys and Hendrick Trip, who built a dynastic powerhouse in
the early 1660s on the Kloveniersburgwal in Amsterdam, known
to this day as the Trippenhuis, the House of Trip. Much of their
fortune had been earned in a few brief decades of mining,
manufacturing and trading, thanks mainly to monopolies they
held in Sweden. The most profitable branch of their commercial
empire was the arms trade. At the outbreak of the devastating
Thirty Years' War in 1618, they boasted that they could
outfit an entire army of 5,000 troops in four weeks. Of course,
the decoration of their supersized mansion could not do
without depictions of their Swedish properties, so Allard
was commissioned to paint four large representations of these.
They include a painting of Hendrick's cannon foundry. There
is no record that Allard visited Sweden at this time, so he may

72

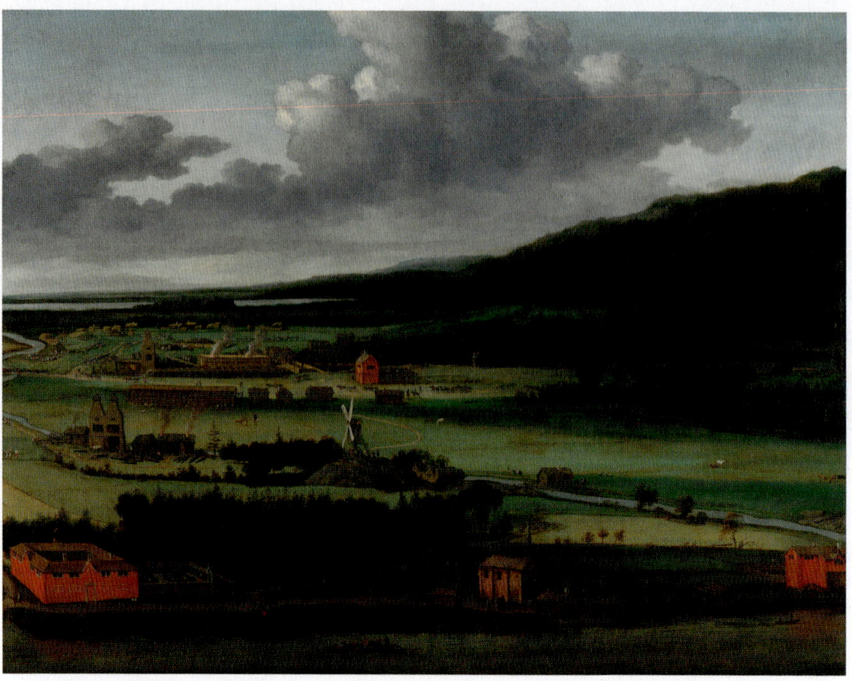

72 Allart van Everdingen, *Hendrik Trip's Cannon Foundry in Julitabruk, Sweden,* c. 1650–75

have worked from drawings provided by an artistic Trip associate, inserted into Scandinavian hill country from Allard's store of motifs.

Great Britain

Of all the countries that imported art and artists from the Low Countries, it was Great Britain where they made the greatest impact. In the sixteenth century, British aristocrats turned to Netherlandish artists for their portraits, a preference that reached royal heights in the seventeenth, with the arrival of Anthony van Dyck. The origins of British seascape painting lay with father and son Willem van de Velde, and although he never visited Britain, Aelbert Cuyp set the style for landscape. Architectural painting was brought to Britain by Hendrick van Steenwijk, *trompe l'oeil* by Edward Collier, flower still life by Simon Verelst. More Dutch artists worked in Rome than in London, but the big difference was that Rome had its own great school, to which Dutch artists could add only in small measure. In Britain, the Flemish and Dutch were the creators of the local specialities. Analysis of ten representative auction catalogues of sales in London between 1689 and 1692 has shown that only five percent were British, the same number as Flemish. The share for Dutch artists was no less than forty-eight percent. There will be few situations in history when a major centre with a rich culture relinquished so much of a given field to practitioners from abroad.

On 18 April 1627, during a visit to London of only a few weeks, the Utrecht artist Claude de Jongh sketched Old London Bridge. In 1630, he transformed the drawing into a large painting, capturing the precarious charm of the bridge, which was built in 1209 and stood until its demolition in 1831. Its eye-catching architecture, with numerous buildings atop the bridge, made it a popular subject for artists. De Jongh met this challenge skilfully, producing at least three painted versions of the scene. Claude was far from a typical Dutch artist. He was named after his maternal grandfather, Claude de Glarges, a Hainaut aristocrat who became Secretary of the Court of Holland after fleeing to the Dutch Republic. His father, Herman de Jonghe, was part of a prominent Utrecht family. Thus, de Jongh grew up within a politically influential, Protestant household. His choice to pursue a career as a professional artist, despite his high-born status, indicates that artistic endeavours were not necessarily deemed inappropriate for someone of his social standing, as discussed by Marten Jan Bok in his study on the artist. This aligns him with other privileged Protestants, such as Hendrick ter Brugghen and Louise Hollandine, who also embraced artistic paths. (Louise Hollandine's path was decidedly sinuous. She converted to Catholicism, moved to France, and with the protection of Louis XIV served for the last forty-five years of her life as abbess of the convent of Maubisson.)

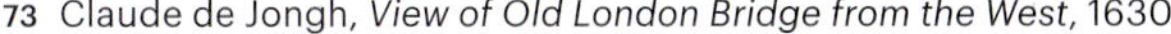

73 Claude de Jongh, *View of Old London Bridge from the West*, 1630

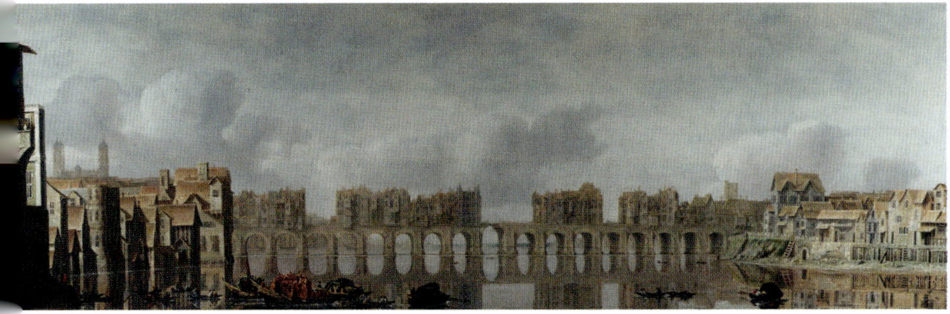

In September 1628, a Dutch fleet of privateers led by Captain Piet Hein achieved one of history's largest heists. Serving the Dutch West India Company (WIC), Hein captured part of the Spanish silver fleet, which annually transported vast wealth from the Spanish colonies in Central and South America. This windfall helped finance significant campaigns, including the capture of coastal Brazil from Portugal in 1630. After struggling with the administration of the colony, in 1637 the WIC appointed Count Johan Maurits van Nassau-Siegen as the governor of New Holland (Dutch Brazil). During his seven-year tenure, he accomplished remarkable feats, such as building forty forts and several palaces, and initiating scientific and artistic studies of Brazil's geography, people, flora and fauna. His governorship had a dark side, however; he introduced the trafficking of enslaved Africans to the colony, engaging in private trade as well.

The illustrated publications that came out of the campaign became crucial early sources of knowledge about Brazil. Unfortunately, as historian Charles Boxer lamented, the manuscripts, drawings and natural collections gathered under Johan Maurits's direction were not preserved together in his town palace in The Hague (now the Mauritshuis museum). Though many items were lost, paintings by Frans Post and Albert Eckhout stand out as unique contributions, enriching Dutch art and expanding knowledge of the seventeenth-century world. Frans Post was the younger brother of the architect Pieter Post, who from 1633 to 1647 worked on the design and construction of Johan Maurits's palace in The Hague. It would seem to be thanks to this connection that in 1636 he was taken by Johan Maurits on a trip to Brazil, where he worked until about 1644. Of his more than 140 surviving paintings of Brazil, all but a few were painted in the Netherlands, after drawings now lost. His painting of Itamaracá is signed and dated 3 November 1637, making it the earliest painting known to have been made by a Dutch master in the Americas.

Working for Johan Maurits in Brazil brought undying fame to another Dutch painter beside Frans Post. Albert Eckhout would have remained an obscure artist from Groningen had he not created some of the most important visual records ever made outside Europe by a European artist. His body of work includes about 800 oil sketches and drawings of plants and animals, compiled in four volumes now housed at the Jagiellonian University in Kraków, Poland. Eckhout collaborated with the young German naturalist Georg Marcgraf, creating a

74

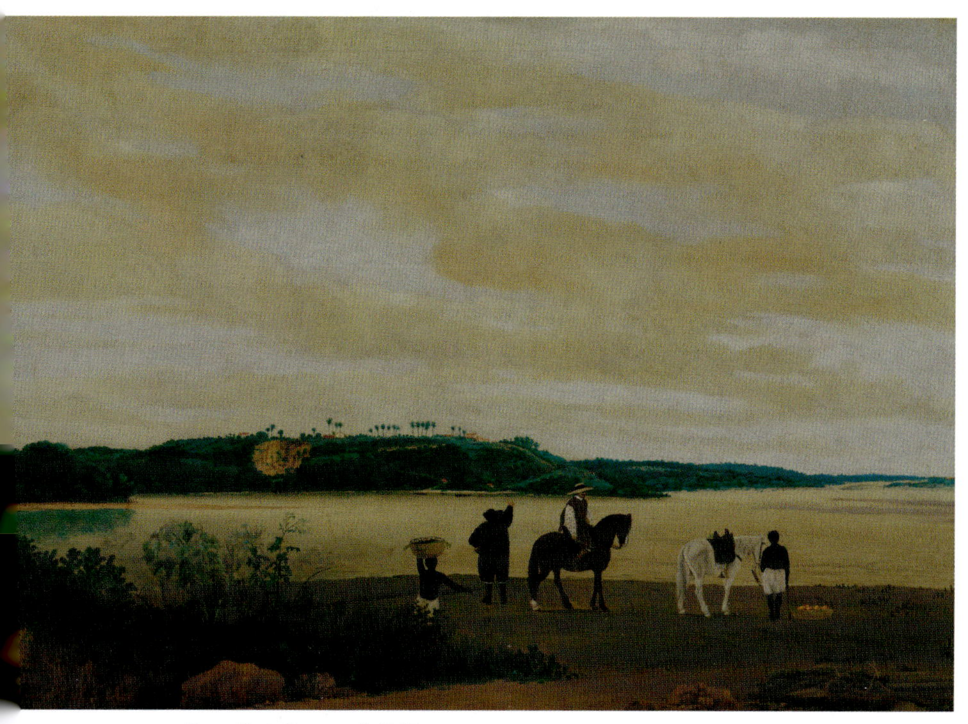

74 Frans Post, *Itamaracá*, 1637

rich documentation of South American flora and fauna. Standing out even more prominently are Eckhout's life-size paintings of Indigenous and mixed-race Brazilians. These eight portraits, plus a ninth depicting a wild dance, have seen a significant shift in scholarly interpretation. Initially, the works were considered straightforward representations of local groups, such as the coastal Tupis, those of mixed race who were semi-assimilated, and the more isolated Tapuyas from the interior. This perspective changed dramatically with a 1979 essay by Ernst van den Boogaart which noted a crucial factor: Eckhout's portrayal reflected each group's relationship with the Dutch colonial administration. Those who submitted to Dutch rule, such as the Tupis and mixed-race individuals, are shown in plantations or maritime settings, clothed and engaged in domestic or hunting activities. Conversely, the Tapuyas, who resisted and attacked settlers, are depicted as wild and naked. His male Tapuya carries a club used in ritual cannibalism, while the woman holds a severed hand, with a foot protruding from her basket. The argument was that these paintings

75

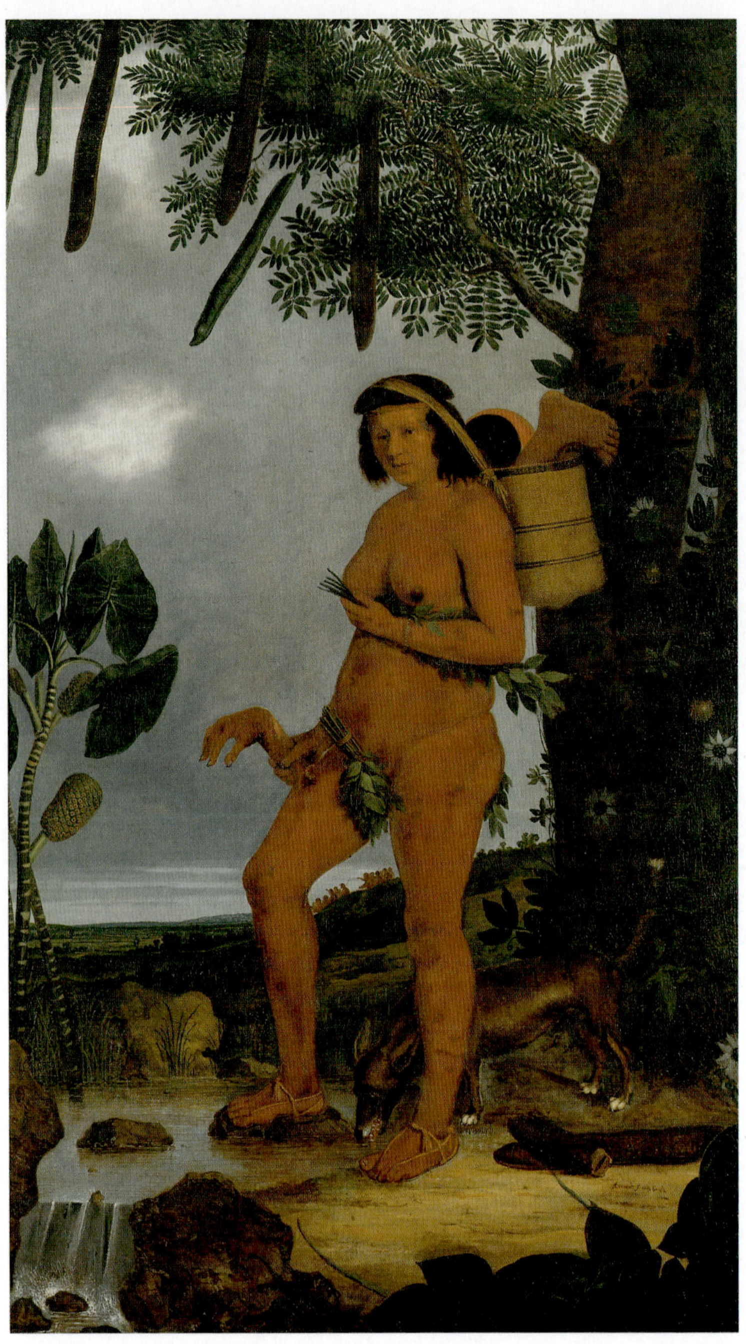

75 ABOVE Albert Eckhout, *A Tapuya Woman at a Creek*, 1641
76 OPPOSITE Jaspar or Jeronimus Becx, *Dom Miguel de Castro, Emissary of the Congo*, between 19 June and 2 July 1643

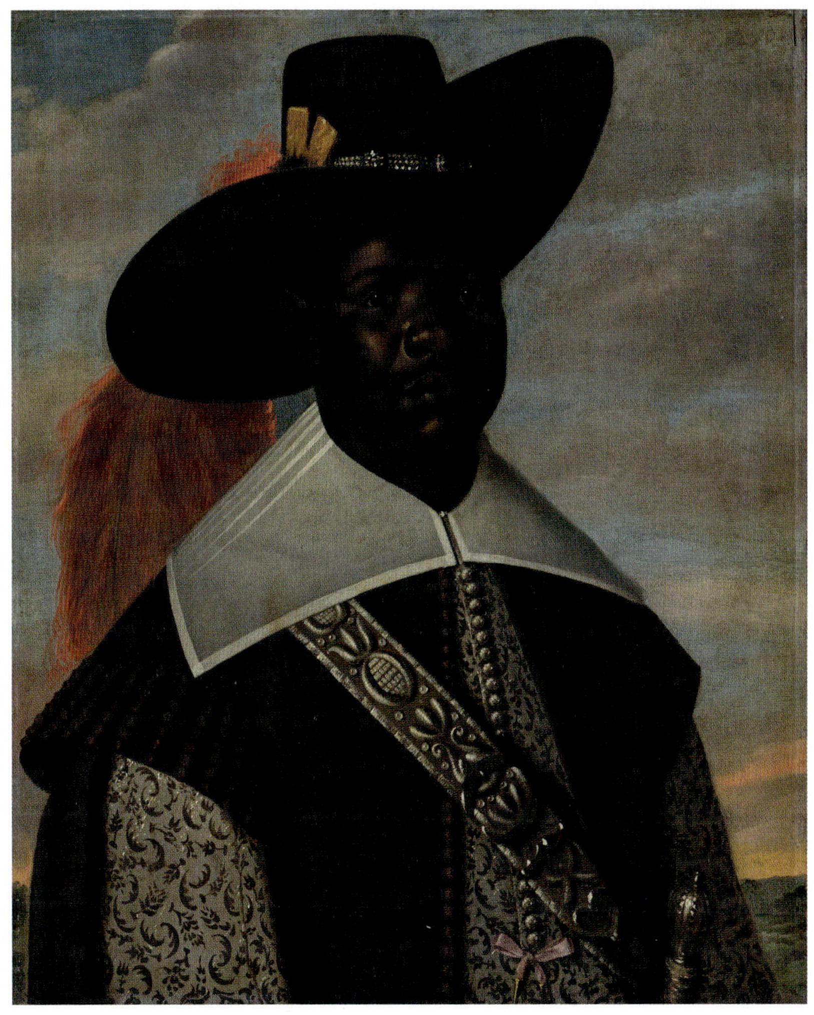

functioned as colonial propaganda rather than objective
documentation. The message, which reinforced colonial
hierarchies and justified Dutch rule, was that the Tupis, along
with Black and mixed-race people, were potential recruits
to 'civility', while the Tapuyas were irredeemable savages.

A portrait of a distinguished Black man long believed
to have been painted in Brazil by Albert Eckhout has been
76 conclusively identified as the work of one of the Becx brothers
in Middelburg. Nonetheless, it remains closely linked to the
history of Dutch Brazil. In the 1640s, the Dutch, Portuguese

and rival Kongo kingdoms were engaged in conflicts in the west
of Africa. In 1643, the count of Sonho, contesting King Dom
Garcia II of Kongo, sent a delegation across the Atlantic to seek
the mediation of Johan Maurits, bringing along two hundred
enslaved individuals as a gift. Among the envoys was Dom
Miguel de Castro, a cousin of the count, who continued to the
Netherlands after the others returned to Africa. Arriving in
Vlissingen in June 1643, Dom Miguel carried a letter for
Stadholder Frederik Hendrik, probably written by Johan
Maurits, his cousin. During a two-week stay in Middelburg as
guests of the WIC, six portraits of the African party were
commissioned: two of Dom Miguel; one each of his servants
Pedro Sunda and Diego Bemba; one showing a sitter 'in
Portuguese clothing'; and another in 'Congoish' attire. The
artist, identified only as 'Becx', could be either Jaspar or
Jeronimus Becx, both active in Middelburg at the time. After
leaving Middelburg, Dom Miguel requested one of his portraits
and a mirror, seemingly to judge the likeness. That painting's
whereabouts are unknown beyond this point, as are the
costume portraits. In August 1644, Johan Maurits, having left
his role as governor of Brazil, visited Middelburg and received
the three remaining portraits. In 1654, he presented them,
along with twenty-three works by Eckhout, to King Frederick III
of Denmark, in an act of personal diplomacy. These portraits,
treasured at the Statens Museum for Kunst in Copenhagen, are
the only known seventeenth-century Dutch paintings depicting
identifiable Black sitters.

Asia

Compared to the Dutch West India Company, which fostered
artistic initiatives, the Dutch East India Company (VOC),
founded in 1602, showed little interest in art. Without a
patron such as Johan Maurits, the VOC did not see art as
valuable to its mission. Most paintings brought back from its
Asian headquarters in Batavia (now Jakarta) were mediocre
portraits of governors-general. In Persia and Mughal India,
the VOC declined requests from local rulers to lend artists
or craftsmen to the royal courts, a decision that astonished
European observers, such as French Capuchin friars in Isfahan,
who viewed such requests as golden opportunities. While the
VOC did bring back some Chinese and Japanese artworks,
its directors mainly focused on acquiring collectibles like
shells, feathers and parrots. They never commissioned Dutch
painters to document the landscapes, peoples or wonders of
the East. The lack of artistic engagement extended to Dutch
artists themselves; only Esaias Boursse and Andries Beeckman

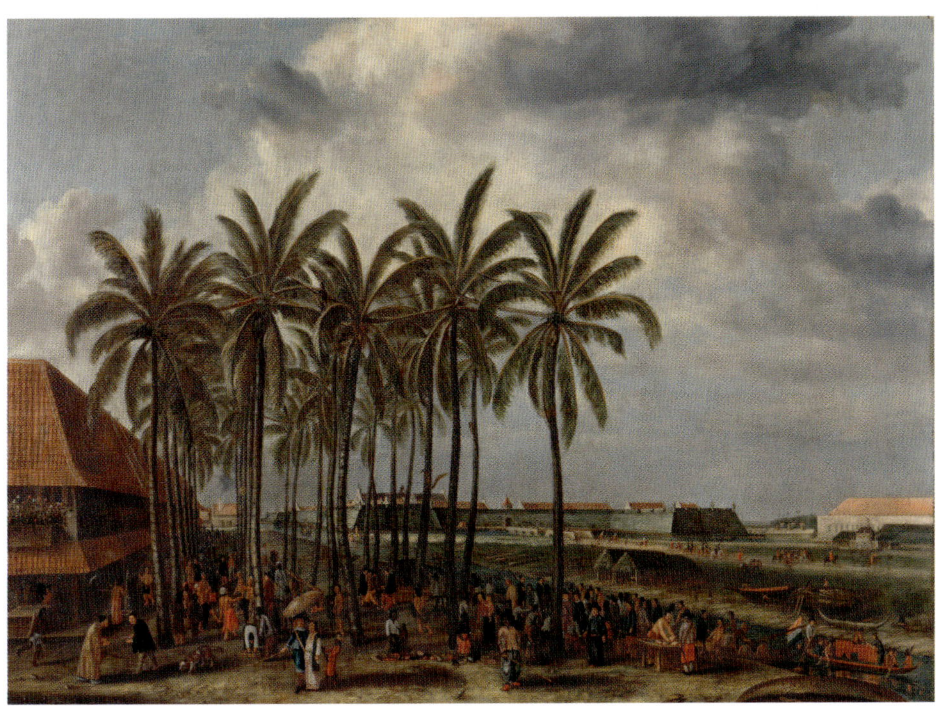

77 Andries Beeckman, *The Castle of Batavia*, c. 1662

are known to have made documentary drawings in the VOC's Asian territories. Their work stands as a rare exception in an otherwise unremarkable artistic legacy left by the VOC.

Looking strictly at the evidence, in the seventeenth century the VOC validated only one image of its presence in Asia. It is a painting by Andries Beeckman that was not even commissioned by the Company: a flattering picture of a multi-cultural society enjoying itself under Dutch auspices. The interaction it evokes between Javanese, Chinese and European persons in a lively outdoor market breathes a spirit of peace and mutual regard. This is how the directors of the Company, the Gentlemen XVII, for whose meeting chamber the painting was bought in 1662, would have liked people to see the settlement they created in the East Indies. Their enterprise brought spices, fabrics, tea and coffee to the motherland, for sale throughout Europe, and muscled its way into local east-east traffic. They obtained the yields and goods in any way necessary. In the Banda Islands – some 'Batavians' were captive islanders – by vicious force, in Japan by the humble acceptance of insultingly constrictive conditions. From 1640 until 1853 the Dutch trade station was confined to an artificial island in the harbour of Nagasaki that was no larger than Dam Square in Amsterdam. They were allowed to leave it only once a year, when they were required to make an onerous journey to pay tribute to the shogun in Edo, a thousand kilometres each way. In Edo, the chief of the Dutch mission would creep on his knees along the presents he had brought, which had been ordered the year before by the shogun. Paintings were seldom among the immense variety of requested gifts. In 1664 the Dutch wished to offer two paintings of battles they thought had been asked for, but which were deemed inappropriate by a Japanese official before they left Deshima and shipped back to Holland.

Chapter 7
The Grand Traditions

In the seventeenth-century Netherlands, certain types of painting were more deeply connected to society, had richer histories, and demanded greater skill from artists than others. This was evident from their status, presence in esteemed collections, and the high prices they fetched. The most respected genre was history painting, which told a narrative. Mastering history painting required proficiency in all aspects of art: figures, perspective, landscapes, plants, animals, and composing diverse elements into cohesive scenes. Karel van Mander emphasized the challenge of depicting movement in static images and, above all, the ability to convey emotions – considered the 'heart and soul of art'.

At the turn of the century, painters gravitated towards history painting, a propensity that later declined. Michael Montias measured this effect in the inventories of collections in Delft. Taking the first and last decades in his sample, in percentages:

Subject category	1610–19	1670–79
Old Testament	15.0	4.1
New Testament	15.9	7.6
Other religious (including allegory)	6.1	2.5
Mythology	4.2	0.9
Other 'history' (including secular allegory)	4.9	1.5
All landscape	25.6	40.9
All still-life	4.2	16.7
All genre	3.8	7.4
Portraits and tronies	16.9	15.0
Other	3.4	3.4

Table 3 Percentage of subjects in 9,623 paintings from Delft inventories, in the decades 1610–19 and 1670–79. Source: John Michael Montias, *Artists and Artisans in Delft*

Between 1610 and 1619, the share of history accounted for nearly half of all paintings; in 1670–79 this had plummeted to one-sixth, ceding the lead to landscape, still life and genre, which now took two-thirds of all painting production. Whether this was a Europe-wide trend is difficult to say. What is apparent is that Dutch painting stopped building on the inheritance of past centuries, during which history had set the standard, and retreated into niche specialities that, except for a small number of landscapes, had not existed at all before the seventeenth century. (That portraiture was the only constant type of painting is not surprising; see p. 142.)

The Bible and Saints

Biblical imagery held the highest esteem in seventeenth-century Dutch art, resonating deeply with the nation's religious values. For Reformed artists, however, portraying biblical themes was a balancing act, as their faith rejected Catholic devotional imagery. The Calvinist painter Jan Victors, for instance, focused solely on Old Testament stories and New Testament parables, reflecting a broader trend in Dutch religious culture. Old Testament figures such as Joseph and Joshua (approved), King David and Samson (cautionary) served as moral examples, featured in sermons, literature and theatre. A Dutch historian of religion even referred to such figures as 'Reformed Saints', indicating their significant role in Protestant moral teachings.

Catholic artists, when commissioned by Catholic patrons, faced no such constraints and freely depicted biblical scenes. One Catholic artist who took full advantage of this freedom was Paulus Bor. Another market for Old Testament scenes in Amsterdam was among the Sephardi Jewish community, who had fled religious persecution in Spain and Portugal. Art collections of Sephardi Jews, such as Manuel Mendes de Crasto and Isacq del Monte, included paintings of the biblical figures Tamar, Samson, Jacob and Esau. For these collectors, such themes carried personal and historical significance beyond moral instruction, reverberant with their experiences of exile and faith. In this context, biblical art not only served as religious expression but also as a bridge between diverse cultural and spiritual identities within Dutch society.

This did not extend in open form to sexual identities, other than unquestioned maleness and femaleness. Art historians have rightly been criticized for overlooking homoerotic themes in Dutch art, which appear strikingly in the oeuvres of such artists as Cornelis Cornelisz van Haarlem and Joachim Wtewael, seen in the latter's *Martyrdom of St Sebastian*. Wtewael was not the only artist to paint St Sebastian as a

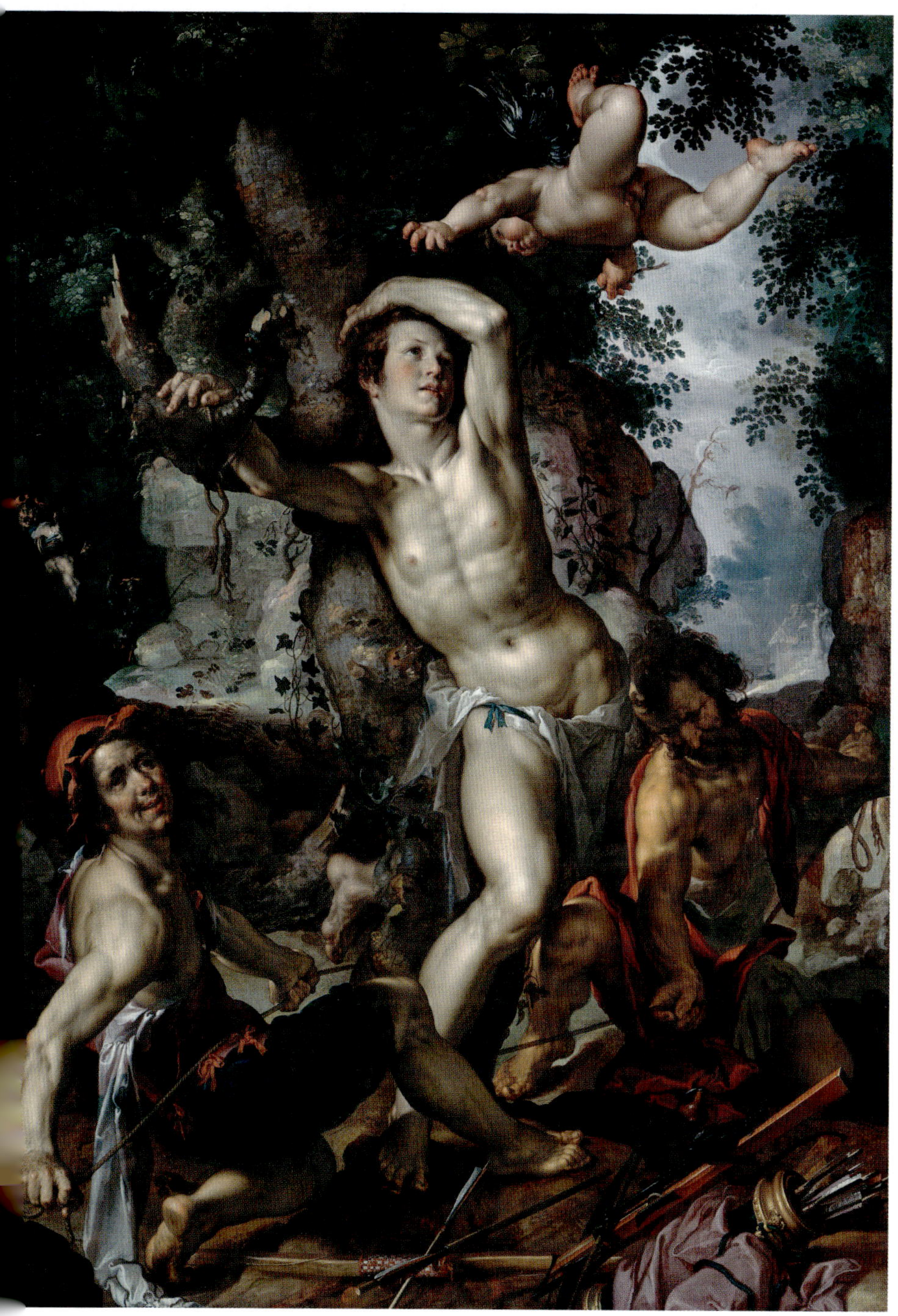

78 Joachim Wtewael, *The Martyrdom of St Sebastian*, 1600

lust object. It is surely time that this phenomenon, with
striking instances in Italian and Flemish art as well as Dutch,
be studied comprehensively and sensitively. Wtewael, born
in the same year as Abraham Bloemaert, was a prominent
figure in Utrecht painting for fifty years. Following a common
tradition, he was the son of a stained-glass artist and father
to a painter who continued his studio after his death.
Untypically, Wtewael showed acute business acumen as a
successful flax dealer and major shareholder in the VOC.
This cut into his production of paintings, much to the
disappointment of Karel van Mander. Alongside his artistic
and business careers, Wtewael was deeply involved in
municipal and religious politics, staunchly supporting
the strict Calvinist faction.

* * *

One of the most unusual works from the Dutch seventeenth
century is a *Crucifixion* by Hendrick ter Brugghen, in a style
reminiscent of a late medieval altarpiece. A summary of the
circumstances behind its creation shows how seemingly
straightforward artworks can have complex and unexpected
origins. In 1987, the Centraal Museum in Utrecht acquired a
smaller version of *The Crucifixion*, featuring the same crucified
Christ, Virgin Mary and St John. In this work, two men kneel
before the Virgin, while four women are placed in front of St
John. An inscription identifies three of the donors: Adriaen
Willemsz Ploos, his son Gerrit, and Nelle, Adriaen's wife. This
type of painting is known as an epitaph, a commemorative
work for a deceased individual. The painting acquired by the
Centraal Museum has been identified as a copy of an earlier
epitaph from a church in Loosdrecht, near Utrecht. The copy
had belonged to Adriaen Ploos (1585–1639), a powerful Utrecht
figure and a descendant of the family commemorated in the
epitaph. The art historians, genealogists and historians who
have since explored the origins of these three related works
hypothesize that Adriaen Ploos commissioned the copy after
the Loosdrecht epitaph with a strategic intent, involving
claims of noble ancestry.

Not satisfied with his influential roles as a canon at St
Mary's in Utrecht and holder of significant political offices,
Adriaen Ploos aspired to nobility. He pursued this aim by
assembling evidence to support his lineage from the van
Amstel van Mynden family, Utrecht aristocrats among whose
titles was lordship of Loosdrecht. When he ordered a copy of
the Loosdrecht epitaph, Ploos had the artist add two coats

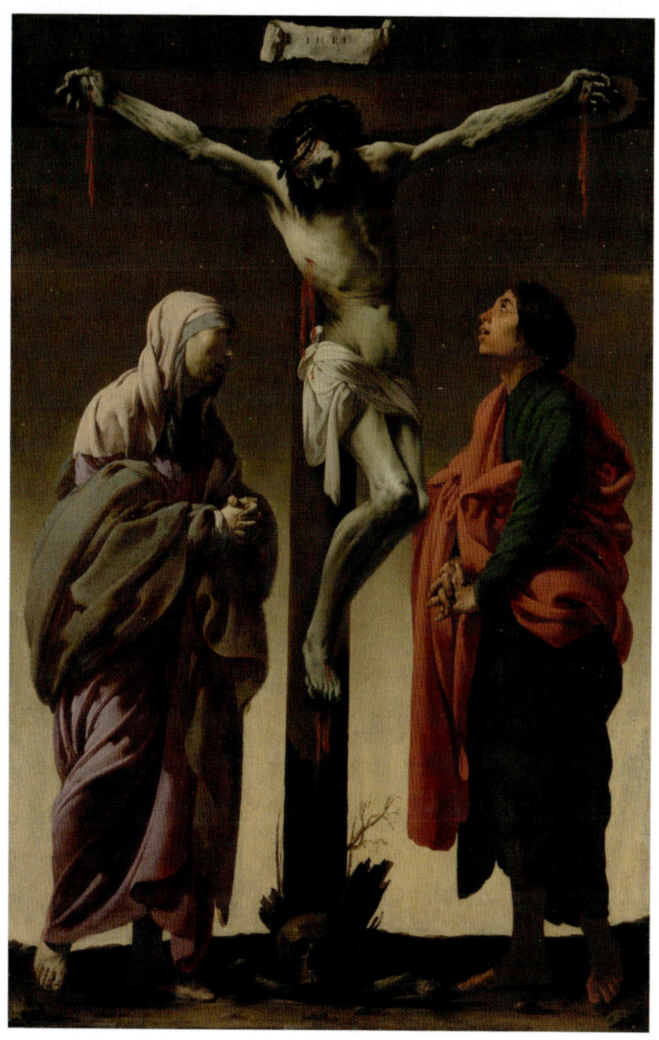

79 Hendrick ter Brugghen, *The Crucifixion with the Virgin and St John*, c. 1618

of arms, one for the van Amstel van Lyndens and another for Nelle's family. This modification was intended to demonstrate that Nelle's descendants, like him, were of noble lineage. The fictive claim was accepted in 1634, allowing Adriaen to change his surname to Ploos van Amstel. This reconstruction of events suggests that Hendrick ter Brugghen's *Crucifixion* was commissioned by Ploos around the same time. With its large scale and refined style, the painting will have been intended for display in a religious setting, possibly a private chapel, serving as a grand tribute to his purported ancestry.

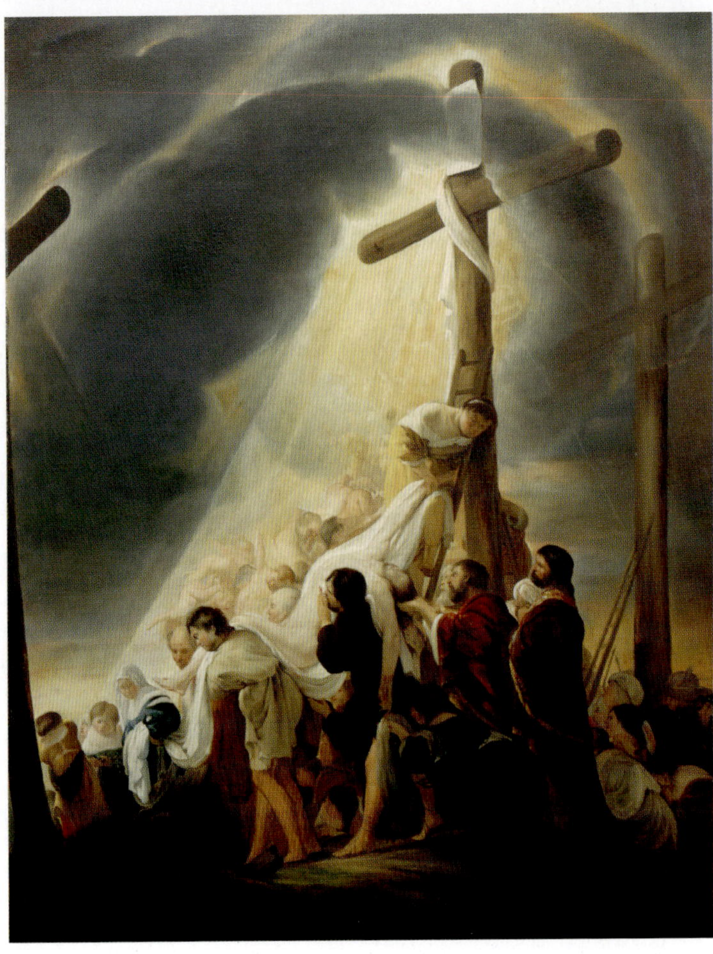

80 LEFT Paulus Bor, *The Descent from the Cross*, c. 1635
81 OPPOSITE Jan Victors, *Jacob Burying the Pagan Idols*, 1646

80 Paulus Bor's *Descent from the Cross* presents a dynamic and emotionally charged contrast to the contemplative mood of ter Brugghen's *Crucifixion*. While ter Brugghen's work evokes calmness through the composed figures of Mary and John, Bor's painting bursts with agitation, portraying the aftermath of Christ's death with heightened drama. The lighting and composition reflect this intensity: a celestial glow bathes Christ's body, still surrounded by the darkness that fell at his death. Instead of the static frontality of ter Brugghen's *Crucifixion*, Bor slashes his composition with a dynamic diagonal. Bor, from a prominent Catholic family in Amersfoort, infused his painting with values rooted in Catholic doctrine. The participation of around twenty figures in the event evokes

the community of the faithful in the mother church, in contrast
to more individual-focused Calvinist representations of the
Passion. However, the comparison between Bor and ter
Brugghen's approaches should not be simplified into a
Protestant versus Catholic dichotomy. Ter Brugghen's
Crucifixion was inspired by an altarpiece intended for a
Catholic church, while Rembrandt's works from the same
period, commissioned by the Protestant Stadholder Frederik
Hendrik, drew heavily on Catholic painters such as Rubens and
Titian. Bor's artistic development was shaped by his
experiences in Rome, where he was a founding member of the
Bentvueghels (see p. 110). During his two Italian years, from
1623 to 1625, he picked up a massive dose of cosmopolitan
knowhow. Upon returning to Amersfoort, he worked alongside
the renowned architect Jacob van Campen, contributing to
significant projects such as the decoration of the stadholder's
palace in Honselaarsdijk. Bor's distinctive stylistic flair had
admirers in high places.

The way that biblical art by a dedicated Calvinist looked is
found in the oeuvre of Jan Victors. For example, he may have
been the only artist ever to have painted the scene of *Jacob
Burying the Pagan Idols*. In Genesis 35, Jacob tells his household

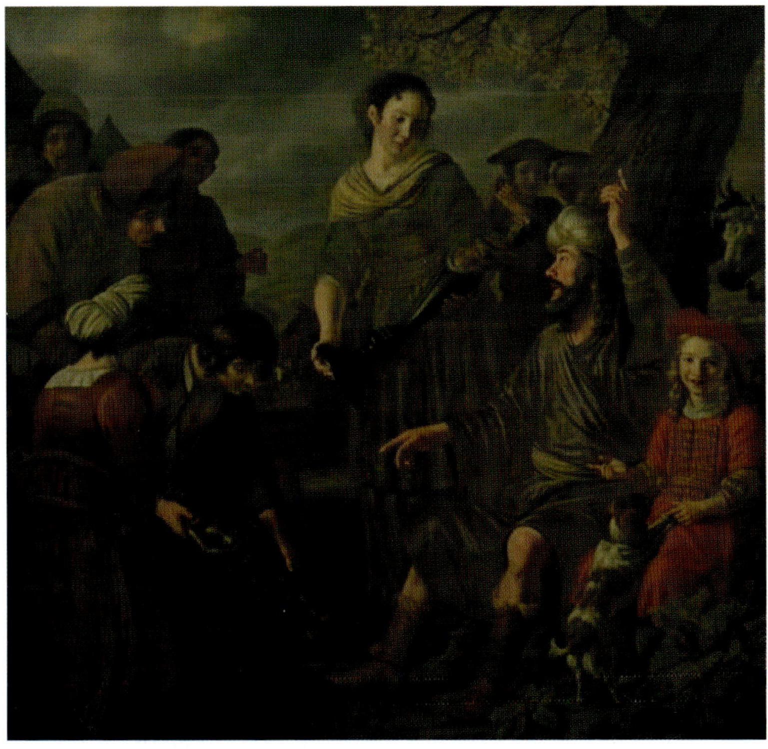

to get rid of their foreign gods. They brought them to him, including the rings in their ears, and Jacob buried them under an oak tree at Schechem. In the painting, a woman and a young man place handsome metal idols into a hole in the ground, while others remove earrings. This can be seen as a foreshadowing of Netherlandish iconoclasm, when Calvinists destroyed what they considered to be idolatrous objects in churches. Victors captures the moment with touches of genre painting, such as a playful child and dog in the foreground. Although there is no documentation linking their names, Victors is considered to be a product of the Rembrandt studio. He shares with Rembrandt pupils of mid-century the habit of dramatizing the stories depicted, as if the personages are actors staging the event. Beyond his art, Victors lived his faith, serving as a *ziekentrooster* (comforter of the sick) for the VOC. The comfort offered may sometimes have alleviated physical pain, but it was mainly spiritual support in a Calvinist mould. He shipped out with the VOC in 1676, and met his end by disease some time later.

∗ ∗ ∗

Jan Victors was among numerous Dutch painters whose work shows a strong Rembrandtesque influence. The German art historian Werner Sumowski (1931–2015) took on the monumental task of cataloguing the works of about fifty artists associated with Rembrandt, publishing comprehensive multi-volume catalogues of their paintings and drawings. Although only twenty of these artists were documented as Rembrandt's students, they are collectively referred to as the 'Rembrandt School'. At the end of his catalogues, Sumowski included a section on Rembrandt-style works with unidentified authors, noting disheartedly that compiling a complete listing would require multiple volumes. This highlights the challenges in categorizing Dutch paintings, many of which remain anonymous, while many documented artists have left no known works.

An Old Testament painting in Salzburg serves as an example of these complexities. Sumowski described it as a 1650s work by an unknown artist, with echoes of Karel van Savoy, dismissing previous attributions to Gerbrand van den Eeckhout, Aert de Gelder or Jan Victors. The subject matter comes from Genesis 38, which recounts the peculiar story of Judah and Tamar. Tamar was married to Judah's firstborn son, Er, who was so wicked in his ways that the Lord killed him. By Jewish law, Tamar was then taken in marriage by the second son, Onan, who because he

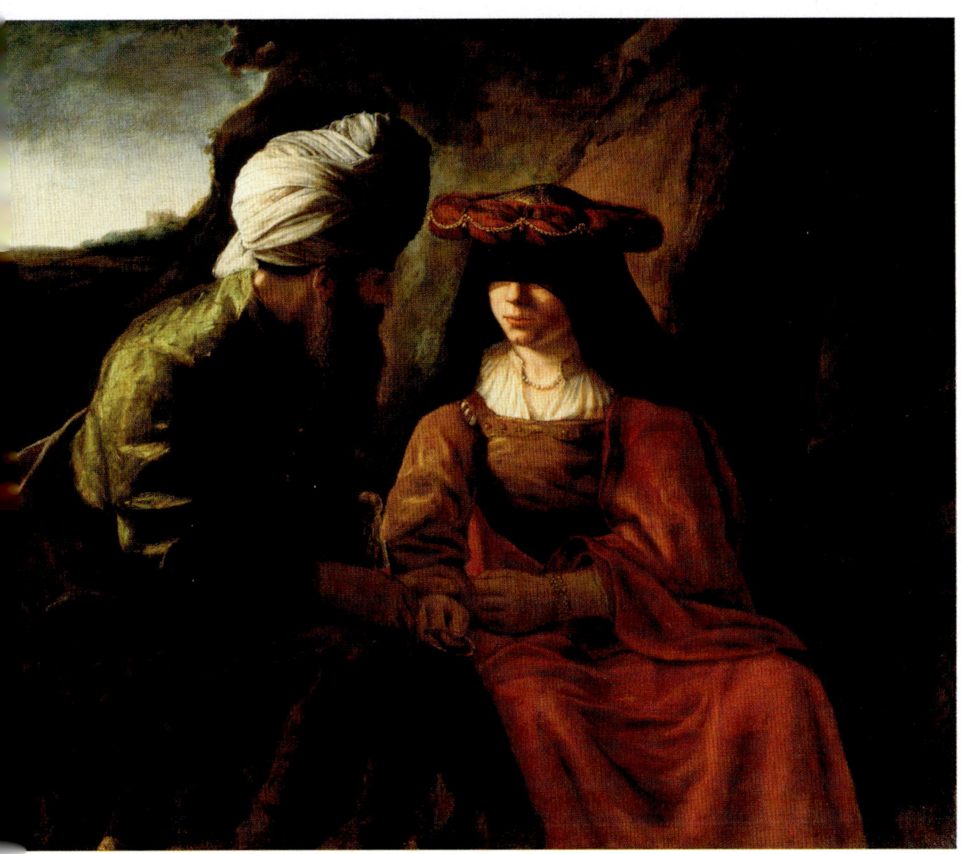

82 Rembrandt school, *Judah and Tamar*, c. 1650–60

refused to father a child with her was also killed by God. When Judah withheld from Tamar his third son, the twice-widowed, childless Tamar took matters into her own hands. She disguised herself as a prostitute and seduced Judah, to secure an heir and bolster her familial status. The painting depicts a crucial detail in the narrative: Tamar's request that Judah turn over to her a seal, cord and staff, which she later implemented as proof of his paternity. For Christian artists this story, morally ambiguous though it may be, carried profound significance. As John Calvin noted, the genealogy of Christ, in Matthew 1, runs through Perez, the fruit of that illicit union. God's plan for salvation, this implies, can unfold even through flawed individuals. This line of thought adds depth to understanding how biblical stories could be used in art to convey not just moral narratives but theological messages as well.

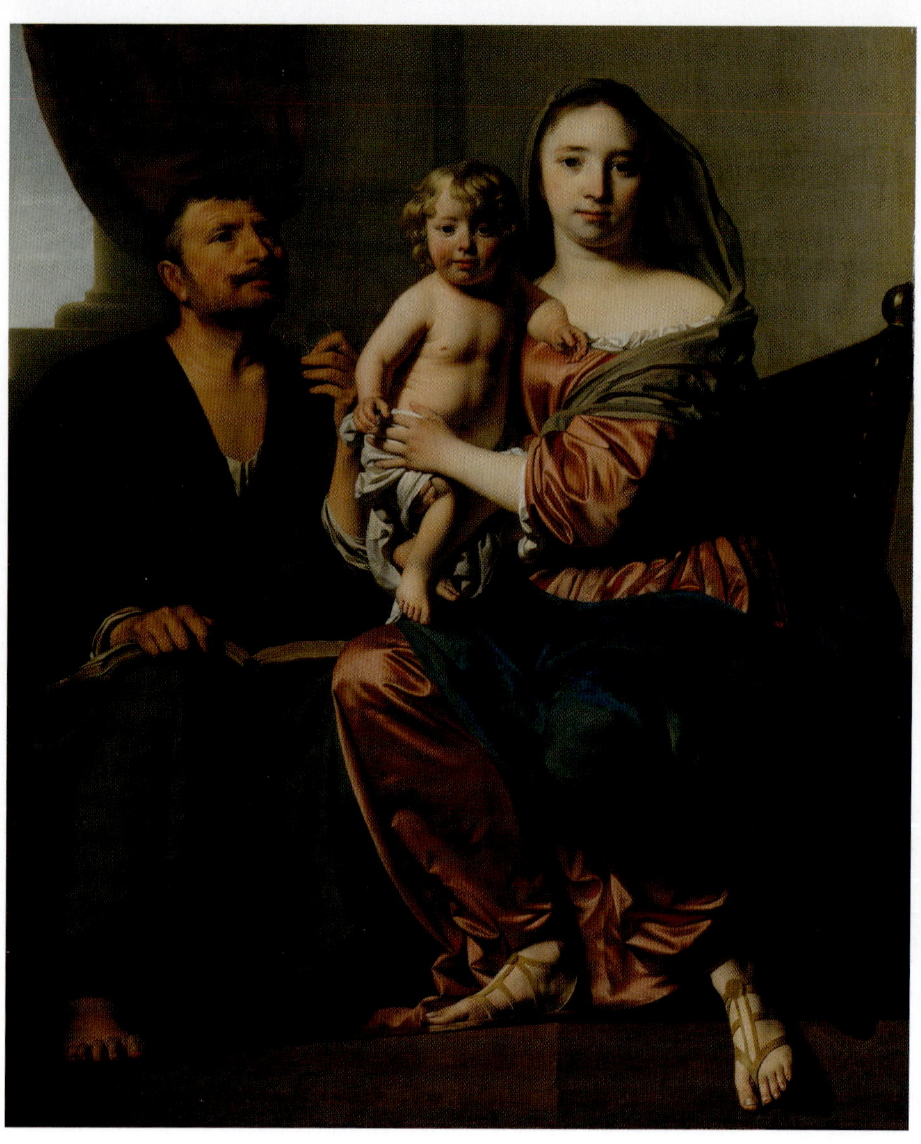

83 Caesar van Everdingen, *The Holy Family*, c. 1660

Not that all Christian art had to be moralizing or theological. A motif often surrounded with miraculous details was pictured by the Reformed Caesar van Everdingen in entirely human terms. But he was not intending, as were some other Dutch painters, to domesticate the holy family. He gives the figures high glamour, dressing Mary in shining satins, with Roman sandals on her feet. Joseph is not a humble carpenter but a studious thinker. And the Christ child takes command of the scene not with the traditional references to his coming sacrifice, but as a baby Master of the Universe. The architecture, with its classical vocabulary, is as far removed as can be from the humble manger of Scripture. Caesar van Everdingen was one of the Dutch painters called upon for the decoration of Huis ten Bosch, where he exerted himself to live up to the classicizing impulse behind that project. That spirit is extended and refined in his more powerful *Holy Family*.

Mythology, History, Allegory

For a Christian artist, painting biblical stories might seem self-explanatory, but depicting pagan mythology required a degree of justification. One common approach was to interpret the figures or narratives as moral lessons. For example, Bacchus could symbolize the dangers of excess, while Mars could serve as a reminder to remain vigilant. Even the more sensual mythological tales were often framed as moral allegories, with emblem books and popular literature providing interpretations that aligned with these lessons. Similarly, stories from classical antiquity often represented ideals or moral concepts beyond the literal narrative. Mythological and historical subjects also allowed artists to evoke strong emotions and display their skills in a wealth of demanding details. Creating allegorical paintings required extensive knowledge of symbolism. Gerard de Lairesse's ceiling paintings in the house of the Amsterdam burgomaster, Andries de Graeff, refers to over 130 motifs, each representing specific values agreed upon by artist and patron. Many of these meanings were drawn from Cesare Ripa's *Iconologia* (1593), a key source for allegorical symbols, which was translated into Dutch in 1644. The symbols in those paintings refer not only to generalities but also to current events, especially those that affected the fortunes of the patron.

The seventeenth century kicked off with a pinnacle of Dutch mythological painting, Hendrick Goltzius's mixed-media masterpiece, *Without Bacchus and Ceres, Venus would Freeze.* Bacchus, the god of wine, and Ceres, the goddess of the harvest, share fruits and grains with Venus, the goddess of love. Her son Cupid holds a burning torch. The painting's message can be interpreted in different ways: one reading endorses the pleasures of food and drink for the enhancement of love, while another warns against overindulgence, reflecting themes common in Christian moral writings. The painting's Latin title, *Sine Cerere et Baccho friget Venus*, taken from Terence's comedy *The Eunuch*, adds a layer of erudition to the mix. Goltzius frequently returned to this theme, creating at least ten versions in various techniques. His virtuosity was renowned across Europe, and his engravings were highly sought after by collectors. The painting now in Philadelphia, along with another version housed in the Hermitage, St Petersburg, were acquired by Emperor Rudolf II in Prague. Both deploy hybrid techniques, in which Goltzius used the brush to imitate the fine effects of engraving. Karel van Mander noted that Rudolf was so impressed by the Philadelphia piece's technique that he summoned other artists to marvel at its craftsmanship.

* * *

While history painting as a genre enjoyed high esteem, even as it declined in frequency, the painting of actual, contemporary history was a rare exception. The first known painting to depict a political event as it was happening is Gerard ter Borch's group portrait of the delegates to the conference in Münster that ended the Dutch revolt against Spain after eighty years, and recognized the Netherlands as a sovereign nation. Ter Borch was not only an eyewitness to the event, he was an actual participant. He came to Münster in the train of the Dutch delegate, Adriaen Pauw, but was released by Pauw to the leading Spanish delegate, with whom he was on friendly terms. Don Caspar de Bracamonte y Guzmán, Conde de Peñaranda, thereupon designated the Zwolle painter as one of his twelve *gentiles-hombres*. Ter Borch painted himself, with falling blond locks, on the left edge of the scene. The painting was assiduously prepared by him with small oval portraits on copper, of the sixty-five delegates. Only eight have survived. (The 88 percent loss over time of even well-documented paintings is on the low side of the rate estimated by economic historians.) The depiction of the space, with its panelling and chandelier, is perfectly true to life, as a visitor to Münster can confirm today. The way in which the delegates swear to the text of the treaty – the Spaniards with a hand on a Bible with a crucifix, the Dutch by raising their right hands – is pictured just as it is documented in first-hand sources. Unable to sell his unique painting for the asking price of six thousand guilders, ter Borch eventually gave or sold it for less to a cousin who was

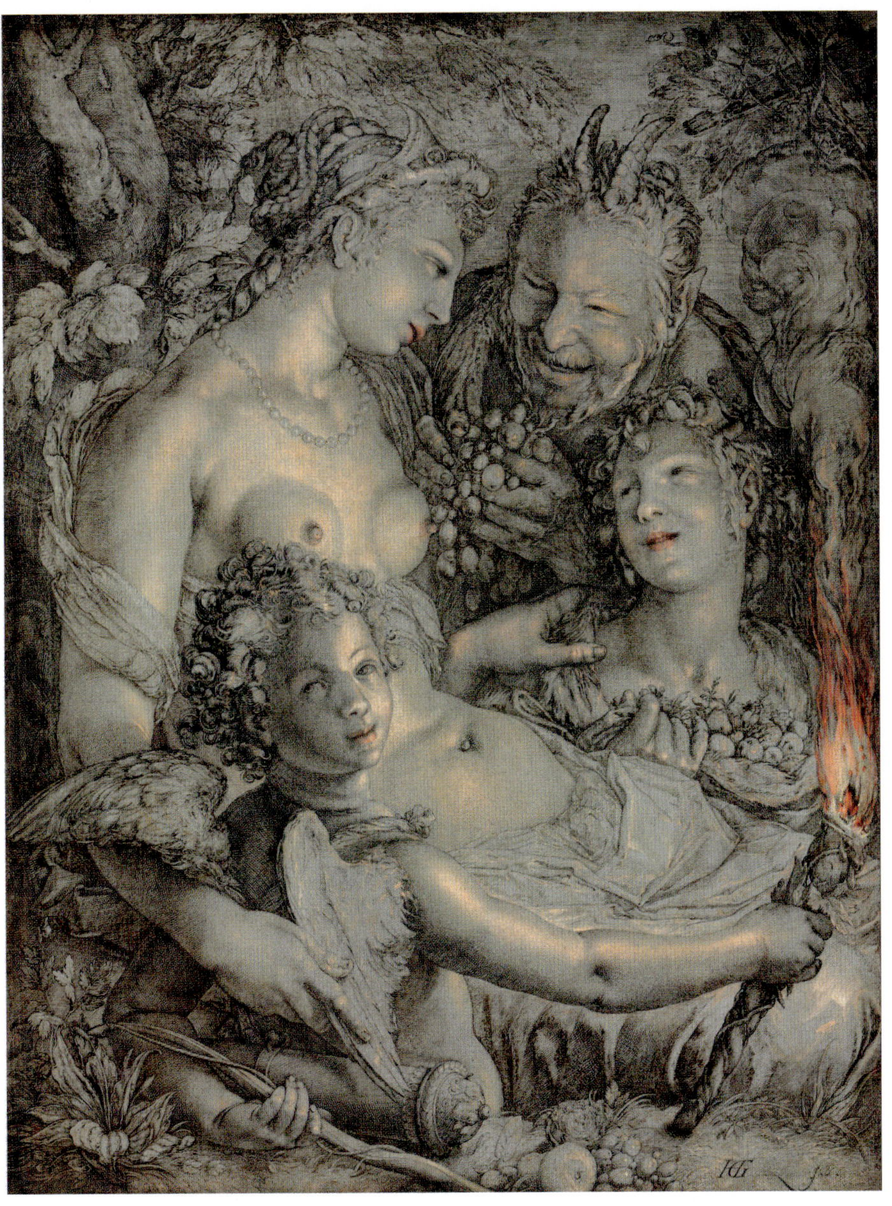

84 Hendrick Goltzius, *Sine Cerere et Baccho friget Venus*, c. 1600

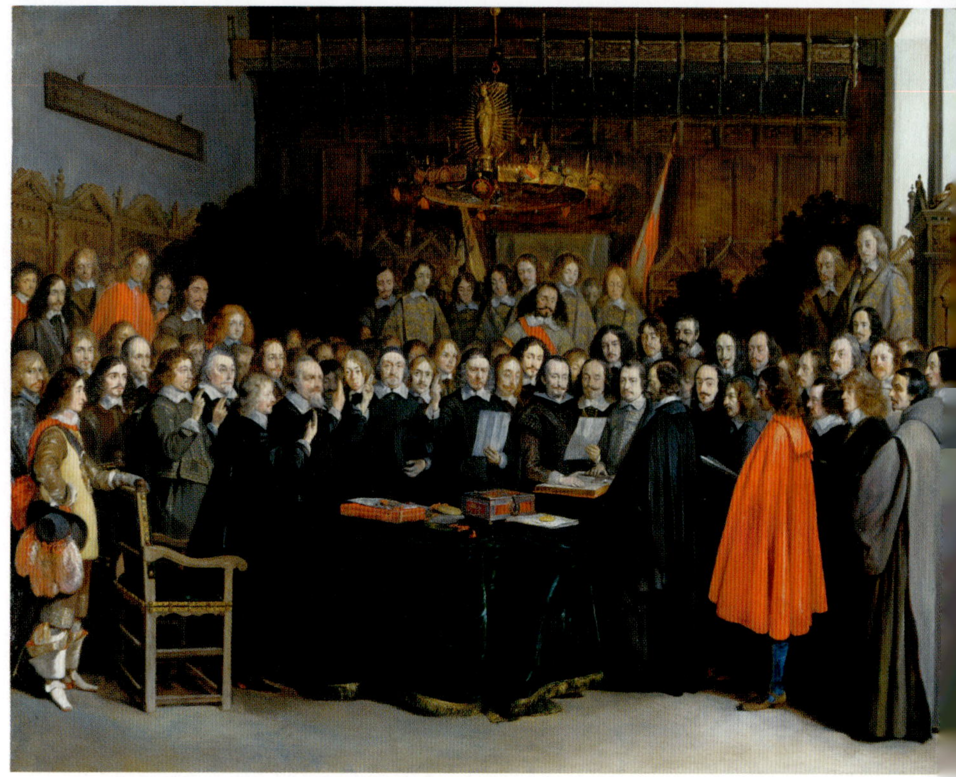

85 Gerard ter Borch, *The Ratification of the Treaty of Münster*, 1648

a burgomaster of Zwolle. A subsequent owner was the French diplomat Talleyrand, who hung the painting in his quarters during the Congress of Vienna in 1814–15, where a new European order was established after the defeat of Napoleon. So this painting witnessed the realignment of Europe twice.

A more conventional way than literal reportage of evoking political developments in paint was to allegorize them. After this treatment was accorded Frederik Hendrik in the Oranjezaal, it also honoured a principled opponent of the House of Orange, Cornelis de Witt. After the early death in 1650 of Stadholder Willem II, the office he held was put in abeyance by the States-General, and the executive authority over the Republic fell step by step to the Grand Pensionary of Holland, the Dordrecht regent Jan de Witt (1625–72). One of the great challenges facing de Witt was fending off the attacks on Dutch shipping by the English. At a given moment during the Second Anglo-Dutch War, he dispatched his brother Cornelis (1623–72) as political attaché to

the fleet. Cornelis had the good fortune to be on duty when, on
23 June 1667, the Dutch fleet conducted a raid on the English in
their home harbour of Chatham on the Medway, capturing the
flagship, the *Royal Charles*. The Dutch commander, Admiral
Michiel de Ruyter, celebrated his part in the victory by having gift
portraits made of himself. Cornelis de Witt did not have to take
the initiative. His home town of Dordrecht commissioned a large
allegory of Cornelis at Chatham, to hang above the chimney
in the great hall of the town hall. That painting was destroyed by
a furious mob five years later, when the de Witt brothers were
lynched and Willem II's son was raised to the stadholdership as
Willem III. The smaller version in the Rijksmuseum, with its
vainglorious frame, was ordered by the sitter. In front of a view
of the battle, winged figures act out Cornelis's glory, blowing
the trumpet of his fame in the heavens, depositing the harvest
of gains at his feet, and crowning him with the laurel wreath of
victory. This, too, is Dutch painting.

Cleopatra stories are perennial favourites in literature,
drama and art, exemplified in Gerard de Lairesse's vision
of her dinner for the Roman general, Mark Antony.

Pliny the Elder:

*The last of the Egyptian queens owned the two largest pearls of
all time, left to her by oriental kings. When Antony was stuffing
himself daily with rare foods, she proudly and impertinently, like
the royal harlot that she was, sneered at his attempts at luxury and
extravagance. When he asked her what could be added in the way
of sumptuousness she replied that she would use up 10,000,000
sesterces at one dinner.*

As she set before Mark Antony a menu of standard palace
fare, he was ready to collect, but Cleopatra removed one of her
earrings, dropped it in vinegar to dissolve it, and swallowed it.
Of all the morals that can be taken from this unedifying story,
de Lairesse chose a humdrum one for the caption to a print he
had made after the painting: *Quem Mars numquam, vincit Venus*
(Venus conquers what Mars never could).

* * *

In his *Treatise on the Art of Painting* (1707, translated into English
in 1712), Gerard de Lairesse urges artists to strive for clarity,
consistency, balance, idealization, dignity, beauty, and respect
for visual inspiration and textual sources. The 'noble' art he
commends he calls antique, as opposed to the 'ignoble' modern.

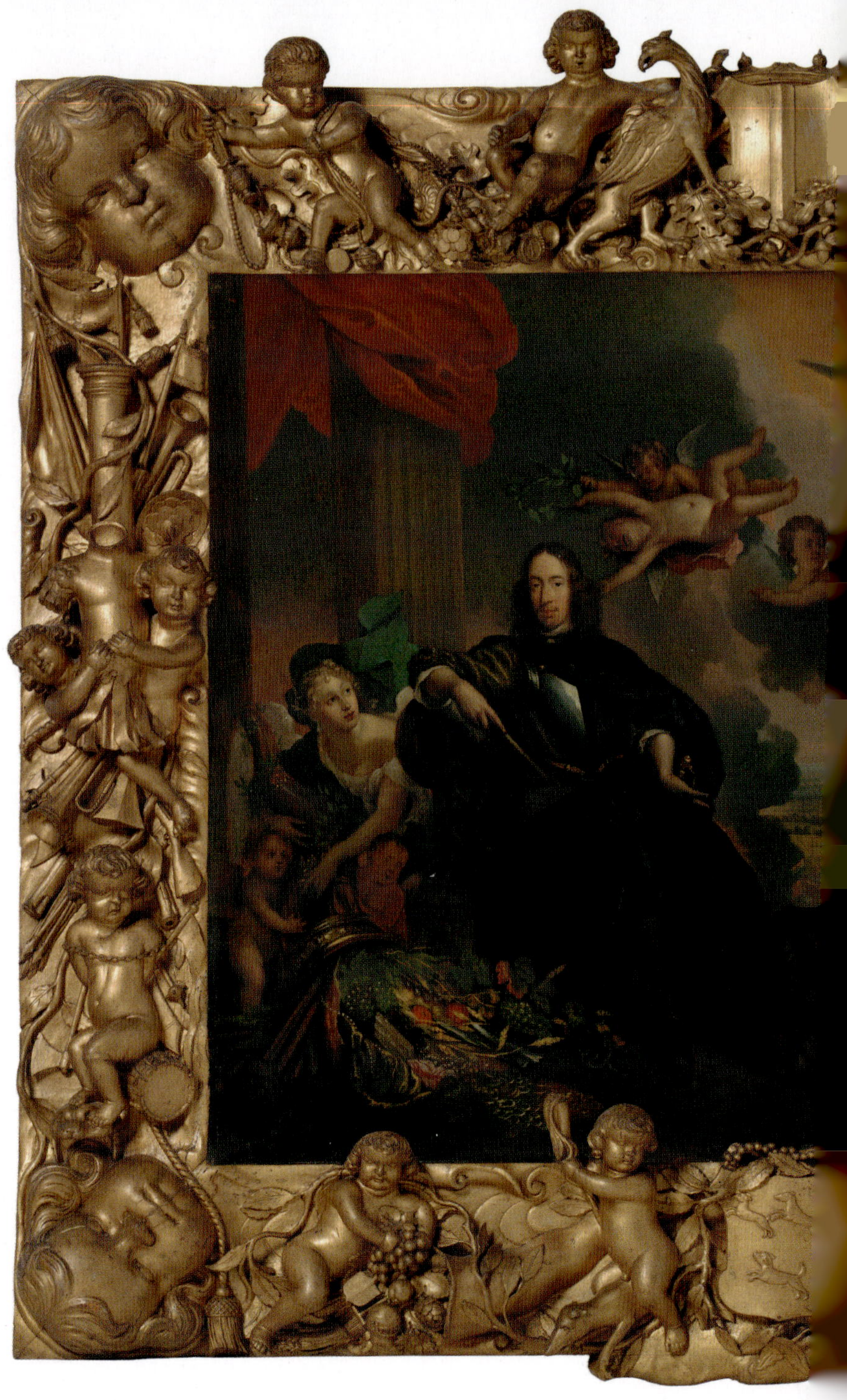

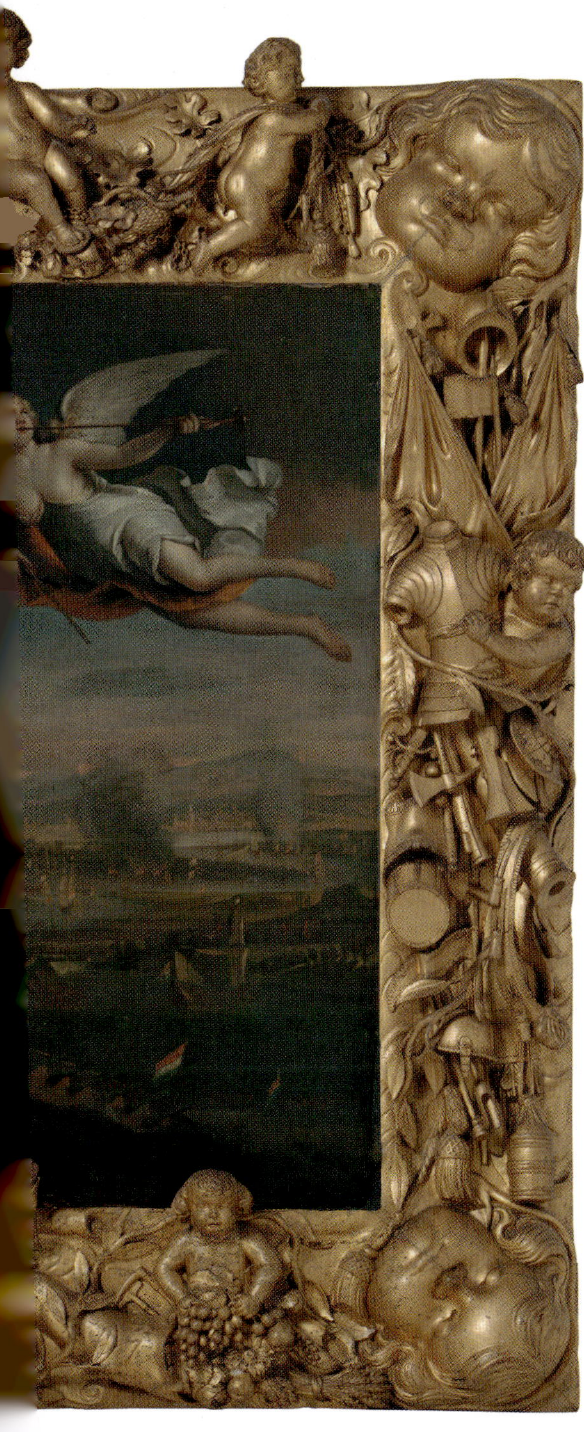

86 By or after Jan de Baen, *The Glorification of Cornelis de Witt, with the Raid on Chatham in the Background*, 1667

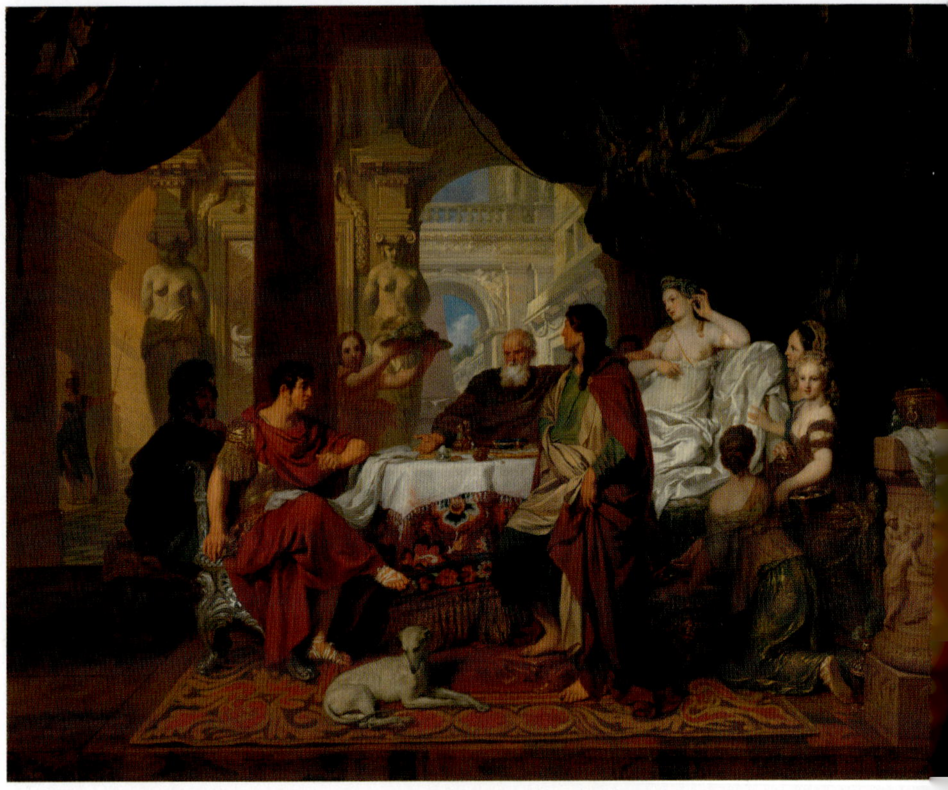

87 Gerard de Lairesse, *Mark Antony at Cleopatra's Table*, c. 1675–80

The antique is unlimited; that is, it can handle *history,*
sacred as well as profane, *fables* and *emblems,* both moral
and spiritual; under which three heads it comprehends,
*all that ever was, is, and shall be; the past, present, and to come;
and that, after an excellent manner, which never alters, but
remains always the same.*

These are exalted aims. In art history, misleadingly,
de Lairesse's 'antique' has been supplanted by the term
'classicistic', a word that did not exist until the nineteenth
century. In writings on art and architecture, 'classicistic'
refers to formal properties, while 'antique', to de Lairesse,
was a philosophical and spiritual concept. These are values
that de Lairesse encountered and embraced in a literary
society to which he belonged, Nil Volentibus Arduum (Nothing
is Difficult for Those Who Try). Living in the 'antique' brings
together artists and those for whom they worked in a shared

ethical and aesthetic space. To live up to the consequent demands, de Lairesse urges artists to adapt the architecture, costume and manners in their works to the particular circumstances of the subject. 'Are you disposed to handle *an ancient story, borrow nothing for it that is new, and of modern invention;* since what is disguised with falsehoods can never be truth.' It was in this spirit that de Lairesse composed *Mark Antony at Cleopatra's Table.* A spirit that contrasted sharply with the 'ignoble' modern one. In contrast, Jan Steen's painting of Cleopatra's feast looks like it could be taking place in a high-class bordello in The Hague.

Chapter 8
Genres and Subgenres

Gerard de Lairesse was not kind to all of his colleagues.

Let me speak plain in spite of others; I say then, that although modern *things seem to have some prettiness, yet they are only to be esteemed as* diversions of art. *I moreover maintain, that such painters as never produce more than one choice of subjects, may truly be ranked among tradesmen*

Writing in 1707, de Lairesse is belittling the work of hundreds of his peers – not only painters by whom just a single work is documented, but also major masters. Michiel van Mierevelt painted only portraits, Jan van Goyen only landscapes, Maria van Oosterwijck only still lifes. De Lairesse may have been dismissive, but he was not altogether wrong. If we leave out his jibe about specialist painters not living the life of the mind, it is true that in a sense they were tradesmen. This led them to adopt profit-seeking methods that art historians are used to explaining as stylistic choices. The grey-brown tonality and looser touch that artists began practising in the 1620s can be seen as a way to increase productivity and lower costs. When artists found that buyers were willing to pay as much for a painting that took two days to make as for one that took three or four, it would be robbing your children of their pocket money, if not tuition fee, not to go that way.

Portraiture

After history painting, with its origins in church art, portraiture is the oldest kind of art made by Dutch painters, beginning in the early fifteenth century. It saw a steady demand, representing around twenty percent of art production. This stability reflected the fact that portraits were typically commissioned by patrons rather than initiated by artists, indicating a consistent desire among Dutch burghers to have pictures of themselves and their families. This dependence on the wishes of others is part of the reason portraiture did not rank very high in the hierarchy of genres. Van Mander, who is not known ever to have painted one, called it rather superciliously, 'a byway of the arts'. While capturing a true likeness was essential, portraits conveyed much more. Clothing, posture and attributes reflected on a sitter's social status, profession and personal qualities. For many, portraits were statements of identity. Painted portraits were commonly reproduced in prints, serving as refined calling cards. Painted copies were often made for family members, underscoring their personal significance. In this capacity, they even enjoyed legal protection. In the liquidation of assets in a bankruptcy, family portraits were excluded, as if a forced sale would be an unethical infringement of one's very person.

A particularly eloquent portrait by Hendrick Goltzius caught the attention of Karel van Mander, who wrote of it: 'He further made some portraits for his own pleasure...in particular a certain Jan Govertsen who lives in Haarlem, a lover of shells, with a mother-of-pearl in his hand and with other horn-shaped shells beside him. In its perfection, this is pre-eminently subtle in execution and likeness.' The sitter lent his features to twelve other works in paint, drawing and print. All are playful, personal works, stressing rather than muffling the wrinkled fleshiness of Govertsen's face. Some show him as a personage in a mythological or biblical subject – St Luke painting the Madonna, but also one of the elders who in the apocryphal Old Testament story falsely accused the virtuous Susanna of adultery and paid for the libel with his life. In 1611 a poem was published whose message seems to pertain to Govertsen's hobby: 'Seashore, or Poem of the Shells' by Philibert van Borsselen.

Just as this noble shell derives its fair lustre
From heaven's greatest light, and in turn reflects it
Upon the face of man, bringing joy to the sorrowful heart,
So too must man, in whose soul a spark
Of heaven's light has mercifully been kindled
And, by God's spirit, nurtured into a holy fire,
Diligently strive to shine that light upon others,
To promote God's glory and edify his neighbour.
Let him not bury the treasure that God has placed in his hands
In the depths of his own heart, but lend it as a pledge,
And seek to increase it...

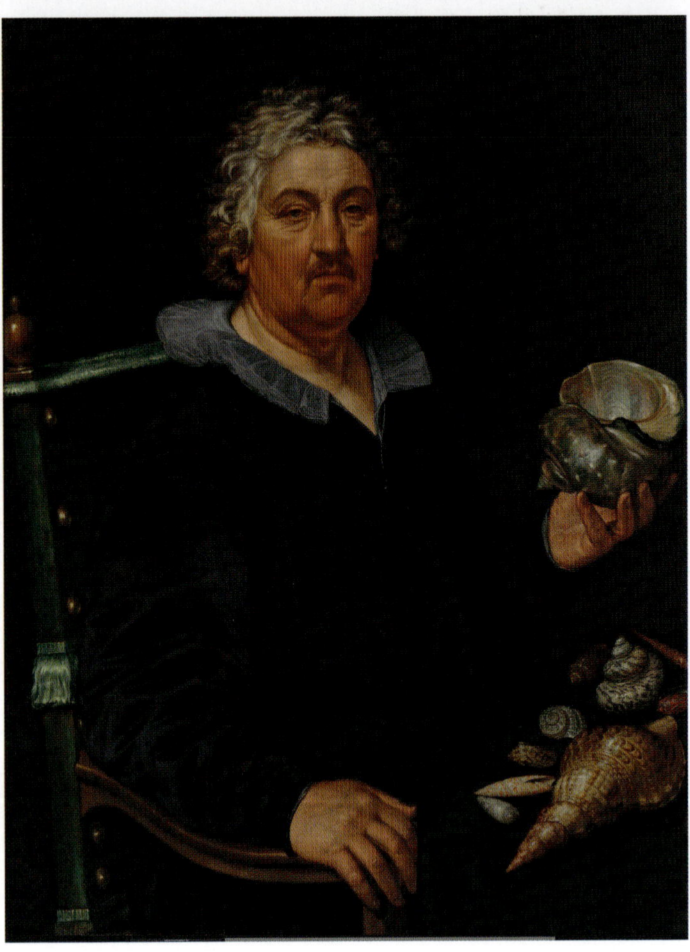

Personal messages were also built into a pair of delicate husband-and-wife portraits by Cornelis Jonson van Ceulen. The male sitter, Willem Thielen, was the Calvinist minister of the Netherlands Reformed Church of Austin Friars in the City of London, the oldest church of that denomination ever founded, in 1550. It was there, in exile, that the most distinctive features of Dutch Calvinism were formulated, so that it was called the 'mother church'. The paintings conform to a widespread format for portraits of a married couple: ovals of a man left and woman right, as in heraldry. Here the armorial bearings of both are added, with name, date and age in the upper outside margin, and on the inside, devotional statements from Scripture appropriate to the two persons. Willem's speaks of resignation,

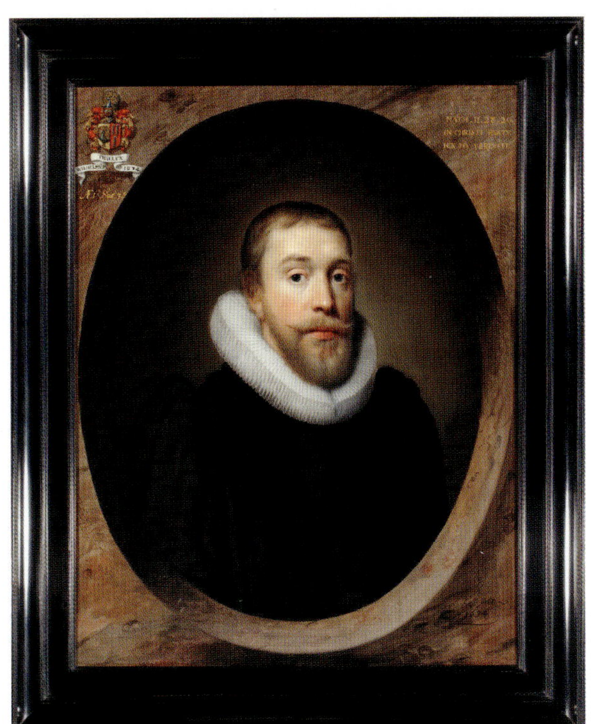

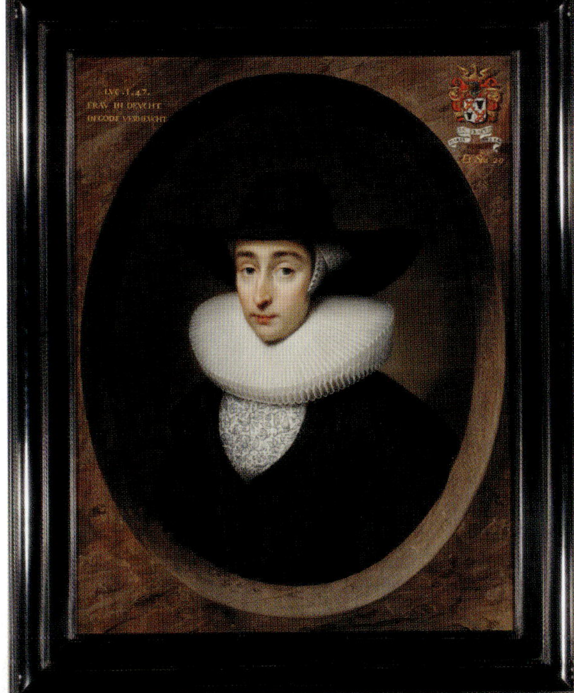

88 OPPOSITE Hendrick Goltzius, *Portrait of Jan Govertsen van der Aer with Shells from his Collection*, 1603

89 ABOVE RIGHT Cornelis Jonson van Ceulen, *Portrait of Willem Thielen, Minister of the Dutch Reformed Church in London*, 1634

90 BELOW RIGHT Cornelis Jonson van Ceulen, *Portrait of Maria de Fraeye, Married to Willem Thielen*, 1634

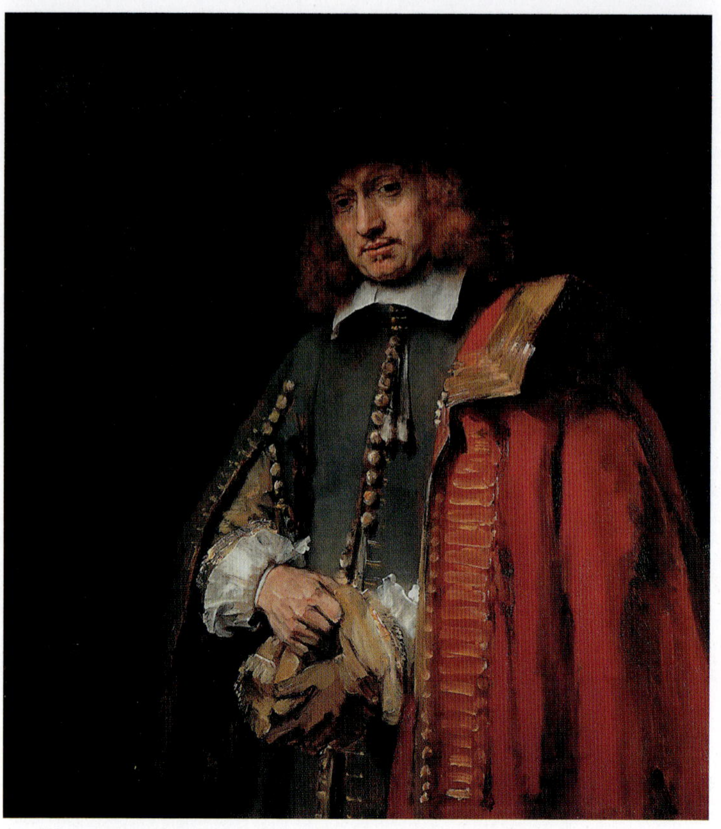

91 Rembrandt van Rijn, *Portrait of Jan Six*, 1654

in reference to the illness that was forcing him into early retirement, four years before his death at the age of forty-two. That of Willem's wife, Maria de Fraeye, builds in a pun on her family name, literally 'the beautiful'.

Born in London to a family of Flemish-German refugees, van Ceulen was probably apprenticed in the Netherlands, where he made his home later in life. He was thus exemplary of a demographic that could be called the North Sea artist, of which there were more than a few. In England he is considered to be the first English-born painter to have left a substantial oeuvre of signed works. At a more modest level than Anthony van Dyck, he set a standard of dignity, refinement and technical prowess that gave English portraiture a distinctive look – at least until the Restoration, when dignity and refinement were no longer the thing. His pendant portraits of the van Thielens were painted in the months before the sitters left London for Middelburg in September 1634. The stiffness of their impeccable Dutch-style ruff collars (Maria's blouse is English) may make the sitters look unapproachable, but the longer you look at them, the more vulnerable and individualized they appear. No wonder that the family had copies made that, like the originals, were kept as heirlooms.

Of all Dutch portraits of the seventeenth century, that of the upper-crust Jan Six by Rembrandt came forth out of the most many-sided relationship between painter and sitter. In 1647 Rembrandt made an etched portrait of Six; the plate is still owned by the sitter's descendants, as is the portrait. They also have Jan Six's friendship album, which has two drawings by Rembrandt, one showing Minerva reading at a desk, the other the poet Homer. A further classical connection between them is Rembrandt's etching for the printed edition of Six's stage play *Medea*. Rembrandt's relationship with the ruling families of Amsterdam had soured after a contretemps around 1640. The portrait of Jan Six was the first sign of favour from an Amsterdam patrician. The pose, action and introverted facial expression withhold closeness from the viewer. Jan has his coat on and when he has pulled on his glove, will turn and take leave of us. In a display of virtuosity, Rembrandt paints so broadly that you can practically count the number of brushstrokes in the painting. The sitter's look is a display of *sprezzatura*, a cool demeanour. This quality, wrote the Italian author Baldassare Castiglione in his book *Il cortegiano* (*The Courtier*; 1528), is the way for a courtier to comport himself if he can. The first Dutch translation of the book, which came out two years before Rembrandt's portrait, was dedicated to Jan Six.

Self-portraits

The self-portrait is the ultimate product of what has been called self-fashioning. This practice, a strategy for presenting oneself as advantageously as possible, was largely a matter of outward appearances. Courtiers took on a certain bearing and had their clothing tailored just so, hoping that others saw them in the desired semblance rather than as laughable poseurs. Artists were uniquely in a position to project images of themselves on their own. To their good fortune, more than one European ruler liked to own self-portraits. The epitome of this practice took form in mid-century when Cardinal Leopoldo de' Medici began purchasing and commissioning self-portraits for the Uffizi, laying the basis for a collection now running to over 2,000 paintings, drawings and sculptures. Of the Dutch painters in this book, the Medici collection includes self-portraits by Pieter van Laer, Job Berckheyde, Abraham Bloemaert, Gerard Dou, Gerard de Lairesse,

Rembrandt (3), Godfried Schalcken, Bartholomeus
van der Helst, Adriaen van der Werff, Frans van Mieris (3)
and Michiel van Musscher, as well as by seven others. On an
incidental basis in his lifetime, self-portraits by Rembrandt
entered the collections of Charles I of England, Louis XIV of
France and Emperor Karl VI of the Holy Roman Empire.
Another ruler-artist link can be seen in Adriaen van der
Werff's self-portrait, in which he wears a gold chain he had
been given by the Elector Palatine Johann Wilhelm.

Self-portraiture fulfilled far more functions than furnishing
royal cabinets. It can be an introspective gesture; a study
of expression or lighting; a manifesto of art or the standing of
the artist; a deed of family devotion, when with parents, spouse
or children; a piece of merchandise with a free model; a
self-advertisement for bourgeois buyers; a combination of the
above, with a dash of vanity thrown in. Or even vanitas – an
avowal of the transitoriness of life and the eternity of death.
The reigning prince of self-portraiture was Rembrandt. In the
wake of his bankruptcy in 1656, he turned to the self-portrait in
what seems like a defiance of adversity. These late works are the
culmination of a lifelong engagement with self-portraiture, in
prints for the masses as well as paintings for royalty. In some
works Rembrandt assumes a given guise. He portrayed himself
as a beggar, an oriental ruler, the prodigal son, the Italian
poet Ludovico Ariosto, St Paul and the Greek painter Zeuxis.
Frequently, he presents himself in the same way that he
portrays his contemporary sitters. One of the rare instances
in which Rembrandt depicts himself with the tools of his craft
is the self-portrait at Kenwood House, London. Unlike typical
representations of an artist at work, the artist is not shown in
his studio. Instead, behind him looms a wall – or perhaps a
canvas – marked by two arcs, one bisected by an oblique line.
These enigmatic symbols have long suggested profound
meaning, though their exact significance remains elusive.
Two stories from the literature of art that have been linked
to these markings seem to be relevant.

The first, recounted by Karel van Mander from Pliny the
Elder, tells of Apelles visiting his fellow artist Protogenes on
the island of Rhodes. Finding him absent, Apelles drew a
fine line on a primed canvas for Protogenes to discover.
Recognizing the exceptional skill displayed, Protogenes
responded with an equally fine line. On a second visit, Apelles,
in friendly rivalry, drew a third line, splitting the previous
two with perfect precision. The story leaves us guessing what
kind of lines they were, but a parallel legend from Vasari's
Lives of the Artists attributes to the Italian master Giotto the

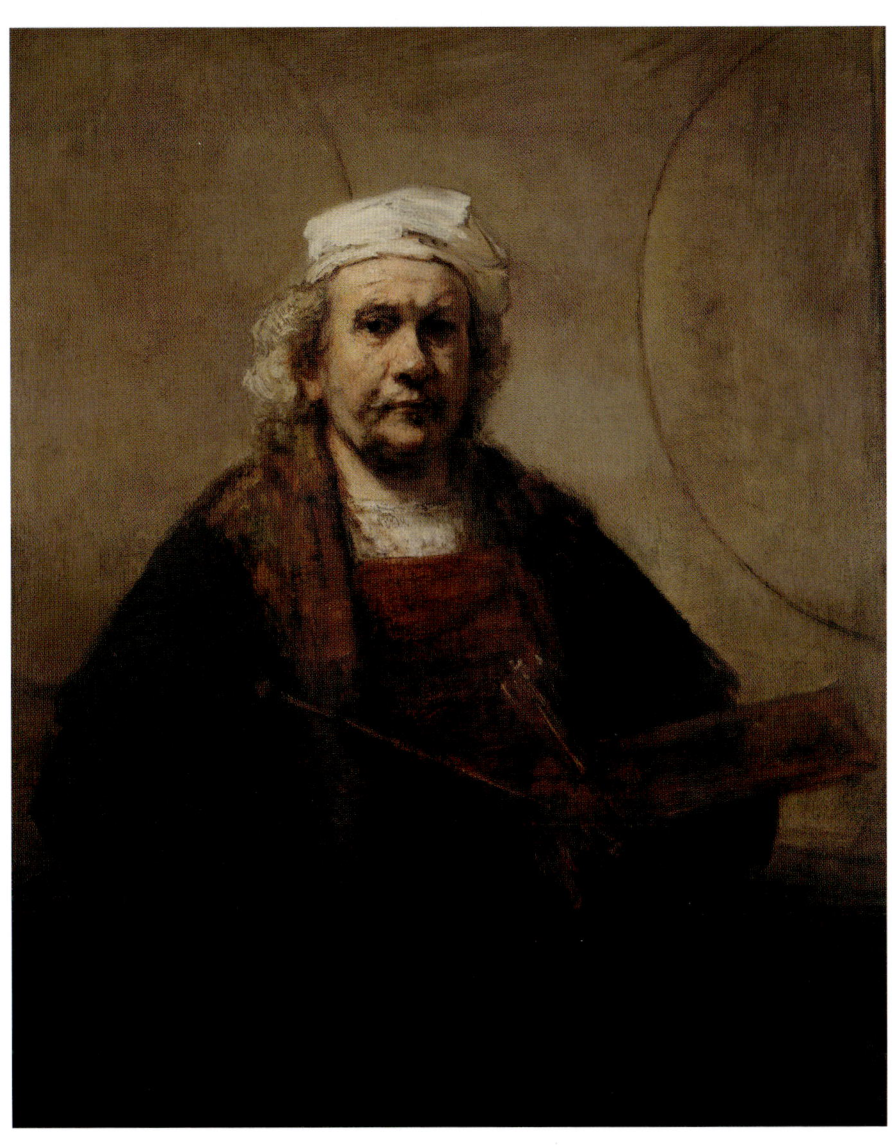

92 Rembrandt van Rijn, *Self-portrait with Two Circles*, c. 1661–62

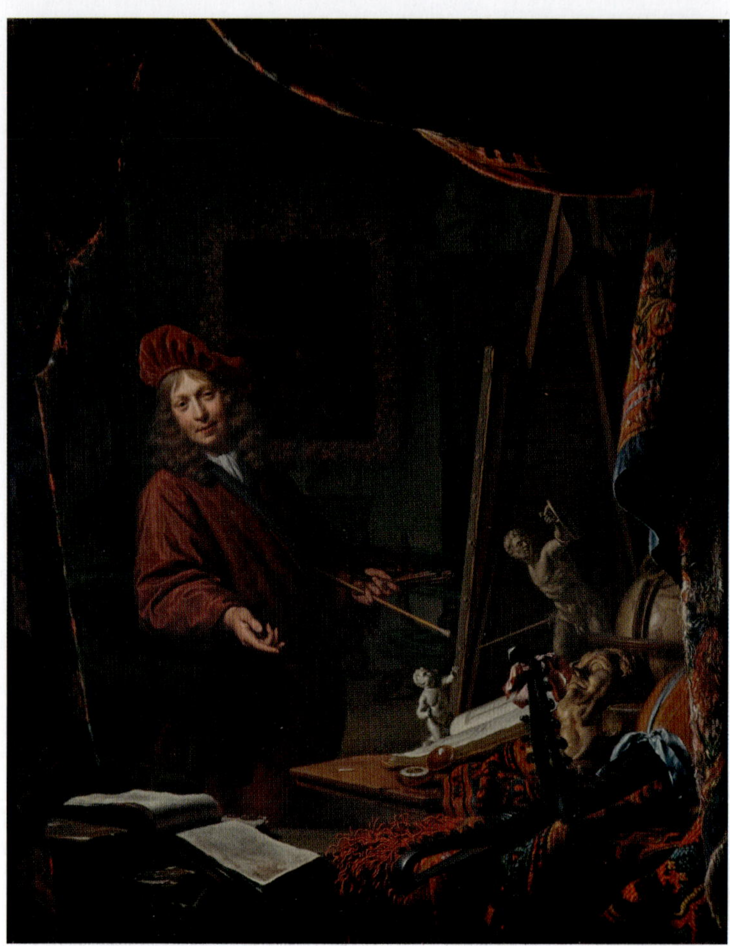

93 Michiel van Musscher, *Self-portrait in the Studio*, 1679

feat of painting a flawless freehand circle, adding specificity to the tale. This has led to the hypothesis that in the Kenwood self-portrait Rembrandt personifies Apelles, standing before a canvas on which he has drawn a circle, with an arc as his rival's answer. He prepares to draw the third, decisive circle. A recent interpretation by Hungarian art historian Andras Renyi offers an intriguing twist: rather than a hypothetical third circle, Rembrandt's ultimate mark is his own likeness. In this reading, the portrait becomes a transhistorical performance, where Rembrandt positions himself proudly as the rightful heir to Apelles, Protogenes and Giotto, challenging the viewer to recognize him as such.

More autobiographical are the self-portraits of Michiel van Musscher. Arnold van Houbraken highly praises a painting of Michiel with his wife, Eva Visscher, and their children. Eva is also portrayed in a pendant to a self-portrait, in which Father Time confronts Michiel with an hourglass and a scythe. Shortly after Eva's death, he painted himself holding a miniature portrait of her. Michiel's estate inventory includes a self-portrait with his deceased great-grandfather. When the artist looked at himself, he thought of his loved ones, time and mortality.

93 In another mode, in a self-portrait in the town museum of his native Rotterdam, van Musscher pulls out all the stops to advertise his distinction and all-roundedness. It begins with the framing device. A large curtain has been pulled aside to vouchsafe us a look into the inner sanctum of the artist. The objects on the tables convey information about his qualities. The open books, one being a Dutch translation of Sebastiano Serlio's treatise on perspective, tell us that he is a learned painter; the plaster casts, including a small copy of the *Borghese Gladiator*, that he studies anatomy and the classics; the celestial globe, a model by Petrus Plancius from about 1625, that he has an interest in astronomy; the lute stands not only for music-making – his estate inventory had more than ten instruments – but also for proper proportion and celestial harmony; the Persian carpet draped over the scene and the Japanese gown he wears are marks of wealth and sophistication. The style in which van Musscher depicts all of this conveys a message in itself. It openly acknowledges a dependence on the model of Gerard Dou, the grand master of fine painting.

Group Portraits

Group portraiture has been treated to the most heavy-going study ever devoted to a genre in Dutch art. In 1902 the Austrian art historian Alois Riegl (1858–1905) published a 205-page article, 'The Dutch Group Portrait', in the leading art periodical in the country. Riegl attached profound importance to these paintings, writing that they establish equality not only among the sitters, but also between them and the viewer. For Riegl, the Dutch group portrait was an index for understanding the nature of communication, the reception of art, and the psyche of people in the past. He associated these qualities with what he saw as the democratic cast of Dutch society. This was too rose-coloured a view of the Dutch polity. A democracy it was not. The only election held in Amsterdam before 1796 was in 1578, when the members of the civic guard chose a town council. Thereafter, the government replenished its ranks by co-optation, with an increasing concentration of power in a few

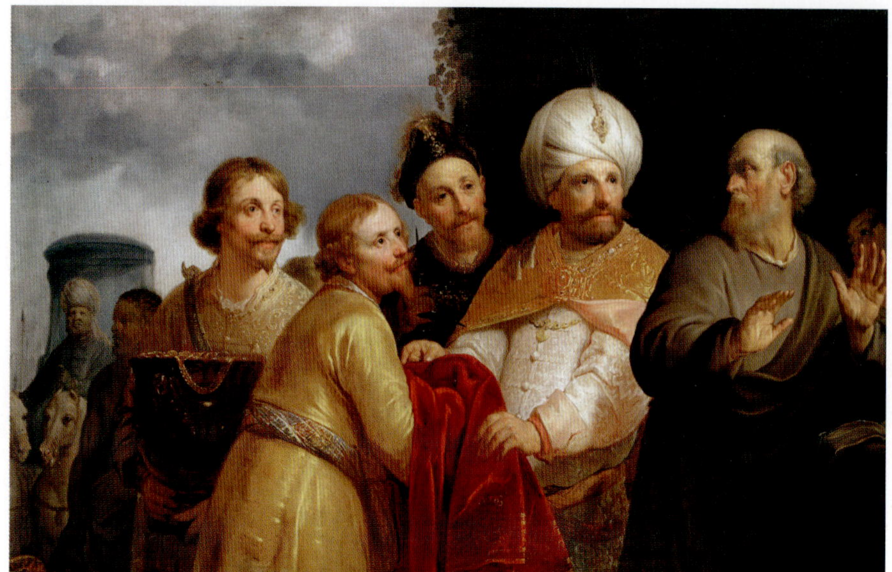

94 Pieter de Grebber, *Elisha Refusing to Accept Presents from Naaman for Curing Naaman's Leprosy*, 1637

families. The impression of equality in group portraits reflects clubbish bonding rather than parity. Nonetheless, the way viewers are drawn into contact with the sitters in Dutch group portraiture can breach barriers of time. What is surely striking about this genre is how civic bodies persisted, sometimes for 150 years, in commissioning portraits of themselves. These paintings played a role in the self-awareness and possibly even the very continuity of the organizations that honoured themselves in this way.

Group portraiture is just as much an exercise in self-fashioning as self-portraiture. For example, in Pieter de Grebber's painting of four board members of the Haarlem lepers' home, the men chose to be depicted as figures in a Bible story, a form known as a *portrait historié*, in which the sitters engage in play-acting. The story (Kings 2: 5) recounts an incident related to the work of the board, and which enabled them to be shown as maintaining a high standard of integrity. Naaman was a Syrian general favoured by his king for all the victories he achieved. He suffered from leprosy, and it transpired that there was a man in Samaria who could cure it. The king therefore gave Naaman a letter of introduction to the king of Israel and a sizeable fortune with which to reward this miracle worker, the prophet Elisha. Elisha initially proved elusive, but eventually he sent Naaman to douse himself in the Jordan, which indeed effected a cure. Returning to the reclusive prophet, Naaman burst in on him and declared, 'Now I know that there is no God in all the world except in Israel. So please accept a gift from your servant.' Elisha declined it, emphatically and curtly: 'As surely as the Lord lives, whom I serve, I will not accept a thing.' That is the subject of de Grebber's painting. Rarely depicted is what happened next. Naaman was on his way home when Elisha's servant, Gehazi, followed and deceitfully informed him that Elisha had changed his mind and was willing to accept his largesse after all. So Naaman gave him gifts that Gehazi took and hid. When Elisha found this out, he placed an everlasting curse on Gehazi: 'Naaman's leprosy will cling to you and to your descendants forever.'

That the story offers an appropriate decoration for the meeting room of a leprosarium board speaks for itself. But there was another reason for the commission, which has to do with Elisha's refusal to accept compensation. The decision of the regents to have themselves painted in 1637 as upright providers of aid followed on a ruling of the Haarlem town council in 1635 to demand financial accountability from the boards of city charities. In this atmosphere, with the suggestion hanging in the air that some regents might be enriching themselves, the sitters wanted to show themselves as Elishas, not Gehazis. And so, as elucidated by Rudie van Leeuwen, the biographies and current circumstances of the sitters can be built into the substance of a *portrait historié.*

In Amsterdam the practice of painting civic guard portraits originated by 1529 and lasted through 1653. No fewer than ninety examples have survived. In Haarlem only twenty are known, the earliest by Cornelis Cornelisz van Haarlem, from 1583, and the latest, by Pieter Soutman, in 1642. Five were painted between 1600 and 1624 by Frans Pietersz de Grebber (1573–1649), the father of Pieter de Grebber, and five by Frans Hals, from 1616 to 1639. By 1633, the date of his *Meeting of the Officers and Subalterns of St George's Civic Guard*, Frans Hals had already painted three group portraits for Haarlem civic guards.

The colourful sashes, flags and weapons provided the painter with welcome features to enliven his compositions. Most paintings of this kind show a meal, the annual 'accounting banquet' held after the body had acquitted itself to the township for its finances. Hals's 1633 painting lacks that element and departs in another way from the previous norm. It is the first to include non-commissioned officers, the sergeants. As we know from an early copy in watercolour, the men are outdoors, in front of a picket fence with a gate leading to a

95

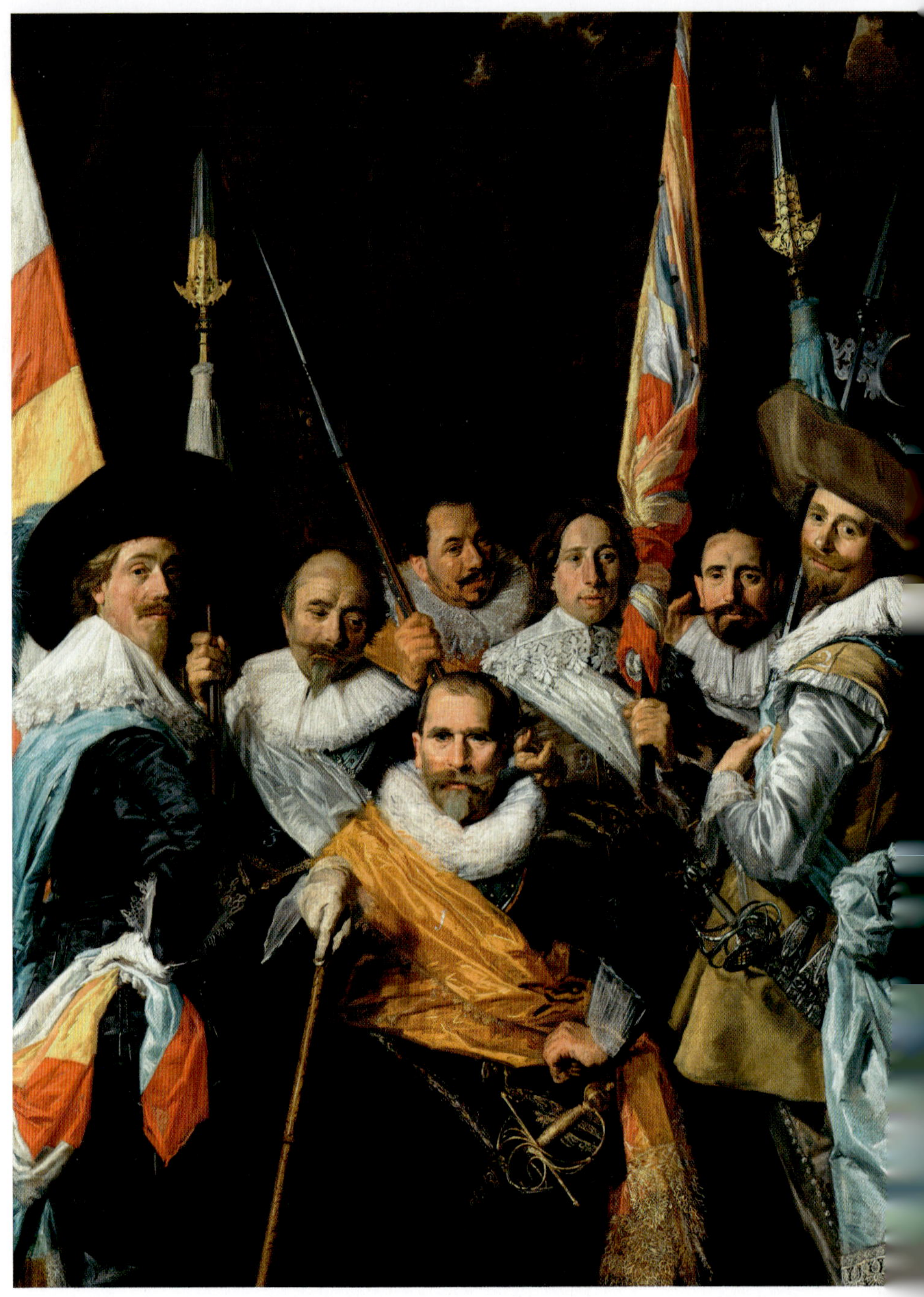

95 Frans Hals, *Officers and Subalterns of St George's Civic Guard*, 1633

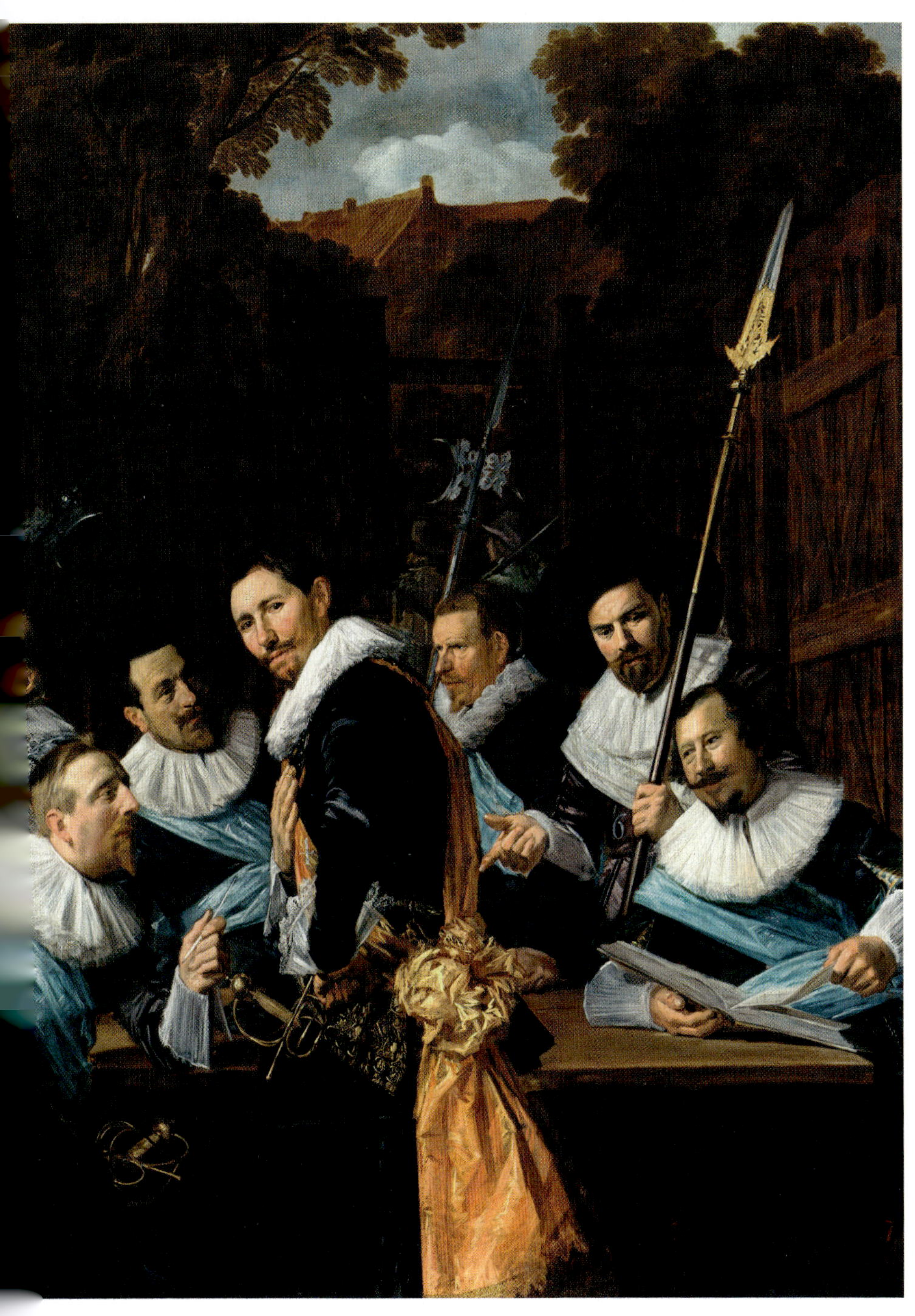

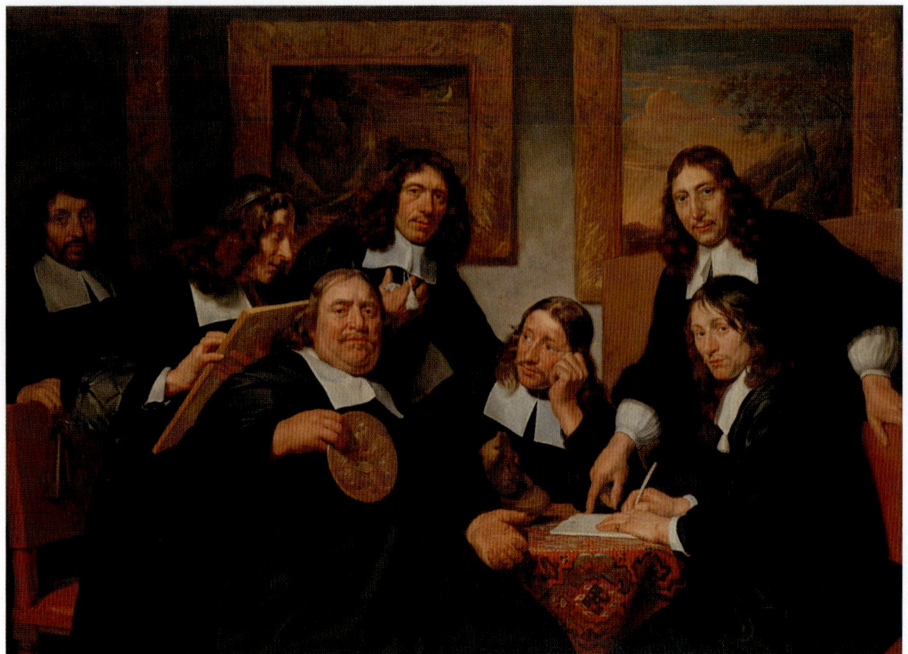

96 Jan de Bray, *Governors of the Haarlem Guild of St Luke*, 1675

tree-lined courtyard. Time has robbed us of the brightness and
spatial effect that were given to the scene by the painter.

Besides the military and charitable civic companies that
commissioned group portraits, there was one board belonging
to the painters themselves: the guilds of St Luke. If anyone in
the country was at home in that milieu, it was the Haarlem
artist Jan de Bray. His father Salomon was an architect, town
planner, painter and poet, and one of the leading figures in the
guild. Jan's brothers Joseph and Dirck were also all-round
artists, and his sister Cornelia was married to Jan Lievens. Jan
de Bray himself served many a term as officer and deacon of the
guild. The de Brays were art-world royalty in Haarlem. Sadly,
this did not save Jan from financial ruin. At the age of sixty-two
he was forced into bankruptcy, even having to sell the grave in
the Bavokerk that he owned. His picture of a routine board
meeting, held in the Painters Room of the town hall, is lively
and engaging. While the Rijksmuseum continues to list the
painting as entirely by Jan de Bray, there is evidence that it has
a four-man authorship. A notation preserved in the museum
identifies the seven sitters by name, adding the name of the one
who painted their likeness. Jan de Bray is given credit only for

the faces of four. The others were painted by Dirck de Bray,
including the profile of Jan himself, and the painters Jan de
Jongh and Jan van Gotingh, who put in self-portraits. Jan took
responsibility for everything else in the painting. The setup – a
small body of officials at a table with a Turkey carpet, attended
by a steward, pausing in their business to look up at the
beholder – is strongly reminiscent of Rembrandt's group
portrait *The Syndics of the Drapers Guild* of 1662. It was one of
Rembrandt's four group portraits in Amsterdam, the others
being two anatomy lessons and *The Night Watch.* All hung
within a few hundred yards of each other and were the only
paintings by Rembrandt in spaces accessible to the public.

Tronies

A type of Dutch art that, until the 1980s, was hard to categorize,
included those studies clearly made after a model, some after
the same model, but which lacked the characteristic look of
the paid portrait. Then, after two prominent English-language
publications seized on a Dutch word that in the seventeenth
century had been used for such images – *tronie* or face – all at
once everyone was using the word, even if they were applying
it differently. As Bob Haboldt, the prominent dealer in Dutch
painting, observed, this shift in art history fitted into an
existing pattern in the market. 'The taste of buyers (including
museum curators) had already begun to turn away from
portraits and genre pieces to freer, less determined subjects,
more in tune with the postmodernist strain in contemporary
art. The label "tronie" accelerated this process to a certain
degree and gave the market a more uniform designation for
paintings that used to be called sketch, *bozzetto*, face study or
tête de caractère.' Academic art historians are not always aware
of this, but they too are participants in an art world where
commerce plays a larger part than historical study.

One of the historical sources for the term is the title given to
a set of seven etchings by Jan Lievens, *Diverse tronikens geets
van J.L. (Various tronies etched by J.L.).* Lievens was also one
of the great painters of tronies. One such is the subject of
a wonderfully appropriate quotation on the subject. It comes
from the prolific pen of Constantijn Huygens. 'There is, in my
Prince's house [the Prince was Stadholder Frederik Hendrik], a
portrait [by Jan Lievens] of a so-called Turkish potentate, done
from the head of some Dutchman or other.' That painting
is known. It passed from the House of Orange to the
Hohenzollern dynasty, who placed it in the picture gallery of
their palace in Potsdam, Sanssouci, where it can be admired
today, although it hangs rather high in a dim corner. Although

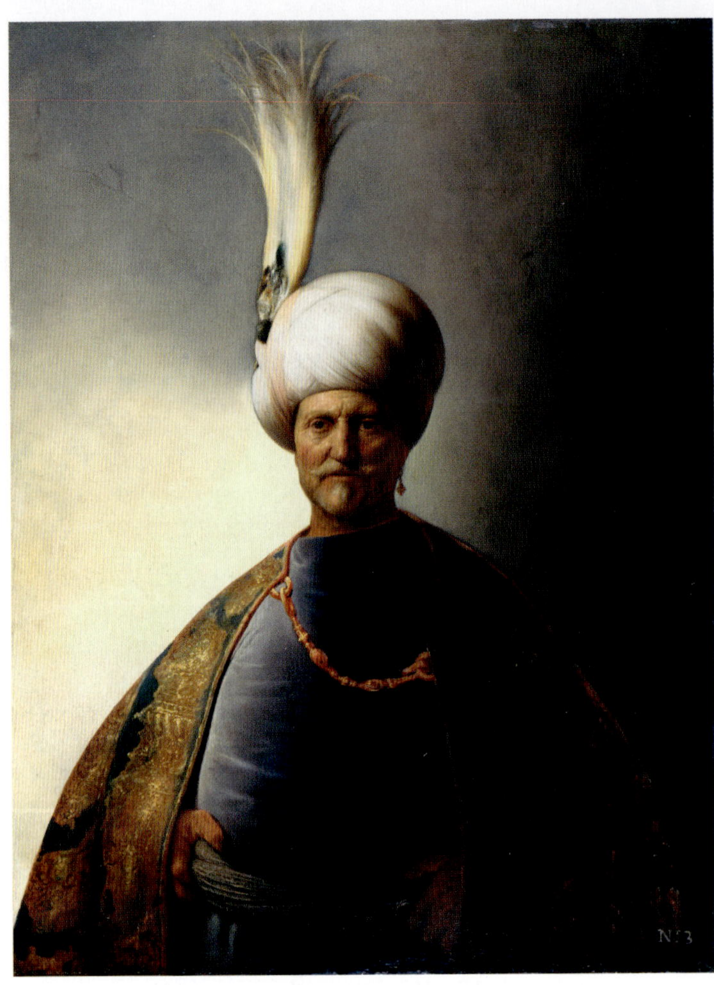

97 Jan Lievens,
*Dutch Model
Dressed as an
Oriental, c.* 1630

all but the most credulous of Huygens's contemporaries would
have seen the painting the same way he did, it was nonetheless
listed in inventories of the House of Orange as 'the Great Turk'
and 'Sultan Soliman by Rembrandt'. (The confusion between
Rembrandt and Lievens around 1630 has not yet been totally
resolved.) Highlighting this case also highlights a certain
unfortunate circumstance. It seems that not a single portrait
of a known personality from the eastern world was ever made
by a Dutch (as opposed to Flemish, French, British, Italian, etc.)
artist in the seventeenth century. Every face or figure painting
of such a person in Dutch art was a tronie.

Most tronies are obvious stereotypes, with a preponderance of men and women of a certain age, painted from models who had lots of time to pose. One strikingly idiosyncratic example is a painting in the National Museum of Sweden of a man with a facial disfigurement. It is often said about Dutch painters, Rembrandt especially, that they show their sitters, including themselves in self-portraits, with 'warts and all'. This is largely untrue. We only have to look for the common minor affliction of bags or dark circles under the sitters' eyes to realize that many likenesses have been flattered. People with disabilities are to be found in peasant and barroom genre scenes, not in portraits. Nice as it would be to give credit for the sympathetic depiction of such a man to a painter whose biography we know, the maker of this work has evaded identification. He or she signed with the letters I and S in ligature. In 1904, the Austrian musicologist and art historian Theodor von Frimmel (1853–1928) admitted defeat, in the name of art history, in giving the artist a name. Since then he or she has been known only as Master or Monogrammist I.S. The indeterminacy extends beyond the name of the artist to their background. Monogrammist I.S.'s

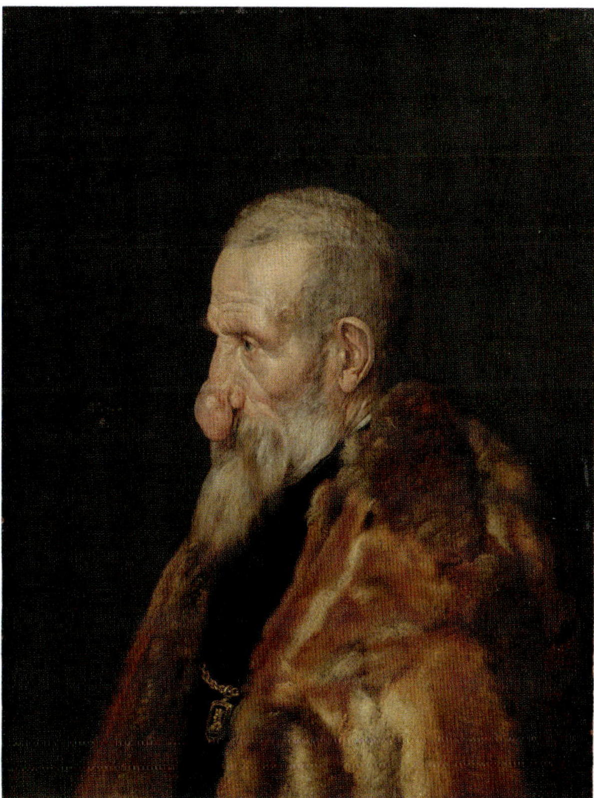

98 Monogrammist I.S., *Man with a Growth on his Nose,* 1645

subject matter and motifs are Dutch, the touch and the
materials point to Germany, the costume of some of the figures
has been called Balkanish, and the provenances tend to come
from Sweden. A master who defies pigeonholing.

Landscape

A Christian believer does not have to be a Calvinist to share
John Calvin's view of the relation between nature and art:
'We must therefore admit in God's individual works – but
especially in them as a whole – that God's powers are actually
represented as in a painting.' The natural world, he went on, is a
'theatre of divine glory', a 'living painting of God's majesty'. The
Flemish Calvinist Guido de Brès put it like this: 'We know God
through two means. First through the creation, maintenance
and governing of the entire world, since our eyes see it as a
beautiful book, in which all creatures, great and small, are
as letters....In the second place he reveals himself to us more
clearly and completely through his holy and divine word, that
is Scripture.' This principle, it has recently been argued, is
taken insufficiently into account in art-historical writings on
landscape painting. In his book *Landscape and Religion from
Van Eyck to Rembrandt*, Boudewijn Bakker sets a theological
interpretation of landscape painting off against all the other
avenues of interpretation he finds in the literature: formal,
descriptive, nationalistic, topographical, allegorical, analogical,
moralizing, iconological, metaphorical, scientific and art
theoretical. The painting of landscape in the Dutch seventeenth
century is not the innovation it appears to be, he writes, but a
continuation of a doctrinal tradition reaching back to the late
Middle Ages and built into the fabric of Calvinism.

Yet the values found in landscape painting by the authors
named, as Bakker courteously admits, are not merely notional.
A painter at his easel and a viewer of a landscape painting
will not always be thinking of God. Invariably, a complexity
of factors is in play. The more we know about a given
work, the more aware we become of ideological and formal
considerations and the reflection in their work of the individual
backgrounds and personalities of the artists, in all their various
environments, interests, beliefs and levels of proficiency and
sophistication.

Landscapes of Known Locations

Among the Flemish immigrant artists to find a home in the
Northern Netherlands were a number of landscape painters.
Their forte, drawing on a rich tradition that included such
founding fathers as Joachim Patinir and Pieter Bruegel, was the

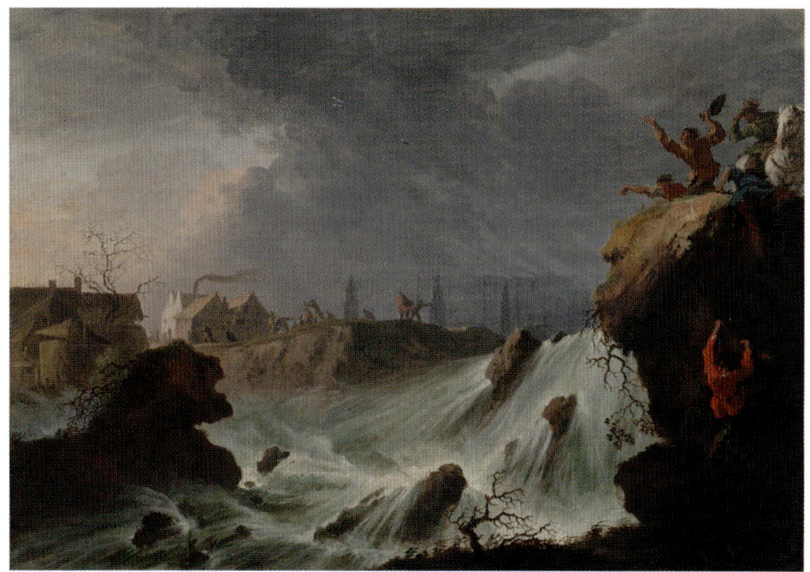

99 Willem Schellinks, *The Breaching of the Sint Anthonisdijk at Houtewael in 1651*, 1651

invention of believable landscapes, combining characteristic elements into a satisfying whole. This was artistic creation 'from the imagination' (*uyt den gheest*), as Karel van Mander called it, distinguishing it from painting after life (*naer 't leven*). One Dutch artist who picked up early on this inspiration was Abraham Bloemaert, of whom van Mander wrote that in his landscapes, well-observed as they may be, he did not hesitate to add invented features 'according to the requirements of the work'.

Printmakers, also perpetuating Flemish forebears, took a different tack. The Haarlem masters Hendrick Goltzius, Esaias van de Velde and Claes Jansz Visscher published series of views in named neighbourhood locations. Draughtsmen too, sometimes in the service of mapmakers, created topographical portraits of locations throughout Europe and the wider world. This practice was seldom taken on by painters. One dramatic exception is a genre we can call the disaster landscape. Several paintings were made, for example, of a dike breach near Amsterdam. One of the artists to paint it was Willem Schellinks, the maker of hundreds of topographical drawings.

On Sunday, March 5ᵗʰ [1651], with a full moon spring tide, the wind from the northwest blew so hard that the water of the North Sea was pushed through openings in the Zuiderzee...Most cellars and various warehouses and sheds [in Amsterdam] were flooded

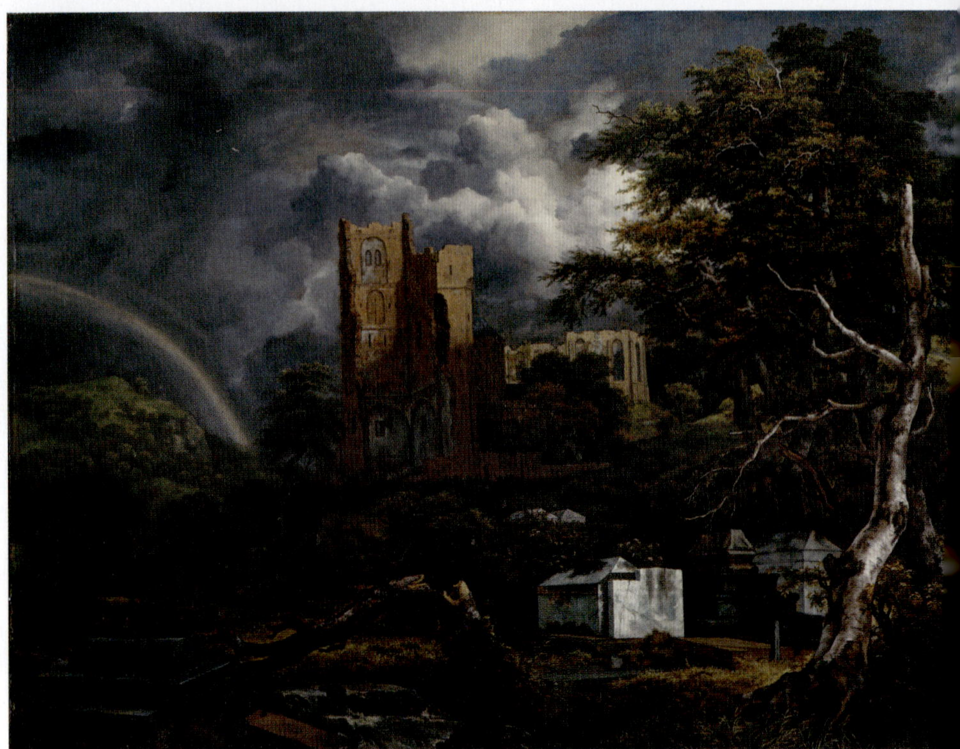

100 Jacob van Ruisdael, *The Jewish Cemetery at Ouderkerk aan de Amstel*, 1654 or 1655

*and lots of merchandise was badly damaged. Other goods, half
ruined, could barely be saved, which was done by people who let
themselves be tempted by the good wages that had to be offered,
and spent hours at a time standing in the water up to their waists.
The St Anthony or Diemer Dike collapsed under the high, powerful
flood, so that two holes were breached in it, one about seventy
roods [265 metres] wide and the other fifteen roods [57 metres].*

The Utrecht delegates to the States General proposed that a
national day of prayer be held to assuage the wrath of God (for
who else would send a northwest storm during a springtide?).
The suggestion was turned down by the States of Holland
because 'days like that tend to be abused, in order to rant
against the government'.

A landscape which has attracted all the analytical and
interpretative approaches criticized by Boudewijn Bakker
is Jacob van Ruisdael's *The Jewish Cemetery at Ouderkerk
aan de Amstel*, of which there is a second version in Dresden.

It combines motifs in an inventive way, though not in the idealizing sense recommended by van Mander. Here, identifiable locations fifty kilometres apart are shown in proximity to each other. In the foreground are tombs in the Portuguese Jewish cemetery outside Amsterdam, founded in 1614. Picturesque as it is, only a handful of artists depicted it, of whom Ruisdael was the first. The view is based on site drawings, with some shifting and mirror-imaging. The dead trees have been added, giving rise to the rather obvious interpretation of the scene as a vanitas image, a comment on the transitoriness of life. The rainbow would then be seen as a promise of Christian salvation and eternal life in the hereafter. There may be another level implied in this imagery. In Christian iconography, dead trees and limbs juxtaposed to Jewish features assert the age-old repudiation of Judaism as a superseded faith. The anti-Judaic interpretation is bolstered by the ruins in the background, which belong to another repudiated faith, Catholicism. The Abbey of St Adelbert at Egmond was demolished in 1573 and its assets sold to finance the founding of the Calvinistic university in Leiden. Ruisdael himself was born into a Mennonite family, but in 1657, shortly after making this painting, he converted to Calvinism. If he was expressing personal commitment to the stricter sect in this painting, it would make this work highly unusual. But then again, it *is* highly unusual, in an oeuvre where allegorical implications are seldom made this explicit. (For a more characteristic landscape from Ruisdael's immense, highly varied oeuvre, see fig. 53.)

Beaches and Dunes

In about 1630, Constantijn Huygens remarked: 'Landscape painters, as I will call the painters who busy themselves mainly with the painting of woods, meadows, hills and villages, are so enormously numerous in the present-day Netherlands, and of such high quality, that it would take all of a small volume to treat each of them individually.' At that time, the beach scene would not have filled more than a page or two, but in later decades it became one of the genres with the best claim to Dutch uniqueness. A pioneer in the genre was Pieter Molijn. Like his close contemporary, Cornelis Jonson van Ceulen, de Molijn was born in London to Flemish parents and came to the Netherlands in his youth. In Haarlem, where he became a prominent member of the art community, he coined a spare style of landscape painting, achieving striking results with minimal means. One effective device, seen for the first time in a painting of 1626, was to avoid the flat horizon in favour of a dynamic diagonal. The painting also displays the reduced range

101

of colours that has been called tonal painting, another means of getting the most out of one's efforts.

The low horizon in a beach scene by Simon de Vlieger puts us on the level of the city-folk wanderers with a dog on the slight rise to the right. With them, we look down at fishermen who make their living from the sea, in modest sailing vessels. The mixture of classes and social roles is a long-standing feature of townscape and landscape painting from deep in the Flemish past. The picture is dominated by a towering cumulus cloud. The depiction of clouds in Dutch landscape paintings has led to an interesting discussion with wider implications. The realism of the clouds in Dutch paintings had long been taken for granted and more recently admired as part of an advance in scientific interest among artists. Then in 1987, the prominent art historian John Walsh questioned their fidelity to nature. He pointed out the distortion of cloud forms in paintings, the imbalance in types of weather and the impossible juxtaposition of stable and unstable formations. He concluded that we should not expect technical accuracy from artists who were interested in picture-making and not meteorology. In 2013 the German meteorologist Franz Ossing published a commentary on Walsh's paper in which he agrees that skepticism is in order, but finds that Walsh goes too far. Skies are always transitioning from stable to unstable and back, he wrote. He found nothing extremely unlikely in the painted skies. In defense of Walsh's standpoint, one can cite van Mander's remark that 'the requirements' of Abraham Bloemaert's work could demand adding 'some sunshine, dark or fiery skies'. So that even if the cloud constellations in Dutch landscapes are not unlikely, it would be a mistake to see this as a result of meteorological rather than picture-making considerations. Ossing's paper is part of a larger project at the German Research Centre for Geosciences in Potsdam, a joint endeavour with the Gemäldegalerie in Berlin. This is important to mention as a collaboration between art and science in an iconographical sense, in addition to the conservation studies that have shown such great advances over the past half-century.

At Sea

Seascape painting is another of the specialities to which Pieter Bruegel made an essential contribution. He pioneered many kinds of composition that were to enter the repertoires of Dutch painters of the sea, ships and battles at sea. He did this not only in drawings and paintings, but also in prints after his work, which were available to all. Two prints of warships after Bruegel were given conspicuous moralizing messages, as Icarus in one

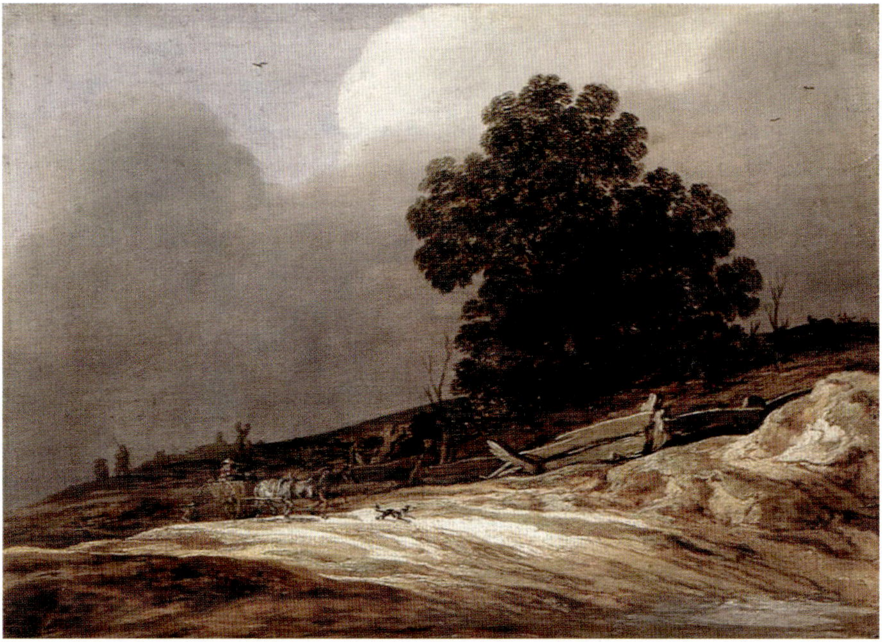

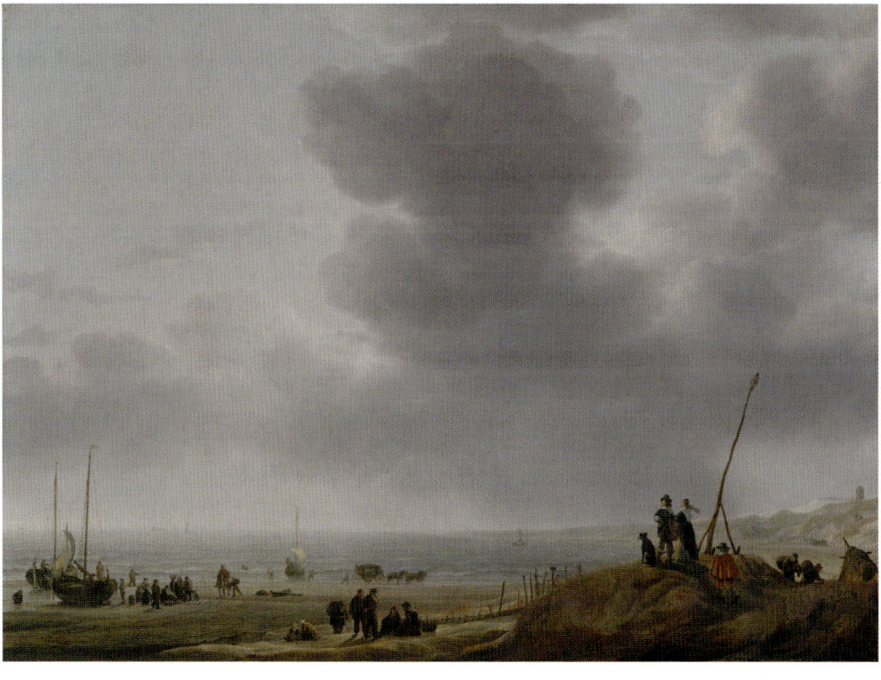

101   TOP   Pieter Molijn, *Road through the Dunes*, 1626
102   ABOVE   Simon de Vlieger, *Beach View with Fishermen and Recreationists*, 1643

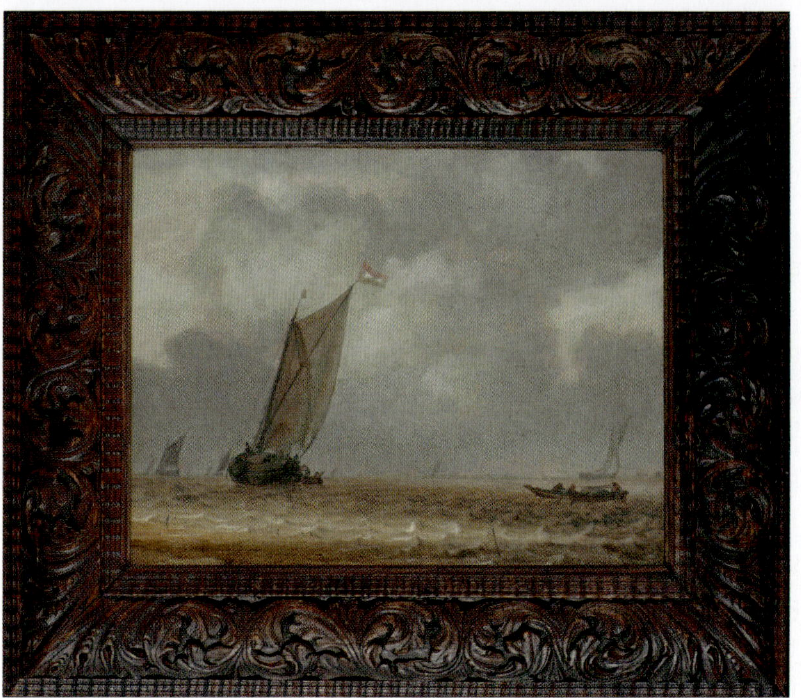

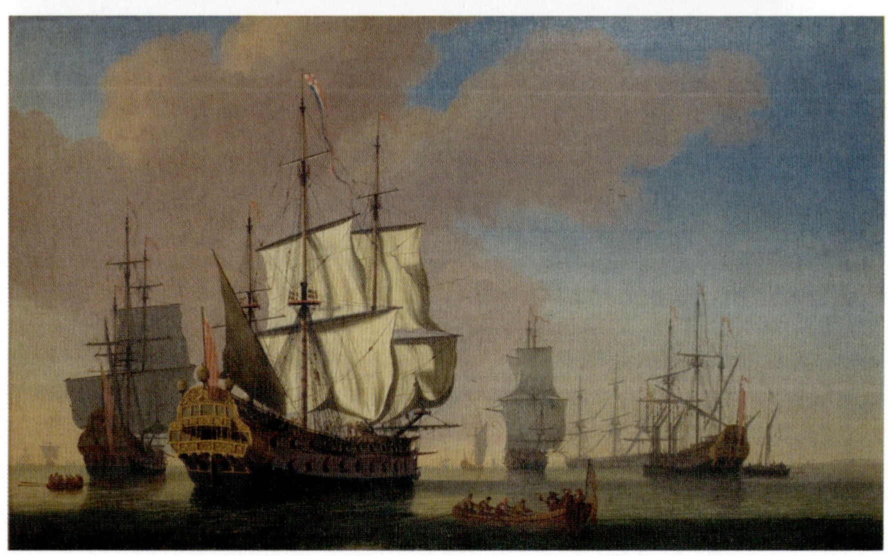

103 TOP Jan Porcellis, *A Sailing Ship and a Rowboat in a Stormy Sea*, 1629
104 ABOVE Jan van Beecq, *English Warships in a Roadstead in Calm Weather*, 1677

and Phaeton in another fall out of the sky into the sea. These
may be taken as warnings against excessive self-confidence in
braving the waters. In Dutch painting, overt morals of that kind
are not found, but writings on the sea are full of them, and it
is assumed that thoughts of peril and salvation were implicit
in these iconographies. Rudi Fuchs, in the previous edition of
the World of Art volume on Dutch painting, asked himself the
question that comes up, unasked for: 'one wonders whether
an image of small ships on a storm-tossed sea is not another
disguised symbol of human life, of "life's uncertain voyage", as
Shakespeare called it.' He wisely refrains from answering the
question categorically.

∗ ∗ ∗

103   Jan Porcellis made some of the most appealing paintings of
the seventeenth century. Even viewers who have never been out
in a small sailing vessel with a storm coming on can feel the
sensation. There is romance in his unassuming pictures, of a
gritty kind. Porcellis worked restlessly in Rotterdam, London,
Middelburg, Antwerp, Ghent, Haarlem, Amsterdam, Voorburg,
The Hague and Zoeterwoude, near Leiden. One of his
marketing procedures gives us insight into his pace of work,
reflecting on that of other artists as well. In a deal with a cooper
in Antwerp in 1615, he contracted to deliver forty panels 'with
various ships and waters' within twenty weeks. The cooper
provided the panels, pigments and the services of an assistant.
The paintings were to be sold by the cooper and the proceeds
split between him and Porcellis. In the event, Porcellis failed to
deliver, but knowing that both men thought he could complete
two paintings a week gives us a starting point for gauging the
rate of production for such relatively simple paintings.

104   The international appeal of Dutch seascape painting is well
illustrated by the career of the Dutch-born painter Jan van
Beecq. After working in London for at least three years, in 1680
he left for Paris, where he was to remain for nearly the rest of
his life. Van Beecq brought to these European capitals the skills
he had acquired in the Netherlands. He is likely to have been
trained in The Hague by Willem van Diest (1610–1668/72), but
in London was little more than an imitator of the Willem van
de Veldes. In France, however, he stood at the lonely top,
recommended by a high naval official to the secretary of the
navy as 'the only one here [in France] to excel in this genre'
– marine painting. He even enjoyed the support of Charles Le
Brun (1619–90), founder of the Académie royale de peinture et
de sculpture, in his application for membership of that body.

Van Beecq's protectors saw him as a valuable asset for the glorification, through tapestries after his designs, of French maritime successes, in the same way that French land battles were being woven after designs by another Netherlandish painter in France: Adam Frans van der Meulen (1632–90). Van Beecq was also an inventor of techniques in shipbuilding, navigation and tapestry weaving. Despite his advantages, none of van Beecq's technical initiatives came to fruition. In French society, he did achieve a historic success, however. He was one of the two, from more than three hundred Dutch and Flemish artists in France, to marry into French nobility.

At War

In 1998, an exhibition devoted to Dutch war art, *Images of a Struggle: War and Peace Before the Treaty of Münster, 1621–1648,* took place in Delft. It was one of several large-scale manifestations in celebration of the 350th anniversary of that world-changing event (see p. 134.) The works selected spoke strongly against the view, as expressed by the Dutch historian, Johan Huizinga, that: 'The renowned military exploits [of our nation] on the ground have hardly been immortalized in painting....This stands to reason....The intimate gaze or refined painter's eye of our artists sought out better subjects than... those that have less beauty, less truth than met the dignity of a Dutch painter.' The 152 displays in the exhibition, most of them paintings, show that, on the contrary, it is to the credit of Dutch artists that they were able to take on such challenging subjects, with such good results.

Most paintings of sieges depict recognizable locations at well-known moments. Paintings of cavalry engagements, however, are nearly all generic, identifying only the weapons and sides of the combatants. In a typical example by Jan Martens de Jonge (in the literature erroneously called Martsen), Orange sashes identify combatants as belonging to the States army, red ribbons to Spain. All of the fallen warriors in the illustrated painting are Spanish, revealing the bias of the artist. Martens was a nephew of Esaias van de Velde (1587–1630), the first artist in the Northern Netherlands to paint battle scenes. The genre was hardly practised in the Republic until 1621. In that year, the Twelve Years' Truce with Spain lapsed, and hostilities resumed. In the first battles he painted, Esaias gave the scene a Roman look, but soon this digression was abandoned. Battle scenes became so popular that by 1640, about one in twenty landscapes in a Dutch household showed a battle. Events in the field had direct impact on the genre. Following the Peace of Münster the soldiers in Dutch art fought less and socialized more.

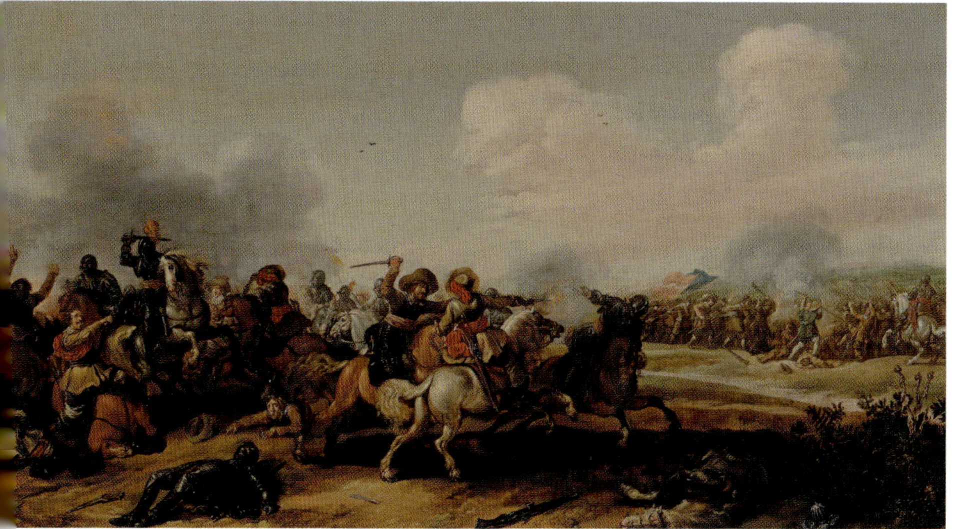

105 Jan Martens de Jonge, *Cavalry Battle Between Dutch and Spanish Troops*, 1630

Soldiers spent a lot more time in the guardhouse than in the field. This was especially the case in the siege warfare practised in the final phase of the Eighty Years' War, from 1621 to 1648. When a town fell to the Dutch, a garrison had to be left in place to ensure it was not retaken. These were tedious assignments, leaving the troops with more free time than they knew what to do with. Their doings reminded Pieter Codde (1599–1678) and Willem Cornelisz Duyster of the hedonistic behaviour of the golden youth during the truce, but shifted from the chic salon to improvised quarters on the land. Between them, they created a speciality that acquired its own name, the *kortegaardje* (guardhouse scene, from the French *corps de garde*), showing officers and soldiers doing the same things – playing cards, carousing, fighting, receiving female company. Lavishing high skills on low subject matter was a way to grab the attention and captivate the feelings of the beholder.

On the Hunt

Historically, the right to hunt was an exclusive privilege of the aristocracy. The House of Orange set the tone, especially after Willem III, a passionate hunter, became stadholder in 1672. The right to hunt was accompanied by the responsibility to police and maintain hunting grounds and their fauna. This was a job for foresters and hunting masters in the service of the nobility. Increasingly, country estates came into the

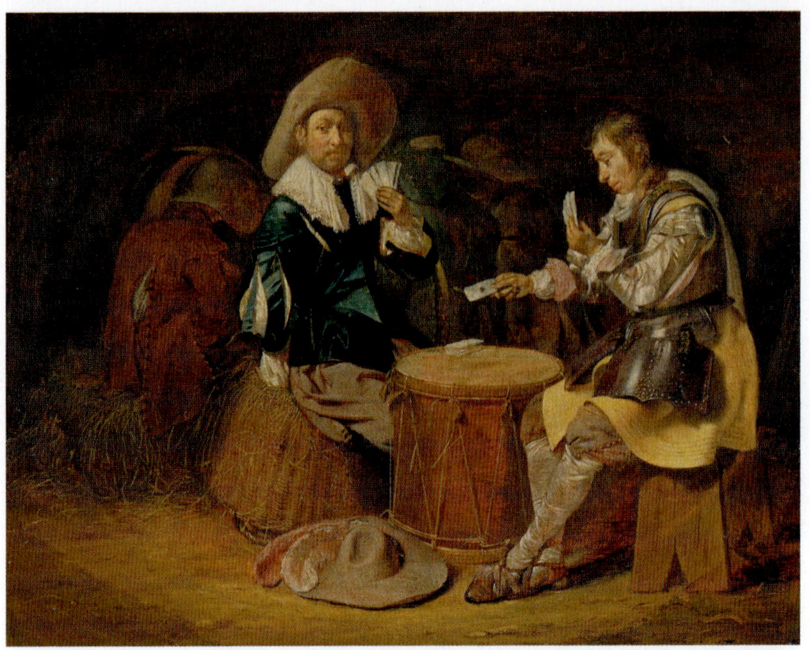

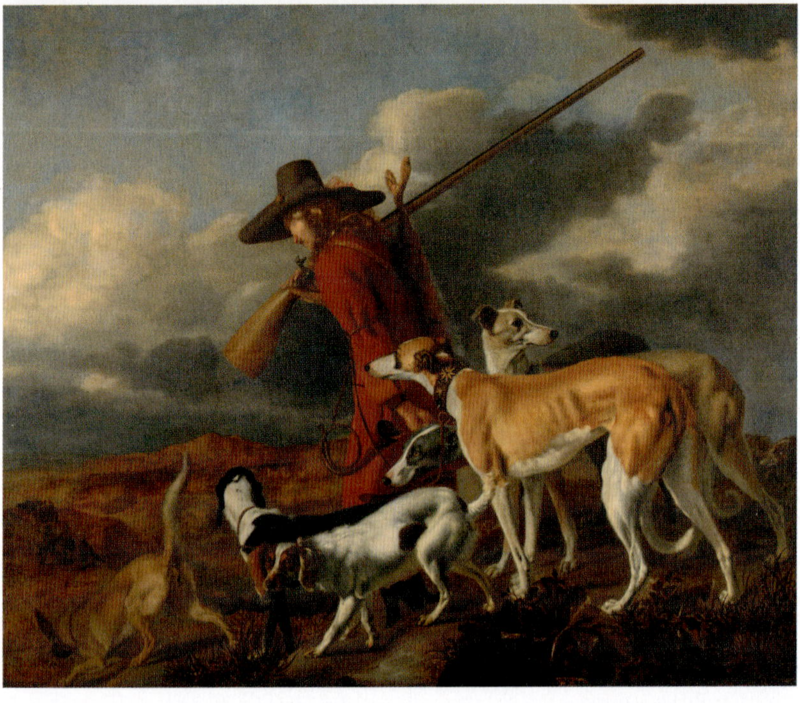

106 TOP Willem Cornelisz Duyster, *Two Officers Playing Cards on a Drum*, c. 1630–35
107 ABOVE Adriaen Beeldemaker, *A Hunter*, 1653

possession of wealthy burghers, who would often acquire
seigneurial rights, including the right to hunt. Province and
township officials would elbow their way into the ranks of
those allowed to hunt. This development was furthered by the
progressive thinning out of the aristocracy. In 1555, there were
about thirty families with that status; in 1800 no more than six
were left. The land holdings and transferable titles of the rest
were up for sale to government bodies and commoners, who
also employed fieldsmen. Hunting was tied into horsemanship,
marksmanship, falconry and other skills for which experts
would be hired. Limited hunting rights could be part of the
fee. One class of huntsman that researchers admit they cannot
quantify is the poacher, who would keep his doings to himself.

Because the large game animals that were the preferred
quarry were rare in low-lying parts of the country, hunters would
go after hares and rabbits, partridges and pheasants. The
hunting of birds along the coast was in fact excepted from the
general prohibition. A large part of hunting culture, and the
noble ethos to which it aspires, is gift-giving. The successful
hunter would be expected to share his catch. In the code-driven
relations governed by patronage some of these gifts would go
to 'clients' – favoured people of lower social standing whose
services put patron and client in mutually beneficial association
with each other. We have already seen some hunters with hounds
and a pair on horseback. The man at the crossroads in Meindert
Hobbema's *Avenue of Middelharnis* is a hunter with rifle on
shoulder; the small group in the distance, it is surmised, were
beaters, who drove the prey to where it could be shot. Riding
their mounts in Berckheyde's *Great Square and Bavokerk in
Haarlem* are two hunters with their hounds. In the best painting
of Adriaen Cornelisz Beeldemaker, showing a man returning
from the hunt with a dead hare dangling from the barrel of his
rifle, the hounds take centre stage. They have been identified
as spaniels, greyhounds and beagles. Other members of the
hunting party can be seen in the distance, on horseback
and in carriages.

While still life was looked down on by writers on art and
valued low in the market, this rule did not apply to paintings of
game or hunting attributes. The tinge of aristocratic privilege
linked to the hunt gave them a status not enjoyed by other still
lifes. Willem van Aelst played to and benefited from this effect.
A painting such as his *Attributes of the Hunt* is an artful and
clean, tasteful image of how aristocrats would like to picture
the end of a hunting day. The mere fact that he used the most
precious of pigments, lapis lazuli from Afghanistan, for the
blue of the velvet hunting bag, places the painting at the acme

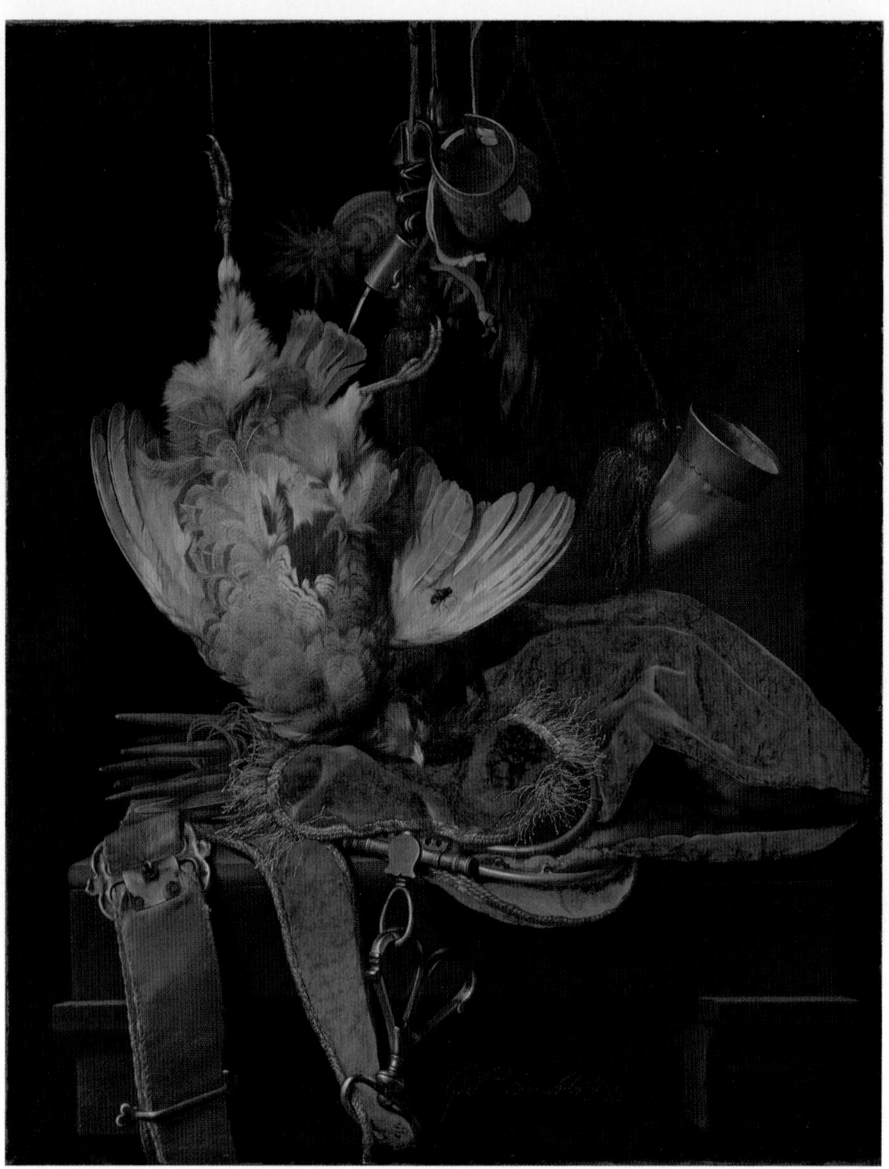

108 Willem van Aelst, *Attributes of the Hunt*, 1668

of collectibles. The utensils represent various traditional hunting methods, such as trapping, driving, hunting, par force hunting and bait hunting. The work is a model of fine painting. A particularly brilliant piece is the fly, which sits on the partridge's wing right in the centre of the picture looking real. This optical illusion is based on a clever trick: while the painter depicted the partridge smaller than life, the fly is life-size. Van Aelst rose to the rank of court painter to Ferdinando de' Medici in Florence. He moved on to Rome, still benefiting from Medici patronage, but within a month got into such a bad fight that he had to flee to stay out of jail.

In the Dutch Countryside

The native landscape offered Dutch painters a vast range of pictorial and iconographical possibilities which they exploited to the full. Undeterred by demographic statistics showing that most people lived in towns, Dutch art lovers thought of their country as a land of farmers, fishermen, herdsmen and villagers. In 1614, when landscape painting as a speciality had barely begun, the thirty lots of paintings that served as prizes in a Delft lottery were mainly landscapes, variously depicting biblical and mythological scenes, plundering soldiers, hunting parties, a sheep meadow and a peasant wedding. The landscape was like a theatre stage, on which performances of any kind could be mounted. Performance is the word. What we are being shown is not only a piece of nature or farmland, but a locus of human activity. This affords the beholder a means of identifying with the scene. It also plays into the most widespread metaphor in art and literature for the meaning of life: the journey. Painters did not have to build such personal profundities into their work. We the viewers do it for them.

It was a landscapist who was the most prolific Dutch painter of all: Jan van Goyen, with nearly 1,200 known paintings. His first panels follow the highly detailed Flemish mode, in series that represent the four seasons or pleasant walks in the country in bright colour. In the 1620s, in line with the development described above (p. 142), he simplified his technique and the extent of detail, reducing the number and size of figures. From 1627 to 1633 he preferred dunes, after which river landscapes took over, furnished from 1634 on with fortresses, ruins and city walls. In the 1640s, van Goyen was grabbed by stormy skies. Some of these motifs came and went in his oeuvre, while panoramas on the water, ice scenes and city views were constant features. In some of these types of painting van Goyen was a clear leader.

109

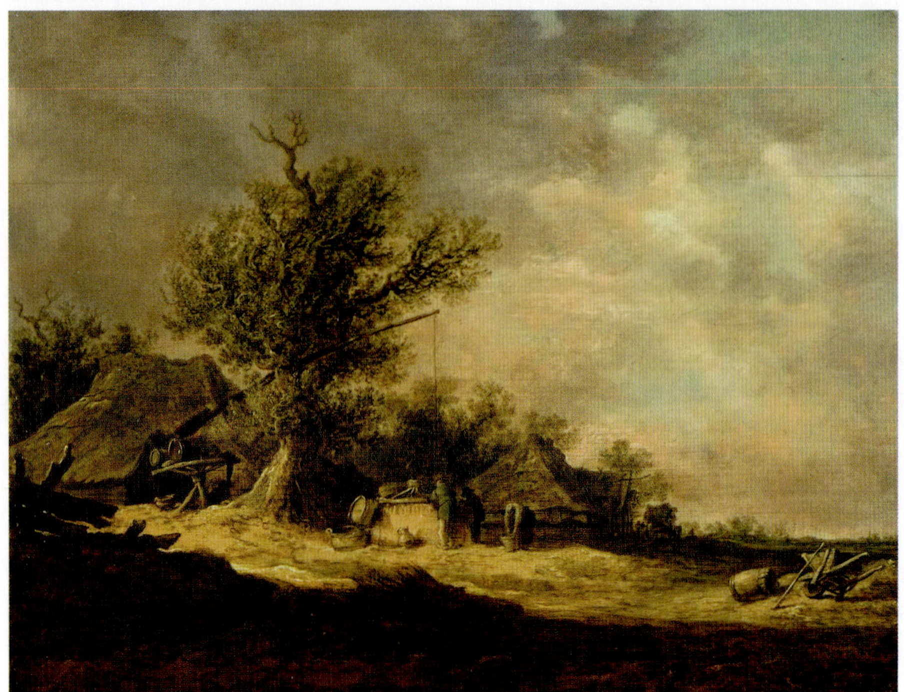

109 Jan van Goyen, *Cottages in a Landscape with a Well,* 1631

The Cowscape
The cow was not just any animal in Holland. It was the main source of farming wealth, with an output of milk that was the envy of the European dairy world. From early on, the cow could symbolize the country itself in allegories of politics, prosperity and the virtue of cleanliness. To a considerable extent, however, this covered a host of disparities and problematic issues.

A close look at Aelbert Cuyp's *Cows in a Watery Landscape,* a painting of a kind that could be called a cowscape, reveals that the cows standing in the water are not very fat. This is true to life. Dutch meadows, including those outside Cuyp's Dordrecht, were used in the summer to fatten scrawny cattle from northern Europe. The water-logged condition of the pasture is also accurate, as the cattle would eat up the grass and trample the ground down to the water table. In other aspects the picture is not representative at all of how things were. This went unnoticed until it became a focus of research for a remarkable scholar who was a specialist in several unrelated fields, Ruth Levitt. The Dutch cowscape in fact typically falsifies grazing behaviour. In the pasture, at any given moment only one or two of ten cattle will have their heads up; the rest are feeding. In painting the ratio is reversed. Cowscapes display all animals at the peak of their prime; exclude the farmer and his heavy labours; present cattle as spotlessly clean and unwounded, though many would be dirty and bruised; and avoid broken-coloured and black-and-white cattle in favour of pure-coloured stock. The paintings emanate peace and harmony, satisfaction with the benevolence of God's creation.

Cuyp, the grandson, son and half-brother of other Dordrecht artists, became one of the most admired Dutch painters of all time. Although he had never been to Italy, he was able to let the golden light that Dutch painters brought back from Italy shine on the local landscape. Cuyp has been called the quintessential country-house Dutch artist, first for patrons in Dordrecht, then, long after his death, for the British aristocracy and landed gentry. The raid on Cuyps led to the total sellout of his paintings from his native country. Alongside the Willem van de Veldes, his example was paramount in forming an ideal of how to depict the sea (Cuyp also painted water scenes) and,

110 Aelbert Cuyp, *Cows in a Watery Landscape*, c. 1650

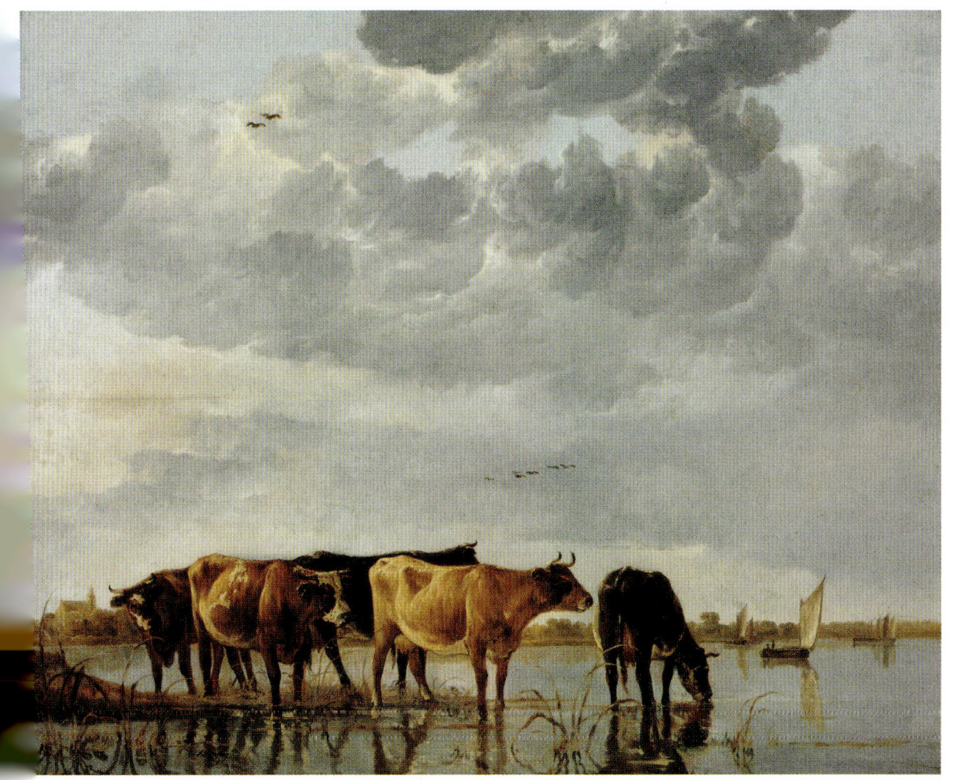

especially, countryside. Not only collectors but also British artists stood in awe of Cuyp and emulated him to the edge of thralldom. The title of an exhibition in the Dordrechts Museum in 2022 says it in a nutshell...*In the Light of Cuyp: Aelbert Cuyp & Gainsborough – Constable – Turner.*

Winters, Nights

Alongside the cowscape, a great favourite in Dutch landscape was the winter scene. This predilection has come to be explained by a meteorological phenomenon called The Little Ice Age, at the climax of which, between 1580 and 1710, the average temperature in Northern Europe is estimated to have been one or one-and-a-half degrees Celsius lower than before 1400, with colder winters and milder summers. Arguably, this only provided artists with more opportunity to paint obviously wintry weather from life. It does not explain why Dutch painters chose to do so, and Flemish and French ones did not. In fact there is a perfect mismatch between the frequency of winter scenes in the meteorologically indistinguishable Northern and Southern Netherlands. From 1580 to 1600, they were painted and printed only in the south, and from 1600 on, nearly exclusively in the north. As I see it, the surprisingly large proportion of such scenes was due mainly to the proliferation of specialities in Dutch painting, in the course of which artists found that winter scenes sold well to people living in well-heated houses.

111   One of the main specialists in the genre is Isaac van Ostade, the younger brother and pupil of Adriaen. Isaac was self-assured in his talent from the start, as one anecdote reveals. The twenty-year-old Isaac accepted a commission to paint seven roundels and six panels for seventy-seven guilders. After two years, he had painted only two roundels and two panels, and wanted to be released from his commitment because the price of his paintings in the market had risen. The contract partner took him to the guild, which allowed Isaac to reduce the number of paintings to be delivered and receive a higher price. The raise was calculated to be from an average of 5.90 to 6.44 guilders. These were the narrow margins on which the living of many a painter depended. Isaac is also notable for carving out a piece of artistic territory for himself. Nothing in his art is unique, except for one motif that he owned: a horse pulling a cart onto an embankment. This has been found to appear only in his works and no others.

Moonlight is so enchanting that hardly a Dutch landscape artist could resist trying his hand at a night scene. The flat Dutch landscape offers ideal circumstances for moonlight

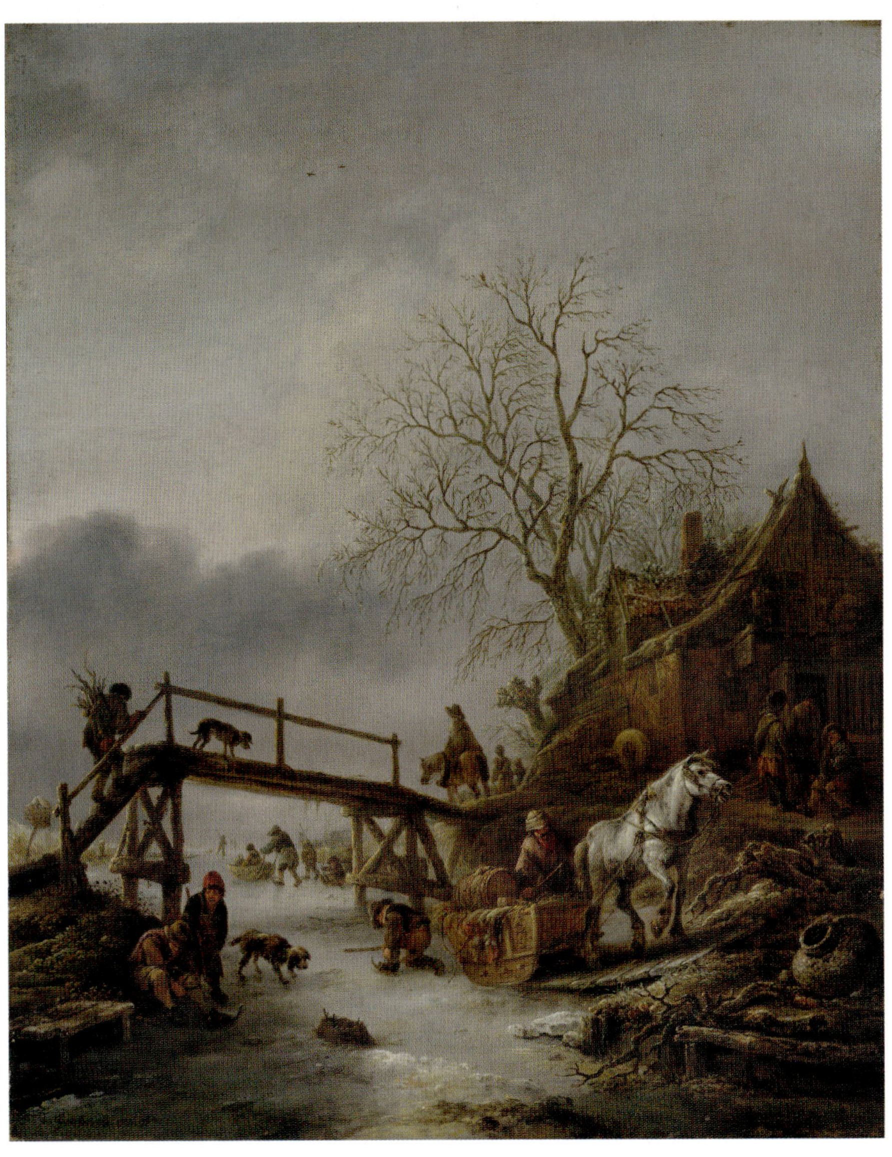

111 Isaac van Ostade, *Winter in the Dutch Countryside*, c. 1640s

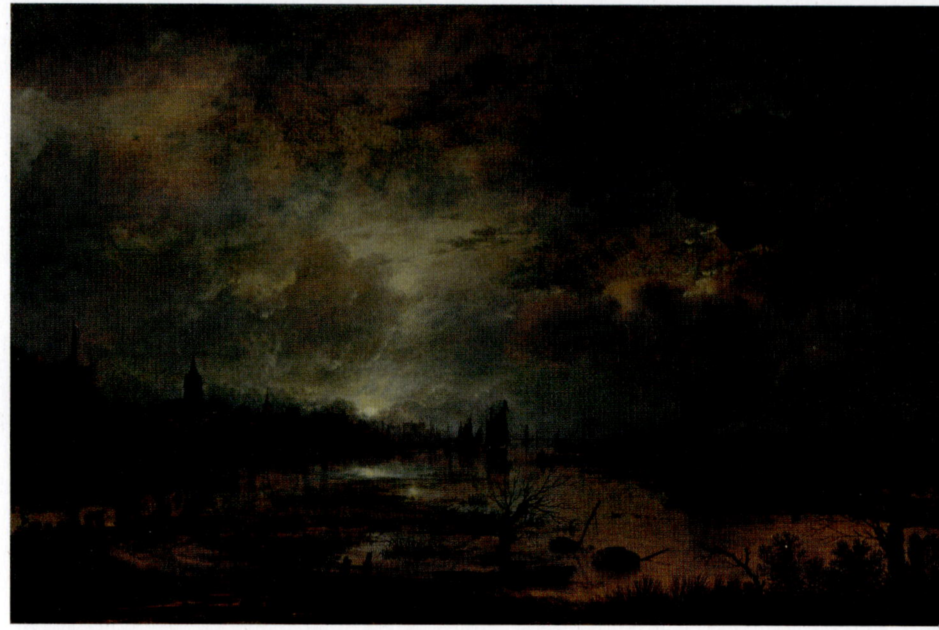

112 Aert van der Neer, *A River near a Town, by Moonlight*, c. 1645

pictures. An entire landscape can be evoked in silhouette or reflection. Local tones are reduced to monochrome that can be enlivened with minimal touches. Only one landscapist made it his main speciality: Aert van der Neer. Night scenes that are difficult to attribute are routinely labelled Follower or Style or Mode of Aert van der Neer. However, he was so unable to make a living from his art that he turned to tavern keeping and eventually had to declare bankruptcy – another of so many under-appreciated Dutch artists unable to support themselves.

In the House of Worship

After the overthrow of Spanish rule, municipalities of the new Dutch Republic took over the Catholic churches and the right to hold services in them was granted to the Calvinists. While not a state religion, Calvinism became the 'public church' of the new Republic. Because the churches had been built for congregations composed of the entire populace of their locales, whereas Calvinism was a minority religion, the buildings were seldom filled. Services would have been attended sparingly, as shown in Pieter Saenredam's *Interior of the Sint Odulphuskerk (Church of St Odolphus), Assendelft*, a town where many inhabitants remained Catholic. Churches that were kept open

during the week functioned as public venues where locals
could socialize and sightseers admire the ornate burial places
of historical figures (see pp. 44–51).

In keeping with the ideal of freedom of conscience
proclaimed in the Union of Utrecht of 1579, a founding
document of the Dutch state, no one was prosecuted for
their beliefs. That did not mean that everyone was allowed to
build a place of worship. Some Protestants, such as Lutheran
immigrants from Germany and Huguenots from France, were
welcome to do so, as were Jews in a few cities. Practitioners
of repudiated faiths such as Catholicism could hold prayer
services only in buildings that did not look like churches from
the street (see pp. 51–54).

The art-historical study of Dutch church painting was
initiated in a major monograph of 1909 by the German
art historian Hans Jantzen. He catalogued 693 paintings
by some fifty artists, thus defining the scope of the field.
His approach was formalistic. He considered the central
contribution of these artists to be the definition of space,
through line, perspective and colour, Not until the 1960s did
more confessional and patronage-related facets of church
painting enter the literature, and have become massively
expanded since. These include, as discussed by Almut Pollmer,
the political, moral, monumental and liturgical aspects of the
genre, as well as the non-ecclesiastical functions of the church,
such as memorials for those buried in them.

Bartholomeus van Bassen, the first Dutch specialist in
church painting, has not yet been accorded his art-historical
due. He was altogether ignored in writings on art until the
nineteenth century, despite having been a prominent architect
as well as a painter. He enjoyed the patronage of Friedrich V
and Elizabeth Stuart, for whom he designed the palace in
Rhenen (1629–31) (see p. 55), as well as one for Stadholder
Frederik Hendrik. In 1638, he became town architect of The
Hague. The churches in his paintings, as in the *Fantasy Church
with Tomb of William the Silent*, are inventions of the painter-
architect. What is real is the funerary monument of William of
Orange. At least, it is real that by 1620 the monument had been
erected, in the Nieuwe Kerk in Delft. However, the sculptures,
an integral part of the design by the sculptor-architect
Hendrick de Keyser (1565–1621), had not been completed.
Bartholomeus must have had drawings of the project, perhaps
through personal contact with the House of Orange. His vision
of the monument is an early tribute to its lasting glory, which
was compounded through the centuries as one member of the
House of Orange after another was buried in the crypt below it.

113

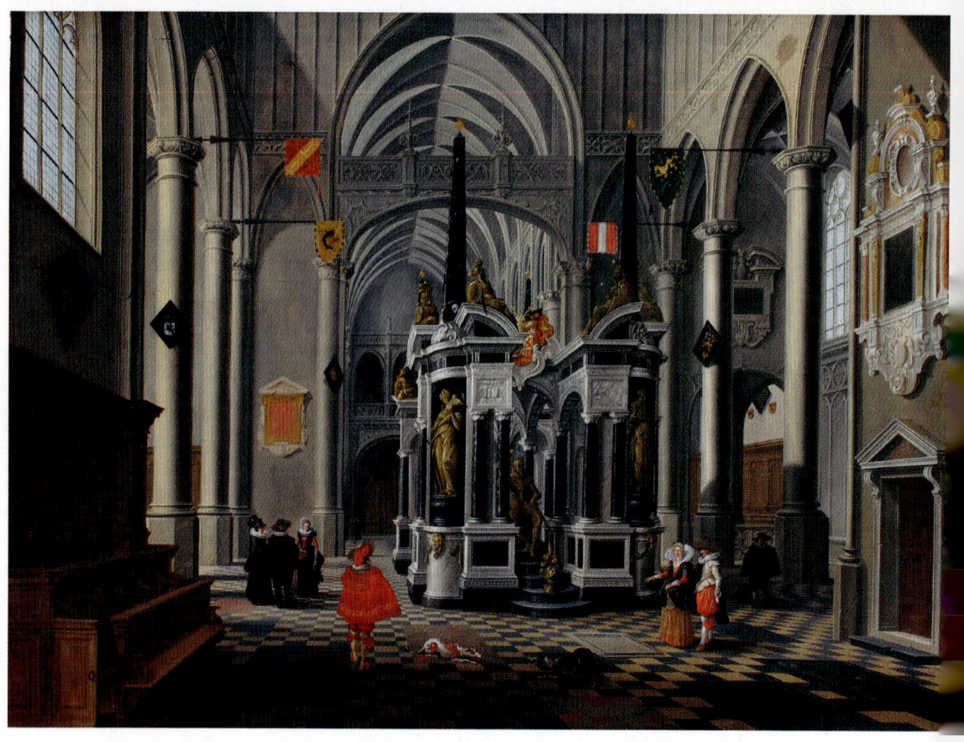

113 Bartholomeus van Bassen, *Fantasy Church with Tomb of William the Silent*, 1620

114   The Delft painter Gerard Houckgeest painted the monument
in its proper place. We see the corner with one of the four
female figures personifying qualities of the assassinated
Father of His Country. She is holding up a hat of the kind that
a liberated slave would be allowed to wear in ancient Rome as a
token of his liberty. Here it stands for William's love of freedom.
As glorious as it is, the tomb is shown as belonging to the
ordinary people of the country. As in some paintings by Pieter
Saenredam, flat surfaces of the base of one of the columns have
been drawn on by children. Below a scarecrow, Houckgeest
placed his monogram, as if to identify himself with a child
compelled to create art.

* * *

While Christians in the seventeenth century, nearly without
exception, persisted in the antagonism to Judaism that helped
define their own religion, the Jews of Amsterdam enjoyed in
increasing measure the effects of what has been called 'everyday

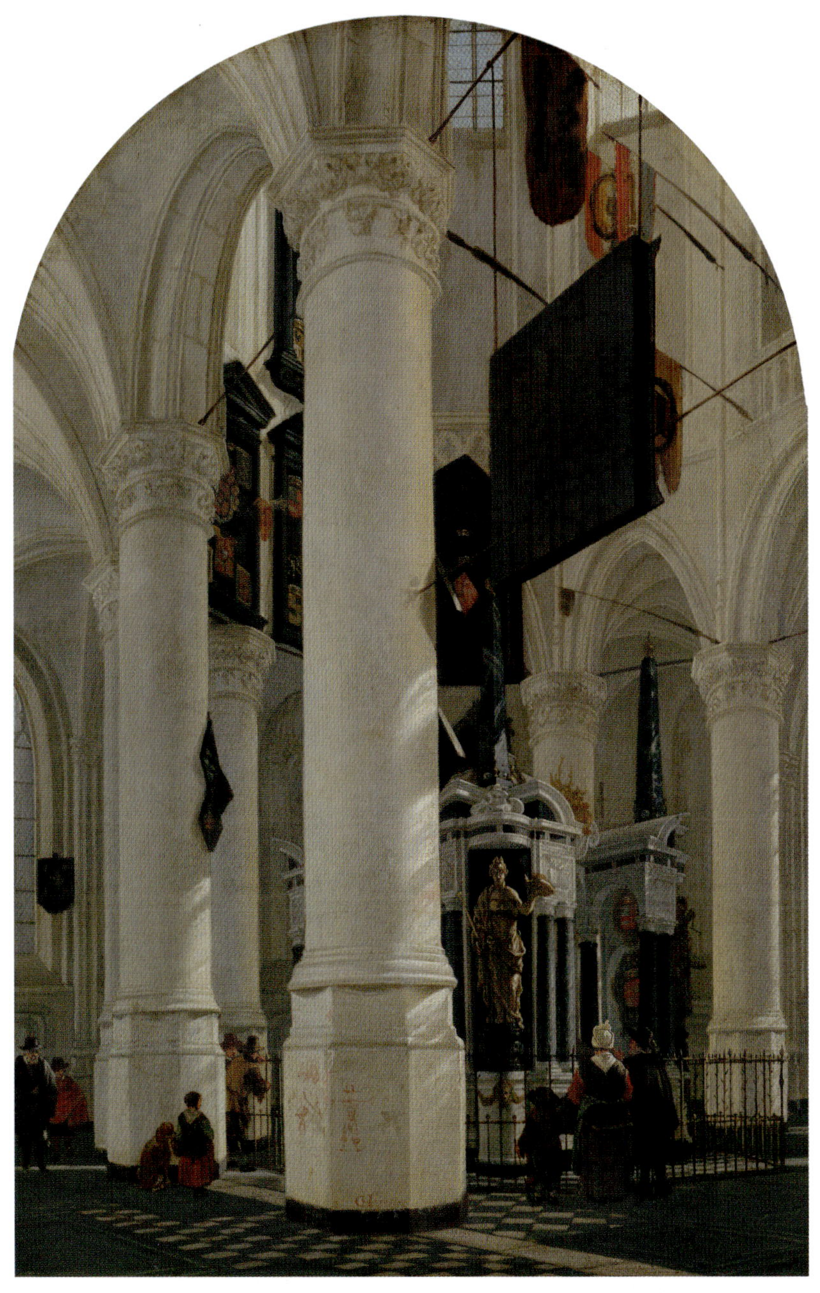

114 Gerard Houckgeest, *Interior of the Nieuwe Kerk, Delft, with the Tomb of William of Orange*, 1651

ecumenism'. That is, as discussed by the Dutch historian Willem
Frijhoff, the way adherents of different faiths could ignore
dogma in their social, financial and even personal relations.
One manifestation of this development was the curiosity that
led many non-Jews to attend services in synagogues. In art, the
earliest record of this practice is not found until 1675, with a
glorified etching of the inauguration of the Portuguese
synagogue by Romeyn de Hooghe. It was followed about 1680 in
three paintings by Emanuel de Witte, in which visitors, dressed
differently from congregants, are watching a service. Concerning
one of Emanuel de Witte's paintings precious documentation
was published in 1996 by Yosef Kaplan, a specialist in Dutch
Sephardi history. On 28 September 1687, the wealthy Sephardi
David de Abraham Cardozo made a testament in which only one
item of movable property was specified: 'Similarly the testator
orders and bequeaths a painting that is in his possession, which
depicts the Portuguese synagogue in this city, which was painted
by Emanuel de Wit, to his good friend Mr Jacob Nunes
Hendriques.' The supposition that de Witte made this painting in
commission is hard to doubt. That Sephardim were enthusiastic
buyers of paintings by Dutch artists has long been known. But
the indication that such a painting might be a commission opens
a new vista on the role of Jewish collectors in the making of
Dutch painting.

On the Street

The appealing genre of street life – markets, fairs, stalls – is one
to which every viewer can relate. Like nearly all specialities, it
began as a background or accessory to history painting, mainly
Bible paintings. Pieter Aertsen (*c.* 1508–75) and his nephew
Joachim Beuckelaer (1534–*c.* 1574) used stories from the life of
Christ as an excuse to create lavish displays of fruit, vegetables,
meat and game laid out in market stalls as well as interiors. In
the seventeenth century, it could be said that these motifs were
liberated, but they never entirely shed the suggestion that they
mean more than meets the eye. To a considerable extent Dutch
prosperity was nourished by the exploitation of animal life.
Fish, cattle, poultry, swine, rabbits, game and whales were
the raw materials of major 'industries' concerning which no
objections were ever raised. Whatever control was exercised
had to do with licensing sellers, fixing locations for the sale of
different kinds of produce and merchandise, and scheduling
and enforcing the terms of daily (in the big cities), weekly,
seasonal and yearly markets. Shopping was a daily chore,
but also a diversion for housewives, their daughters and
maidservants. It brought all layers of society into contact

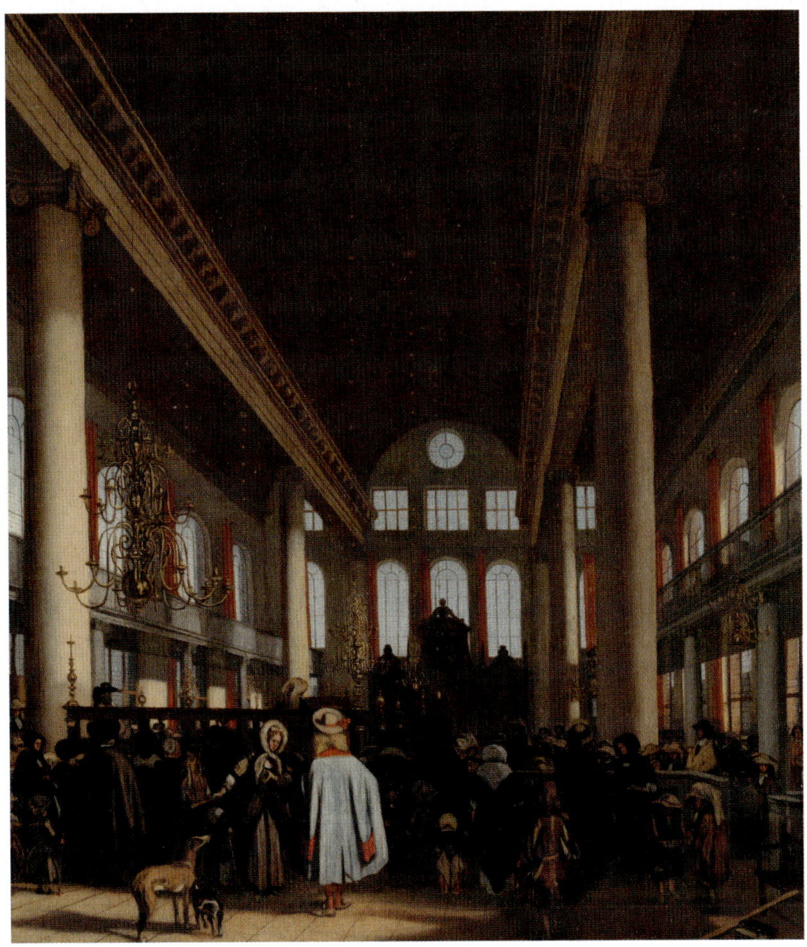

115 Emanuel de Witte, *Interior of the Portuguese Synagogue in Amsterdam*, 1680

with each other. The variety of persons and their dress was a
magnet for painters, and the recognizability of locations a
draw for buyers. The central location painted by Sybrand van
Beest was known to everyone in The Hague. The building
behind the open-air market was built in 1355 as a chapel for the
St Nicholas Guesthouse, and converted into a meat hall in 1615.
In the centre of the painting, a man in an expensive red suit,
accompanied by two fashionable women, is shaking hands with
someone who looks not like a butcher, but a trader in meat.

* * *

In the sixties and seventies a revolution took place in the study
of Dutch genre painting. Until then, genre was understood as
an uncomplicated expression of the pride that the Dutch took
in the small things of life. Hegel lauded it as being unburdened
by the demands of religion. Then the Utrecht art historian Eddy
de Jongh revamped that picture. He demonstrated that Dutch
genre paintings and prints are not straightforward description
at all, and certainly not uncomplicated, but embedded
with moral messages. An exhibition of 1976 was given the
programmatic title *Tot lering en vermaak* (For Instruction and
Amusement), a characterization of art from Roman antiquity
that was taken for granted in the Dutch seventeenth century.
De Jongh showed that over time we viewers had lost sight of the
instructional dimension of genre painting, but sources existed
to enlighten us about that.

117   Gabriël Metsu's painting was one of de Jongh's key exhibits.
A poultryman is offering a woman customer a cockerel, but we
are meant to understand that she also has a sexual interest
in him. To support this interpretation, the catalogue was
illustrated with a print of about 1600 by Gillis van Breen,
showing the same confrontation between a fashionable woman
shopper and a poultry seller. The dialogue in the caption read:
'"How much for that bird, birdsman?" "It's sold." "To whom?"
"To a lady innkeeper who I bird all year."' The clue is the
double entendre in the verb *vogelen*: 'dealing in poultry' but also
'fornicating'. Metsu enriches his composition with live and dead

116 Sybrand van Beest, *A Hog Market in The Hague*, 1638

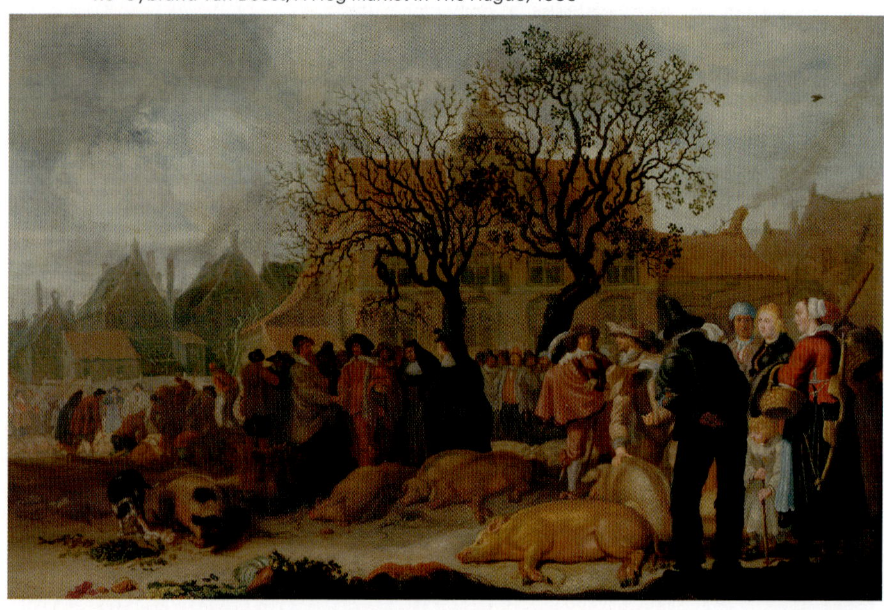

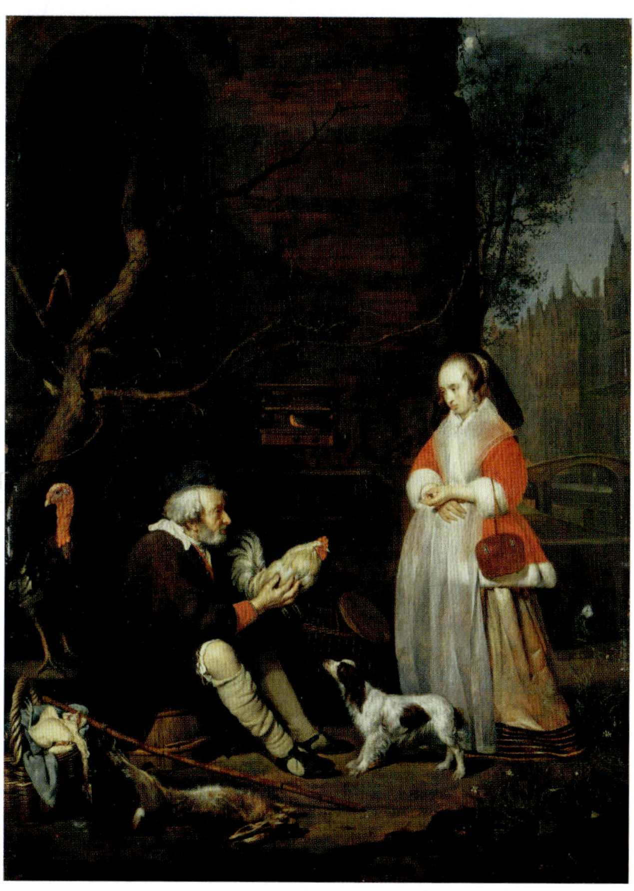

117 Gabriël Metsu, *Old Seller of Game and Poultry Showing a Cock to a Young Woman*, 1662

animals and birds, and a city canal. This is to the benefit of the literal meaning of the scene, which stands on its own without schoolboy wit.

The Poor

Wealth inequality in the Netherlands at this time was among the most extreme for any society in history. Ten percent of the households possessed nearly all the wealth, and the richest one percent about forty percent of the total figure. The overwhelming majority of households was too poor even to be assessed for their possessions. These shocking figures cast a different light on the Netherlands from what we see in the art produced there. At a time when the Dutch Republic was the leading financial power in Europe, its regent class was able to keep the lion's share of everything being earned.

That it did not share its wealth with those dependent on it
can be seen in these pages. Even painters whose work was
collected enthusiastically by the upper crust, whose art created
a flattering picture of their way of life were allowed to fall
into unpayable debt. For example, when Jan Steen died, he
was worth less than the amount he had inherited. And as
mentioned earlier, Rembrandt went bankrupt and Hals died in
penury, while Johannes Vermeer, creator of timeless images of
domestic tranquillity, was seized by fatal despair at his inability
to support his children, so that 'in a day and a half he had gone
from being healthy to being dead' (see p. 19).

The painters, most of whom had periods of good earnings,
were not the worst off. Most people lived from hand to mouth
all their lives. One Amsterdammer in four required charitable
assistance at one time or another. For women especially, it was
well-nigh impossible to rise above a situation of total
dependence. The largest single group of wage earners in
seventeenth-century Amsterdam were women in domestic
service – as many as the membership of all fifty or so of the
city's guilds. Little evidence of this found its way into art. The
figures conceal another shock. In 1614, of 2,500 families
registered in Amsterdam as recipients of municipal charity,
only 200 were Dutch. More than ninety percent of the poor in
the city were immigrants from abroad. This did not warm the

118 David Vinckboons, *Distribution of Bread Outside an Almshouse*, c. 1610

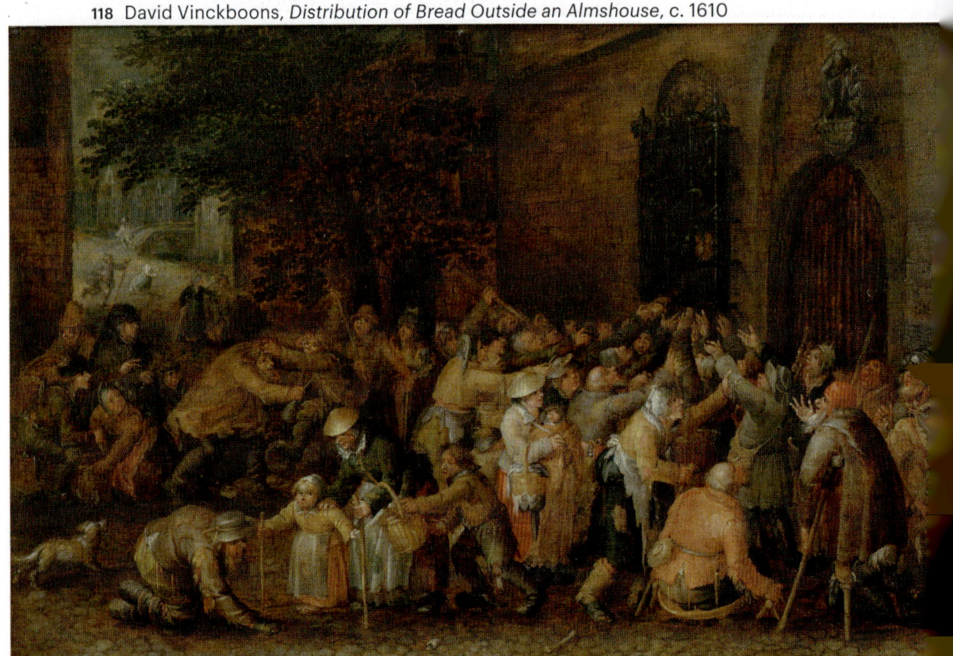

hearts of the established citizenry. Because Amsterdam never closed its doors to migrants, they had to be taken care of in one way or another to keep them off the streets. (In 1596, the single year for which the records survive in the Amsterdam archives, the authorities registered the arrest of 1,783 beggars.) In 1613, a new function was instituted – that of almoners, supervisors of the poor. The supervision entailed distinguishing between the honest poor, deserving of charity – bread, a pair of shoes and some change – and the rest. A dystopic vision of how bad things might become was painted by David Vinckboons. It seems to have an unattractively reactionary message: give bread to the poor and this is what you get. In other paintings and prints, Vinckboons's beggars and peasants stand for coarseness, stupidity and sinfulness.

In grisailles (monochrome works) and polychrome panels of the 1630s and 1640s by the remarkable Adriaen van de Venne, the poor once again beat each other's brains out. The motif of fighting peasants and beggars is derived from German and Flemish prints of the sixteenth century (again including Pieter Bruegel), but van de Venne made it his own in Dutch art. The genre can be called moralizing, but it is primarily satirical, cynical and prejudicial. A 1613 edition of prints of disabled dancers has a title page telling the smug reader that the people portrayed are feigning impairment to receive alms and live a lazy life. Whatever misery they suffer they have brought on themselves. The caption *All'-arm!* is found in other paintings by van de Venne and on the title page of a collection of engravings after compositions by him. The phrase can be read as 'Everybody's poor', but read as one word *all'-arm* is a cognate to the English 'alarm'. Verbal-visual games like this were played by van de Venne not only on panel. He also theorized about them in writings that worked out the concept from antiquity, *ut pictura poesis*, that painting and poetry are sister arts. In Middelburg, where Adriaen lived from 1614 to 1624, this took on commercial and near-institutional form. His brother Jan had a printing and publishing house called The Painting Shop, which became a centre for literary life. Adriaen put his thinking into ambitious aesthetic form in an illustrated poem of nearly three hundred pages, *A Pictorial Account of the Absurd World*. A further distinction of Adriaen van de Venne is that he was the only Dutch painter of the century to produce an entire branch of his oeuvre in the grisaille technique, painting in tones of one and the same colour. Van de Venne's first venture in the technique was a large canvas of Friedrich V and Elizabeth Stuart, with Frederik Hendrik and Amalia van Solms in the background.

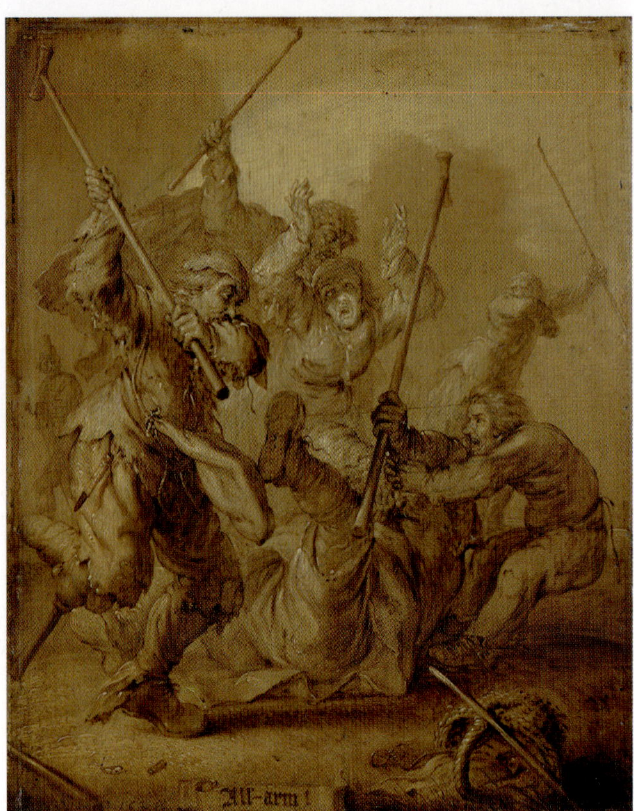

119 Adriaen
van de Venne,
All-arm, 1631

If it was intended to be sold to the royals, the deal fell through
and Adriaen was left with this tour de force.

There are numerous paintings of rowdy beggars, but only
one group portrait of poor people: Jan van Bijlert's *Inmates and
Officials of the St Job Hospital and Old Men's Home in Utrecht*.
The seven men on the left are indigent elders who were housed
in the almshouse. Three of them hold vessels for the collection
of donations, while one points heavenward, a reminder of
the divine injunction to share one's wealth with the poor.
The three men on the right are the regent, steward and
housemaster of the home.

The severely tried hero of the Book of Job seems to be the
only figure from the Old Testament to become a fully fledged
Christian saint. His dreadful tribulations led to his being
embraced as the patron saint of sufferers from leprosy and
other gruesome conditions. So when syphilis reached Utrecht
in 1495 with the Spanish army, and the city opened a hospital

for its victims in 1504, it was to St Job that it was dedicated. In
the seventeenth century this function was displaced and the
hospital became a home for worthy old men. Between 1626
and 1642, more than thirty-five paintings were donated to the
institution by Utrecht artists to be hung in its rebuilt refectory,
which became a showcase for the Utrecht school. A key figure
in this development was Jan van Bijlert, the son of a stained-
glass artist. After a stay of four years in Rome (1620–24; his
Bentvueghel name was the Roman hero, Aeneas) he spent the
rest of his life in Utrecht, where he joined the board of the St
Job home and served a term as its director. Van Bijlert was a
versatile painter, with works in all genres. A second donation
of his to the home, from 1628, was a painting now lost with a
unique iconography: the comforting of Job's wife.

At Work

In a country with a reputedly high work ethic, Dutch painters
showed disappointingly little interest in depicting people on
the job. Only when commissioned by patrons like a city
government, Johan Maurits or the Trips did Dutch painters
portray enterprises. The only book on the subject, by Annette
de Vries, laments the 'limited volume, wayward distribution in
the oeuvres of very different artists, and the near lack of major
showpieces. Moreover, [depictions of labour] show little
correspondence with economic sectors...Beer brewing, which
was all over the place, has to content itself with a stray hint on

120 Jan van Bijlert, *Inmates and Officials of the St Job Hospital and Old Men's Home in Utrecht*, c. 1630–35

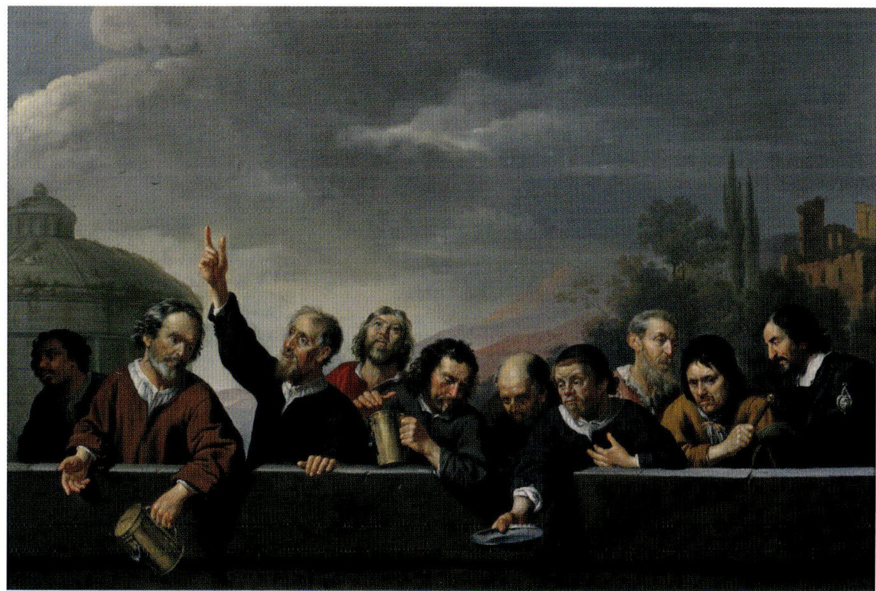

a portrait, townscape or pen drawing.' When artists went into the countryside, they ignored the highly efficient raising of crops, the largest sector in the country, in favour of cows and cottages. The images we have of soap-making came into being only because one factory was burnt down in a fire. Paintings of people at work declined over the course of the century. This reflects a change in the lives of art patrons; fewer and fewer of them worked at all. Why should they, when they had ample income from investments and sinecures. Still, random as it may be, there is a lot to enjoy in portraits and genre scenes of people at work.

121 An engaging portrait of a city official at work, by an unknown artist, is preserved by the township of Amsterdam. The sitter, Jacob de Vogelaer, was one of the seven to twelve secretaries in the service of the town government at the height of its worldwide standing. He is seated at a desk with a sealed charter and a book in which transcripts of the resolutions of the burgomasters, aldermen, council and committees are bound. The folded papers hanging next to Jacob are headed 'Minutes | 1655'. That tells us that he is sitting in an office of the new town hall, opened in May of that year (see pp. 75–76). The rich frame, adorned with symbols of secretaryship, is attributed to Artus Quellinus, who made the marble carvings for the building. In 1655, Jacob de Vogelaer became a governor of the lepers' hospital. Given his prestige and personal wealth – Jacob's father, Marcus, was one of the foremost traders with Russia – it is surprising that the portrait was not entrusted to one of the major painters working on the town hall. On the other hand, it adds to our enjoyment to know that a painter unidentifiable by his style was capable of making such a satisfyingly charming picture.

In mid-century, a small group of Haarlem painters inspired each other to go to the workshops and forges of craftspeople. 122 Cornelis Beelt was the most fervent of them. Three versions of his interior of a blacksmith's shop have survived. Interestingly, Cornelis Beelt's own workshop was not that of a typical painter. The year before he registered with the Haarlem guild of St Luke in 1635, he took out membership as a woodcarver. The three men and a boy hammering away in turn at the hot metal on the anvil have been connected to an emblem on this theme by Jacob Cats, 123 the most popular poet in the country. His emblem book, *Mirror of Old and New Times* (1632), includes an engraving, designed by Adriaen van de Venne, that could be a model for the painting. It is an illustration for the proverb, 'Where many work the forge, you have to keep the beat'. Everyone has to take his turn, in time with the others. One of several explications, in five languages,

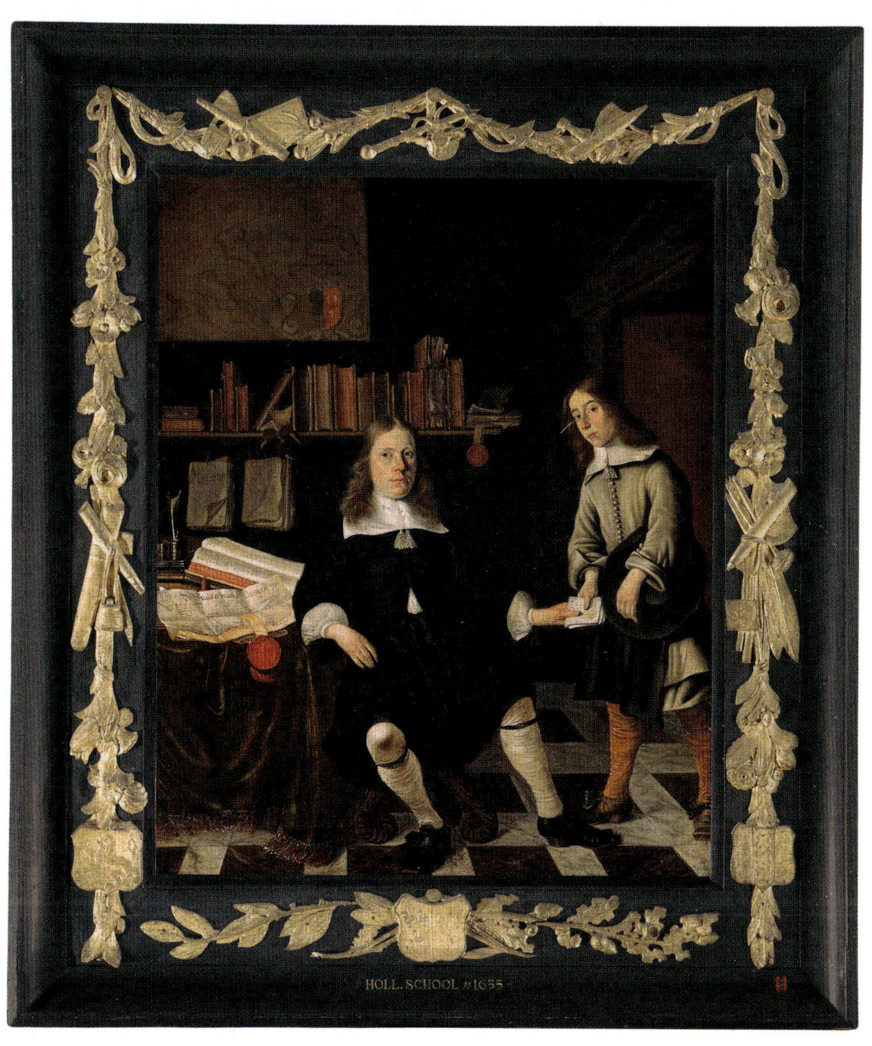

121 Unknown artist, *Portrait of Jacob de Vogelaer, Town Secretary of Amsterdam*, 1655

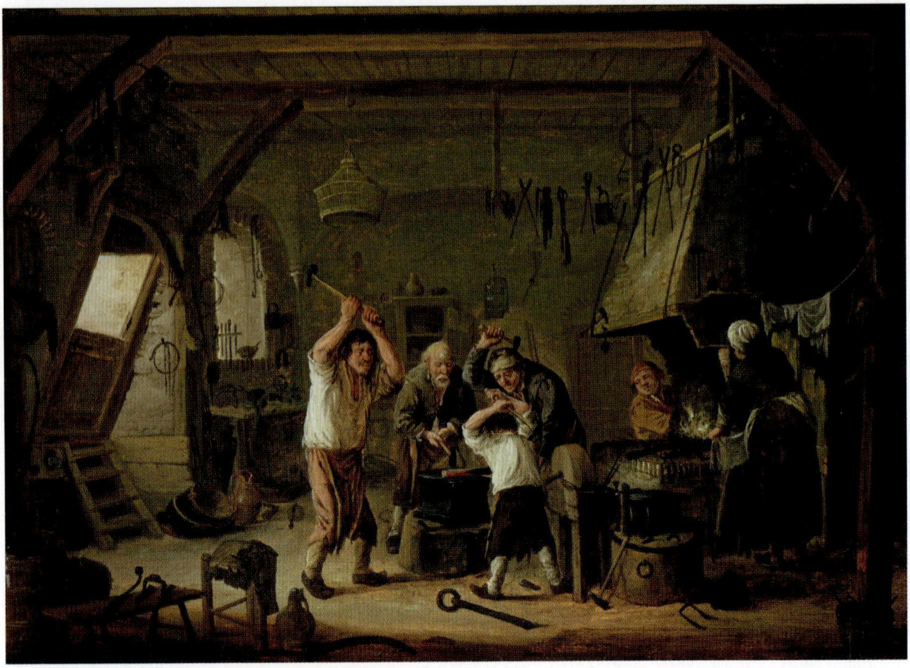

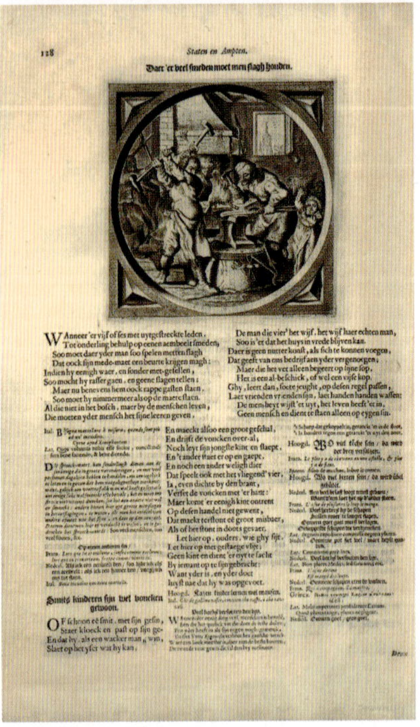

122 ABOVE Cornelis Beelt, *A Smithy*, c. 1650–60
123 LEFT Jacob Cats, *Spiegel van den ouden en nieuwen tyt*, Book III (*Staten en ambten*), Amsterdam, 1657. Later edition, with different layout, of his book of 1632. The engraving was designed by Adriaen van de Venne
124 OPPOSITE Cornelis Gerritsz Decker, *The Weaver's Workshop*, 1659

says: 'This proverb is particularly applicable to those who deal day by day with large assemblies and lots of people, to allow everyone that which he deserves.' The comparison is valuable evidence for the interweaving of painting with printmaking, book publishing, emblem literature, poetry and moral writings. It should never be assumed that a Dutch painting is proffering only what meets the eye.

53 Some of the cloth that was laid out on the bleaching fields outside Haarlem was woven in the city. In Haarlem this did not take place in factories, as in Leiden, but in the modest quarters of weavers with one or two looms. In 1643, the authorities counted no fewer than 3,350 linen looms in the city. The weaver 124 in a painting by Cornelis Gerritsz Decker also had a spinning wheel, so that he could perform two steps in weaving flax into linen. Typically, looms would be installed on the ground floor of the house where a weaver lived. The wicker cradle on the floor in this painting suggests that a baby would be left there when the weaver's wife was doing the shopping. It was not an establishment that would be visited by anyone but cloth jobbers and chums, so no excessive care was taken with maintenance or neatness. Decker was cushioned from the ups and downs in the art market by his real estate holdings. The inventory of his properties after his death included seven houses. Two of them were in the Haarlem weavers' quarter. Knowing this adds a touch of personality to an otherwise generic picture.

A retail establishment, such as a tailor's shop, would have had to be neater than a workshop. Despite the scraps and tools on

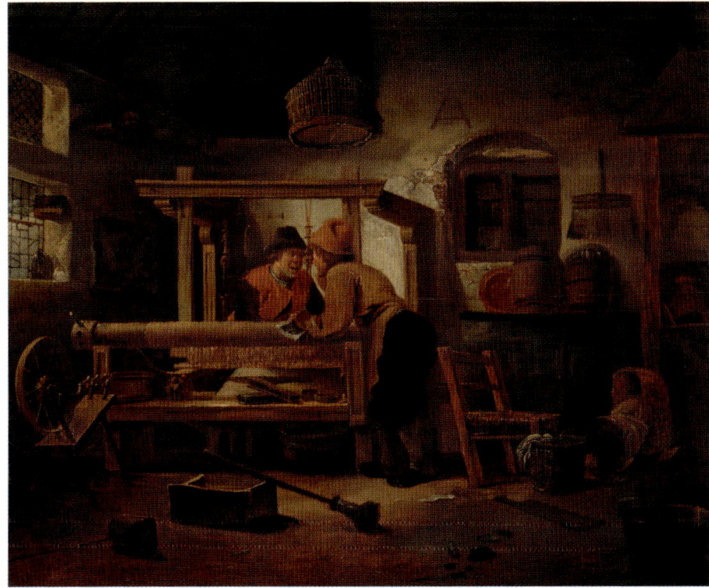

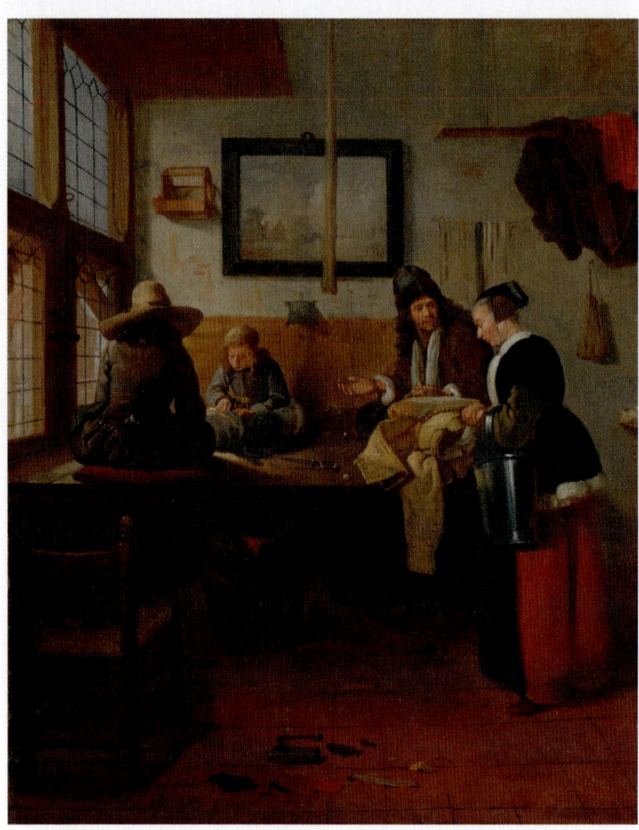

125 the floor, Quiringh van Brekelenkam's *Interior of a Tailor's Shop* is notably tidy and respectable-looking. Even the two assistants seated on cushions near a window, without the broken panes so often seen, are well-dressed. To chat with the customers, as the tailor is doing with a lady, calls for good manners. After all, they are talking about the role of the craftsman in how a proper housewife shows herself in public. That the tailor has an ebony-framed landscape on the wall is a true-to-life detail. Craftsmen were regular buyers at art auctions. In 1640, the English traveller Peter Mundy was impressed that shopkeepers and artisans, even blacksmiths, adorned their places of work with paintings. Quiringh van Brekelenkam painted tailors' shops a number of times, in addition to his hundreds of other genre scenes and a few family portraits and still lifes. Income from his prolific production was insufficient for the support of his family of nine children, however. In the mid-1650s he took out a license for the sale of beer and brandy.

There is something important to be told about the history of Brekelenkam's *Tailor's Shop*. It was bought in 1833 for 495 guilders by the Amsterdam banker Adriaan van der Hoop (1778–1854), who in 1855 established a museum in his name to house his collection. He bequeathed 224 paintings to the city of Amsterdam, which assigned them a room of their own in the new Rijksmuseum building in 1885. Other paintings in this volume from that unrivalled collection are Cornelis Bega's *Saying Grace* and Rembrandt's *Jewish Bride*. Van der Hoop was one of the Dutch collectors who staunched the flood of Dutch seventeenth-century paintings to buyers abroad. In 1858–60, when the French art critic Théophile Thoré-Bürger, taking political refuge in the Netherlands, published his fundamental two volumes on *Les musées de la Hollande*, those museums housed only eight paintings by Rembrandt. The example of collectors like van der Hoop and exposés like that of Thoré-Bürger led to the formation in 1883 of the Rembrandt Society, for preserving or buying back national heritage. Today, the museums of Holland have some fifty paintings by Rembrandt.

In the 1650s, Nicolaes Maes in Dordrecht and Quiringh van Brekelenkam in Leiden began painting young women making lace. The motif spread like wildfire, and within a few years it was picked up by Caspar Netscher in The Hague, Gerard Dou in Leiden, Gabriël Metsu in Amsterdam and Johannes Vermeer in Delft, to name the foremost. Each gave it a twist of their own. Lacemaking was not only a profession. It was part of the upbringing of girls in well-off families. The qualities it was intended to foster are those we see in the paintings: diligence, correctness, mastering a demanding challenge. That was extended to feminine virtue in general. Caspar Netscher's *Lace-maker* has been called a paragon of virtue, with all details marshalled in support of this laudatory reading. There is room for doubt. If she is the mistress of the household, she has paid more attention to her clothing than to the shabby condition of her house, with the cracks in the wall. She can also be seen as a servant girl who has put her broom aside and kicked off her shoes to sit down and practise lacemaking. Are we seeing an overambitious servant who in her dress and chosen hobby is aspiring to a status above her class?

In 2017–18, an inspiring exhibition on Dutch genre painting was held in Paris, Dublin and Washington. It was arranged thematically, showing at a glance how different painters conceived of similar motifs. Netscher's *Lace-maker* is discussed in the catalogue as a response to Vermeer's *Milkmaid* of 1658–59 and a forebear of the latter's *Lacemaker* of 1669–70. With a touch

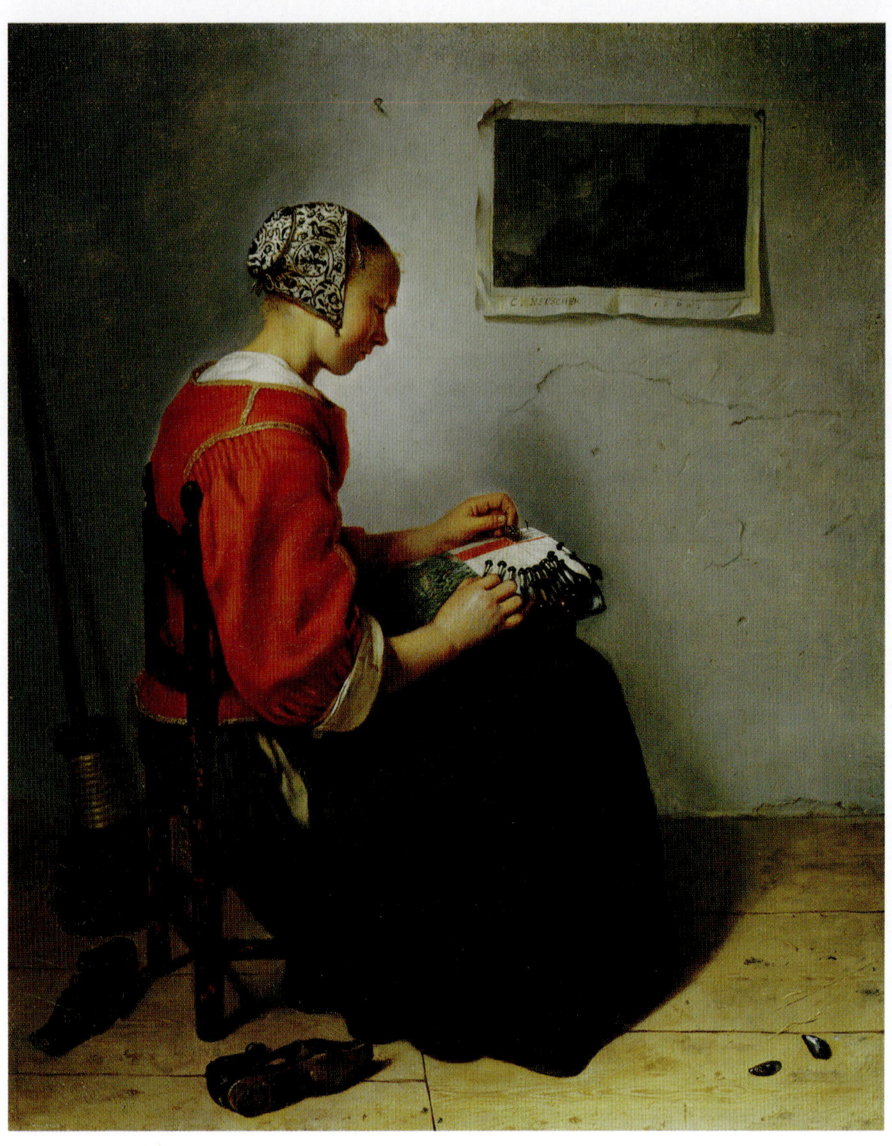

126 Caspar Netscher, *The Lace-maker*, 1662

of bravado, Netscher signed and dated his ultra-finely executed painting on the lower margin of the curling print on the wall.

At Play

The game of games in the Dutch seventeenth century may have been the blood sport of the hunt, but few people (that is, men) could play at it. For everyone, there were numerous other varieties of recreation. Country outings, full of pastoral make-believe and flirting, were popular with young people of means. Every large city had its labyrinths and menageries, and ice skating was practised by all. Ball games thrived, with courts for playing them. Golf originated in the Dutch game of *kolf*. At home, families entertained themselves with parlour games. The year was punctuated not only by seasons, with their appropriate sports, but also by holidays with a kermis – a fun fair that had its roots in religious feasts in the past. Each province and each city had its favourites. A good measure of Dutch prosperity, it can be said, was invested in free time.

The most playful of the major Dutch masters was Jan Steen. He often seems to be enjoying himself while at work, playing games with us. For indoor fun, see his family in fig. 66. He also painted outdoor games, as in *A Bowling Game*. The pitch is set up for a game of nine-pin skittles. The pose of the bowler, as he is about to roll the ball, creates a palpable sense of tension, introducing the time element into a static picture. There is more happening than the game. Children are at play in the left, couples are keeping company with each other on the right and in mid-background. Gentlefolk, such as the horseman and the distinguished figure in black, share the space with peasants and beggars. The background moves from a country cottage to woods to a gate into a small city. A painting that could serve as an advertisement for harmony between people and environments.

Quiet conviviality also speaks in Adriaen van Ostade's *The Courtyard of an Inn with a Game of Shuffleboard*. Van Ostade is the model of how we would like to think of the Dutch painter. He was eminently industrious, creating a hefty oeuvre of which some eight hundred paintings have survived. Moreover, after Rembrandt, Adriaen was the major Dutch etcher of the century. His trademark motif was the life of poor countryfolk making the best of modest circumstances. In contrast to the ridiculing mode of earlier in the century, van Ostade depicts his peasants and villagers with sympathy, if an occasional jibe. The van Ostade painter's workshop illustrated above is not autobiographical. For once, it can be said that an artist's honest dedication to his career paid off. Adriaen owned not only his

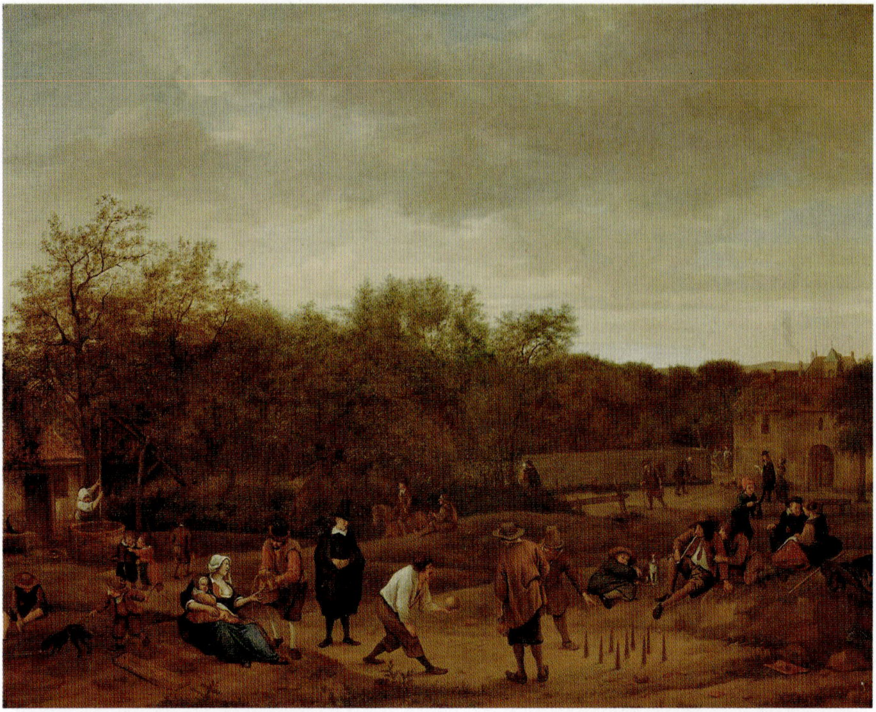

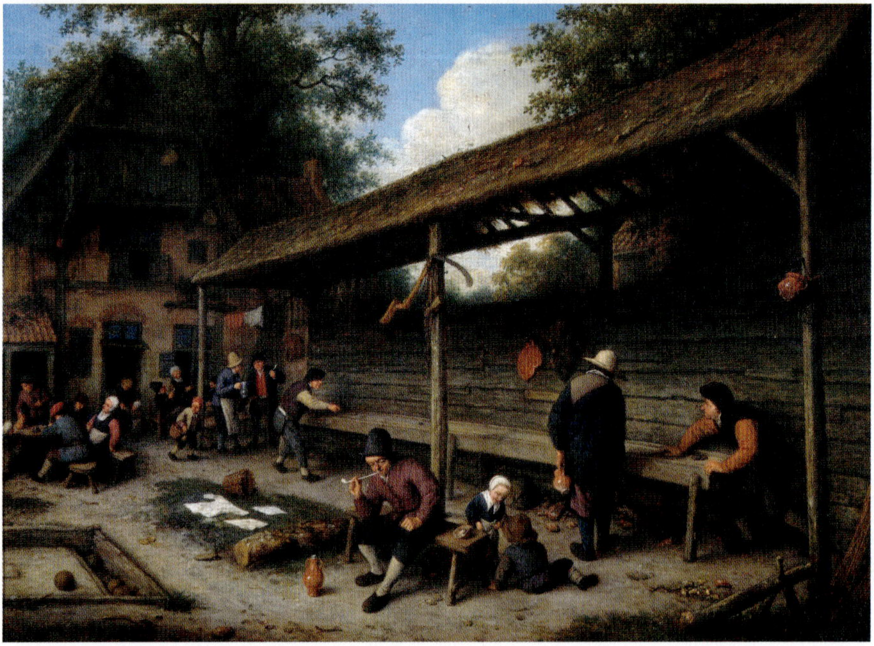

127 TOP Jan Steen, *A Bowling Game*, 1655
128 ABOVE Adriaen van Ostade, *The Courtyard of an Inn with a Game of Shuffleboard*, 1677

own house but several others as well. He served in the civic guard, which demanded a certain level of prosperity, and for several terms was an officer of the guild of St Luke. On the occasion of his first marriage in 1638, he converted from the Dutch Reformed church, into which he was born, to Catholicism, maintaining the new allegiance throughout life. This had no deleterious effect on his social standing or livelihood, which speaks well of Dutch tolerance.

At Home

The Dutch have been credited, in a wide-reaching cultural history of the home by Witold Rybczynski, with the invention of domestic life itself. In the arrangement of space in their houses and the way they presented it in paintings, they replaced the late medieval town house as a semi-public space with a realm of seclusion and privacy. It is easy to see how this impression could be created. Specialists in the matter have corrected the premise, but with however much salt it is to be taken, it does live in art. One testimony is the room of his own dwelt in by a student of modest means, in Jan Davidsz de Heem's *The Student, or Interior of a Room with a Young Man Seated at a Table*. This image of 1628 has a lot in common with a literary form being cultivated at the time. In 1623, Constantijn Huygens wrote a collection of rhymed character sketches that he called 'moral prints' (*zedeprinten*). Eighteen types of person were dismembered into their constituent parts. The origins of this kind of writing lie in ancient Greece, in the thirty 'Characters' by the scholar-philosopher-writer Theophrastus of Lesbos (*c.* 371–*c.* 287 BCE). In de Heem's painting, the young man is defined by his daydreaming pose and his attributes. The books and papers on the table identify him as a student, the rundown interior as a poor one. On the wall above his head are what look like a board for the game of mills and a sack for the pieces. Therefore, a poor student who goes in for distraction.

The key detail is the print portrait beside the board. It depicts Duke Christian of Braunschweig-Lüneburg (1599–1626), a swashbuckling military man who made a name for himself through daring in the field, although it usually ended badly. The student's sword, leaning on a travelling chest, beneath a map, rounds out the picture of a would-be daredevil who wants to live fast and die young like Christian (who died at the age of twenty-six – in his bed) – but is too lazy to do anything about it. Confusingly, de Heem has given the student his own features. Perhaps, it has been suggested, to say that he too is indecisive in life choices. One choice on which he indeed sat

129

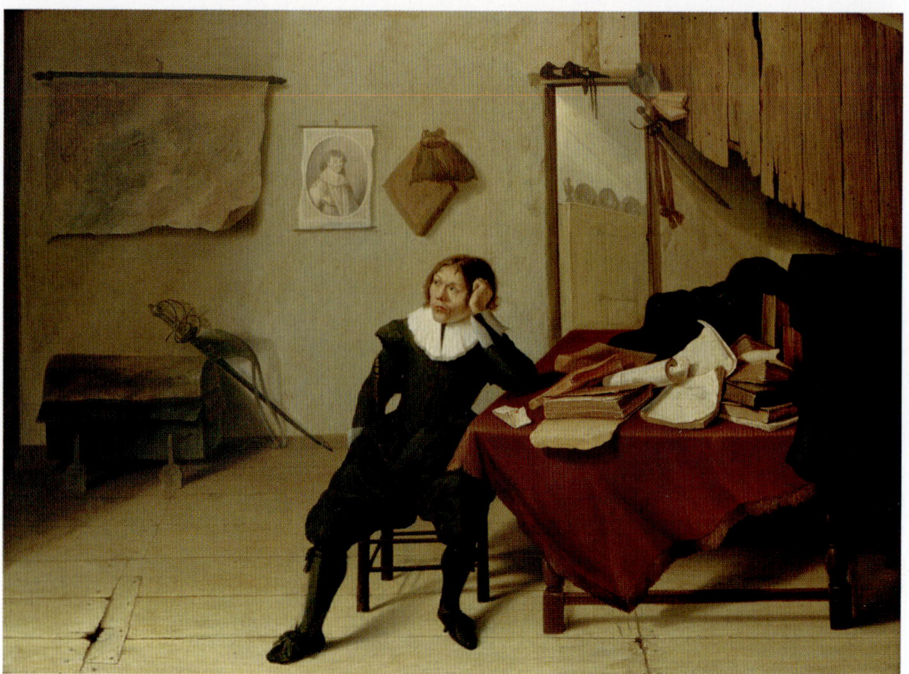

129 Jan Davidsz de Heem, *The Student, or Interior of a Room with a Young Man Seated at a Table*, 1628

on the fence is whether to live in the Northern or Southern Netherlands (see p. 13).

130　　A more touching picture of a penurious interior is Cornelis Pietersz Bega's family saying grace before a meal. Not all Dutch people were churchgoers, but nearly all, it seems safe to say, would say grace. That quiet ritual is especially moving for the meagreness of the meal for which they are thanking the Lord: a loaf of bread, half a wheel of cheese, perhaps porridge in the bowl, eaten in a dilapidated attic room. To judge by their age, the man behind the table is not the husband but the (widowed) father of the young woman. Bega came from a Catholic family of master builders, silversmiths, woodcarvers and painters. He was a pupil of Adriaen van Ostade, with whom he shared a dedicated temperament and preference for sympathetic depictions of the life of ordinary people. Cornelis's mother was the daughter, born out of wedlock, of Cornelis Cornelisz van Haarlem, one of the great figures in Haarlem painting. Family relations were open and warm. Bega was named after his grandfather, and he and his family lived in a house owned by Cornelis Cornelisz, who bequeathed it to them, with other

properties. Sadly, Bega died at the age of thirty-two, it is
thought of the plague.

***

Until mid-century, the great majority of female subjects in
Dutch genre paintings were barmaids, prostitutes, demi-
mondaines, camp followers and other types associated with
anything but home life. Then, all of a sudden, they became
caring housewives and loving mothers. The transition
coincided with the end of the Eighty Years' War, which may
have been a contributory factor in the domestication of the
image of the Dutch woman. Thanks to this shift in what
womanhood means in art, paintings such as Pieter de Hooch's
Woman with Maid at Linen Cabinet could start looking typically
Dutch. Whatever the character of the women at the cupboard,
the interior is typical only for the uppermost crust of society.
A floor in red and grey Swedish stone would almost never be
found in a private residence. Reserved for the rich are the oak
cupboard, inlaid with ebony, the Chinese Wanli (porcelain)

131

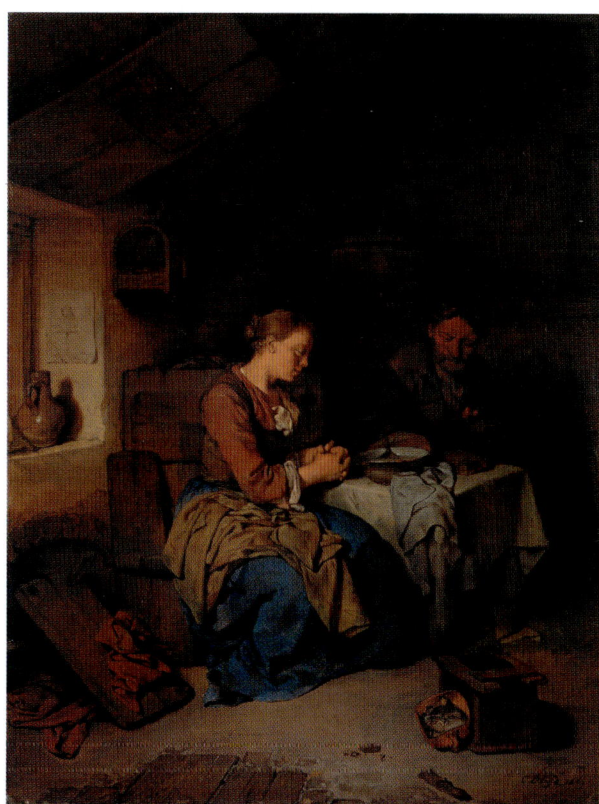

130 Cornelis
Pietersz Bega,
Saying Grace, 1663

bowl on the cupboard, and the sculpture above the richly framed door. It is a copy of Benvenuto Cellini's *Perseus with the Head of Medusa* (1545–54) on the Loggia de' Lanzi in Florence, perhaps a souvenir from a voyage through Italy by the missing father of the family. As Herman Roodenburg observed: 'When such cupboards were opened, costly fragrances came out, since sachets of sweet-smelling flower petals and spices – sometimes called musk-bags – were customarily placed among bed linen and clothing.' Roodenburg has noted that the air on the canal seen through the doors would have been unbearably fetid in the summer. However we analyze the painting, it remains as inviting an image of home comfort as any ever made.

Music-making

In 2016, a small exhibition was held of Dutch genre paintings from the British Royal Collection. Taking those twenty-seven paintings as a random sample, we find in twelve of them three lutes, three violins, three drums, two bass viols, one cello and one pipe. There is singing and dancing in more than one painting. Not encountered here, but occurring elsewhere, are pages of printed and written sheet music. From households to family groups to tavern scenes to sets of the five senses to merry companies, music-making may be the most common genre motif of all. The range of symbolic possibilities is also broad. What springs first to mind is harmony, although music has its dubious side as well, as in scenes of seduction and vanity. What it always brings is a suggested accompaniment in sound to what we are seeing.

132The serious music-making on the left of an architecturally fanciful interior by the Zeeland artist Dirck van Delen is set off against a lively discussion on the right. The five central figures, from the woman playing the theorbo to the man seated at the table, are lifted, with slight variations, from a genre piece by Pieter Codde, in which they are the only figures. In the ill-defined moral rights of authorship in Dutch art, appropriating motifs was not only tolerated but recommended. Yet we seldom see it in such blatant form. Van Delen was another artist-officeholder. He served nearly twenty terms as burgomaster of Arnemuiden, in addition to numerous administrative and churchly functions.

* * *

In Dutch genre paintings, as in Hollywood romantic comedies, you cannot introduce a man and a woman into the picture

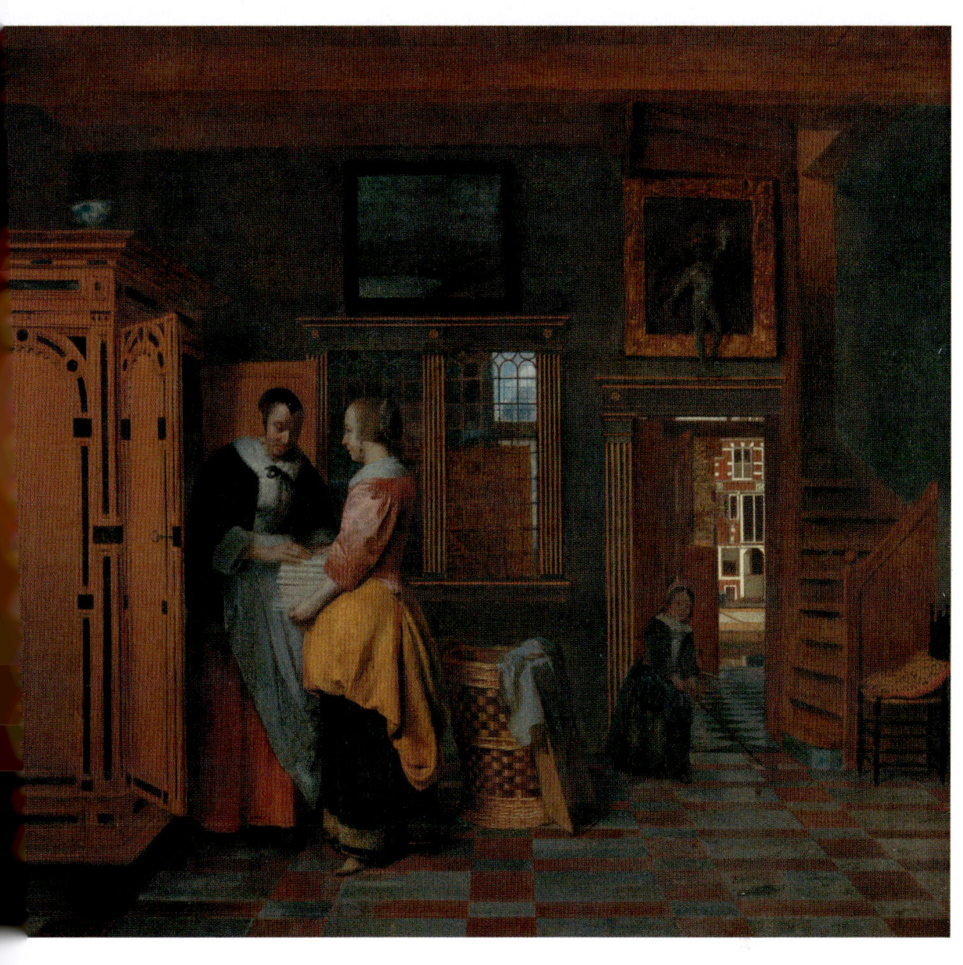

131 Pieter de Hooch, *Woman with Maid at Linen Cabinet*, 1663

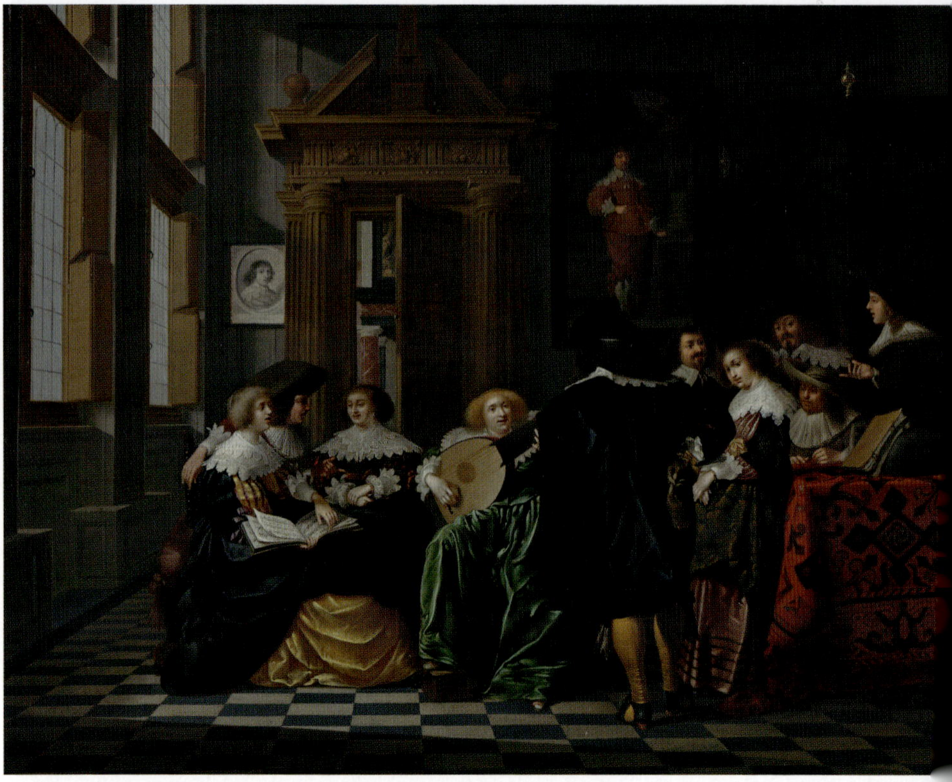

132 Dirck van Delen, *A Musical Company*, 1636

without the viewer musing on the possibility of intimate
involvement. That is especially the case with paintings where
music is involved. That wondering does not always lead to a
simple answer. Two opposing forces are built into Jan Steen's
A Young Woman Playing a Harpsichord to a Young Man. The
inscription just below the young woman's hands, *Soli • Deo •
Gloria* (Glory Only to God), suggests a nun-like chastity. The
text on the inner side of the harpsichord, nearer the man,
reads *ACTA VIRUM PROBANT* (Actions Prove the Man), as if
encouraging a move from him. This duality has been related
to Dutch upper-class social conventions derived from the
love lyrics of the much-admired Italian poet Petrarch (1304–74).
His ideal woman, musically gifted, made herself unavailable
to unworthy admirers, who were destined to be frustrated
by unreciprocated affection. If that is what Jan Steen's would-be
beau is undergoing, all hope may not be lost. In the doorway,
a young servant approaches with a large theorbo. This

133

suggests that the suitor will soon join the young woman for
a duet, a metaphor for being in love. One detail that lends
credence to the idea that Jan Steen had literary associations
in mind is his signature. In the spot on the harpsichord where
the instrument-maker would usually place his name, the artist
signs in Latin, perhaps for the only time, with a show of
learning, *Johanis Steen fecit*.

There does not even have to be a man in the picture for the
image of a woman making music to suggest romance. Vermeer
insistently plants the idea in the head of the viewer in his *Young
Woman Standing at the Virginal*. The painting above and behind
her of a naked little Amor does the job. But what is he saying?
Are we to think that the woman is prey to the desire that an
arrow from the bow of Amor can kindle? A knowledgeable
viewer might well have thought the opposite. In a famous book
of love emblems (1608) by the learned artist Otto van Veen
(1566–1629), illustrating personifications of love in 124 Amors,
the very first one holds up a card like that in the Vermeer, with
the number 1. The accompanying quatrain, in Latin, Dutch and
French, says that the number stands for faithful love to one

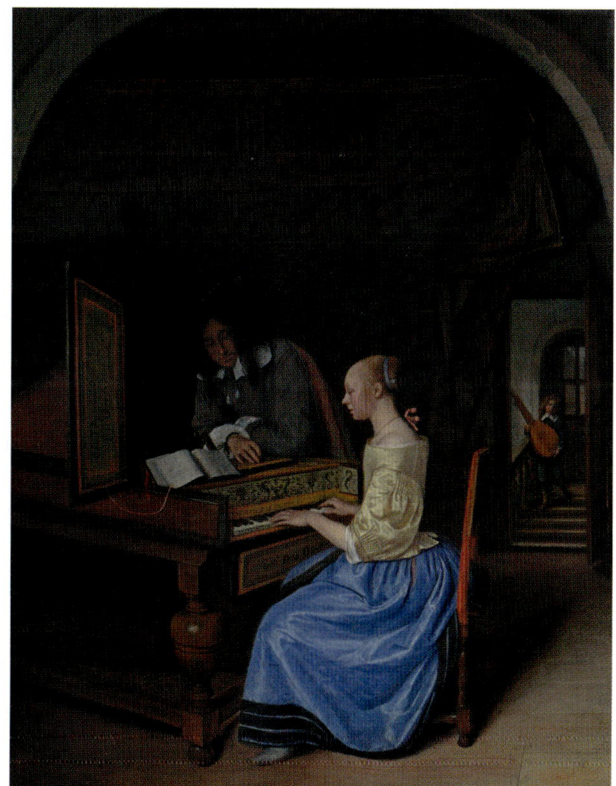

133 Jan Steen,
*A Young Woman
Playing a Harpsichord
to a Young Man,*
probably 1659

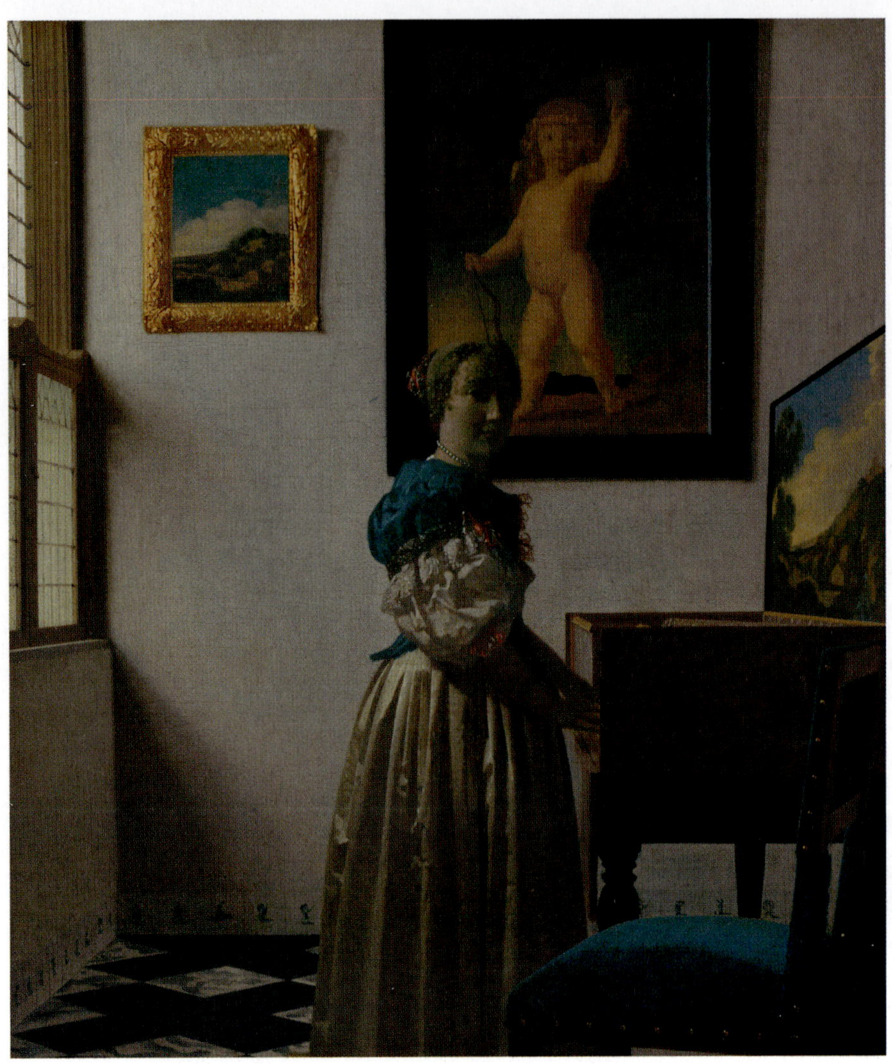

134 Johannes Vermeer, *Young Woman Standing at the Virginal*, c. 1670–72

partner. This reading does not sit well with the inviting gaze that Vermeer's woman casts on the viewer and the empty chair – for whom? The painting of Amor recurs in another Vermeer canvas, mounted above a young woman reading a letter. That Amor was painted over early on, to be restored to view in 2021. The painting of the love god itself is thought to have been a copy after a work by Caesar van Everdingen, now lost, that belonged to Vermeer.

Sex

It cannot be said they were not warned. Not a treatise on painting was written in which painters were not told that they had the power to excite the libido of the viewer, but that they should definitely not do so. Samuel van Hoogstraten reported the case of a 'young man who, it is said, seeing paintings of the abduction of Ganymede, shameless Nais cuddling Hylas, and Apollo and Hyacinth, was so moved that he cried out: "It's no bad thing to imitate the gods."' To the painter, van Hoogstraten says: 'Thou shalt not put into a painting anything that is not fit to see.' Hordes of artists to whom this message was addressed appeared to have deaf ears. Prurient intentions could easily be disguised. Mythology and the Bible are full of motifs that call for naked women and sexual doings. In Andor Pigler's compendium of subject matter in art of the early modern period, ten pages in small type are filled with references to Susanna and the Elders, in which the chaste and beautiful woman, having undressed to bathe, is propositioned by two lecherous old men. (The books of Leviticus, Numbers and Deuteronomy have three pages in total.) The end of the story – the execution of the two elders – seems never to have been depicted in art. When they ran out of Bible stories (such as Lot and his Daughters, Joseph and Potiphar's Wife, the Prodigal Son), artists could turn to moralizing messages, which opened vast opportunities, showing all kinds of things not to do. Certain limits were observed. No depictions of actual intercourse are known, or love between people of the same sex.

There was no taboo – quite the opposite – on images of unequal love, especially of young women entrapping older men. The motif has hoary antecedents. In his play *The Merchant*, the Roman playwright Plautus (*c.* 254–184 BCE), puts it thus: 'Any man over the age of sixty, regardless of marital status, who consorts with harlots...shall be considered stupid, and will come running for help only after the harlots have wasted his property and possessions.' Hendrick ter Brugghen's painting of the subject looks at first sight like everyday transactional sex. But that is not what is happening. The grey-bearded old face is a

135

mask worn by a brown-haired young man. What seems to be going on is that a young man wants the girl to think he is a rich old codger. Her laugh could mean that she is on to the ruse but is not unhappy about it. Ter Brugghen was born into a distinguished family. His father was appointed secretary to the States of Holland on the recommendation of William of Orange. That he chose to become a painter, when he could have had a good career in government, shows how serious art was taken as a profession. In his teens he spent some years in Rome, where he was excited by the innovations of Caravaggio. Back in Utrecht, he was one of the chief exponents of the spirit of that master, as in the unapologetic sensualism of this painting.

The most sensitive and touching visualization in Dutch painting of libidinous propositioning was made by Judith Leyster. It would be denying the obvious to avoid saying that this is thanks to the gender of the artist. The all-too-familiar occurrence is centred for once on the feelings of the woman, a woman attracting sexual attention that repels her. There can be no doubt what the man wants, coming from behind in the dark

135 BELOW Hendrick ter Brugghen, *Unequal Lovers*, c. 1623
136 OPPOSITE Judith Leyster, *A Man Offering Money to a Woman*, 1631

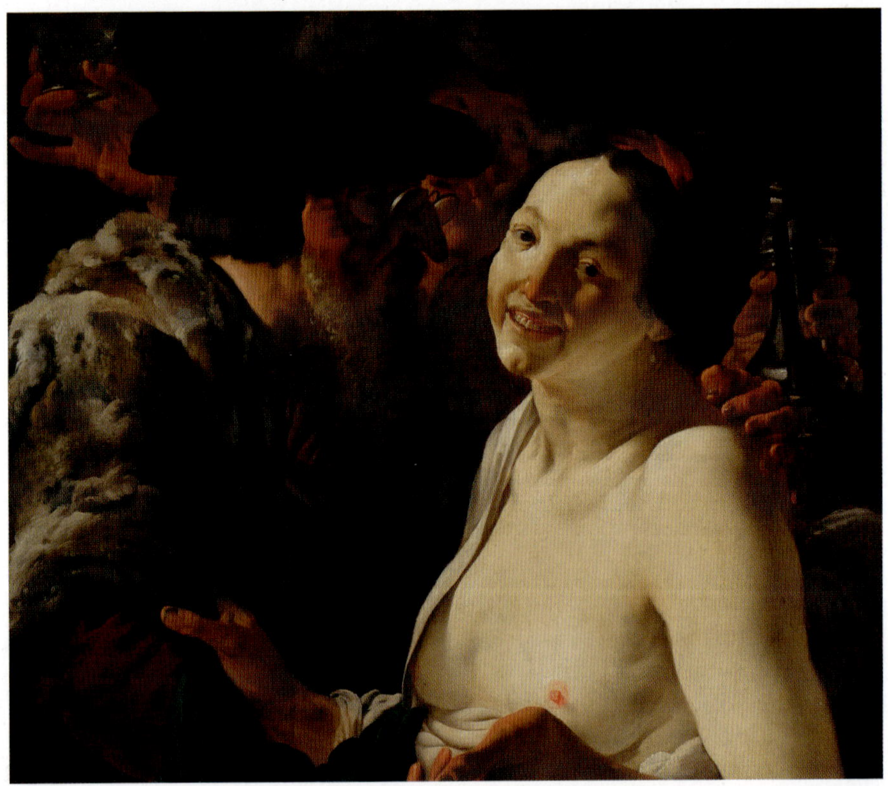

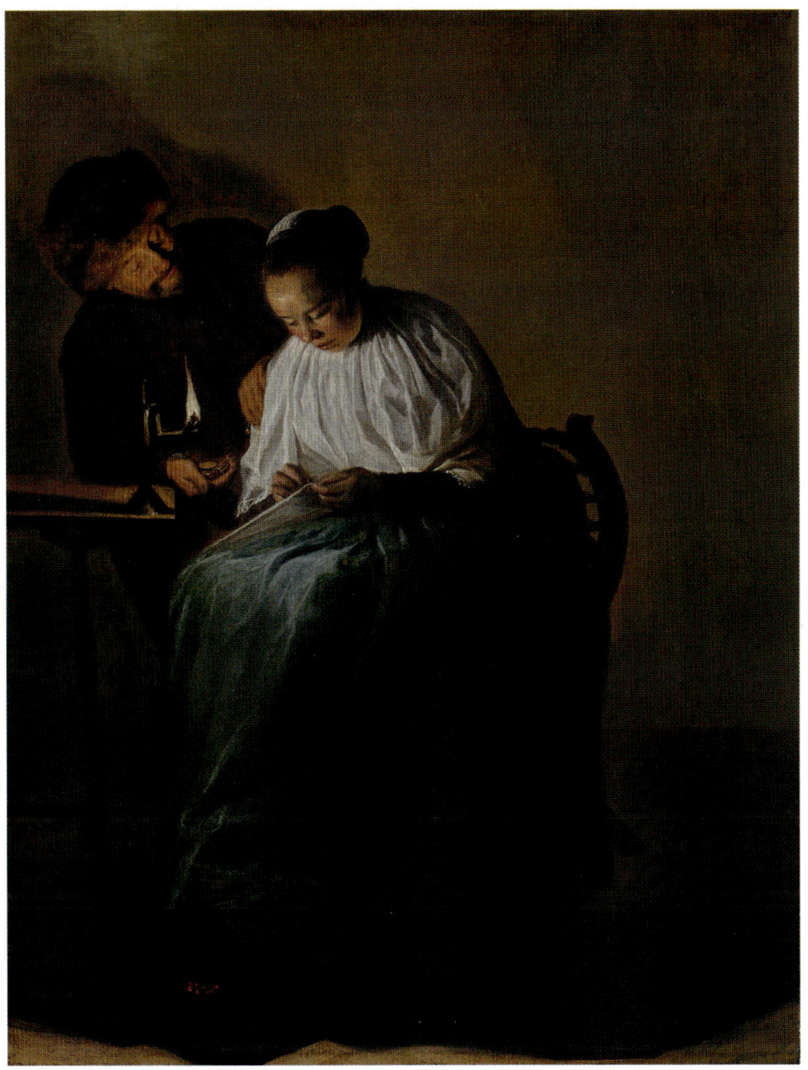

to the young servant and offering her a palmful of coins. Her reaction is *not* to react, to ignore him. In her vulnerable situation as a household servant, it takes courage to behave contrarily to a man whose unwelcome presence was surely made possible by her employers.

Judith Leyster was a star of Haarlem painting. In 1628, when she was nineteen years old, she was mentioned in the section on artists in *the* book on Haarlem, by Minister Samuel Ampzing, a major reference work to this day. In a line about the studio of

94

Frans Pietersz de Grebber, Ampzing mentions his artist children, a boy (Pieter) and a girl (Maria), adding 'and here [in this studio] is another one [another female] who paints with good and keen skill'. Leyster's stardom was also a punning function of her name, which can be read as 'guiding star'. She signed some of her paintings with a star attached to the monogram *JL*. Her career as an independent artist came to a halt when, in 1636, she married the more famous Jan Miense Molenaer, who commanded better prices in the market (see p. 94.) Incomprehensibly, she was written out of art history for some two centuries after her death. Fortunately, she has now benefited from the attention of a sterling group of art historians, most of them women.

135, 137

A painting by Jacob van Loo mirrors Hendrick ter Brugghen's masquerade scene, presenting a pivotal moment from Giovanni Battista Guarini's *Il pastor fido* (*The Faithful Shepherd*), a pastoral tragicomedy first published in 1590. By 1601, a Dutch adaptation captivated audiences with its tale of love and divine decree. The goddess of the hunt, Diana, has ordained that the dwellers in Arcadia sacrifice a virgin once a year until a marriage takes place between two inhabitants who were descendants of the gods. The nymph Amaryllis is one of the designated victims, but she is also, as a descendant of Pan, a potential bride. To meet the condition of the gods, a marriage is planned for her with a hunter who has the right credentials. She is, however, in love with the shepherd Mirtillo. In the course of the complicated events, Amaryllis holds a contest to see which of the Arcadian nymphs can kiss her the best. To be able to participate, Mirtillo dresses as a woman. He is the last contestant, and his kiss is so sweet that Amaryllis gives him the crown of victory. Jacob van Loo merges the kiss with the crowning. (Mirtillo turns out to be noble as well, so that his marriage to Amaryllis saved Arcadia.)

More paintings of scenes from *Il pastor fido* were made in Holland than anywhere else. This preference corresponded with the taste of the Orange and Stuart courts, which were charmed by the idea that, uncontestably noble though they may be, they were as simple at heart as nymphs and shepherds. The first known depiction in art of the kissing contest was made towards 1630 by Anthony van Dyck for Stadholder Frederik Hendrik. Another attraction of the subject, which is never spoken of explicitly, is the apparently lesbian lovemaking it depicts. Jacob van Loo's career took an unusual turn after 1660, when he killed an innkeeper in a tavern brawl. To flee the capital punishment that threatened him, he went to France. There he became the patriarchal founder of a dynasty of French artists that flourished throughout the seventeenth and eighteenth centuries, injecting a Dutch element into the heart of French painting.

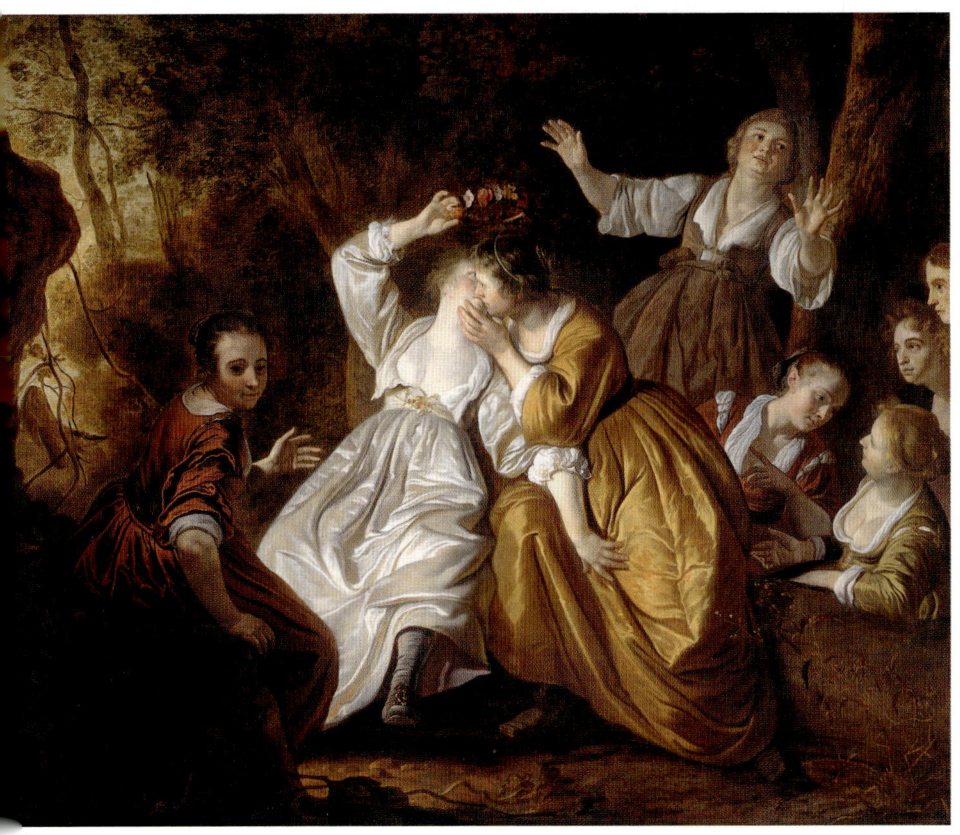

137 Jacob van Loo, *Amaryllis Crowning Mirtillo*, c. 1648

138   Nothing much is left to the imagination in Frans van Mieris's scene of mutual seduction in a bedroom. The oysters, with their reputedly aphrodisiac quality, cannot even be called symbolic. Intriguingly, the enactors of this foreplay are the artist and his wife, Cunera van der Cock. Their appearance is known from two oval portraits made shortly after their marriage. Van Mieris's face has been found by his cataloguer in no fewer than thirty-one paintings, mainly genre scenes. Artistic behaviour of this kind teases the always-present question of the relation of art to life.

66   As we have seen, Jan Steen's use of his own features in disorderly family scenes damaged the artist's posthumous reputation. Arnold Houbraken wrote of him: 'In general I must say that his paintings were like his lifestyle, and his lifestyle like his paintings.' He reserves comment on Frans van Mieris giving his features to debauched characters, but he does relate that he and

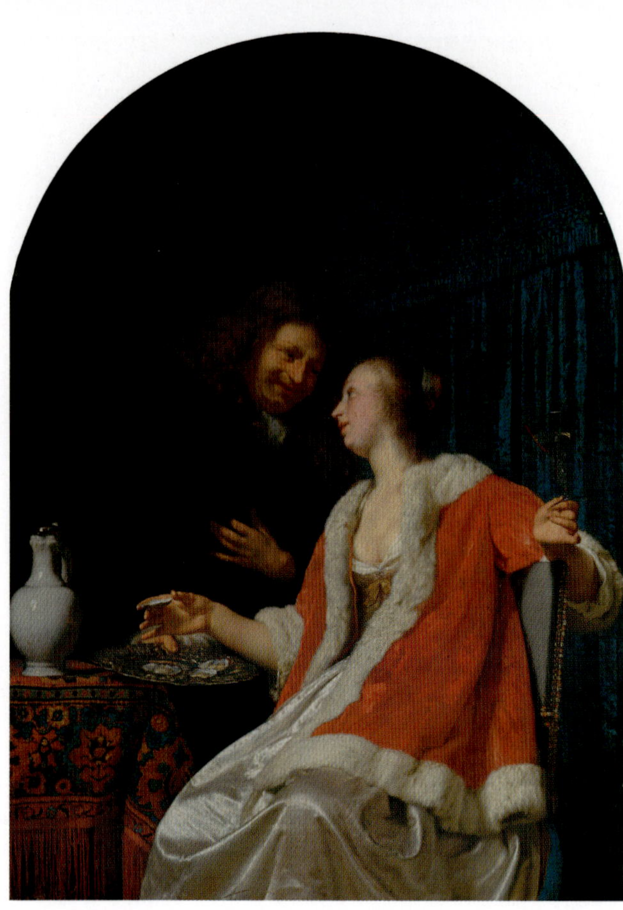

138 LEFT Frans van Mieris, *The Oyster Meal*, 1661
139 OPPOSITE Eglon van der Neer, *Interior of a Brothel, with a Woman Washing Her Hands*, 1675

Jan Steen were drinking buddies and that Frans would pour alcohol into Jan until deep in the night, to hear more and more of his stories.

* * *

While Gerard de Lairesse (see pp. 139–40) might insist on clarity in painting a story, ambiguity could serve its purposes. In Eglon van der Neer's *Interior of a Brothel, with a Woman Washing Her Hands*, the unclear relation between the elegant main figures in the foreground and the raw action in the background is a sure recipe for animated conversation between the owner and his guests. A man is pushing his way into a room that looks like a high-class brothel, apparently to reach the semi-dressed woman by the bed on the left. She holds out her arm in apparent

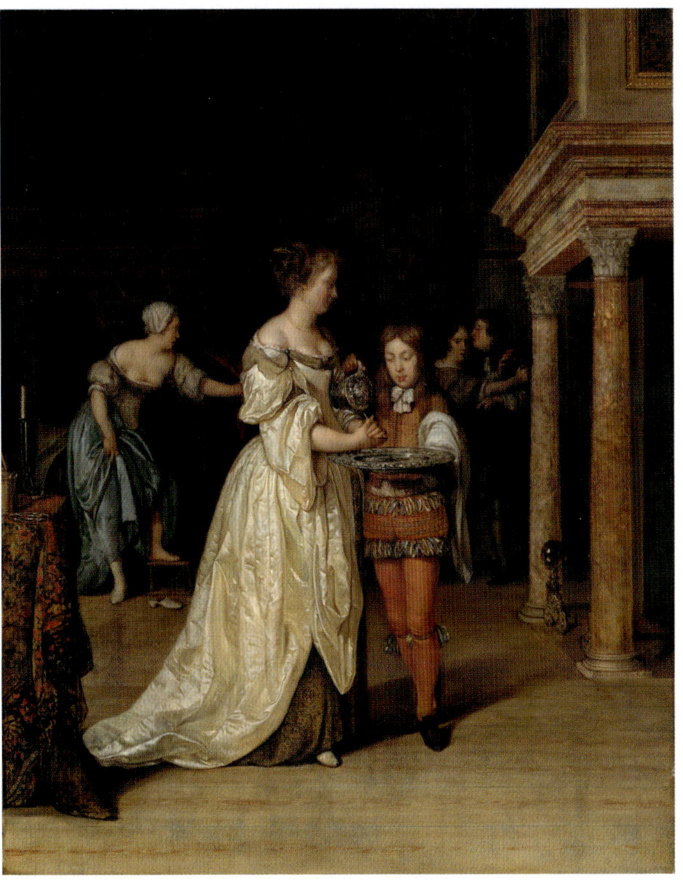

protest, while another woman seems to be blocking the man. Is he ignoring the opening hours of the establishment? The woman's hand-washing has been seen as a deliberate attempt to distance herself from the sinful behaviour of the figures behind her, but it can also be seen as a hypocritical pretence of innocence.

Leaving that matter to rest, it is interesting to tell about how the painting came to be in the Mauritshuis. Before the Second World War it belonged to the German Jewish banker Fritz Mannheimer (1890–1939), who lived in Amsterdam from 1916 and became a Dutch citizen in 1936. Mannheimer was a flamboyant man who operated at the highest level of international finance and led a personal life that fed the gossip columns for decades. In his art purchases from 1921 onwards, he competed with the most important collectors in the world. As tension grew in

Europe in the late 1930s, he engaged in failing speculations with national currencies, so that within hours of his sudden death, his firm was declared bankrupt. Much of the art in his Amsterdam villa (which now houses the executive offices of the Rijksmuseum) was bought by Nazi agents for Hitler. The Eglon van der Neer was reserved for the museum that Hitler planned to build in his native city of Linz, the aborted Führermuseum. After the war it was sent back to the Netherlands, in the drive to recuperate art stolen or bought under duress by the Nazis from its owners, most of them Jewish. The curator assigned to the case decided that the Mannheimer properties should not go to his heirs; half was sold and half went to the Rijksmuseum, with a few odds and ends placed in other Dutch museums. The Eglon van der Neer was one of those that was transferred in ownership to the Mauritshuis in 1960, by then a state museum.

On the Table

The painting of eatables and kitchen instruments has a long history in Dutch art, from the fifteenth century on. We find it in accessory details in biblical stories that call for it, such as Esther's Banquet or The Multiplication of the Loaves and Fishes, or with symbolic meanings of their own, such as ears of wheat standing for the Resurrection. Not until the early seventeenth century did artists do away with the excuse of a Bible link to paint tables of food on their own. Ironically, this had the effect of calling more attention to the individual items, their combinations and associations. In 1611, when the Amsterdam grain dealer, rhetorician and poet Roemer Visscher (1547–1620) published a volume of more than a hundred emblems, *Sinnepoppen* (Moral Marionets), the first one was a general lesson about the meaning of things. This matters, because no one with enough cultural sensitivity to buy a painting would not have known *Sinnepoppen*.

A hand pushing an empty glass or glass bottle under water with the mouth downwards; the bottle will not fill up with water, because it is full of compressed air. Which means that God fills everything, even if it doesn't seem so, confirming the truth of the saying: Nihil est in rebus inane, *which is: 'Nothing in things is empty or in vain.'*

The print is captioned *Iovis omnia plena* (God fills everything), and the canteen being pushed into the water shows the name of God in Hebrew. In that context, a message that will have been known to every Dutch believer emphatically relates the belief in God's omnipresence to representational art. In this regard, still life is like landscape, in which nature is painted as part

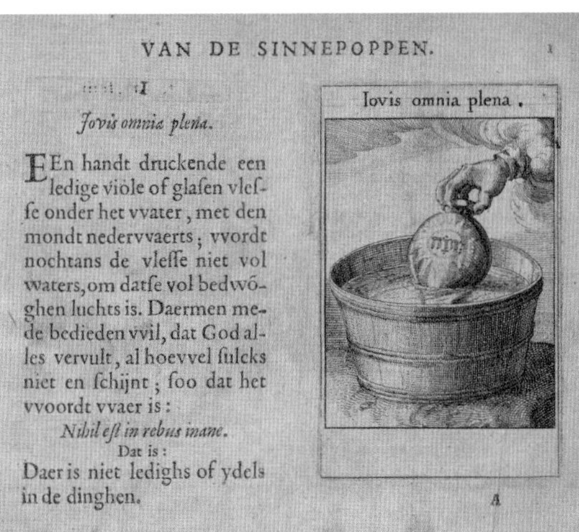

140 Claes Jansz
Visscher, Emblem 1
in Roemer Visscher,
Sinnepoppen, 1614

of Creation. These observations cast doubt on the too-easy
assumption that Dutch artists were pioneering a secular art,
categorically distinct from sacred art.

The English designation 'still life', which seems self-
explanatory to us, is taken from the Dutch word *stilleven*,
which did not enter the language until about 1650. (In English
it was first found by the Oxford English Dictionary in 1693).
Before then, lacking a word that fits all, still-life paintings
were called by their main motif: a fish piece, a breakfast
piece, or as Cornelis Jacobsz Delff's *Still Life of Kitchen Utensils*
would have been called, a kitchen piece. The early speciality
practised by him and Floris van Schooten, of gleaming copper
cooking vessels, did not catch on as a semi-genre in itself,
although other artists later included them as details. Delff
reused some of the objects here in different constellations,
which lessens one's expectation that he means anything in
particular. But we cannot help asking why the strainer is
sticking out into the air from under the cauldron with water,
standing on a stool, or whether the doused candle on the
shelf is a bearer of meaning. That the artist was after certain
painterly effects seems clear. The fall and reflection of light
on the various surfaces is a tour de force, and the dried fish,
with their glimmering scales, provide an organic counterpart
to the shiny metal vessels.

A kitchen sampler of another kind is Floris van Dijck's
breakfast piece *Still Life with Fruits, Nuts and Cheese*. The slanting
table in itself, allowing an overview of the ingredients, is enough
to tell us that the picture is not intended to be taken literally. It is

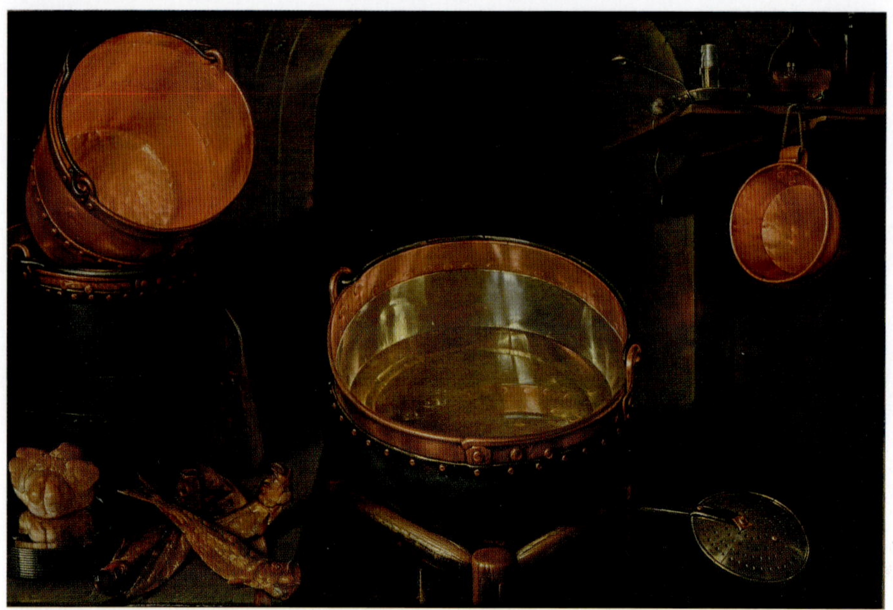

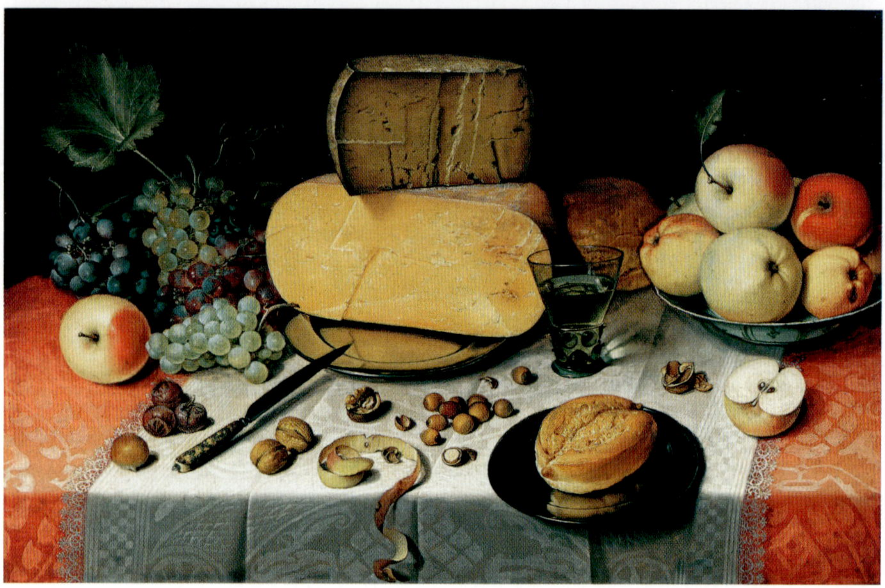

141 TOP Cornelis Jacobsz Delff, *Still Life of Kitchen Utensils*, 1610–45
142 ABOVE Floris van Dijck, *Still Life with Fruits, Nuts and Cheese*
(A 'Breakfast Piece'), 1613

a display of, among other things, tastes: sour apples, salty cheese, sweet grapes and bitter nuts. Laid tables with all the comestibles and tableware we see here were first painted in Antwerp. The innovation credited to Floris van Dijck is the arrangement of the cheeses, one on top of another. The display on this table, with apples plumped unceremoniously into an expensive Chinese blue-and-white bowl, is decidedly lavish. Unexpectedly for a painting of this quality, it is a copy by the master himself of a previous version dated 1610. This practice does not seem to be widespread, but its very existence complicates the connoisseur's attempt to distinguish originals from copies.

Floris van Dijck, who was born into a prosperous Catholic family, was an interesting person. In his twenties he spent some time in Rome, in the studio of Giuseppe Cesari, known as Cavaliere d'Arpino (1568–1640), who drew a portrait of Floris that became a family heirloom. He served several terms on the board of the Haarlem guild of St Luke and presented to it a head by Michelangelo that he had brought from Rome. Although only still lifes by him have survived, paintings of sacred subjects, in a Catholic strain, were documented in his lifetime.

143

It may come as a surprise that pictures of truly modest table fare (*banketjes*), such as Pieter Claesz's *Still Life with Herring and Beer*, are relatively hard to find. This offering recalls Arnold Houbraken's description of how Rembrandt, 'when he was at work, would often take his meal with a piece of cheese and bread, or with a pickled herring'. There is a kind of pride attached to this modesty. Pieter Claesz was born in a town near Antwerp, where he was trained before moving to Haarlem by 1620. It seems likely that he began painting food still lifes in Antwerp. He was not well off, and was always being sued by landlords and grocers. It would have done him good that his artist son, Nicolaes Berchem, was so much more successful. Berchem took up completely different specialities from his father. He painted heavily atmospheric landscapes and histories in a self-invented, lyrical mode. Most are peopled with shepherds and shepherdesses, but he also conjured up glamorous figures in classical surroundings. The nods at Italy are so emphatic that art historians have found it difficult to accept the evidence that he never went there. This is a fascinating turn for the son of an artist who never painted anything that he was not looking at. What does it say about Dutch buyers, that they prized the son's fantasies more highly than the father's descriptions?

144

With Willem Kalf, the average cost of an object in a *banketje* went through the ceiling. Rather than products that could be bought around the corner, such as earthen pots and linen tablecloths, Kalf served up exotic rarities. The objects in his

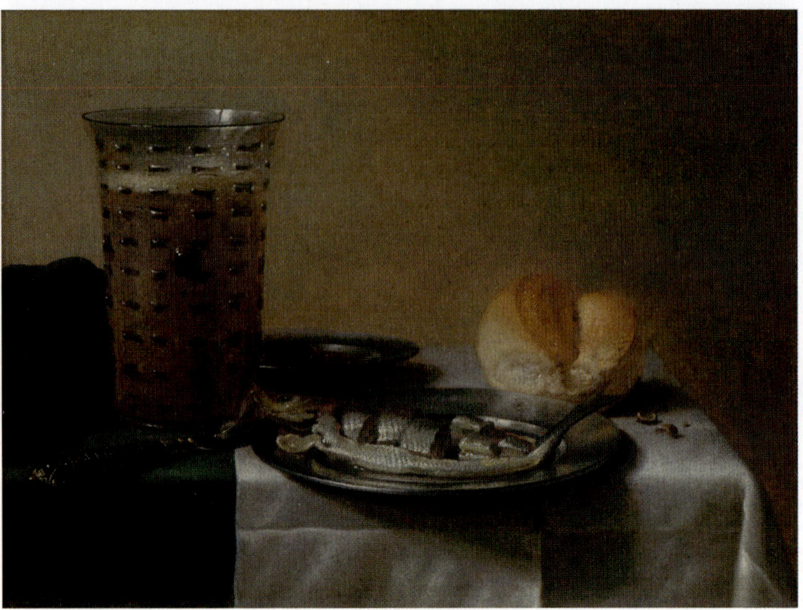

143 Pieter Claesz, *Still Life with Herring and Beer*, 1636

Still Life with a Chinese Bowl, Nautilus Cup and Other Objects, laid out on a marble table-top decked with a Persian carpet, are a Ming bowl with reliefs of the eight Taoist immortals; a wine glass made in the Netherlands by Venetian artisans; and a nautilus shell from the East Indies in a silver mount, incorporating a mermaid and merman, a dolphin's tail and Neptune, the god of the sea, riding on a whale's head with a man escaping from the mouth. Although Kalf's father, a prosperous cloth merchant, may have had goods like this at home, Willem did not start out painting them. He spent his youth in the Dutch-Flemish artists' milieu in Paris, where he painted rustic interiors said to have been emulated by the famed Le Nain brothers. His earliest rich *banketje*, from about 1653 when he moved to Amsterdam, includes the drinking horn of the Amsterdam calivers' civic guard, suggesting that it may have been a commission.

While the details in Kalf's *Still Life with a Chinese Bowl* beg for interpretation, we have a protestation from Gerard de Lairesse that none was intended:

Although I have before said, that the famous Kalf excelled above all others in still life, yet he could give as little reason for why he included this or that as his predecessors and followers: he only exhibited what occurred to his thoughts (as a Porcelain pot or

*dish, gold cup, mum-glass or rummer with wine, a lemon-peel
hanging on it, a clock, a mother-of-pearl horn on a gold or silver
foot, a silver dish of peaches, or else cut China Oranges or lemons,
a carpet, and other usual things), without any thought of doing
something of importance carrying some particular meaning, or
applicable to something.*

What would Roemer Visscher have said about this? (see p. 214).

* * *

145   In Dutch art history, Adriaen Coorte occupies a place of his
own. He is the archetypal rediscovered artist, the proof that we
can change our minds and recognize quality where it was once
ignored. Until 1952, Coorte was virtually unknown and little

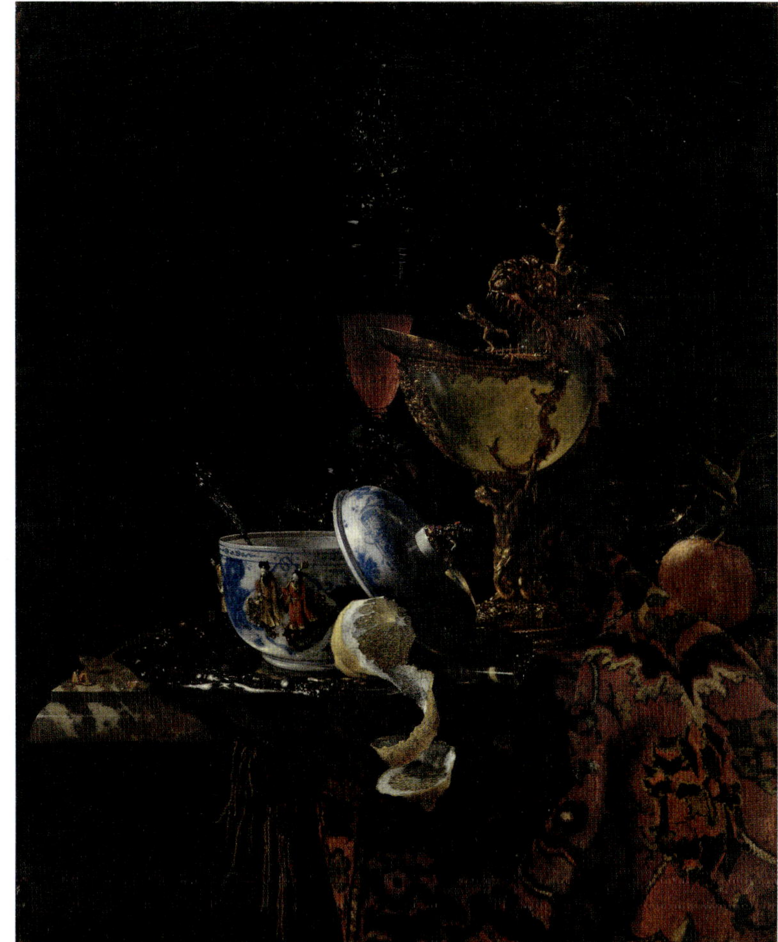

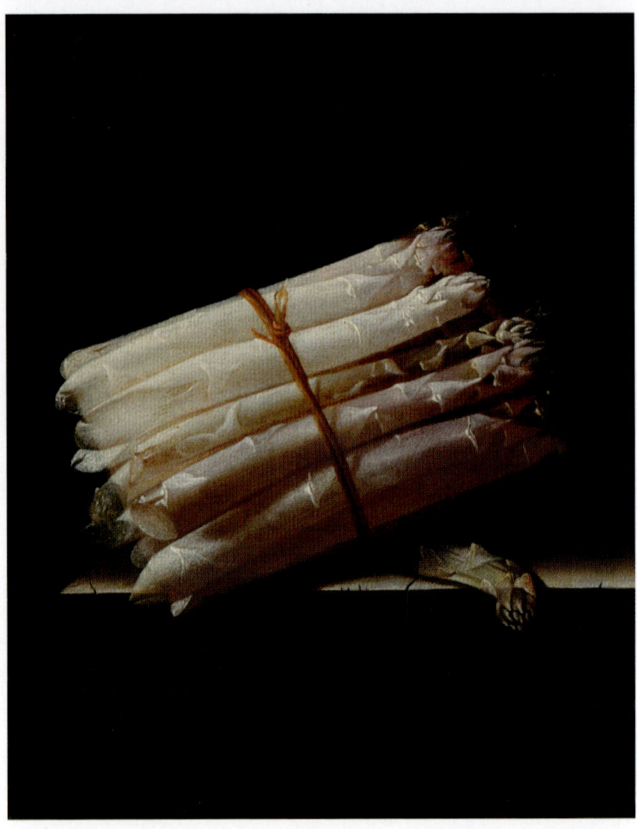

145 Adriaen Coorte,
Asparagus, 1697

sought after by collectors. At that point he benefited from the attention of Laurens J. Bol, an art historian from Zeeland who did pioneering research into the painters of the provincial capital, Middelburg. In that year, Bol published an article on Coorte that combined biographical research and the reconstruction of an oeuvre of eighty paintings with a lyrical appreciation and a dose of Zeeland chauvinism. The kernel of the new appreciation lay in what Bol later called, in the title of a small book, *The Charm of Little Things* (*Bekoring van het kleine*).

While Dutch fruit and flower still lifes piled entangled things on higher and higher or became a pretty decorative game, Coorte aspired to a purer simplicity. Not for him was the grand gesture, the verbose display of feeling; he is understatedly intimate, a tender soul, sensitive without sentimentality, secure and unwavering, out for the miracle of sheer looking.

In stages, Bol's encomium inspired a veritable Coorte cult.
Over the past half century, more books and articles have
been written about, more videos filmed and more exhibitions
held on Adriaen Coorte, with what art historian Hanneke
Grootenboer has called his 'inexplicable vastness' and
'indefinable sublimity', than any but the most famous five or so
Dutch artists. The artist and art critic Peter Jochems describes
Coorte's 'monumental simplicity', comparing his *Asparagus* to a
Crucifixion or a Head of Christ.

From the Garden, on the Forest Floor

The subject of flowers attracted artists long before the
seventeenth century. Think only of the margins in medieval
books of hours. Once again it was in the Southern Netherlands
that a feature was extracted from religious iconographies to
become a genre of its own. While that was going on, botanical
illustrators were at work, creating compendious plant atlases.
As the study of natural history advanced, a point was eventually
reached where artists had little more knowledge to contribute.
An exception was the representation of species in parts of
the world where others did not come. Flower painters were
particularly indebted to the concept of the Book of Nature, the
world as Creation, and to the moral messages that a flower
or a bouquet could convey. Foremost among them was the
transience of floral beauty, a perennial theme in poetry and
patrology, emblem books and pastoral plays. Texts of this kind
are more about human ageing than other natural processes.

The study of flower painting was enriched greatly by the
input of the biologist and art historian Sam Segal. He identified
and commented on the cultivars in 32,000 paintings, prints
and drawings, and entered into art-historical discussion on
attributions and the development of the genre. Coming from
him, a general observation that had been made by others
carries extra conviction:

*'Nature' as such does not play much of a part in flower still lifes.
The flowers are isolated from the place where they were grown.
Most of them are cultivated blooms, meaning that they came
from a garden or nursery....Furthermore, until well on into the
nineteenth century, the depicted bouquets were composed of
flowers which do not bloom at the same time.*

The artists had other priorities – in the case of this genre,
the sheer delectation that a good flower painting offers.
In his systematic spirit, Segal tabulated the specific nature
of successive periods of flower painting. In the period 1600–20,

he found twenty-eight defining features, of which a few that help us understand an early example, such as Ambrosius Bosschaert's *Vase with Flowers*, are quoted below.

Both the total composition and the bouquet are symmetrical; there is one distinct vertical main axis.

The flowers are more or less arranged in layers.

There is little overlapping of the individual flowers.

The relative proportions of the flowers are often unrealistic.

The length of stems was often not borne in mind, so that a short-stemmed flower sometimes protrudes from the top of a bouquet.

The palette is varied, and the colours are not usually distributed in accordance with a clear plan. There are a lot of colours, but few intermediate shades. Adjacent colours often contrast sharply.

Fragrant herbs play a relatively important part. In big bouquets the number of species can be in excess of a hundred.

Flowers and leaves are generally depicted in pristine state and full development.

Butterflies, caterpillars, dragonflies and grasshoppers occur, but with relatively little variation of the species.

Bosschaert brought to the Northern Netherlands a background in flower painting from Antwerp, where he was born and trained. After twenty years in Middelburg, he went on to live a peripatetic life in Amsterdam, Bergen op Zoom, Utrecht and Breda. He died in the saddle, in The Hague, where he had gone to deliver a painting.

Although some artists continued adhering to the formula of the early years, more austere variants came into fashion between 1620 and 1650. The rainbow effect was replaced by limited schemes of related colours, and the number of blooms was reduced, sometimes to a single flower. In the second half of the century more atmospheric variants came into sway, with studied and subtle transitions between hues and tints. The foremost master in this mode was the Utrecht-Antwerp artist Jan Davidsz de Heem. Illustrated is an outstanding example by one of his best pupils, Maria van Oosterwijck. The unwed daughter of a Reformed minister, Maria practised her art wherever it took her, from Delft to Leiden to Utrecht to Amsterdam to London, then back to Amsterdam. Stadholder-King William III is reported to have paid her nine hundred florins for one of her flower pieces. She also sold paintings to King Louis XIV of France, Emperor Leopold in Vienna, Grand Duke Cosimo III of Tuscany and the king of Poland. Maria retired to the village house of a minister nephew she had raised after the death of his parents. Another nice thing we know

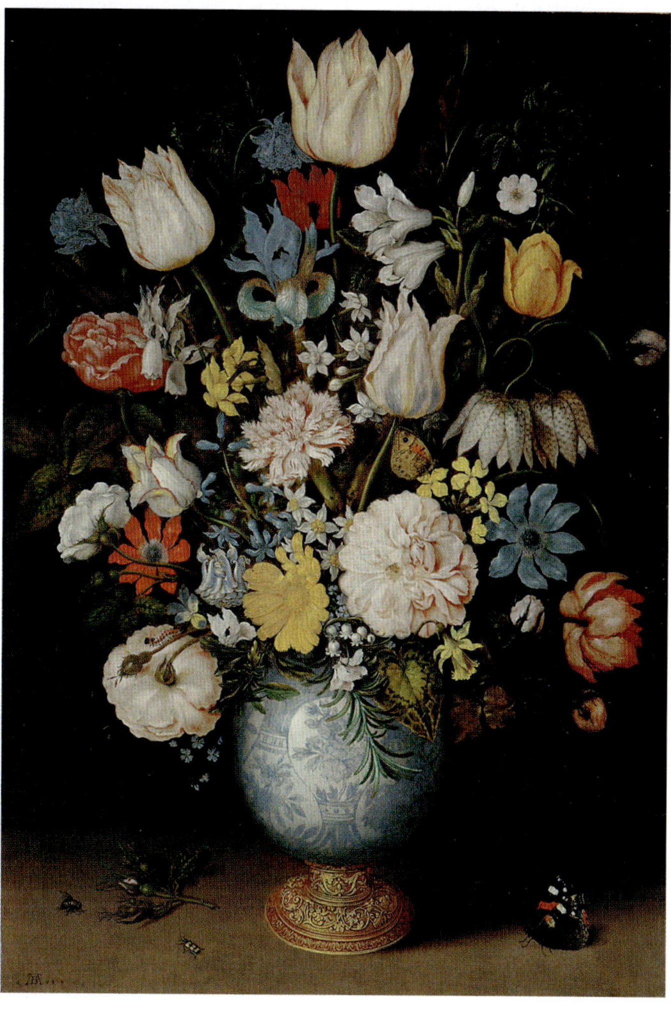

about her is that she taught flower painting to her maidservant, Geertje Pieters. Arnold Houbraken tells us that Maria was 'virtuous and more than usually devout, yet buoyant'. This has led interpreters to look for religious symbolism in her paintings, which once sought can always be found. A bouquet of sunflowers in Dresden has been related to an emblematic meaning of the flower, in which the way it turns its face to follow the sun is likened to believers who align their lives in accord with the teachings of Christ. The single grain of wheat falling over the front edge of the table in that painting also lends itself to a Christian reading, as a promise of resurrection.

In the early 1650s in Rome, Otto Marseus van Schrieck looked at what Italian artists and his Netherlandish comrades in the Bentvueghels were doing, and decided to do something else. Having traced so many genres of Dutch painting back to Flemish antecedents, we now come across an undisputedly individual Dutch invention. Arnold Houbraken wrote that Otto Marseus 'painted hardly anything besides poisonous snakes, toads and chameleons, and always (because he could depict them so well) did well by it'. Houbraken could have added lizards, butterflies, fungi, insects and other creatures that make people squirm, as in *Forest Floor Still Life with Insects and Amphibians*. In 1655, Otto Marseus exchanged the raucous company of the Bentvueghels for the distinguished Medici court in Florence, where Cosimo III, himself a collector of living things, was entranced with his work and bought one painting after another. In 1663, van Schrieck moved back to Holland and settled in Amsterdam. There he entered yet another distinguished milieu, that of the leading natural historians and philosophers in the country. The biologist and microscopist Jan Swammerdam credited van Schrieck with one of the most important discoveries of the time: that flies deposit minuscule eggs in the wounds of caterpillars. No one before the Dutch artist had observed this crucial instance of parasitism in the life cycle of the fly. The discovery provided Swammerdam with vital evidence in his lifelong campaign against the belief that lower forms of life came into being through spontaneous generation. The issue was not only biological, but also theological. To believe in contingency and chance, Swammerdam wrote, in miracles and spontaneous generation, was to deny that nature obeyed unimpeachable laws instituted by God at the creation.

Perhaps because of advances in the fieldwork of investigators, artists began worrying about the accuracy of their nature paintings. Rather than putting cut flowers in a vase, some began to depict herbs, animals and insects as if in a native environment. Their efforts did not go all the way; they too combined plants and animals, often exotic species, that never shared the same spaces. Rachel Ruysch was an exponent of this subgenre. As the granddaughter of the architect Pieter Post, the daughter of the Leiden professor of anatomy and botany Frederik Ruysch, the wife of the portrait painter Jurriaen Pool, and the court artist of Johann Wilhelm of the Palatinate (in southern Germany), she lived in a world of learning, art and high patronage. It commands respect that she pursued a major career in painting and also gave birth to ten children.

147 RIGHT Maria van Oosterwijck, *Flowers and Shells*, c. 1685
148 BELOW Otto Marseus van Schrieck, *Forest Floor Still Life with Insects and Amphibians*, 1662

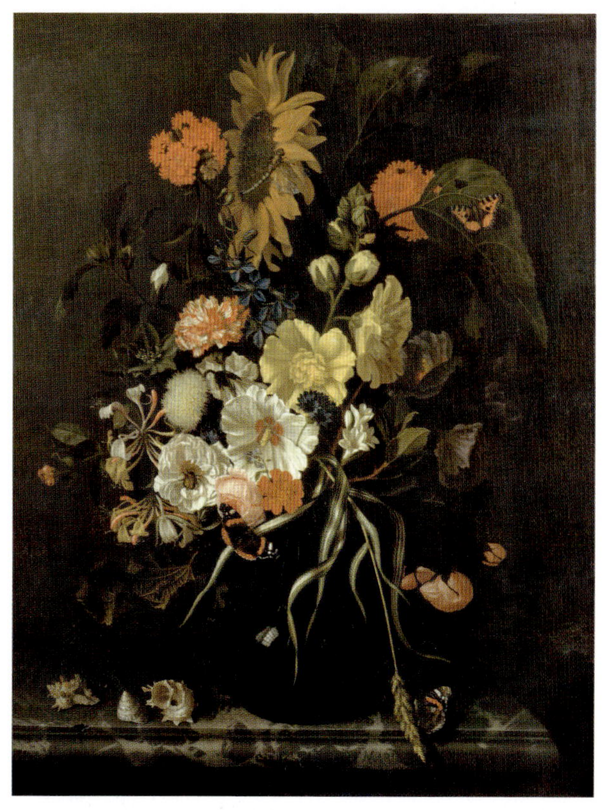

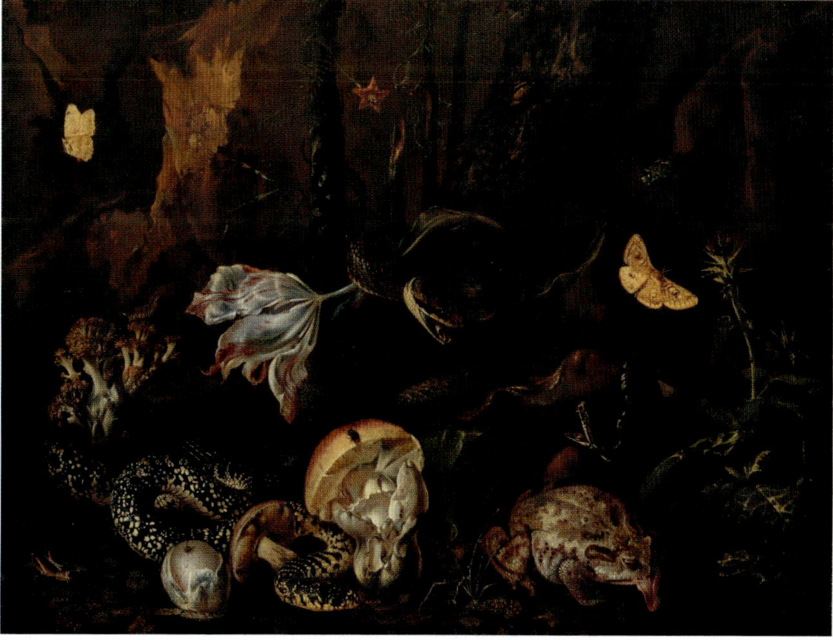

149-50

It is a pleasure, in a field where so much is left to guessing and filling in the blanks, to be able to offer a concrete identification, on the authority of Sam Segal, of the plants and animals in a painting by Rachel Ruysch in the Museum Boijmans Van Beuningen.

Animals, Birds

In the preceding pages we have seen lots of animals and birds. Just about all of these have been harnessed for work, domesticated or caged for pleasure, killed for sport or the table, or otherwise instrumentalized. One powerful impetus for looking at animals on their own was the commission to document the fauna and wild life of Brazil for Johan Maurits van Nassau. Some serious animal students, such as Otto Marseus van Schrieck and Melchior d'Hondecoeter, raised the bar for ecological accuracy, but it was Maria Sibylla Merian, who from 1699 to 1701 performed a service of documentation like none ever seen, in her artistic work in Surinam. She was the first to draw insects and other small creatures in their proper ecological niche. Because she made no paintings of that sort, she is absent from this volume, but it would be remiss not to honour her achievement.

151

In the paintings of Aelbert Cuyp and other cowscapes, the animals are seen in a picturesque pasture. But they were not there all the time. To pay for themselves during their lifespan, they had to be milked twice a day. Mostly this was done in a dark cowshed. In earlier art, we find spaces of that kind only in images of the Nativity. Roelant Savery's *Cows in a Stable, with Witches in the Corners* makes stranger use of the motif. Five cows, one of them relieving herself, share the stable with a ram, a goat, some sheep, and – what is he doing there? – a small sleeping bear. A lizard and a toad can also be made out. The back door, at which a man is playing a pipe, opens onto a farmyard and the farmer's house. The stable is painted in a circle, leaving spandrels in the corners in which spooky figures disport themselves. In the left lower corner is an ice-breathing witch on a broomstick; in the upper left, a witch riding a fire-farting animal, while she holds a forked pole with a flame. In the upper right is a serpentine knight with a fire-spewing dragon; in the lower right, a bird of prey standing between the spread-eagled legs of a woman. They undoubtedly represent the four components of a quartet, but of what we do not know.

Roelant Savery was born and trained in the Southern Netherlands, then worked in Amsterdam before entering the service of Emperor Rudolf II (1552–1612) in Prague in 1603. Under Rudolf, the visual arts were practised at a stratospheric level,

149 RIGHT Rachel Ruysch,
Tree Trunk Surrounded by Flowers, Butterflies and Animals, 1685
150 BELOW RIGHT Sam Segal, *Flowers and Nature, Netherlandish Flower Painting of Four Centuries*, 1990, p. 236.
Key: 1 Ink mushroom, *Coprinus spec.*; 2 White Water Lily (leaves), *Nymphaea alba*; 3 Arrow Head (leaves), *Sagittaria sagittifolia*; 4 Bur reed (leaves), *Sparganium erectum*; 5 Ground Ivy (leaves), *Glechoma hederacea*; 6 Fairy-ring (mushroom), *Marasmius*; 7 Oak, *Quercus robur*; 8 Herb Robert, *Geranium robertianum*; 9 Hedge Parsley, *Torilis japonica*; 10 Snapdragon, *Anthirrinum majus*; 11 Provins Rose, *Rosa x provincialis*; 12 Small Morning Glory, *Convolvulus tricolor*; 13 Reed grass, *Phalaris arundinacea var. picta*; 14 Polyanthus Narcissus, *Narcissus x intermedius*; 15 White Lily, *Lilium candidum*; 16 Opim Poppy, *Papaver somniferum*; 17 White Rose, *Rosa x alba*; 18 Sulphur Rose, *Rosa haemisphaerica*; 19 Opium Poppy, *Papaver somniferum*; 20 Wheat, *Triticum aestivum*; 21 Scentless Mayweed, *Matricaria perforata*; 22 Opium Poppy, *Papaver somniferum*; 23 mushroom, *Tricholoma?*
a Frog (2), *Rana esculenta*; b Sand Lizard (2), *Lacerta agilis*; c Garden Snail (2), *Cepaea hortensis*; d Red Admiral, *Vanessa atalanta*; e Painted Lady, *Cynthia cardui*; f Hawker (dragonfly), *Aeschna juncea*; g Stag Beetle, *Lucanus cervus*; h Damsel Fly, *Coenagrion puellum*; i Demoiselle Fly, *Ischnura elegans*; j Grasshopper, *Chortippus brunneus*

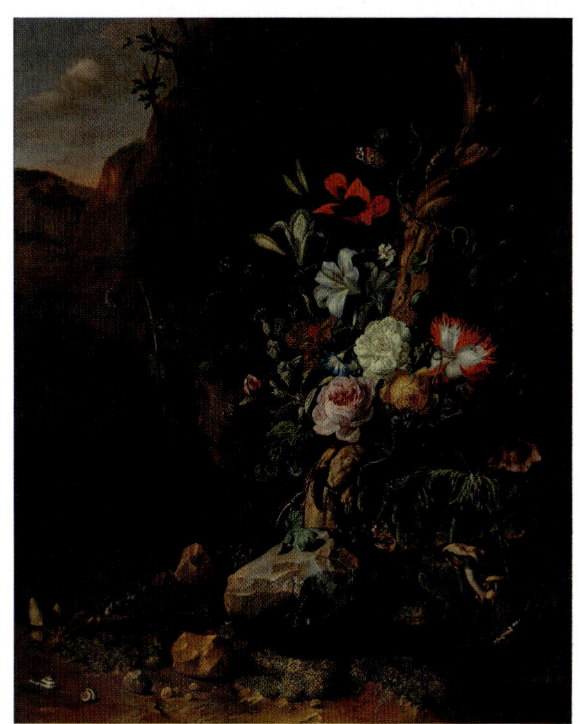

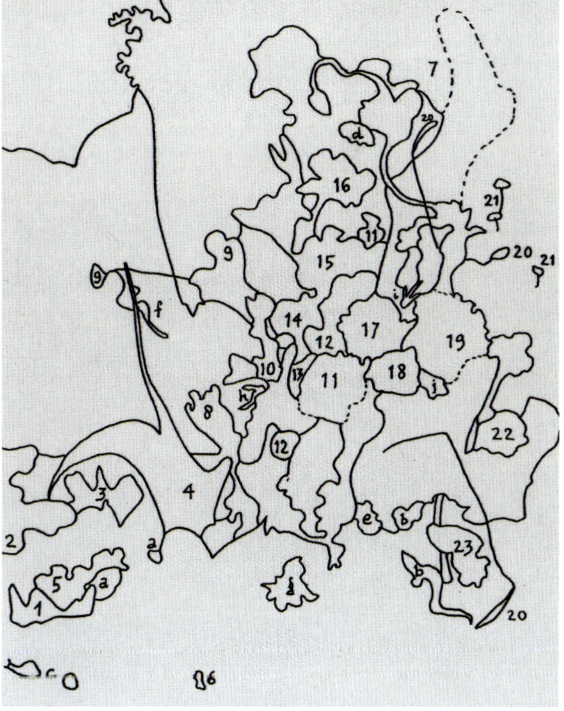

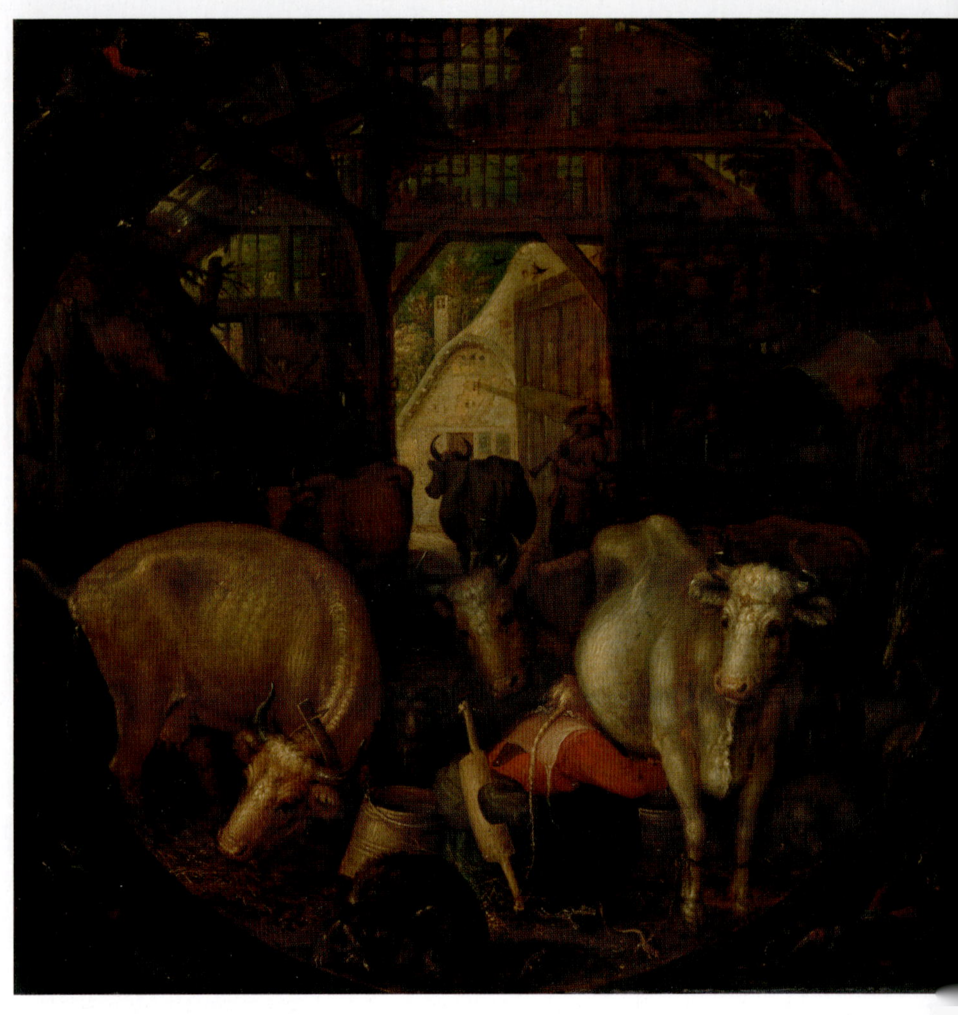

151 Roelant Savery, *Cows in a Stable, with Witches in the Corners*, 1615

sweeping from earthly delights below to esoteric mysteries above. In his conviction that all existences were united, Rudolf encouraged artists, alchemists, astronomers, humanists, curators of flora and fauna and others to collaborate. In the year of his *Cows in a Stable*, Savery travelled back and forth from Amsterdam to Prague, where Rudolf had been succeeded by his brother, Matthias. The centre of the composition, we could say, fits the Amsterdam scene, the spandrels that of Prague. The idea that a cowshed housed spectral beings would have appealed to the emperor. Once re-established in Amsterdam, and from 1619 until his death, in Utrecht, Savery remained more down to earth, though the intellectual spiritedness of Prague never left him.

152 Barnyard and menagerie could supply satirical as well as genre and occult motifs. In Cornelis Saftleven's *Satire on the Trial of Johan van Oldenbarnevelt*, twenty-four animals stand in as mocking portrayals of the judges who, in 1619, ordered the execution of the foremost politician in the Dutch Republic, the grand pensionary of Holland. Johan van Oldenbarnevelt was one of the most respected people in the country, until his side was defeated in an internal struggle over the course to be followed on the battlefield and in religious matters. In opposition to Stadholder Maurits, van Oldenbarnevelt supported the more tolerant brand of Calvinism, the Remonstrant movement (see p. 46). When the dispute came down to armed control of the cities, van Oldenbarnevelt took a step that enabled Maurits to accuse him of high treason. He was tried on these charges and, with three thousand people watching, beheaded in the government quarter of The Hague. He remained a martyr for the Remonstrant cause.

 Saftleven was probably the biggest animal-lover of all Dutch artists. The catalogue of his works lists more than two hundred drawings of animals, categorized under the headings elephants, bears, camels, monkeys, lions and tigers, foxes, deer, oxen, horses, donkeys, pigs, goats, sheep, rabbits, cats, dogs (his favourite, with fifty-seven entries) and birds. Love them though he might have, when he painted them in the guise of corrupt judges, he suffused them with nasty characteristics.

153 The member of the House of Orange who took the natural world most seriously was Stadholder-King William III. This finds expression in *The Floating Feather*, a painting made for him by Melchior d'Hondecoeter. Of the sixteen bird species depicted, several are varieties that belonged to William: the cassowary from the East Indies, the king vulture from South America, and the Asian white peacock. They are painted with a degree of ornithological accuracy that raised the bar for the

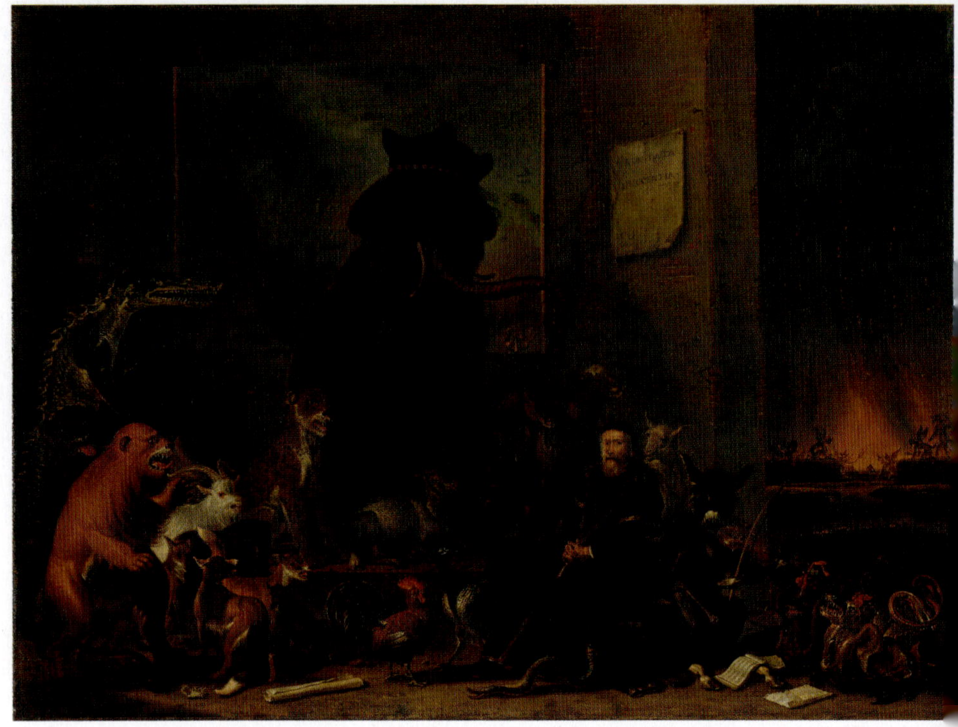

152 Cornelis Saftleven, *Satire on the Trial of Johan van Oldenbarnevelt*, 1663

depiction of birds and fowl. Commissions of this kind could not have been better extended to anyone other than Melchior d'Hondecoeter, the son and grandson of painters with fowl and poultry in their stock of motifs. Their work was rather conventional and still symbolic or allusive. Melchior did sometimes force birds to band together unnaturally to sing a concert, but he distinguished himself with a studious approach, not only to the feathers, but also the typical behaviours and stances of birds. He kept an aviary of his own for that purpose. In this he was the counterpart of Otto Marseus van Schrieck. Neither of them was a systematic thinker, but through their connections with collectors and natural philosophers, they rose above the inherited limitations of the genres in which they worked.

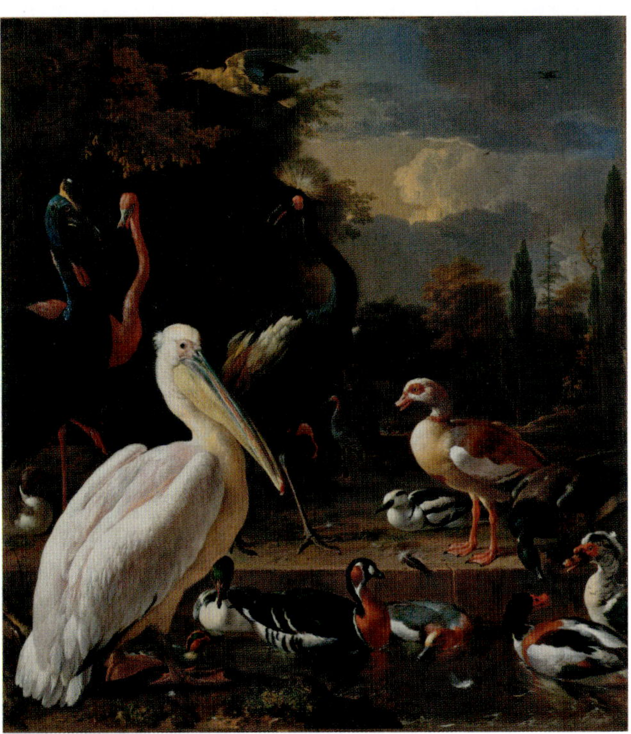

153 Melchior d'Hondecoeter, *A Pelican and Other Birds near a Pool, known as 'The Floating Feather'*, c. 1680

Optical and Conceptual Special Effects

The skills a youngster learned to become a painter could be put to more use than making easel paintings in standard genres. Most looked no further, but there were adventurous spirits eager to do more. One obvious extension was applying a knowledge of perspective to create more convincing illusions of space on a flat picture surface. Another way to push the boundaries was to deceive not the eye but the expectations, by playing with techniques or motifs in novel ways that were not explained in the handbooks. Hendrick Goltzius's *Sine Cerere et Bacchus friget Venus* is an example of the former, David Bailly's *Vanitas Still life with Portrait of a Young Painter* of the latter. This section begins, however, with an artist whose pretensions defied the natural order itself, and who nearly paid for it with his life.

The lyrics on the sheet of music in Johannes Torrentius's *Emblematic Still Life with Flagon, Glass, Jug and Bridle* read: *ER * wat bui-ten maat be-staat, int on-maats qaat ver-ghaat*. ER* has been read as an abbreviation of *Eques Rosae Crucis*, Knight of

the Rose Cross, or a fellow of the secret mystical confraternity
of the Rosicrucians, founded shortly before 1614, the date on
the painting. This is, however, inconclusive, as is everything
about the painting. The Dutch text means, 'That which exists
beyond measure, will perish in evil beyond measure', playing
on the geometrical and moral meanings of 'measure' (*maat*).
The musical notation in the lower centre is itself off beat, giving
the message an added twist. Music of another kind, Torrentius
claimed, was emanated by the painting itself. The sceptical
Constantijn Huygens wrote that the artist 'spread the
nonsensical rumour that the pigment, when rubbed by his
nearly divine hand, can be made to bring forth harmonious
sounds, something like the harmony of the spheres'. An
association that is difficult to downplay (although some do)
is that the three vessels on the shelf are the same that Roemer
Visscher illustrated in the first emblem of the second book
of *Sinnepoppen* (see p. 214). The message there – *Elck wat wils*
(To Each Their Own) – was Visscher's personal motto, giving
it that much more weight. It is the first of Plutarch's *Sayings
of the Spartans*, praising the moderation and wisdom of King
Agesilaus the Great. The bridle in the painting seems to tell us
to rein ourselves in, to allow others to have their fill.

Insofar as the image admonishes us to moderation,
Torrentius would have done well to take his own advice.
Huygens, who knew him personally and disliked him, wrote
that Torrentius gathered followers into a sect. They called
him 'Sire' and believed him when he said that the secret of
his unusual technique, which leaves no visible brushstrokes,
was revealed to him in an instant of heavenly rapture.
This pretence, seen as devil worship, formed part of the
charges brought against him in 1627 in Haarlem: blasphemy;
membership of the forbidden order of the Rosicrucians; and
creating pornography. Following hideous torture, Torrentius
was sentenced to be burned at the stake, a sentence later
reduced to twenty years imprisonment. At the request of
Charles I, he was allowed to go to England in 1629; in token of
his gratitude, he brought the painting now in the Rijksmuseum
as a gift to the king (who twenty years later was beheaded).

A mystery of another order was offered by the 67-year-
old Leiden painter, David Bailly, at the end of a long and
honourable career, mainly as a portraitist. In a painting of
composite genres, he comments on the way he has spent
his life. Above his signature and the date 1651, he paints in
professionally written capitals (his father was a calligrapher)
one of the most quoted lines in the Bible: *VANITAS. VANI[TA]
TVM. | ET. OMNIA. VANITAS* (Ecclesiastes 1:2; 'Vanity of vanities,

155

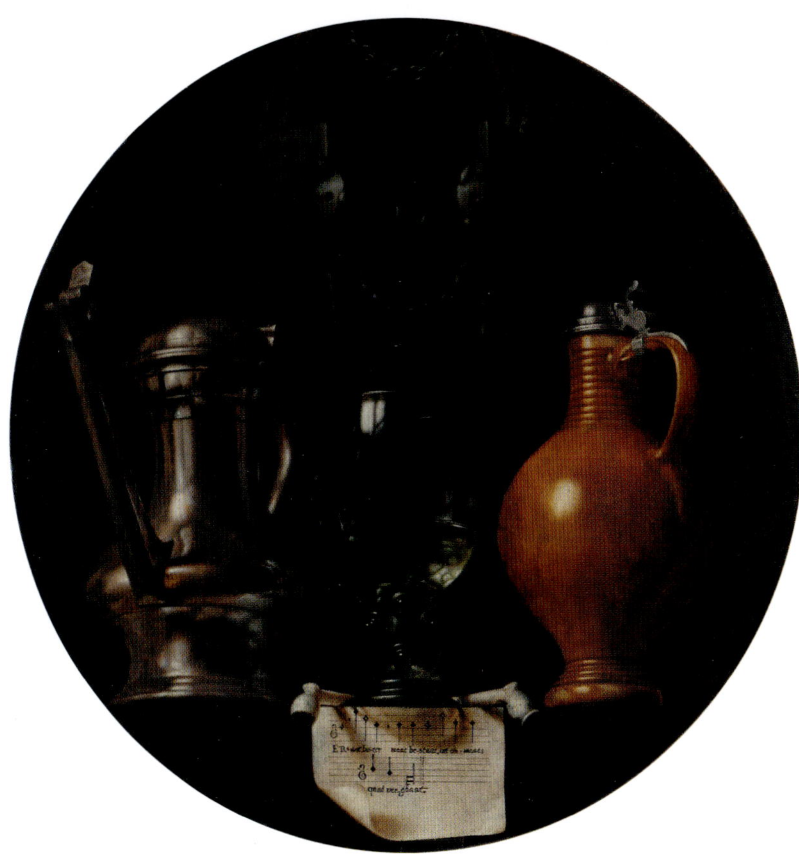

154 Johannes Torrentius, *Emblematic Still Life with Flagon, Glass, Jug and Bridle*, 1614

all is vanity'). The message was conveyed in thousands of Dutch still lifes, genre paintings and even portraits, but seldom as engrossingly as here. The painting recalls not only the profession of his father, but also a speciality he learned from his first master, Jacques de Gheyn (1565–1629), the main exponent in Dutch art of vanitas motifs. In fact, Bailly's father had once produced a print after a vanitas theme by de Gheyn. These incidental details typify the richly biographical and introspective content of one of the most intriguing paintings of the seventeenth century.

The composition offers a profusion of vanitas motifs. Standard symbols of transience are the skull, the bubbles, the cut flowers, the snuffed candle. The coins on the table stand for wealth to be spent or lost, the pearls for expensive, selfish luxuries. The meaninglessness of sensory pleasure is alluded

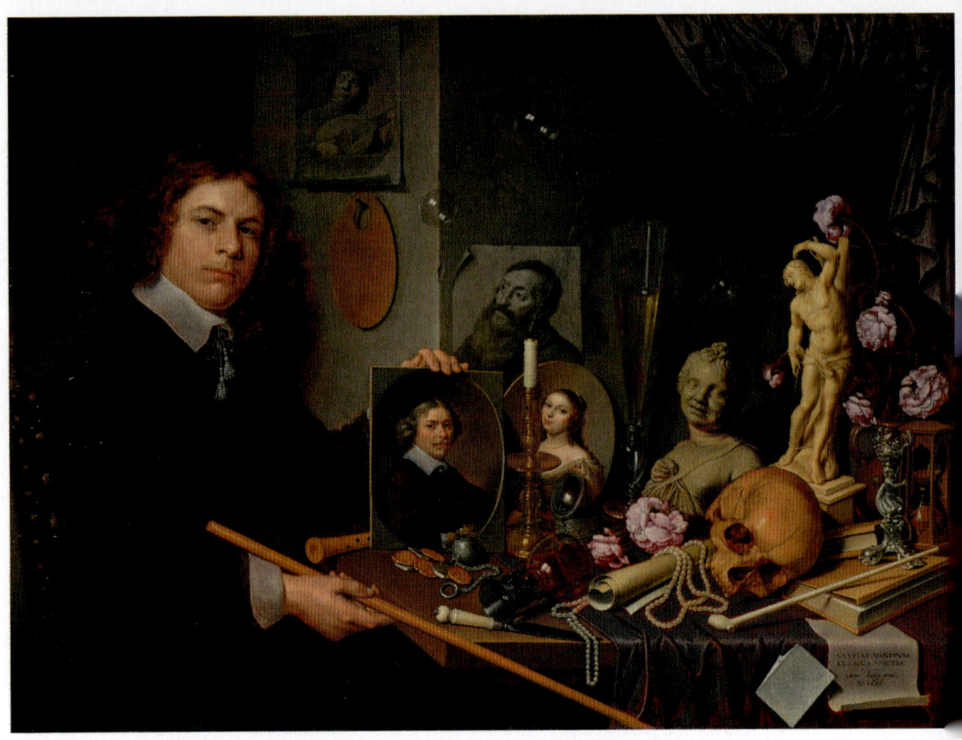

155 David Bailly, *Vanitas Still Life with Portrait of a Young Painter*, 1651

to in the pipe, the glass of wine and the pomander. Aesthetic enjoyment goes by the wayside in the recorder, the lute played by the young man in a copy (drawn by Bailly) after a painting by Frans Hals, and the works of art. The vanity of intellectual endeavour is symbolized in the book, and of artistic creation in the clean palette. Personalities are in play as well. The oval portraits are of Bailly himself and his wife, Agneta van Swanenburg. This leaves the main motif to explain. The small painting being displayed on the table is a self-portrait of Bailly. Who though is the young man holding it and looking us in the eye? Although some doubt it, those who call it a portrait of the artist as a young man are probably correct. The painting is about the inexorable passage of time, which relativizes all things. How fitting, then, that the artist would illustrate the passage of a near half-century of his own life, displaying himself as an exemplar of transience and mortality. His young self looking at his own progress to the grave. A clinching clue is that he dresses the young man in the garb worn by the old one.

The 67-year-old is imposing himself on the twenty-five-year-old, and vice versa. This is *Back to the Future* in 1651!

Vanitas still life was practised more particularly in Leiden than elsewhere, and David Bailly was its main proponent. Ingvar Bergström has suggested that the Leiden propensity to indulge in this depressing sentiment was a function of the commanding presence of a university with a Calvinist mission. Bailly had indeed lifelong links to the university, where his father had worked, and he seems to have been a dedicated Calvinist. Debating Bergström, one could say that for a Calvinist the thought that earthly things are in vain is not depressing, but an uplifting promise of everlastingness in the world to come.

Leiden was also the home of an artist who has haunted these pages. Gerard Dou was, simultaneously, one of the most typical and most exceptional of Dutch painters. A superlative realist whose fine touch was a wonder of the age, he was also praised by a contemporary biographer, Cornelis de Bie, as a conceptualist, who 'resolves the muddle that our minds benights / and elevates the intellect to otherworldly heights'. In his largest painting, he inserts himself into what looks like a typical genre scene – a mountebank hawking a fake cure – but that is also an apology for the deception that the artist himself perpetrates. The comparison is emblematized by two trees, one leafless and dead, the other green and protective. The underlying concept is found in Roemer Visscher's *Sinnepoppen*, in an image of two trees just like those in the painting, with the title 'Choice engenders anxiety'. Choosing the better of two alternatives is not always a matter-of-fact business. 'Whoever wishes to go to the choice tree, often arrives at the foul tree.' The purveyors of choice are the mountebank with his monkey and his false wares, and behind him in the window, the painter, palette in hand. Do not confuse the deceptions I create, he is saying, with those of outright deceivers.

There is a certain irony built into this choice. The quacksalver priced his pills and lotions at a level that could be afforded by the small crowd gathered outside the Leiden Blauwpoort (Blue Gate) – the hunter, farmer, maidservant and housewife (being robbed of her purse by a boy on the right edge; the group is full of significances). On the other hand, a painting by Dou, who charged a small fortune for his work, would have cost a decade or more of their earnings. Famously, Dou was on a generous retainer from the Dutch agent of the Swedish crown for the right of first refusal on his paintings, which were coveted throughout Europe, as well as at home.

In 1665, an enthusiastic Leiden collector opened a private museum housing twenty-seven of his paintings.

More irony: Dou was the first documented pupil of Rembrandt. There are paintings of about 1630 whose authorship is still in the balance between them. Soon thereafter, Rembrandt moved to the money capital of the world, Amsterdam, where he fell into penury, while Dou, staying behind to become Mr Leiden Painting, died a wealthy man. The two were also set off against each other in art writings. Rembrandt's impasto was so thick you could hang your coat on it; in a Dou the brushstrokes were not even visible. Rembrandt delved into the soul, Dou celebrated superficialities. This framing of Dou, which was unjust, had dire consequences for his reputation in the centuries when individuality was the sought-after quality in art. It became bon ton for writers on Dou to praise his technique, while letting the reader know that his art was not to their taste. Only in the 1960s, starting with an article by the Utrecht art historian Jan Emmens, was there renewed recognition of Dou's intellectual sophistication, his command of emblematic and philosophical literature, and what art historian and curator Ronni Baer has called 'the uncanny congruence of medium and message' in his paintings.

If Leiden painting was famous for vanitas subjects, Delft made its mark with perspective tours de force. Around the time Gerard Houckgeest painted his innovative interior of the Nieuwe Kerk and paving the way for the town view from a gallery by Daniël Vosmaer, Carel Fabritius created an alluring view into Delft space. We are on a terrace looking onto the choir of the Nieuwe Kerk, in the company of a man who seems to be the instrument maker who crafted the lute leaning against the wall and the violin under our nose. The optical idiosyncrasy of this small canvas calls for an explanation. All commentators agree that it was not meant to be seen in as distorted a form as it appears. The most widely accepted explanation is that it was made to be installed on a hemicylindrical panel in a perspective box. Viewed through a peephole, the apparent distortions are corrected. Although this is the only known painting of its kind by Fabritius, it was for his excellence in perspective that he was praised by Samuel van Hoogstraten ('in which he performed wonders'), and by Arnold Houbraken ('famous for being the best in his time as a painter of perspective, as well as a good portraitist').

Samuel van Hoogstraten praised Fabritius for his perspective 'wonders' as a past master of the art himself. If any Dutch painter felt that his training, even if it came from Rembrandt, did not exhaust the possibilities he saw in himself, it was he.

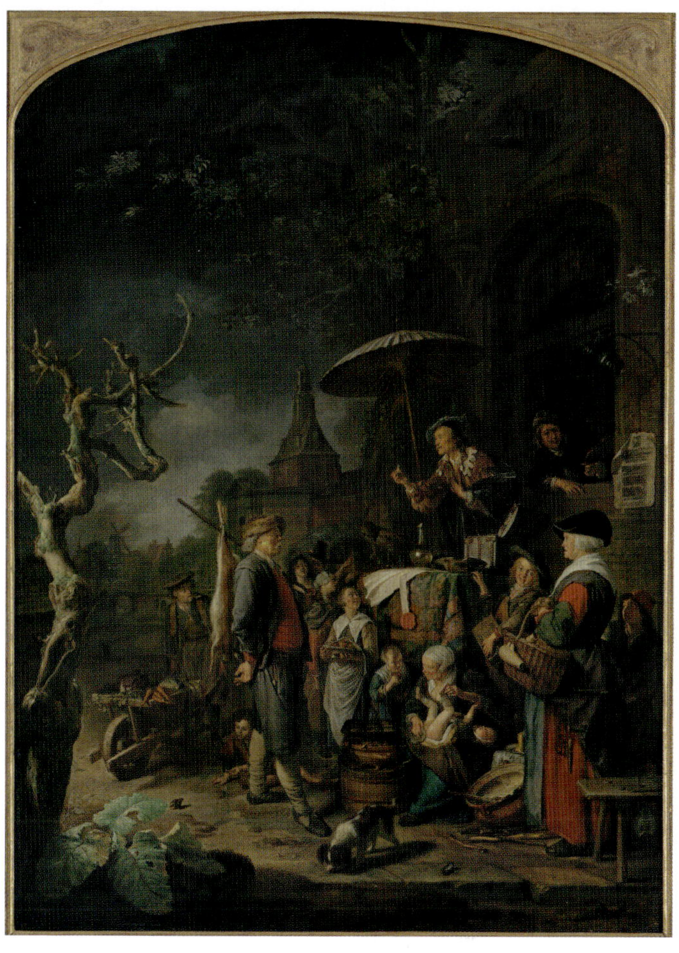

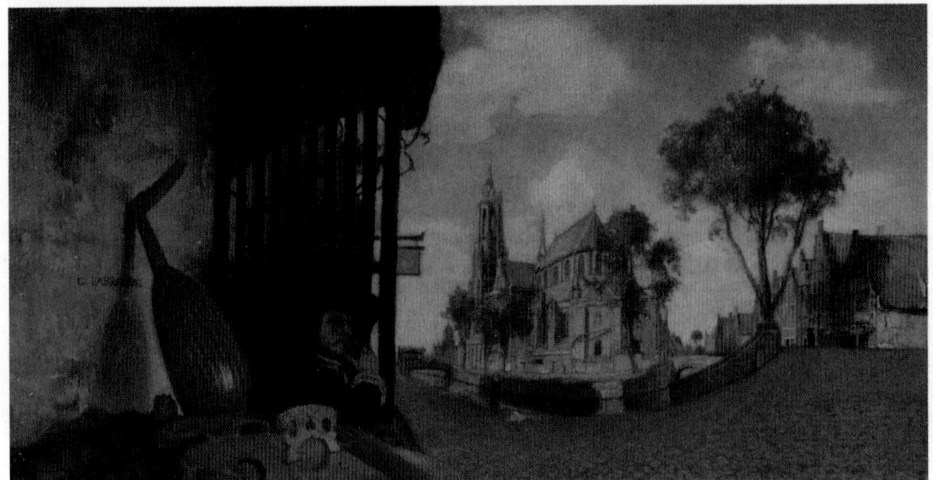

157 Carel Fabritius, *View in Delft, with Music Shop*, 1652

Not only did he write the best book on Dutch painting since van Mander's some seventy-five years earlier, as well as stage plays and poetry, he also pushed the boundaries of artistic possibilities in witty and challenging ways. The highpoint was his peepshow with the interior of a Dutch house. He wrote of this kind of object: 'Through mastery of this science [of perspective] one can also make the amazing perspective cabinet, which, if painted properly and knowledgably, can make a figure no taller than a finger look life-size.' Of the six extant Dutch perspective cabinets, all made in the third quarter of the seventeenth century, van Hoogstraten's is the most complete and complex, and the best painted. The main feature is a household salon with a black-and-white marble floor. We view it and its adjoining spaces on five surfaces. The front is open, giving a view with anamorphic distortions. These resolve themselves when you look through one of the peepholes on either side. From the right side the view is extended into the room of the man of the household, with attributes of his position and learning. From the left one looks into the bedroom. The outsides are painted with putti enacting what van Hoogstraten calls the 'Three desires [that] are the stimuli to learn the arts: for love, for profit and to be respected by everyone'. On the top is a recumbent nude woman accompanied by Eros, in a severely anamorphic image. The interior is adorned with paintings and household appurtenances that also call for explanation.

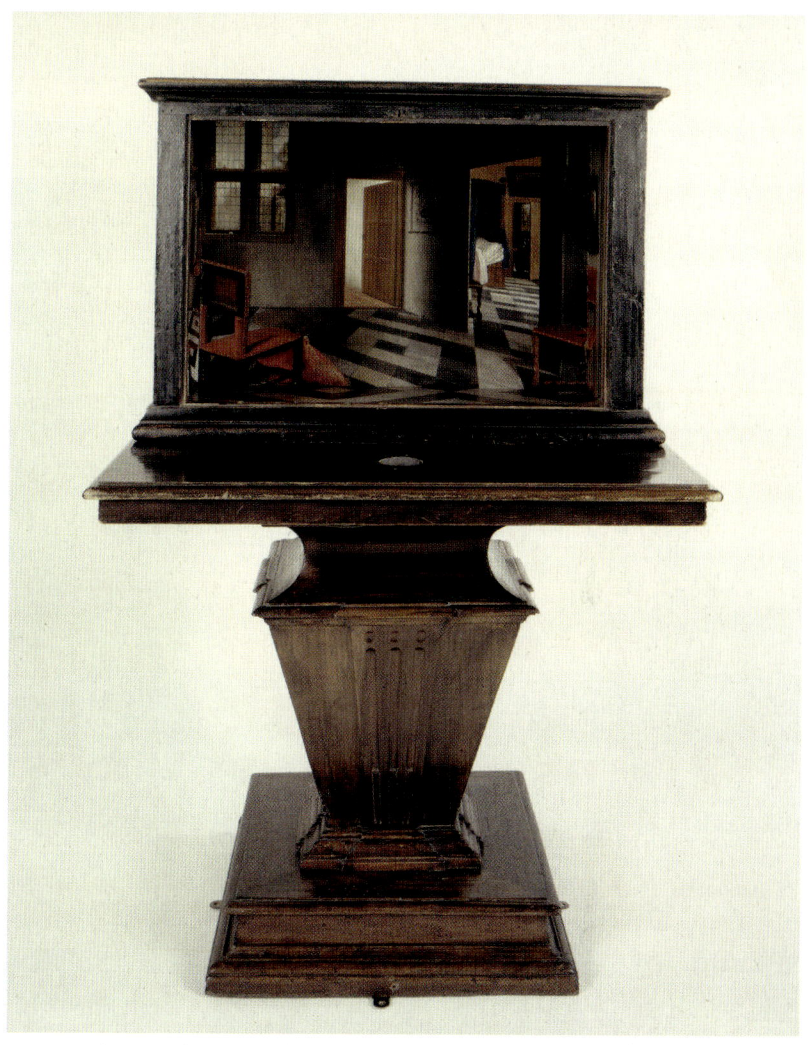

158 Samuel van Hoogstraten, *A Perspective Box with Views of the Interior of a Dutch House*, c. 1655–60

That explanation may have been written up by Samuel van Hoogstraten himself, in a lost manuscript. The treatise from which we quote, *Introduction to the Academy of Painting*, has a subtitle: *The Visible World*. It was to be accompanied by a second volume, *The Invisible World*, the manuscript of which was owned by van Hoogstraten's pupil, Arnold Houbraken, before it disappeared. Those invisible values were likely to be moral lessons. Of the competing interpretations of this

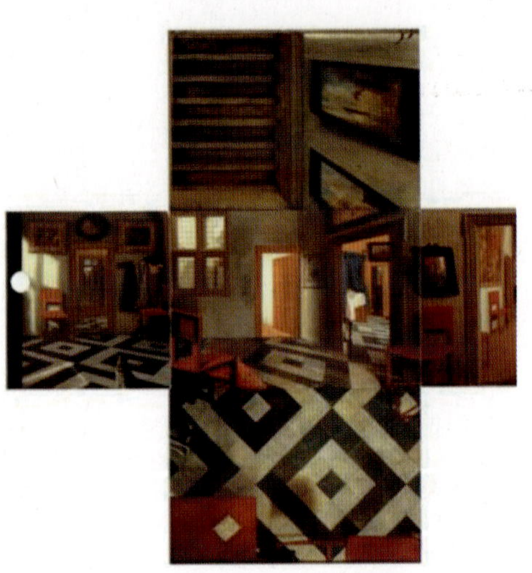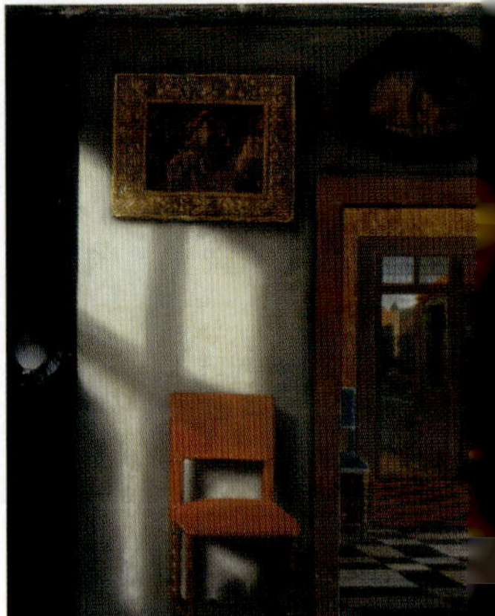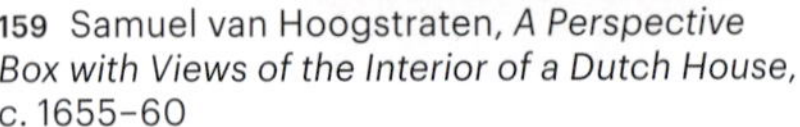

159 Samuel van Hoogstraten, *A Perspective Box with Views of the Interior of a Dutch House,* c. 1655–60

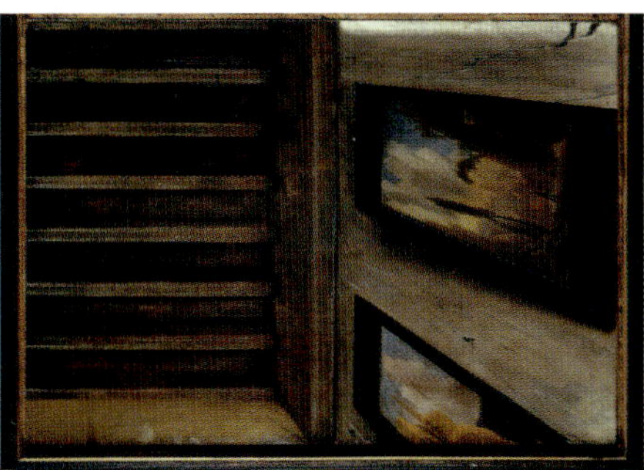

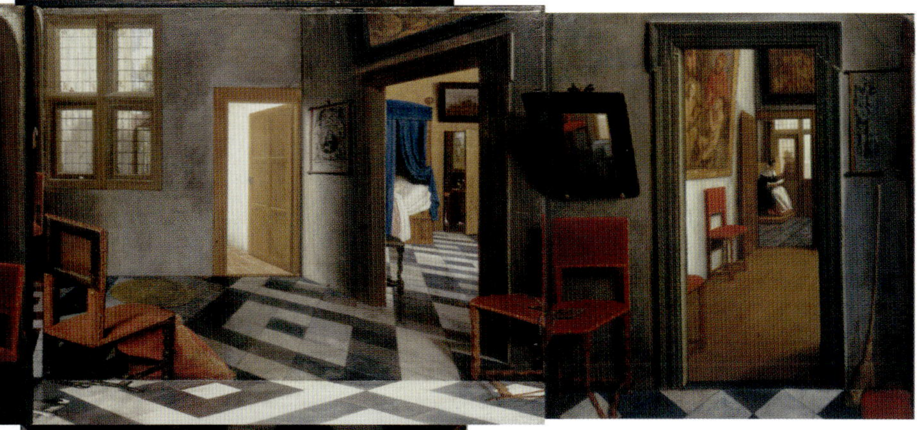

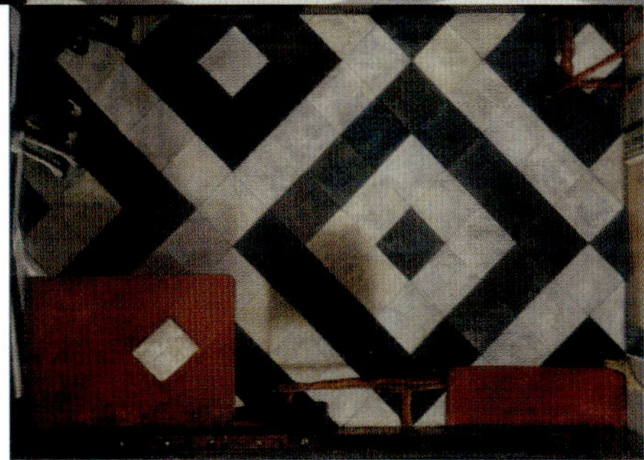

complex object, the most appealing is the most romantic one. Herman Colenbrander finds the clue in the coats of arms of the artist and Sara van Balen, whom he married in 1656. He links them to images within the house of lovemaking, childbirth and birth rituals, the education of children, as well as proud domesticity, to arrive at this conclusion: 'It is my contention that the perspective box was van Hoogstraten's marriage gift to his bride.'

Chapter 9
Afterword on Attribution

In the above, I have captioned and discussed some 150 paintings under the name of an individual artist. This carries with it the assumption that the painting was conceived and executed by a single creative mind and capable hand, and that we can identify, enjoy and study it as an expression of a unique artistic personality. However, this assumption is not always backed up by the facts. Consider this case: Daniël Vosmaer (see p. 79), a Delft artist born and bred, the grandson of a painter, son of a goldsmith and brother of two other painters, was a friend of Carel Fabritius (see pp. 38, 238), with whom he and his brother Nicolaes collaborated. One of their joint efforts gave rise to a dispute about the relative share of the three, which affected the appraisal of the painting. The notarial document concerned, dated 13 July 1666, was correctly paraphrased in an article of 1932 by Wilhelm Valentiner. At issue was the relative value of the contribution of three painters in

a large representation of land and sea which Carel had executed with two other Delft painters, Daniël and Nicolaes Vosmaer. It appears that the two brothers, who had received the order for the composition, were not getting on very well with it. They begged Carel to lay the painting on for them, or, as the document says, to draw it in with chalk; then Daniël executed the landscape, Nicolaes Vosmaer the seascape, which presumably did not turn out so well; at the end, Fabritius went over the entire painting, which only in this way received unity and life. Our artist [Fabritius] received a certain share in the painting, the size of which was later quarrelled over.

The painting has not been identified, but if it emerged, could we attribute it properly? And do we know how common it was

that paintings underwent such a complicated genesis or bore
the autograph signature of someone other than the maker?
In 1629 Johannes Porcellis, in buying a house from the weaker
seascape painter Cornelis Stoter, paid off part of the sum with
the production of fourteen days of his work, leaving Stoter
free to sell them as his own. Publishing the document in 1913,
Abraham Bredius wrote: 'The more details the archives reveal
about our old painters, the trickier it becomes for the art critic,
and the more cautious we should be in our judgments.' This
sensible warning to himself did not save Bredius from falling
prey to deliberate fraud in 1937, when in an influential article
he praised Han van Meegeren's infamous Vermeer forgery,
The Supper at Emmaus, as not merely a masterpiece, but as
'*the* masterpiece of Johannes Vermeer of Delft'.

The 'art critic' might also take to heart a stunning thought
on the matter by the Leiden artist, Philips Angel, in his address
to the Leiden painters' guild on St Luke's Day, 1641, published
the next year:

*Shall we paint so that everyone can see that a work was made by
this or that master? No, absolutely not. If...the hand is identifiable,
then the master is putting in rather too much of his own. On the
other hand, if he follows nature so closely that his work approaches
real life, without allowing the determination of the manner of the
master who made it – that artist deserves praise and honour and
should be regarded more highly than others.*

That has not kept connoisseurs from insisting on putting a
name to a manner, even when a painter has lived up to Angel's
ideal.

A famous case of attributional uncertainty is a woman's
portrait in the Rijksmuseum, of evidently high quality. In 1976,
with the appearance of a complete catalogue of the paintings in
the Rijksmuseum, opinion since 1880 broke down thus:

Rembrandt: 7
Rembrandt?: 1
Bol: 11
Bol?: 1
Backer?: 1

The Rijksmuseum and the RKD currently label the painting as
by Ferdinand Bol. This opinion would carry more force if the
attribution to Bol had been accepted by Albert Blankert, the
leading authority on the master. But he turned the possibility
down pointedly. In his 1982 monograph on Bol, he endorsed the
attribution to Rembrandt, with the possible participation of
workshop assistants.

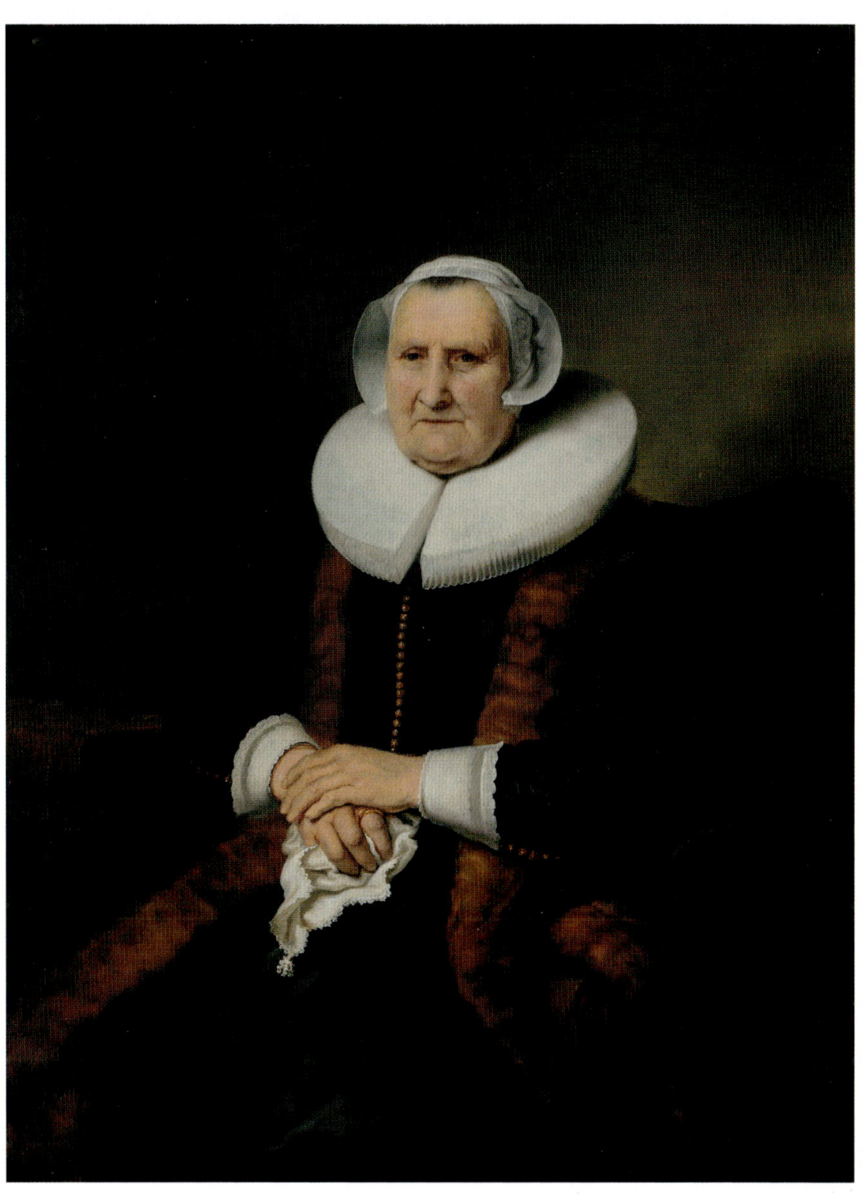

160 Rembrandt? Ferdinand Bol? *Portrait of an Old Woman, possibly Elisabeth Bas,* c. 1640–45

This situation tells us that the confident conviction of the connoisseur, as described by one of the greatest, Max J. Friedländer, that 'the artist…at bottom remains the same, and…something which cannot be lost reveals itself in his every expression' is open to question. The tools presently available for the determination of authorship and quality fail to deliver unassailable proof when connoisseurs disagree. Other tools are in development, and probably someday we will be able to distinguish individual hands at a microscopic, perhaps even an atomic level, or via artificial intelligence by a multitude of features. When that day comes, we will be able to say which parts of that seascape were by Fabritius and which by one of the Vosmaer brothers. At that point, consensus among specialists will no longer be the last word in attributionism. We will finally then be able to test hypotheses concerning studio participation and unfailingly distinguish originals from copies and forgeries. This will probably subvert much received opinion, and I look forward to it.

At the time, it mattered to buyers whether a painting was by a known master or not – but not as much as it has come to matter since. In his exhaustive research on art auctions in Amsterdam, Michael Montias found that unattributed landscapes averaged 9.73 guilders in appraised value and those by known masters 53.70 – so, 5½ to one. The figures for still lifes are 13.55 and 45.41 guilders respectively, about 3½ to one. This modest differential is dwarfed today, when a perfectly good unattributed Dutch painting may go for under five thousand euros, while top pieces by established masters start at five million. Authorship has been fetishized to a degree that has blinded us to the value attached to paintings by their original audience.

My hope in presenting the Dutch paintings in this book is that readers will admire and enjoy them not for the reputation of their makers or of 'Dutch Painting', but for their intrinsic interest; their seldom rivalled level of craftsmanship; the knowledge and wit they convey; their fortunes in culture, collecting and scholarship; the personal associations some of them will have for each of you; and for their charm. I leave it to Melchior d'Hondecoeter to sum up, with a flourish and a quip, some of what has been said and shown.

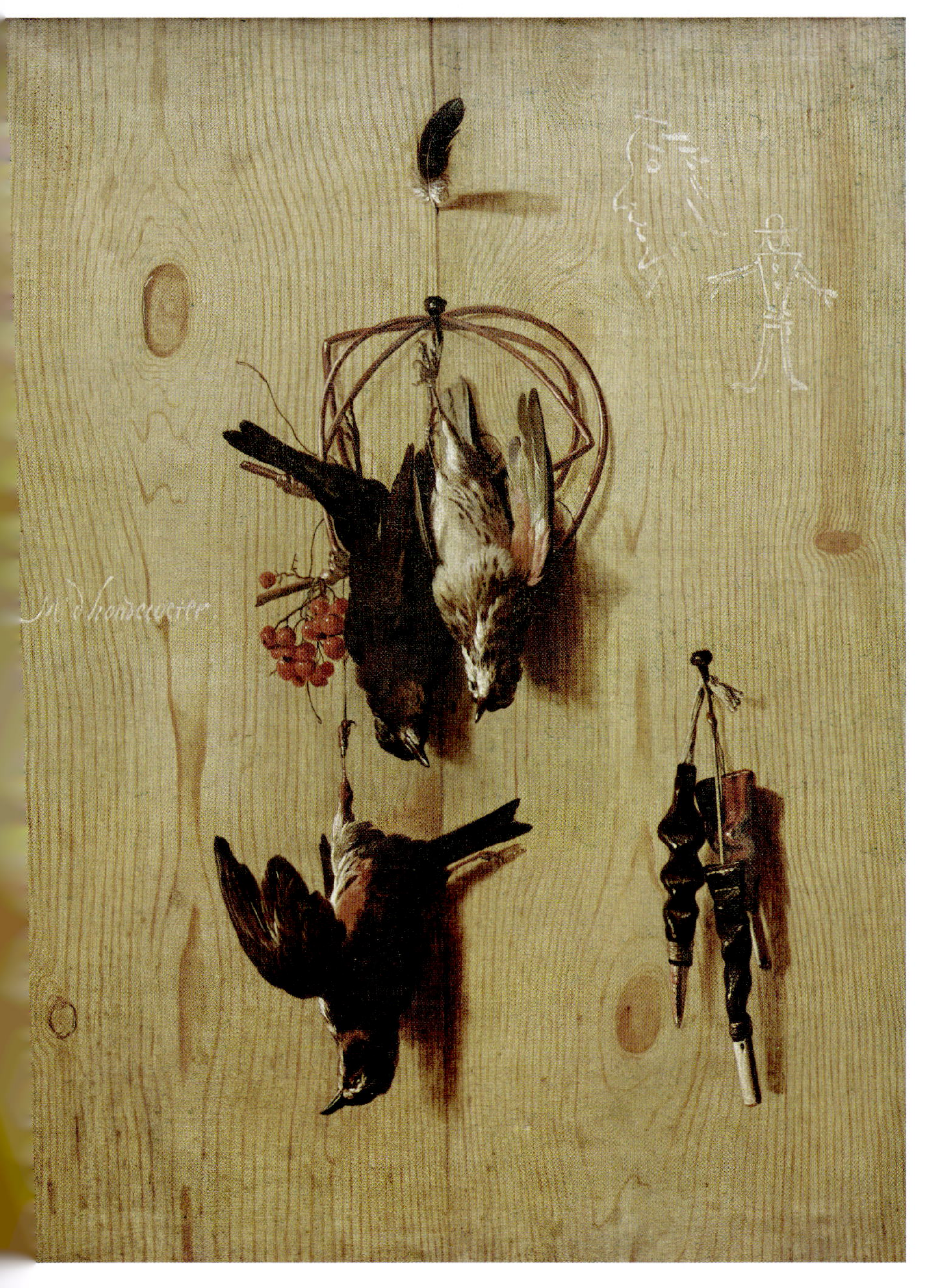

161 Melchior d'Hondecoeter, *Trompe l'oeil with Three Dead Thrushes, Currants and Decoy Flutes Hung on a Wooden Plank*, c. 1670

References

Rather than a bibliography, I provide here references to the main sources consulted for this volume, section by section. Each title is listed only once, although I may have drawn on it elsewhere as well. Museum exhibitions are given by venue, with credit to the main curator.

For museum information on the paintings illustrated, a search action including the inventory number will mostly take you straight to the entry.

Historical Sources

Ampzing, Samuel, *Beschryvinge ende lof der stad Haerlem in Holland*, Haarlem 1628. Available online

Angel, Philips, *Lof der schilder-konst*, Leiden 1642. Available online

Bie, Cornelis de, *Het gulden cabinet van de edel vrij schilder const, inhoudende den lof vande vermarste schilders, architecte, beldthowers ende plaetsnijders van deze eeuw*, Antwerp 1661. Available online

Hoogstraten, Samuel van, *Inleyding tot de hooge schoole der schilderkonst: anders de zichtbaere werelt*, Rotterdam 1678. Available online

–, *Samuel van Hoogstraten's Introduction to the Academy of Painting; or, The Visible World*, Celeste Brusati (ed.), Jaap Jacobs (trans.), Los Angeles 2021

Houbraken, Arnold, *De groote schouburgh der Nederlantsche konstschilders en schilderessen*, 3 vols., Amsterdam 1718–21. Available online

Houbraken Translated. Arnold Houbraken's Great Theatre of the Netherlandish Painters and Paintresses, Hendrik J. Horn and Rieke van Leeuwen (trans., eds.). Online at the website of RKD – Netherlands Institute for Art History

Huygens, Constantijn, *Mijn leven, verteld aan mijn kinderen*, Frans Blom (ed., trans.), 2 vols., Amsterdam 2003

Lairesse, Gerard de, *A Treatise on the Art of Painting in All Its Branches...*, revised, corrected, and accompanied with an essay by W.M. Craig, 2 vols., London 1817, a translation of de Lairesse's *Groot schilderboek waar in de schilderkunst in al haar deelen grondig werd onderweezen, ook door Redeneeringen en Prentverbeeldingen verklaard*, Amsterdam 1707. Available online. [Translated quotations revised by Gary Schwartz]

Mander, Karel van, *Den grondt der edel vrij schilder-const*, 2 vols., Hessel Miedema, ed., Utrecht 1973

–, *The Lives of the Illustrious Netherlandish and German Painters*, Hessel Miedema (ed.), Michael Hoyle (trans.), 6 vols., Doornspijk 1994–99

–, *Het schilder-boeck: waer in voor eerst de leerlustighe Iueght den grondt der edel vry schilderconst in verscheyden deelen wort voorghedraghen*, Haarlem 1604. Available online

Melion, Walter, *Karel van Mander and his Foundation of the Noble, Free Art of Painting: First English Edition, with Translation and Commentary*, Leiden/Boston 2023

Orlers, I.I. [Jan], *Beschrijvinge der stadt Leyden, inhoudende 't begin, den voortgang, ende den wasdom der selver:...*, 2d ed., Leiden 1642. Available online

Ripa, Cesare, *Iconologia of uytbeeldinge des verstands*, Amsterdam [1641]. Translated from *Iconologia*, Rome 1593. Available online

Visscher, Roemer, *Sinnepoppen*, Amsterdam 1614. Available online

Wagenaar, Jan, *Amsterdam in zyne opkomst, aanwas, geschiedenissen, voorregten, koophandel, ...*, 4 vols., Amsterdam 1760–1802. Available online

Multi-essay Publications

Art in History, History in Art: Studies in Seventeenth-century Dutch Culture, David Freedberg and Jan de Vries (eds.), Santa Monica and Chicago 1992. Proceedings of a symposium held at the Getty Center for the History of Art and the Humanities, Santa Monica, in 1987. Cited as *Art in History, History in Art*. Online at the website of the Getty Research Institute

Blankert, Albert, *Selected Writings on Dutch Painting: Rembrandt, Van Beke, Vermeer and*

Others, with a Foreword by John Walsh, Zwolle 2004. Cited as Blankert, Albert, *Selected Writings*

DaCosta Kaufmann, Thomas and Michael North (eds.), *Mediating Netherlandish Art and Material Culture in Asia*, Amsterdam 2014

Face Book: Studies on Dutch and Flemish Portraiture of the 16th–18th Centuries. Liber Amicorum Presented to Rudolf E.O. Ekkart on the Occasion of his 65th Birthday, Leiden 2012. Cited as *Face Book*

Preface

Knuttel Wzn, G., 'Het Nederlandsche karakter in de beeldende kunst', in *De Nederlandsche Geest*, H. Edelman (ed.), Naarden 1941, pp. 205–25

Schwartz, Gary, 'Art in History', in *Art in History, History in Art*, pp. 7–16. Online at the website of the Getty Research Institute

Chapter 1
Making an Art World
Painters of the Seventeen Provinces

Rotterdam (Museum Boijmans Van Beuningen) and Frankfurt (Städelsches Kunstinstitut), exh. cat. *Dutch Classicism in Seventeenth-century Painting*, Albert Blankert, Beverly Jackson (trans.), Rotterdam 1999. Focused on a strain in Dutch painting that many felt was 'unDutch'.

Utrecht (Centraal Museum), exh. cat. *Nederlandse 17e eeuwse Italianiserende landschapschilders*, Albert Blankert (uncredited author), Utrecht 1965. The first survey of a major subgenre in Dutch landscape painting, depicting Mediterranean topographies.

Washington (National Gallery of Art), Detroit (Detroit Institute of Arts) and Amsterdam (Rijksmuseum), exh. cat. *Gods, Saints and Heroes: Dutch Painting in the Age of Rembrandt*, Albert Blankert and Arthur Wheelock, 1980/81. A breakthrough exhibition of paintings in the genre that in its time was the most highly regarded and expensive of all, in later centuries to be devalued in favour of more vernacular subjects.

Migration from South to North

Amsterdam (Koninklijk Paleis), exh. cat. *Het kunstbedrijf van de familie Vingboons: Schilders, architecten en kaartmakers in de gouden eeuw*, Jacobine E. Huisken and Friso Lammertse, Maarssen/The Hague 1989. On the many cultural activities of the Vingboons 'art factory'.

Briels, Jan, *Vlaamse schilders in de Noordelijke Nederlanden in het begin van de Gouden Eeuw*, Antwerp 1987. A pioneering study of the Flemish immigrants who gave shape to what we think of as Dutch art.

Groenendijk, Pieter, *Beknopt biografisch lexicon van Zuid- en Noord-Nederlandse schilders, graveurs, glasschilders, tapijtwevers et cetera van ca. 1350 tot ca. 1720*, Utrecht 2008. The most complete, concise biographical lexicon in print of Dutch and Flemish artists in all fields.

Klippel, Carolien De, 'Adriaen Brouwer, Portrait Painter: New Identifications and an Iconographic Novelty', *Simiolus: Netherlands Quarterly for the History of Art*, vol. 30, 2003, pp. 196–216. Available on JSTOR. Good insights into Brouwer's painting of himself and his Dutch and Flemish buddies, here identified.

Oudenaarde (MOU–Museum van Oudenaarde en de Vlaamse Ardennen), exh. cat. *Adriaen Brouwer, meester van emoties*, Karolien Lichtert, 2018. The first exhibition devoted to this important master, held in his birthplace.

Shaping a Canon, Setting Terms: Karel van Mander
See under Historical Sources

Becoming a Painter: The Studio

Amsterdam (Rijksmuseum), San Francisco (Fine Arts Museum of San Francisco) and Hartford (Wadsworth Atheneum), exh. cat. *Michael Sweerts (1618–1664)*, Guido Jansen and Peter C. Sutton, Zwolle 2002

Blankert, Albert, 'Michael Sweerts, Painter of Silence and Secrecy', Diane Webb (trans.), in *Selected Writings*, pp. 287–96

Miedema, Hessel, *De archiefbescheiden van het St Lukasgilde te Haarlem*, 2 vols., Alphen aan den Rijn 1980. Complete transcriptions of the best preserved archive of a painters' guild.

Wetering, Ernst van de, *Rembrandt: The Painter at Work*, Amsterdam 1997. Research into studio practice in connection with Rembrandt's technique.

Woude, Ad van der, 'The Volume and Value of Paintings in Holland at the Time of the Dutch Republic', in *Art in History, History in Art*, pp. 285–329. An investigation by an economic historian that upended conventional assumptions about the size and shape of painting production in the Netherlands.

Materials and Manufacture

Hendriks, Ella, 'Haarlem Studio Practice', in *Painting in Haarlem, 1500–1850: The Collection of the Frans Hals Museum*, Neeltje Köhler, Ghent 2006, pp. 65–96. Systematic discussion that is valid for all of the Netherlands, not only Haarlem.

Taylor, Paul, 'The Concept of Houding in Dutch Art Theory', *Journal of the Warburg and Courtauld Institutes*, vol. 55, 1992, pp. 210–32. Available on JSTOR. Shows how much can be learned from the careful interrogation of a common but unstudied term in art writings.

Drawings, Prints, Paintings

Amsterdam (Rijksmuseum), exh. cat. *The Glory of the Golden Age: Dutch Art of the 17th Century. Painting, Sculpture and Decorative Art*, Judikje Kiers and Fieke Tissink, Zwolle 2000

Amsterdam (Rijksmuseum) and New York (Metropolitan Museum of Art), exh. cat. *Hercules Segers, Painter, Etcher*, 2 vols., Huigen Leeflang and Pieter Roelofs, 2016

The Europeanness of Dutch Art

Gerson, Horst, *Ausbreitung und Nachwirkung der holländischen Malerei des 17. Jahrhunderts*, Haarlem 1942. A reprint with an introduction by B.W. Meijer and additional illustrations was published in Amsterdam in 1983. The latter online on the website of RKD – Netherlands Institute for Art History.

Gerson Digital. On the basis of Horst Gerson, *Ausbreitung*, the RKD – Netherlands Institute for Art History has an ongoing project called Gerson Digital, with sections on the countries where Dutch painters worked.

Frames and Contexts

Amsterdam (Rijksmuseum), exh. cat. *Framing in the Golden Age: Picture and Frame in 17th-century Holland*, Pieter J.J. van Thiel and C.J. de Bruyn Kops, Andrew P. McCormick (trans.), Zwolle 1995

Eikema Hommes, Margriet, *De Oranjezaal in Huis ten Bosch: een zaal uit loutere liefde*, Zwolle 2013. The most complete publication on a key architectural-painting-political ensemble.

Modes

Schwartz, Gary, *Rembrandt's Universe: His Art, His Life, His World*, London 2006

The Diversity of Dutch Art, by Decade

1601–10

Blankert, Albert, 'Hendrick Avercamp', in: *Selected Writings*, pp. 127–46

Welcker, Clara J., *Hendrick Avercamp 1585–1634 bijgenaamd 'De stomme van Campen' en Barent Avercamp 1612–1679, 'schilders tot Campen'*, Zwolle 1933

1611–20

Franits, Wayne, *Dutch Seventeenth-Century Genre Painting, its Stylistic and Thematic Evolution*, New Haven/London 2004

1621–30

Dudok van Heel, S.A.C., 'Een minne met een kindje door Frans Hals', *Jaarboek van het Centraal Bureau voor Genealogie en het Iconografisch Bureau*, vol. 29, 1975, pp. 146–59. Identification of the woman and child in a Frans Hals portrait.

Slive, Seymour, *Frans Hals*, 3 vols., London 1970

1631–40

Broos, Ben and Ariane van Suchtelen, *Portraits in the Mauritshuis, 1430–1790*, The Hague/Zwolle 2004

Duparc, Frederik, *Uit de doeken: een biografie van het Mauritshuis*, Amsterdam 2015. Tells the inside story of how the Mauritshuis acquired Jacob van Campen's portrait of Constantijn Huygens and his wife.

1641–50

Gent, Judith van, *Bartholomeus van der Helst: Een studie naar zijn leven en werk*, Zwolle 2011

1651–60

Broos, Ben, *Meesterwerken in het Mauritshuis*, The Hague 1987

1661–70

Smith, John, *A Catalogue Raisonné of the Works of the Most Eminent Dutch, Flemish, and French Painters, …*, vol. 7, *The Life and Works of Rembrandt van Rhyn*, London 1836. Available online

1671–80

Robinson, M.S., *Van de Velde: A Catalogue of the Paintings of the Elder and Younger Willem van de Velde*, 2 vols., Greenwich 1990

1681–90

Moser, Benjamin, *The Upside-down World: Meetings with the Dutch Masters*, New York 2023. A present-day encounter with Meindert Hobbema's masterpiece.

1691–1700

Gaehtgens, Barbara, *Adriaen van der Werff, 1659–1722*, Munich 1987

Chapter 2
Patronage and the Market
Protestant Churches – Paintings For and Of
The Hague (Mauritshuis), exh. cat. *A Choice Collection: Seventeenth-century Dutch Paintings from the Frits Lugt Collection*, Quentin Buvelot and Hans Buijs, Zwolle 2002

Liedtke, Walter A., *Architectural Painting in Delft: Gerard Houckgeest, Hendrick van Vliet, Emanuel de Witte*, Doornspijk 1981

Pollmer, Almut, *Kirchenbilder: Der Kirchenraum in der holländischen Malerei um 1650*, Weimar 2018. Trade edition of dissertation, Leiden University, 2011. Dissertation edition available online. Church painting seen through a multitude of criteria.

Ruyven-Zeeman, Zsuzsanna van, *Stained Glass in the Netherlands Before 1795*, 2 vols., Amsterdam 2011

Schwartz, Gary and Marten Jan Bok, *Pieter Saenredam: The Painter in His Time*, London 1989

Catholic Places of Worship
Eck, Xander van, *Clandestine Splendor: Paintings for the Catholic Church in the Dutch Republic*, Zwolle 2008

The Court
Judson, J. Richard and Rudolf E.O. Ekkart, *Gerrit van Honthorst, 1592–1656*, Doornspijk 1999

Cologne (Wallraf-Richartz Museum) and Dordrecht (Dordrechts Museum), exh. cat. *Schalcken: gemalte Verführungkunstenaar*, Anja Ševčík, Stuttgart 2016

City Governments
Blankert, Albert, 'Art and Authority in Seventeenth-century Amsterdam: Paintings for Public Places by Ferdinand Bol and Others', Diane Webb (trans.), in *Selected Writings*, pp. 45–92

Darnell, Lorne, 'A Sacred History for Dutch Classicist Architecture: The Paintings of Pieter Saenredam in the Collection of Constantijn Huygens', Research master thesis, University of Leiden, 2016

Civic Bodies
Alkmaar (Stedelijk Museum Alkmaar), exh. cat. *Caesar van Everdingen, schilder met een vleiend penseel (1616/1617–1678)*, Christi Klinkert and Yvonne Bleyerveld, Zwolle 2016

Private Patrons
Montias, John Michael, *Vermeer en zijn milieu*, Hans Bronkhorst (trans.), Baarn 1993. A Dutch translation, with transcriptions of the archival sources, of *Vermeer and his Milieu: A Web of Social History*, Princeton 1989

Naumann, Otto, *Frans van Mieris the Elder (1635–1681)*, 2 vols., Doornspijk 1981

Schwartz, Gary, *Rembrandt, His Life, His Paintings: A New Biography*, New York 1985

Slager, H.G. [Hans], 'Johannes Vermeer and his Neighbors'. Online at Essential Vermeer, 2017

The Market
Alpers, Svetlana, *Rembrandt's Enterprise: The Studio and the Market*, Chicago 1988. Makes a case for Rembrandt's role in liberating the painter from the constraints of patronage.

Bok, Marten Jan, *Vraag en aanbod op de Nederlandse kunstmarkt, 1580–1700*. Dissertation, Utrecht University, 1994. Basic contribution to the re-examination of the Dutch art market.

Goosens, Marion Elisabeth Wilhelmina, *Schilders en de markt: Haarlem 1605–1635*. Dissertation, Leiden University, 2001. In an exhaustive study, the author performs the cited calculation concerning Isaac van Ostade.

Montias, John Michael, *Artists and Artisans in Delft: A Socio-Economic Study of the Seventeenth Century*, Princeton 1982. Pioneering reconnoitering by an economist of the facts of financial life for the Dutch artist.

Schwartz, Gary, 'The Shape, Size and Destiny of the Dutch Market for Paintings at the End of the Eighty Years' War', in *1648: War and Peace in Europe*, essay vol. 2: *Art and culture*, Münster and Osnabrück 1998, pp. 235–44. Online at the website Westfälischer Friede

Chapter 3
The City Environments
Bièvre, Elisabeth de, *Dutch Art and Urban Cultures, 1200–1700*, New Haven/London 2015. Delves deeply into the distinguishing characteristics of the seven main artistic centres in the Netherlands.

Prak, Maarten, 'Urbanization', in *The Cambridge Companion to the Dutch Golden Age*, Cambridge 2018, pp. 15–31. Available online

Dordrecht
Dordrecht (Dordrechts Museum), exh. cat. *De Zichtbaere Werelt: schilderkunst uit de Gouden Eeuw in Hollands oudste stad*, Celeste Brusati, Zwolle 1992

Amsterdam

Frijhoff, Willem and Maarten Prak (eds.),
    *Geschiedenis van Amsterdam, Centrum van de
    wereld, 1578–1650*, 2 vols., Amsterdam 2004–05

Delft

Delft (Stedelijk Museum Het Prinsenhof), exh.
    cat. *Delftse meesters, tijdgenoten van Vermeer:
    een andere kijk op perspectief, licht en ruimte*,
    Michiel Kerstens, Zwolle 1996. With a
    reinterpretation of Daniël Vosmaer's view
    by curator Michel van Maarseveen.

Haarlem

Köhler, Neeltje (ed.), *Painting in Haarlem, 1500–
    1850: The Collection of the Frans Hals Museum*,
    Ghent 2006. With a wealth of information,
    including authoritative biographies by Irene
    van Thiel.
Leeflang, Huigen, 'Dutch Landscape, the Urban
    View: Haarlem and its Environs in Literature
    and Art, 15th–17th century', *Netherlands
    Yearbook for History of Art*, vol. 48, 1997,
    pp. 52–115. Available on JSTOR
Stechow, Wolfgang, *Dutch Landscape Painting of
    the Seventeenth Century*, London 1966

The Hague

Buijsen, Edwin, *Haagse schilders in de Gouden
    Eeuw: Het Hoogsteder lexicon van alle schilders
    werkzaam in Den Haag, 1600–1700*, Zwolle 1998.
    A model publication on all the documented
    painters in The Hague, with and without
    known work.

Leiden

Schaeps, Jef and Mart van Duijn, *Rembrandt en de
    Universiteit Leiden*, Leiden 2019. The university
    archivist Mart van Duijn found Rembrandt's
    registration for a second year of study.
Zoeteman, M. 'De studentenpopulatie van de
    Leidse universiteit, 1575–1812: "Een volk op
    zyn Siams gekleet eenige mylen van Den Haag
    woonende"'. Dissertation, Leiden University,
    2011. Available online

Utrecht

Kettering, Alison, *The Dutch Arcadia: Pastoral Art
    and Its Audience in the Golden Age*, Montclair
    1983
Meyere, Jos de, *Utrechtse schilderkunst in de gouden
    eeuw : honderd schilderijen uit de collectie van
    het Centraal Museum te Utrecht*, Utrecht 2006

An Inland City: Zwolle

Zwiers, Saskia, 'Het Raadsel EM: Schilder zonder
    oeuvre of oeuvre zonder schilder', *Zwols
    Historisch Tijdschrift*, vol. 1, 2014, pp. 4–12.
    Available online. Disentangles documentation
    concerning master of Hendrick ten Oever.

**Chapter 4
The Female Brush**

Hove, Jan van and Saskia Zwiers, *Het Vrouwenhuis
    van Aleida Greve: hofje vol historie*, Zwolle 2023
Los Angeles (Los Angeles County Museum of Art),
    Austin (University Art Museum), Pittsburgh
    (Carnegie Museum of Art) and Brooklyn
    (Brooklyn Museum), exh. cat. *Women Artists:
    1550–1950*, Ann Sutherland Harris and Linda
    Nochlin, Los Angeles and New York 1976.
    Available online
Russell, Margarita, 'The Women Painters in
    Houbraken's Groote Schouburgh', *Woman's Art
    Journal*, vol. 2, no. 1, 1981, pp. 7–11. Available
    on JSTOR
Stighelen, Katlijne van der and Mirjam Wester,
    *Elck zijn waerom: Vrouwelijke kunstenaars in
    België en Nederland, 1500–1950*, in connection
    with exh. Antwerp (Koninklijk Museum voor
    Schone Kunsten) and Arnhem (Museum voor
    Moderne Kunst), Ghent 1999

**Chapter 5
Families and Children in Paintings**

The database of 1,823 European paintings was
    built by the author with an associate, Trudy
    van den Oosten, in a research group led by
    Willem Frijhoff and Marijke Spies.
Eaker, Adam, *Gesina ter Borch*, London 2024
Haarlem (Frans Hals Museum) and Antwerp
    (Koninklijk Museum voor Schone Kunsten
    Antwerpen), exh. cat. *Pride and Joy: Children's
    Portraits in the Netherlands, 1500–1700*, Jan
    Baptist Bedaux and Rudi Ekkart, Ghent and
    Amsterdam 2000
Kettering, Alistair McNeil, *Drawings from the
    Ter Borch Studio Estate*, 2 vols., The Hague
    1988
Meijer, Fred and Carla van de Puttelaar, *Gesina
    ter Borch (1631–1690): A Testimony of Love*,
    Amsterdam 2024. Available online
Muizelaar, Klaske and Derek Phillips, *Picturing
    Men and Women in the Dutch Golden Age:
    Paintings and People in Historical Perspective*,
    New Haven/London 2003
Raleigh (North Carolina Museum of Art),
    Indianapolis (Indianapolis Museum of Art)
    and Manchester, NH (Currier Museum of Art),

exh. cat. *Jan Miense Molenaer: Painter of the Dutch Golden Age*, Dennis P. Weller, 2002
Washington (National Gallery of Art) and Amsterdam (Rijksmuseum), exh. cat. *Jan Steen, Painter and Storyteller*, Perry Chapman, Wouter Kloek and Arthur Wheelock, New Haven/London 1996

Chapter 6
Dutch Painters Abroad
Italy
Repertory of Dutch and Flemish Paintings in Italian Public Collections, four volumes to date, published by the Netherlands Art History Institute in Florence, 1998–
Utrecht (Centraal Museum), exh. cat. *De Bentvueghels: Een berucht kunstgenootschap in Rome, 1620–1720*, Liesbeth Helmus, Amsterdam 2023

Scandinavia
Alkmaar (Stedelijk Museum Alkmaar), exh. cat. *Allart van Everdingen, meester van het ruige landschap, 1621–1675*, Christi Klinkert and Yvonne Bleyerveld, Rotterdam 2021
Klein, P.W., *De Trippen in de 17e eeuw: Een studie over het ondernemersgedrag op de Hollandse stapelmarkt*, Assen 1965

Great Britain
Bok, Marten Jan, 'Claude de Jongh, "Painter, Sorely Incapacitated in His Arms": A Study of His Milieu', *Hoogsteder-Naumann Mercury*, vol. 10, 1989, pp. 41–55. Available online
Close Encounters: Cross-Cultural Exchange between the Low Countries and Britain 1600–1830, online on the website of RKD – Netherlands Institute for Art History
Karst, Sander, *Painting in a Country without Painters: The Netherlandish Contribution to the Emergence of the British School of Painting, 1520–1720*. Dissertation, Utrecht University, 2021. Dutch edition available online

Brazil
Amsterdam (Rembrandt House Museum), exh. cat. *Black in Rembrandt's Time*, Elmer Kolfin and Epco Runia, Zwolle 2020
Boogaart, E. [Ernst] van den (ed.), *Johan Maurits van Nassau-Siegen, 1604–1679*, The Hague 1979. Signalled the political dimension in Albert Eckhout's paintings of Indigenous Brazilians.
Middelburg (Zeeuws Museum), exh. cat. *Terug naar Zeeland: Topstukken uit de 16e en 17de eeuw*, Katie Heyning, 2008. Discussion of the portraits of Blacks made by one of the Becx brothers in Middelburg.
Monteiro C., Odegard E. L. L., 'Slavery at the Court of the "Humanist Prince": Reexamining Johan Maurits van Nassau-Siegen and his Role in Slavery, Slave Trade and Slave-smuggling in Dutch Brazil', *Journal of Early American History*, vol. 10, no. 1, 2020, pp. 3–32. Available online

Asia
Jonker, Menno, Erlend de Groot and Caroline de Hart, *Van velerlei pluimage: Zeventiende-eeuwse waterverftekeningen van Andries Beeckman*, Nijmegen 2014
Schwartz, Gary, 'Terms of Reception: Europeans and Persians and Each Other's Art', in: Da Costa Kaufmann, Thomas and Michael North, pp. 25–63. Available online
Vialle, Cynthia, '"To Capture Their Favor": On Gift-Giving by the VOC', in Da Costa Kaufmann, Thomas and Michael North, pp. 291–319

Chapter 7
The Grand Traditions
The Bible and Saints
Alpers, Svetlana, *The Art of Describing: Dutch Art in the Seventeenth Century*, Chicago 1983. Draws a sharp distinction between Dutch and Italian art.
Exalto, John, *Gereformeerde heiligen: De religieuze exempeltraditie in vroegmodern Nederland*, Nijmegen 2005. Biblical heroes as positive and negative models for Dutch Calvinists.
Lubow, Arthur, 'The Lusty Creativity of Cornelis Cornelisz van Haarlem', *The New York Times*, 13 January 2021. Available online for subscribers. Challenges art historians to acknowledge homosexual themes in Dutch art.
Schnabel, Paul, *Anders gekeken: Het beste en het boeiendste uit de Hollandse schilderkunst van de Gouden Eeuw*, Zwolle 2021. Does not look away from homoerotic subject matter.
Sumowski, Werner, *Gemälde der Rembrandt-Schüler*, 6 vols., Landau/Pfalz 1983–94

Mythology, History, Allegory
Eikema Hommes, Margriet, *De hemel van Gerard de Lairesse: een plafondschildering uit het rampjaar 1672*, Amsterdam 2023. Exhaustive discussion of symbolic and emblematic details.

Sluijter, Eric Jan, *De 'Heydensche Fabulen' in de Noordnederlandse schilderkunst circa 1590–1670: Een proeve van beschrijving en interpretatie van schilderijen met verhalende onderwerpen uit de klassieke mythologie.* Dissertation, Leiden University, 1986

Ullman, Berthold, 'Cleopatra's Pearls', *The Classical Journal*, vol. 52, no. 5, February 1957, pp. 193–201. Available online

Chapter 8
Genres and Subgenres

Montias, John Michael, 'The Influence of Economic Factors on Style', *De Zeventiende Eeuw*, vol. 6, no. 1, 1990, pp. 49–57. Available online

Sluijter, Eric Jan and Nicolette Sluijter-Seijffert, 'Jan van Goyen: Virtuoso, Innovator, and Market Leader', *Journal of Historians of Nether-landish Art*, vol. 13, no. 2, 2021. Online only

Portraiture

Amsterdam (Rijksmuseum), exh. cat. *Dawn of the Golden Age: Northern Netherlandish Art, 1580–1620*, Ger Luijten, Amsterdam 1993. Cites Philip van Borsselen in connection with Goltzius portrait of Jan Govertsen.

Knotter, Mirjam, 'Sephardi Jewish Life and Material Culture in Rembrandt's Time', in *Rembrandt Seen Through Jewish Eyes: The Artist's Meaning to Jews from His Time to Ours*, Amsterdam 2024, pp. 23–44. Available online

Nichols, Lawrence W., *The Paintings of Hendrick Goltzius, 1558–1617: A Monograph and Catalogue Raisonné*, Doornspijk 2013

Priem, Ruud, 'Een "begaaft en seer ijverich man": Willem Thielen en zijn echtgenote Maria de Fraeye, geportretteerd door Cornelis Jonson van Ceulen', in *Face Book*, pp. 215–26

Reznicek, Emil, 'Het begin van Goltzius' loopbaan als tekenaar', *Oud Holland*, vol. 75, 1960, pp. 65–120. Available on JSTOR

Thiel, P.J.J. van, 'Andermaal Michiel van Musscher: zijn zelfportretten', *Bulletin van het Rijksmuseum*, vol. 22, no. 4, 1974, pp. 131–49. Available on JSTOR

Self-portraits

Amsterdam (Museum Van Loon), exh. cat. *Michiel van Musscher (1645–1705): The Wealth of the Golden Age*, Robert E. Gerhardt and Francis Griep-Quint, Zwolle 2012

Florence (Gli Uffizi), *Gli Uffizi, catalogo generale*, Florence 1979

Group Portraits

Giltaij, Jeroen, 'Het vriendschapsschilderij van Jan de Braij en drie andere schilders', in *Face Book*, pp. 431–42

Haarlem (Frans Hals Museum), exh. cat. *Salomon, Jan, Joseph en Dirck de Bray: vier schilders in één gezin*, Pieter Biesboer, Zwolle 2008

–, exh. cat. *Portretten van echt en trouw: Huwelijk en gezin in de Nederlandse kunst van de zeventiende eeuw*, Eddy de Jongh, Zwolle 1986

Leeuwen, Rudie van, *Beeltenissen van bestuurders en burgers als bijbelfiguren: Het bijbelse portret historié in de Noordelijke en Zuidelijke Nederlanden van de zestiende en zeventiende eeuw.* Dissertation, Radboud University, Nijmegen, 2018. Available online. Essential study of the *portrait historié* in Dutch painting.

Middelkoop, Norbert E., *Schutters, gildebroeders, regenten en regentessen: Het Amsterdamse corporatiestuk, 1525–1850*, 3 vols. Dissertation, University of Amsterdam, 2019. Available online. Complete catalogue of Amsterdam group portraits for civic institutions.

Riegl, Alois, *The Group Portraiture of Holland*, introduction by Wolfgang Kemp, Evelyn M. Kain and David Britt (trans.), Los Angeles 1999

Tronies

Gottwald, Franziska, *Das Tronie, Muster, Studie und Meisterwerk: Die Genese einer Gattung der Malerei vom 15. Jahrhundert bis zu Rembrandt*, Berlin 2011

Hirschfelder, Dagmar, 'Portrait or Character Head: The Term "Tronie" and its Meaning in the Seventeenth Century', in Kassel (Gemäldegalerie Alte Meister) and Amsterdam (Rembrandt House Museum), exh. cat. *The Mystery of the Young Rembrandt*, Bernhard Schnackenburg and Ernst van de Wetering, 2011, pp. 82–90

–, *Tronie und Porträt in der niederländischen Malerei des 17. Jahrhunderts*, Berlin 2008

Landscape

Amsterdam (Rijksmuseum), Boston (Museum of Fine Arts) and Philadelphia (Philadelphia Museum of Art), exh. cat. *Masters of 17th-Century Dutch Landscape Painting*, Peter S. Sutton, 1987

Bakker, Boudewijn, *Landscape and Religion from Van Eyck to Rembrandt*, Diane Webb (trans.), Farnham 2012. First published in Dutch, Bussum 2004

Jorink, Eric, *Reading the Book of Nature in the Dutch Golden Age, 1575–1715*, Peter Mason (trans.), Leiden/Boston 2010. In Dutch, as Groningen University dissertation, 2004, available online

Landscapes of Known Locations
Freedberg, David, *Dutch Landscape Prints of the Seventeenth Century*, London 1980
Slive, Seymour, *Jacob van Ruisdael: A Complete Catalogue of His Paintings, Drawings, and Etchings*, New Haven 2001

Beaches and Dunes
Ossing, Franz, 'Realities in the Skies: A Comment on John Walsh's Article "Skies and Reality in Dutch Landscape Painting" (1991)'. Available online
Walsh, John, 'Skies and Reality in Dutch Landscape', in: *Art in History, History in Art*, pp. 94–117

At Sea
Bredius, A. [Abraham], 'Porcellis sluit een curieus contract', *Oud Holland*, vol. 31, 1913, pp. 135–36. Online at JSTOR
Fuchs, R.H. [Rudi], *Dutch Painting*, London 1978
Levert, Stephanie Leontine, *'Étrangers, mais habitués en cette ville de Paris': Les artistes néerlandais à Paris (1550–1700), une prosopographie*. Dissertation, Utrecht University, 2017. Available online. Discovered van Beecq's marriage.
Schwartz, Gary, 'J. van Beecq, Amsterdam Marine Painter, "The Only One Here [in France] Who Excels in this Genre"', in *Les échanges artistiques entre les anciens Pays-Bas et la France 1482–1814*. Proceedings of a conference held in Lille in 2008, Gaëtane Maës and Jan Blanc (eds.), Turnhout 2010, pp. 17–31. Available online
–, 'There is no such thing as "Dutchness" or "Flemishness" in seascape painting', *The Low Countries*, vol. 23, 2015, pp. 88–97. Available online
Sluijter, Eric Jan, 'Dien grooten Raphel in het zeeschilderen!': Over de waardering voor Jan Porcellis' sobere kunst door eigentijdse kenners', in *Liber Amicorum Marijke de Kinkelder: Collegiale bijdragen over landschappen, marines en architectuur*, The Hague 2013, pp. 343–58

At War
Delft (Stedelijk Museum Het Prinsenhof), exh. cat. *Beelden van een strijd: oorlog en kunst vóór de Vrede van Munster, 1621–1648*, Michel van Maarseveen, Zwolle 1998
Rosen, Jochai, *Soldiers at Leisure: The Guardroom Scene in Dutch Genre Painting of the Golden Age*, Amsterdam [2010]

On the Hunt
Gietman, Conrad et al., *De jacht: Een cultuurgeschiedenis van jager, dier en landschap*, Hilversum 2021

In the Dutch Countryside
Valkenburg, Reindert, 'Onweer bij Jan van Goyen: Artistieke wedijver en de markt voor het Hollandse landschap in de 17de eeuw', *Netherlands Yearbook for History of Art*, vol. 48, 1997, pp. 116–61. Available on JSTOR

The Cowscape
Dordrecht (Dordrechts Museum), exh. cat. *In het licht van Cuyp: Aelbert Cuyp & Gainsborough Constable Turner*, Zwolle 2021
Levitt, Ruth L., 'Cuyp's Cattle: Aesthetic Transformations in Dutch 17th-century Art'. Dissertation, University of London, 1989. Scan available on the website of the British Library

Winters, Nights
Bachmann, Fredo, *Aert van der Neer, 1603/4–1677*, Bremen 1982
The Hague (Mauritshuis), exh. cat. Winters van weleer: Het Hollandse winterlandschap in de Gouden Eeuw, Ariane van Suchtelen, Zwolle 2001

In the House of Worship
Jantzen, Hans, *Das niederländische Architekturbild*, Braunschweig 1909
Kaplan, Yosef, 'For Whom did Emanuel de Witte Paint his Three Pictures of the Sephardic Synagogue in Amsterdam?', *Studia Rosenthaliana*, vol. 32, no. 2, 1998, pp. 133–54. Available online
Knotter, Mirjam, 'Sephardi Jewish Life and Material Culture in Rembrandt's Time', in *Rembrandt Seen Through Jewish Eyes: The Artist's Meaning to Jews from His Time to Ours*, Amsterdam 2024, pp. 23–44. Available online
Rüger, Axel and Rachel Billinge, 'The Design Practices of the Dutch Architectural Painter Bartholomeus van Bassen', *National Gallery Technical Bulletin*, vol. 26, 2005, pp. 23–42. Available online

On the Street

Amsterdam (Rijksmuseum), exh. cat. *Tot lering en vermaak: betekenissen van Hollandse genrevoorstellingen uit de zeventiende eeuw*, Eddy de Jongh, 1976

Zumthor, Paul, *Daily Life in Rembrandt's Holland*, Simon Watson Taylor (trans.), London 1962. Sheds light on a vast array of topics.

The Poor

Bok, Marten Jan, *Vijfendertig Utrechtse kunstenaars en hun werk voor het Sint Jobs Gasthuis, 1622–1642*. Master's thesis, Utrecht University, 1984

Buijsen, Edwin, *Ick soeck en vind: De schilderijen van Adriaen van de Venne, 1590–1662*, Zwolle 2023

Huys Janssen, Paul, *Jan van Bijlert, 1597/98–1671: Catalogue Raisonné*, Amsterdam/Philadelphia 1998

Luiten van Zanden, Jan and Lee Soltow, *Income and Wealth Inequality in the Netherlands 1500–1990*, Amsterdam 1998

Phillips, Derek, *Well-Being in Amsterdam's Golden Age*, Amsterdam 2008

Schwartz, Gary, *A Pregnant Past: The Dutch Seventeenth-Century in the Global Twenty-First*, Amsterdam 2014. Available online

At Work

Amsterdam (Amsterdams Historisch Museum), exh. cat. *De Hollandse meesters van een Amsterdamse bankier: De verzameling Adriaan van der Hoop (1778–1854)*, Ellinoor Bergvelt, Zwolle 2004

Franits, Wayne E., *Paragons of Virtue: Women and Domesticity in Seventeenth-Century Dutch Art*, Cambridge 1993

Paris (Musée du Louvre), Dublin (National Gallery of Ireland) and Washington (National Gallery of Art), exh. cat. *Vermeer and the Masters of Genre Painting: Inspiration and Rivalry*, Adriaan E. Waaiboer, 2017–18

Vries, Annette de, *Ingelijst werk: De verbeelding van arbeid en beroep in de vroegmoderne Nederlanden*, Zwolle 2004

At Play

Haarlem (Frans Hals Museum), exh. cat. *De Gouden Eeuw viert feest*, Anna Tummers, Rotterdam 2011

At Home

Boston (Museum of Fine Arts), exh. cat. *Class Distinctions: Dutch Painting in the Age of Rembrandt and Vermeer*, Ronni Baer, 2015

Denver (Denver Art Museum) and Newark (The Newark Museum), exh. cat. *Art & Home: Dutch Interiors in the Age of Rembrandt*, Mariët Westermann, Zwolle 2001

Meijer, Fred G., *Jan Davidsz. de Heem 1606–1684*. Dissertation, University of Amsterdam, 2016. Available online

Roodenburg, Herman, 'Smelling Rank and Status', in exh. cat. *Class Distinctions*, pp. 41–53

Rybczynski, Witold, *Home: A Short History of an Idea*, New York 1986

Stoett, F.A., *Nederlandsche spreekwoorden, spreekwijzen, uitdrukkingen en gezegden*, 2 vols., Zutphen 1923–25. Available online

Music-making

The Hague (Hoogsteder & Hoogsteder) and Antwerp (Hessenhuis Museum), exh. cat. *The Hoogsteder Exhibition of Music & Painting in the Golden Age*, Edwin Buijsen and Louis Peter Grijp, Zwolle 1994

London (The Queen's Gallery, Buckingham Palace), Edinburgh (The Queen's Gallery, Holyroodhouse) and The Hague (Mauritshuis), exh. cat. *Masters of the Everyday: Dutch Artists in the Age of Vermeer*, Desmond Shawe-Taylor and Quentin Buvelot, Brussels 2016

Sex

Haarlem (Frans Hals Museum), exh. cat. *Judith Leyster, schilderes in een mannenwereld*, Zwolle 1993

The Hague (Mauritshuis), exh. cat. *Frans van Mieris, 1635–1681*, Quentin Buvelot, Zwolle 2005

Noorman, Judith, *Art, Honor and Success in The Dutch Republic: The Life and Career of Jacob van Loo*, Amsterdam 2020

Pigler, A., *Barockthemen: Eine Auswahl von Verzeichnissen zur Ikonographie des 17. und 18. Jahrhunderts*, 3 vols., Budapest 1974. Available online

Roberts, Benjamin B., *Sex and Drugs before Rock 'n' Roll: Youth Culture and Masculinity During Holland's Golden Age*, Amsterdam 2012. Available online

Stewart, Alison, *Unequal Lovers: A Study of Unequal Couples in Northern Art*, New York 1978. Available online

Suchtelen, Ariane van and Quentin Buvelot, *Genre Painting in the Mauritshuis*, The Hague and Zwolle 2016

Utrecht (Centraal Museum), exh. cat. *Het gedroomde land: Pastorale schilderkunst in de Gouden Eeuw*, Peter van den Brink, Zwolle 1993

On the Table

Auckland (Auckland City Art Gallery), exh. cat. *Still-life in the Age of Rembrandt*, Eddy de Jongh, 1982

Bergström, Ingvar, *Dutch Still-life Painting in the Seventeenth Century*, Christina Hedström and Gerald Taylor (trans.), New York 1956. First published in Swedish, Göteborg 1947

Bol, L.J. [Laurens Johannes], *Bekoring van het kleine*, Amsterdam 1963

Grimm, Claus, *Stilleben: Die niederländischen und deutschen Meister*, Stuttgart/Zürich 1988

Grootenboer, Hanneke, 'Sublime Still Life: On Adriaen Coorte, Elias van den Broeck, and the *Je ne sais quoi* of Painting', *Journal of Historians of Netherlandish Art*, vol. 8, no. 2, 2016. Online only

Jochems, Peter, *Still Life with Asparagus – 1697 – Art Talk.* On YouTube

Utrecht (Centraal Museum), exh. cat. *Vis: Stillevens van Hollandse en Vlaamse meesters 1550–1700*, Liesbeth M. Helmus, Utrecht 2004

From the Garden, on the Forest Floor

Osaka (Nabio Museum of Art), Tokyo (Tokyo Station Gallery) and Sydney (The Art Gallery of New South Wales), exh. cat. *Flowers and Nature: Netherlandish Flower Painting of Four Centuries*, Sam Segal, The Hague 1990, no. 65, pp. 235–37

Taylor, Paul, *Dutch Flower Painting 1600–1720*, New Haven/London 1995

Animals, Birds

Kearney, Joy, 'Ornithology and Collecting in the Dutch Golden Age: Captured Specimens and the Collecting of Exotica', in proceedings of congress *Collecting Nature*, held at Schwabenakademie Irsee in 2013, Newcastle upon Tyne 2014. Available online

Optical and Conceptual Special Effects

Bruijnen, Yvette, 'Johannes Torrentius, *Emblematic Still Life with Flagon, Glass, Jug and Bridle*, 1614', in Jonathan Bikker (ed.), *Dutch Paintings of the Seventeenth Century in the Rijksmuseum*, Amsterdam and New Haven/London 2007. Available online

Colenbrander, Herman, 'A Pledge of Marital Domestic Bliss: Samuel van Hoogstraten's Perspective Box in the National Gallery, London', in *The Universal Art of Samuel van Hoogstraten (1627–1678): Painter, Writer, and Courtier*, Thijs Weststeijn (ed.), Amsterdam 2013. Available online

Emmens, Jan, 'Natuur, onderwijzing en oefening: Bij een drieluik van Gerrit Dou', in *Kunsthistorische opstellen*, vol. 2, Amsterdam 1981. First published in 1963

's-Hertogenbosch (Het Noordbrabants Museum), exh. cat. *Schijn bedriegt: Trompe-lóeil en de kunst van illusie*, Paul Huys Janssen, Eindhoven 2013

Keith, Larry, 'Carel Fabritius' *A View in Delft*: Some Observations on its Treatment and Display', *National Gallery Technical Bulletin*, vol. 15, 1994, pp. 54–78. Available online

Leiden (Museum de Lakenhal), exh. cat. *David Bailly: Time, Death and Vanity*, Christiaan Vogelaar, Zwolle 2023

Liedtke, Walter, '*The View in Delft* by Carel Fabritius', *The Burlington Magazine*, vol. 118, 1976, pp. 61–73. Available on JSTOR

Nakamura, Jun P., 'Seeing Outside the Box: Reexamining the Top of Samuel van Hoogstraten's London Perspective Box', *Journal of Historians of Netherlandish Art*, vol. 12, no. 2, 2020. Online only

Washington (National Gallery of Art), London (Dulwich Picture Gallery) and The Hague (Royal Cabinet of Paintings Mauritshuis), exh. cat. *Gerrit Dou, 1613–1675: Master Painter in the Age of Rembrandt*, Ronni Baer, Washington and New Haven/London, 2000

Weststeijn, Thijs, *The Visible World: Samuel van Hoogstraten's Art Theory and the Legitimation of Painting in the Dutch Golden Age*, Beverley Jackson and Lynne Richards (trans.), Amsterdam 2008

Chapter 9
Afterword on Attribution

Amsterdam (Rijksmuseum), *All the Paintings of the Rijksmuseum: A Completely Illustrated Catalogue*, Amsterdam and Maarssen 1976. Available online

Blankert, Albert, *Ferdinand Bol (1618–1680), Rembrandt's Pupil*, Doornspijk 1983

Friedländer, M. [Max J.], *On Art and Connoisseurship*, London 1942. Available online

Lopez, Jonathan, *The Man Who Made Vermeers: Unvarnishing the Legend of Master Forger Han van Meegeren*, Orlando etc. 2008

Montias, John Michael, *Art at Auction in 17th Century Amsterdam*, Amsterdam 2002

Tummers, Anna, *The Eye of the Connoisseur: Authenticating Paintings by Rembrandt and his Contemporaries*, Los Angeles 2011

Valentiner, W.R., 'Carel and Barent Fabritius', *The Art Bulletin*, vol. 14, no. 3, 1932, pp. 197–241. Online at JSTOR

List of Illustrations

Dimensions are given in centimeters (inches), height
before width before depth where relevant.

1   Caspar Netscher, *The Lace-maker*, 1662. Oil on
canvas, 33 × 27 (13 × 10½). The Wallace Collection,
London (P237)
2   Abraham Goos, map of the seventeen provinces
of Southern and Northern Netherlands (with
north to the right), 1621. Published by Ian Iansen,
Amsterdam 1621
3   Karel van Mander, *Dance Around the Golden Calf*,
1602. Oil on canvas, 98 × 213.5 (38½ × 84). Frans
Hals Museum, Haarlem (os 52-26a)
4   David Vinckboons, *A Country Fair*, 1629. Oil on
panel, 40.2 × 67.4 (16 × 26½). Mauritshuis, The
Hague (542)
5   Adriaen Brouwer, *Self-portrait Among Artist
Friends, known as 'The Smokers'*, c. 1636. Oil on
panel, 46.4 × 36.8 (18¼ × 14½). Metropolitan
Museum Art, New York. The Friedsam Collection,
Bequest of Michael Friedsam (1931, 32.100.21)
6   Adriaen van Ostade, *A Modest Painter's Studio*,
c. 1647–50. Oil on panel, 36.5 × 34.5 (14½ × 13½).
Rijksmuseum, Amsterdam (SK-A-298)
7   Jan Miense Molenaer, *The Painter's Workshop*,
1631. Oil on canvas, 82 × 127 (32¼ × 50).
Gemäldegalerie, Staatliche Museen zu Berlin (873)/
Jörg P. Anders
8   Michael Sweerts, *An Artist's Studio*, 1652. Oil on
canvas, 73.5 × 58.8 (29 × 23). Detroit Institute of
Arts. City of Detroit Purchase (30.297)
9 and 10   Gerrit Lundens, *Miniature Portraits of a
Fifty-year-old Woman and a Fifteen-year-old Boy*, 1650.
Oil on silver, 4.8 × 5.0 × 0.2 (2 × 2 × ⅛). Rijksmuseum,
Amsterdam (SK-A-4338 and SK-A-4337)
11   Hercules Segers, *Landscape with a Waterfall,
First Version*, c. 1627. Drypoint etching, 14.3 × 19.1
(5½ × 7½). Rijksmuseum, Amsterdam (RP-P-H-
ON-826)
12   Willem van de Velde the Elder, *Council of War
Aboard 'The Seven Provinces', the Flagship of Michiel
Adriaensz de Ruyter, 10 June 1666, Preceding the
Four Days' Battle: Episode from the Second Anglo-
Dutch War*, 1666–93. Ink on canvas, 117 × 175
(46 × 69). Rijksmuseum, Amsterdam (SK-A-4289)
13   Gabriël Metsu, *Portrait of the Family of Jan
Jacobsz Hinlopen and Leonora Huydecoper*, 1663.
Oil on canvas, 72 × 79 (28 × 31). Gemäldegalerie,
Staatliche Museen zu Berlin (792)/Jörg P. Anders
14   Juan Bautista Martinez del Mazo, *Family of the
Artist*, c. 1664–65. Oil on canvas, 149.5 × 174.5
(59 × 69). Kunsthistorisches Museum, Vienna
(320)
15   The Hague, Huis ten Bosch, the Oranjezaal,
1645–52. Royal Collections of the Netherlands/
Koninklijke Verzamelingen
16   Ferdinand Bol, *Michiel de Ruyter*, 1667. Oil on
canvas,157 × 135 (62 × 53). Mauritshuis, The Hague
(585)
17   Adriaen van Nieulandt, *Allegory of the Peace
under Stadholder Willem II*, 1650. Oil on canvas,
136 × 105 (54 × 41). Rijksmuseum, Amsterdam
(SK-A-1995)
18   Rembrandt van Rijn, *The Mill*, c. 1648. Oil on
canvas, 87.6 × 105.6 (34½ × 42). National Gallery
of Art, Washington (1942.9.62)
19   Hendrick Avercamp, *Winter Landscape with Ice
Skaters*, c. 1608. Oil on panel, 77.3 × 131.9 (30 × 52).
Rijksmuseum, Amsterdam (SK-A-1718)
20   Willem Buytewech, *Merry Company*, c. 1617–
20. Oil on canvas, 49.3 × 68 (19 × 27). Museum
Boijmans Van Beuningen, Rotterdam. Gift A.C.
Mees (1103(OK))/Photo Studio Tromp
21   Frans Hals, *Portrait of a Man, known as 'The
Laughing Cavalier'*, 1624. Oil on canvas, 83 × 67.3
(33 × 26½). The Wallace Collection, London (P84)
22   Jacob van Campen, *Double Portrait of
Constantijn Huygens and Suzanne van Baerle*,
c. 1635. Oil on canvas, 98 × 78.5 (39 × 31).
Mauritshuis, The Hague (1089)
23   Bartholomeus van der Helst, *Militia Company
of District VIII under the Command of Captain Roelof
Bicker*, c. 1640–43. Oil on canvas, 235 ×
750 (92½ × 295). Rijksmuseum, Amsterdam
(SK-C-375)
24   Carel Fabritius, *The Goldfinch*, 1654. Oil on
panel, 33.5 × 22.8 (13 × 9). Mauritshuis, The Hague
(605)
25   Rembrandt van Rijn, *Isaac and Rebecca, known
as 'The Jewish Bride'*, c. 1665. Oil on canvas, 121.5
× 166.5 (48 × 66). Rijksmuseum, Amsterdam (SK-
C-216)

26 Willem van de Velde the Younger, *The Cannon Shot*, c. 1668. Oil on canvas, 78.5 × 67 (31 × 26). Rijksmuseum, Amsterdam (SK-C-244)
27 Meindert Hobbema, *The Avenue at Middelharnis*, 1689. Oil on canvas, 103.5 × 141 (40¾ × 55½). National Gallery, London (NG830)
28 Adriaen van der Werff, *Self-portrait with the Portrait of his Wife, Margaretha van Rees, and their Daughter Maria*, 1699. Oil on canvas, 81 × 65.5 (32 × 26). Rijksmuseum, Amsterdam (SK-A-465)
29 David Colijns, *Organ Shutters with Depiction of David with the Head of Goliath*, c. 1635–40. Oil on canvas, 202 × 182 (79½ × 71½). Museum Catharijneconvent, Utrecht (ABM s 163)
30 Thomas de Keyser, after a lost stained-glass window of 1611 in the Zuiderkerk, Amsterdam, by Pieter Lastman, *Cyrus Restores the Treasures of the Temple*, 1660. Oil on canvas, 118.8 × 92 (46¾ × 36). Fondation Custodia, Paris (Collection Frits Lugt; 6781)
31 Pieter Saenredam, *Interior of the Sint Odulphuskerk (Church of St Odolphus), Assendelft*, 1649. Oil on panel, 49 × 73.6 (19 × 29). Rijksmuseum, Amsterdam (SK-C-217)
32 Hendrick van Vliet, *The Tomb of Admiral Jacob van Wassenaer in the Choir of the Jacobskerk*, 1667. Oil on canvas, 93 × 71.1 (36½ × 28). Bowdoin College Museum of Art, Brunswick, Maine (1971.6)
33 Abraham Bloemaert, *The Supper at Emmaus*, 1622. Oil on panel, 145 × 215.5 (57⅛ × 85). Royal Museum of Fine Arts of Belgium, Brussels (3705). Rapp Halour/Alamy Stock Photo
34 Adriaen van de Velde, *The Annunciation to the Virgin*, 1667. Oil on canvas, 128 × 176 (50 × 69). Rijksmuseum, Amsterdam (SK-A-2688)
35 Wybrand de Geest, *Ernst Casimir, Count of Nassau-Dietz*, 1631. Oil on canvas, 196 × 121 (77 × 47½). Royal Collection, The Hague (on display in the Royal Palace, Amsterdam) (SC-0312)
36 Gerard van Honthorst, *Portrait of Frederik Hendrik, Prince of Orange, his Wife Amalia van Solms and their Three Youngest Daughters Albertina Agnes, Henrietta Catharina and Maria*, c. 1647. Oil on canvas, 263.5 × 347.5 (103¾ × 137). Rijksmuseum, Amsterdam (SK-A-874)
37 Godefridus (Godfried) Schalcken, *Candlelit Portrait of Stadholder-King William III*, c. 1692–97. Oil on canvas, 76.5 × 65 (30⅛ × 25½). Rijksmuseum, Amsterdam (SK-A-367)
38 Pieter van Bronckhorst, *The Judgement of Solomon*, 1622. Oil on panel, 135 × 187 (53⅛ × 73½). Prinsenhof Museum, Delft. The Picture Art Collection/Alamy
39 Christiaen van Couwenbergh, *The Capture of Samson*, 1630. Oil on canvas, 156 × 196 (61½ × 77).

Dordrechts Museum, transfer Municipality of Dordrecht 1975 (DM/975/502)
40 Govert Flinck, *The Roman Consul Marcus Curius Dentatus Refusing the Gifts of the Samnites*, 1656. Oil on canvas, 485 × 377 (191 × 148½). Royal Palace, Amsterdam
41 Jan Victors, *Dining Hall of the Reformed Diaconate Girls' Orphanage*, 1659–60. Oil on canvas, 146 × 221 (57½ × 87). Amsterdam Museum, Amsterdam (SB 5398)
42 Caesar van Everdingen and Pieter Post, *Count Willem II Granting its Charter to the Rijnland Water Board*, 1655. Oil on canvas, 218 × 212 (86 × 83½). Museum De Lakenhal, Leiden (B 1491). Photo Rob Lumen Captum/Dreamstime.com
43 Johannes Vermeer, *A Kitchen Maid Making Bread Pudding, called 'The Milkmaid'*, c. 1658/59. Oil on canvas, 45.5 × 41 (18 × 16⅛). Rijksmuseum, Amsterdam (SK-A-2344)
44 Frans van Mieris, *An Officer in a Fabric Shop*, 1660. Oil on panel, 54.5 × 42.7 (21½ × 17). Kunsthistorisches Museum, Vienna (586)
45 Rembrandt van Rijn, *Aristotle with a Bust of Homer*, 1653. Oil on canvas, 143.5 × 136.5 (56½ × 53¾). Metropolitan Museum of Art, New York (61.198)
46 Nicolaes Maes, *The Eavesdropper*, 1657. Oil on canvas, 92 × 121 (36 × 47½). Dordrechts Museum, on loan RCE, 1953 (DM/953/135)
47 Pieter Saenredam, *The Old Town Hall of Amsterdam*, 1657. Oil on panel, 65.5 × 84.5 (26 × 33¼). Rijksmuseum, Amsterdam, on loan from the city of Amsterdam (SK-C-1409)
48 Emanuel de Witte, *Courtyard of the Exchange in Amsterdam*, 1653. Oil on panel, 49 × 47.5 (19 × 18½). Museum Boijmans Van Beuningen, Rotterdam. Loan Foundation Willem van der Vorm (VdV 91)/Photo Studio Tromp
49 Johannes Lingelbach, *Dam Square in Amsterdam, with the New Town Hall under Construction*, 1656. Oil on canvas, 122.5 × 206 (48¼ × 81⅛). Amsterdam Museum, Amsterdam (SA 3044)
50 Gerrit Berckheyde, *The Two Synagogues in Amsterdam*, c. 1680–85. Oil on panel, 32.3 × 45.3 (12½ × 18). Städel Museum, Frankfurt (259)
51 Daniël Vosmaer, *View of Delft*, 1663. Oil on canvas, 90 × 113 (35½ × 44½). Museum Prinsenhof, Delft
52 Gallery above the tribunal chamber, town hall of Delft. Photo Florian Monheim/ Bildarchiv Monheim GmbH/Alamy stock photo
53 Jacob van Ruisdael, *View of Haarlem from the Northwest, with Bleaching Fields in the Foreground*, c. 1670–75. Oil on canvas, 62 × 55 (24 × 21½). Kunsthaus Zürich (R 32)

54 Gerrit Berckheyde, *The Great Square and Bavokerk in Haarlem*, 1696. Oil on canvas, 69.5 × 90.5 (27½ × 35¾). Frans Hals Museum, Haarlem (os 75-316)

55 Paulus van Hillegaert, *The Princes of Orange and their Families on Horseback, Riding Out from the Buitenhof, The Hague*, c. 1621–22. Oil on canvas, 144.6 × 214 (57 × 84¼). Mauritshuis, The Hague (546)

56 Isaac Claesz van Swanenburg, *Spinning, Shearing the Warp and Weaving Wool*, c. 1607. Oil on panel, 137.5 × 196 (54⅛ × 77). Museum De Lakenhal, Leiden (S 421)

57 Abraham van den Tempel, *The Leiden Maiden Receives the Broadcloth Industry*, 1651. Oil on canvas, 207 × 266.5 (81½ × 105). Museum De Lakenhal, Leiden (S 427)

58 Hendrik van der Burch, *The Conferring of a Degree at Leiden University*, c. 1650. Oil on canvas, 71.5 × 59 (28⅛ × 23¼). Rijksmuseum, Amsterdam (SK-A-2720)

59 Paulus Moreelse, *Pastoral Portrait of Two Little Girls*, 1622. Oil on canvas, 121 × 95.8 (47½ × 37½). Centraal Museum, Utrecht (10240)

60 Hendrick ter Brugghen, *Lazarus and the Rich Man*, 1625. Oil on canvas, 168.2 × 207.3 (66 × 81½). Centraal Museum, Utrecht (11241)

61 Hendrik ten Oever, *Landscape Outside Zwolle with Cows and Bathers*, 1675. Oil on canvas, 66.7 × 87 (26¼ × 34¼). University of Edinburgh (EU0727). ARTGEN/Alamy stock photo

62 Aleida Greve, *Self-portrait in a Landscape*, 1686. Oil on canvas, 115 × 100 (45 × 39½). Stichting het Vrouwenhuis, Zwolle, The Netherlands

63 Gerrit van Honthorst, *Margaretha Maria de Roodere with her Mother Maria van der Putten and the Portrait of her Father Gerard de Roodere*, 1652. Oil on canvas, 142.3 × 168.3 (56 × 66¼). Centraal Museum, Utrecht (20088)

64 Frans Hals, *Catharina Hooft and Nurserymaid*, c. 1620. Oil on canvas, 86 × 65 (34 × 25½). Gemäldegalerie, Staatliche Museen zu Berlin (801G)/Christoph Schmidt

65 Jan Miense Molenaer, *Self-portrait with Family*, c. 1635–36. Oil on panel, 62.3 × 81.3 (24½ × 32). Frans Hals Museum, Haarlem (os 75-332)

66 Jan Steen, *As the Old Sing, so Pipe the Young*, c. 1663. Oil on canvas, 133.7 × 162.5 (52½ × 64). The Hague, Mauritshuis (742)

67 Gesina ter Borch, *Memorial Portrait of Moses ter Borch as a Two-year-old in 1647*, 1667. Oil on canvas, 56 × 45 (22 × 17½). Rijksmuseum, Amsterdam (SK-A-5124)

68 Jan Weenix, *Agnes Block with her Husband Sybrand de Flines and Two Children in the Garden at her Estate, the Vijverberg in Loenen aan de Vecht*, c. 1694. Oil on canvas, 84 × 111 (33⅛ × 43½). Amsterdam Museum (A 20359)

69 Gerrit van Honthorst, *The Liberation of St Peter*, c. 1616–18. Oil on canvas, 129 × 179 (51 × 70½). Gemäldegalerie, Staatliche Museen zu Berlin (431)/Jörg P. Anders

70 Pieter van Laer, *The Flagellants*, c. 1635. Oil on panel, 53.5 × 82 (21⅛ × 32). Alte Pinakothek, Munich (4833). Photo Scala, Florence/bpk, Bildagentur für Kunst, Kultur und Geschichte, Berlin

71 Caspar van Wittel, *View of Castel Sant' Angelo in Rome*, late seventeenth century. Oil on canvas. Musée des Beaux-Arts, Rouen (821.1.20)

72 Allart van Everdingen, *Hendrik Trip's Cannon Foundry in Julitabruk, Sweden*, c. 1650–75. Oil on canvas, 192 × 254.5 (75½ × 100). Rijksmuseum, Amsterdam (SK-A-1510)

73 Claude de Jongh, *View of Old London Bridge from the West*, 1630. Oil on panel, 50.8 × 167.6 (20 × 66). Kenwood House, London (88028831)

74 Frans Post, *Itamaracá*, 1637. Oil on canvas, 63.5 × 89.5 (25 × 35¼). Rijksmuseum, Amsterdam (SK-A-4271)

75 Albert Eckhout, *A Tapuya Woman at a Creek*, 1641. Oil on canvas, 272 × 165 (107⅛ × 65). Nationalmuseet, Copenhagen (N.38.a2)

76 Jasper or Jeronimus Becx, *Dom Miguel de Castro, Emissary of the Congo*, between 19 June and 2 July 1643. Oil on panel, 75 × 62 (29½ × 24). Statens Museum for Kunst, Copenhagen (KMS7)

77 Andries Beeckman, *The Castle of Batavia*, c. 1662. Oil on canvas, 108 × 151.4 (42½ × 59½). Rijksmuseum, Amsterdam (SK-A-19)

78 Joachim Wtewael, *The Martyrdom of St Sebastian*, 1600. Oil on canvas, 169.2 × 125.1 (66½ × 49¼). Nelson-Atkins Museum of Art, Kansas City (F84-71)

79 Hendrick ter Brugghen, *The Crucifixion with the Virgin and St John*, c. 1618. Oil on canvas, 154.9 × 102.2 (61 × 40¼). Metropolitan Museum of Art, New York (56.228)

80 Paulus Bor, *The Descent from the Cross*, c. 1635. Oil on canvas, 109.8 × 151.5 (43¼ × 59½). Centraal Museum, Utrecht (8284 a)

81 Jan Victors, *Jacob Burying the Pagan Idols*, 1646. Oil on canvas, 180 × 194 (71 × 76½). Statens Museum for Kunst, Copenhagen (1759)

82 Rembrandt school, *Judah and Tamar*, c. 1650–60. Oil on canvas, 108.5 × 130 (42½ × 51). Residenzgalerie, Salzburg (570)

83 Caesar van Everdingen, *The Holy Family*, c. 1660. Oil on canvas, 129 × 105 (51 × 41).

Museum Catharijneconvent, Utrecht (BMH x115)
84 Hendrik Goltzius, *Sine Cerere et Baccho friget Venus*, c. 1600. Ink and oil on canvas, 105.1 × 80 (41½ × 31½). Philadelphia Museum of Art (1990-100-1). Purchased with the Mr. and Mrs. Walter H. Annenberg Fund for Major Acquisitions, the Henry P. McIlhenny Fund in memory of Frances P. McIlhenny, bequest (by exchange) of Mr. and Mrs. Herbert C. Morris, and gift (by exchange) of Frank and Alice Osborn, 1990
85 Gerard ter Borch, *The Ratification of the Treaty of Münster*, 1648. Oil on copper, 45.4 × 58.5 (18 × 23). National Gallery, London (NG896)
86 By or after Jan de Baen, *The Glorification of Cornelis de Witt, with the Raid on Chatham in the Background*, 1667. Oil on canvas, 75.5 × 102 (29½ × 40). Rijksmuseum, Amsterdam (SK-A-4648)
87 Gerard de Lairesse, *Mark Antony at Cleopatra's Table*, c. 1675–80. Oil on canvas, 74 × 95.5 (29⅛ × 37½). Rijksmuseum, Amsterdam. H.A. Insinger-van Loon Bequest, Amsterdam (SK-A-2115)
88 Hendrick Goltzius, *Portrait of Jan Govertsen van der Aer with Shells from his Collection*, 1603. Oil on panel, 102.5 × 82.7 (40½ × 32½). Museum Boijmans Van Beuningen, Rotterdam (3450 (OK)). Loan P. & N. de Boer Foundation/ Photo Studio Tromp
89 Cornelis Jonson van Ceulen, *Portrait of Willem Thielen, Minister of the Dutch Reformed Church in London*, 1634. Oil on panel, 78.7 × 62.7 (31 × 24½). Museum Catharijneconvent, Utrecht (RMCC S348a)
90 Cornelis Jonson van Ceulen, *Portrait of Maria de Fraeye, Married to Willem Thielen*, 1634. Oil on panel, 78.7 × 62.7 (31 × 24½). Museum Catharijneconvent, Utrecht (RMCC S348b)
91 Rembrandt van Rijn, *Portrait of Jan Six*, 1654. Oil on canvas, 112 × 102 (44⅛ × 40). Six Collection, Amsterdam. incamerastock/alamy stock photo
92 Rembrandt van Rijn, *Self-portrait with Two Circles*, c. 1661–62. Oil on canvas, 116.3 × 97.2 (46 × 38¼). Kenwood House, London
93 Michiel van Musscher, *Self-portrait in the Studio*, 1679. Oil on panel, 57 × 46.5 (22½ × 18). Museum Rotterdam (10567-A-B)
94 Pieter de Grebber, *Elisha Refusing to Accept Presents from Naaman for Curing Naaman's Leprosy*, 1637. Oil on canvas, 120 × 185.5 (47¼ × 73). Frans Hals Museum, Haarlem (os i-103). Album/Alamy Stock Photo
95 Frans Hals, *Officers and Subalterns of St George's Civic Guard*, 1633. Oil on canvas, 207 × 337 (81½ × 132½). Frans Hals Museum, Haarlem (os i-112)

96 Jan de Bray, *Governors of the Haarlem Guild of St Luke*, 1675. Oil on canvas, 130 × 184 (51 × 72½). Rijksmuseum, Amsterdam (SK-A-58)
97 Jan Lievens, *Dutch Model Dressed as an Oriental*, c. 1630. Oil on canvas, 135 × 11 (53⅛ × 4). Sanssouci, Potsdam (Stiftung Preussische Schlösser und Gärten Berlin-Brandenburg; GK 4-184)
98 Monogrammist I.S., *Man with a Growth on his Nose*, 1645. Oil on panel, 48 × 47 (19 × 18½). Nationalmuseum, Stockholm (NM645). Photo Cecilia Heisser/Nationalmuseum
99 Willem Schellinks, *The Breaching of the Sint Anthonisdijk at Houtewael in 1651*, 1651. Oil on canvas, 47 × 68 (18½ × 26¾). Amsterdam Museum (SB 5456)
100 Jacob van Ruisdael, *The Jewish Cemetery at Ouderkerk aan de Amstel*, 1654 or 1655. Oil on canvas, 142.2 × 189.2 (56 × 74½). Detroit Institute of Arts (26.3)
101 Pieter Molijn, *Road through the Dunes*, 1626. Oil on panel, 26 × 23 (10¼ × 9). Herzog Anton Ulrich Museum, Braunschweig (GG 338). ARTGEN/Alamy Stock Photo
102 Simon de Vlieger, *Beach View with Fishermen and Recreationists*, 1643. Oil on panel, 60.6 × 83.5 (24 × 33). Mauritshuis, The Hague (558)
103 Jan Porcellis, *A Sailing Ship and a Rowboat in a Stormy Sea*, 1629. Oil on panel, 27 × 35.9 (10½ × 14⅛). Museum De Lakenhal, Leiden (S877)
104 Jan van Beecq, *English Warships in a Roadstead in Calm Weather*, 1677. Oil on canvas, 79 × 132 (31⅛ × 52). Statens Museum for Kunst, Copenhagen (KMSsp656)
105 Jan Martens de Jonge, *Cavalry Battle Between Dutch and Spanish Troops*, 1630. Oil on panel, 82 × 44 (32 × 17). Museum Boijmans Van Beuningen, Rotterdam. From the estate of C.M. Caster (1494 (OK))/Photo Studio Tromp.
106 Willem Cornelisz Duyster, *Two Officers Playing Cards on a Drum*, c. 1630–35. Oil on panel, 36 × 44 (14 × 17). Alte Pinakothek, Munich (302)
107 Adriaen Beeldemaker, *A Hunter*, 1653. Oil on canvas, 183.5 × 221 (72¼ × 87). Rijksmuseum, Amsterdam (SK-A-750)
108 Willem van Aelst, *Attributes of the Hunt*, 1668. Oil on canvas, 68 × 54 (26¾ × 21¼). Kunsthalle, Karlsruhe (350)
109 Jan van Goyen, *Cottages in a Landscape with a Well*, 1631. Oil on panel, 42.5 × 54.5 (16¾ × 21½). The Barber Institute of Fine Arts, Birmingham (59.4)
110 Aelbert Cuyp, *Cows in a Watery Landscape*, c. 1650. Oil on panel, 59 × 74 (23¼ × 29⅛). Museum of Fine Arts, Budapest (408)

111 Isaac van Ostade, *Winter in the Dutch Countryside*, c. 1640s. Oil on panel, 48.8 × 40 (19 × 15¾). National Gallery, London (NG848)
112 Aert van der Neer, *A River near a Town, by Moonlight*, c. 1645. Oil on panel, 30.3 × 48.4 (12 × 19). National Gallery, London (NG239)
113 Bartholomeus van Bassen, *Fantasy Church with Tomb of William the Silent*, 1620. Oil on canvas, 112 × 151 (44⅛ × 59½). Museum of Fine Arts, Budapest (1106). The Artchives/Alamy Stock Photo
114 Gerard Houckgeest, *Interior of the Nieuwe Kerk, Delft, with the Tomb of William of Orange*, 1651. Oil on panel, 56 × 38 (22 × 15). Mauritshuis, The Hague (58)
115 Emanuel de Witte, *Interior of the Portuguese Synagogue in Amsterdam*, 1680. Oil on canvas, 110 × 99 (43 × 39). Rijksmuseum, Amsterdam (SK-A-3738)
116 Sybrand van Beest, *A Hog Market in the Hague*, 1638. Oil on panel, 44 × 68 (17 × 26¾). Mauritshuis, The Hague (541)
117 Gabriël Metsu, *Old Seller of Game and Poultry Showing a Cock to a Young Woman*, 1662. Oil on panel, 61.5 × 45.5 (24 × 18). Gemäldegalerie Alte Meister, Dresden (1733). Photo Scala, Florence/bpk, Bildagentur für Kunst, Kultur und Geschichte, Berlin
118 David Vinckboons, *Distribution of Bread Outside an Almshouse*, c. 1610. Oil on panel, 35 × 53 (14 × 21). Nationalmuseum, Stockholm (NM 6679)
119 Adriaen van de Venne, *All-arm*, 1631. Oil on panel, 37.4 × 30 (14½ × 12). Amsterdam Museum (SA 7422)
120 Jan van Bijlert, *Inmates and Officials of the St Job Hospital and Old Men's Home in Utrecht*, c. 1630–35. Oil on canvas, 76.3 × 115.3 (30 × 45). Centraal Museum, Utrecht (7372)
121 Unknown artist, *Portrait of Jacob de Vogelaer, Town Secretary of Amsterdam*, 1655. Oil on canvas, 64.5 × 54 (25 × 21¼). Amsterdam Museum (SA 7266)
122 Cornelis Beelt, *A Smithy*, c. 1650–60. Oil on panel, 33.5 × 55 (13 × 21½). Frans Hals Museum, Haarlem (os 84-425)
123 After Adriaen van de Venne, Illustration for *Cats, Jacob. Spiegel van den ouden en nieuwen tyt*, Book III, p. 128. Jan Jacobsz. Schipper, 1657
124 Cornelis Gerritsz Decker, *The Weaver's Workshop*, 1659. Oil on panel, 45 × 55.7 (17½ × 22). Rijksmuseum, Amsterdam (SK-A-2562)
125 Quiringh van Brekelenkam, *Interior of a Tailor's Shop*, c. 1661–62. Oil on panel, 66 × 53.5 (26 × 21⅛). Rijksmuseum, Amsterdam (SK-C-112)
126 Caspar Netscher, *The Lace-maker*, 1662. Oil on canvas, 33 × 27 (13 × 10½). The Wallace Collection, London (P237)
127 Jan Steen, *A Bowling Game*, 1655. Oil on panel, 67 × 85.5 (26½ × 33½). Kunsthistorisches Museum, Vienna (6319)
128 Adriaen van Ostade, *The Courtyard of an Inn with a Game of Shuffleboard*, 1677. Oil on panel, 33.7 × 47 (13¼ × 18½). English Heritage, The Wellington Collection, Apsley House (WM.1521-1948). Historic England/Bridgeman Images
129 Jan Davidsz de Heem, *The Student, or Interior of a Room with a Young Man Seated at a Table*, 1628. Oil on panel, 60 × 82 (23½ × 32). Ashmolean Museum, Oxford (WA1940.2.34)
130 Cornelis Pietersz Bega, *Saying Grace*, 1663. Oil on canvas, 37.5 × 30 (14¾ × 12). Rijksmuseum, Amsterdam (SK-C-95)
131 Pieter de Hooch, *Woman with Maid at Linen Cabinet*, 1663. Oil on canvas, 70 × 75.5 (27½ × 29½). Rijksmuseum, Amsterdam (SK-C-1191)
132 Dirck van Delen, *A Musical Company*, 1636. Oil on panel, 41.3 × 61.8 (16¼ × 24). Museum Boijmans Van Beuningen, Rotterdam (1158 (OK))/ Photo Studio Tromp
133 Jan Steen, *A Young Woman Playing a Harpsichord to a Young Man*, probably 1659. Oil on panel, 42.3 × 33 (16½ × 13). National Gallery, London (NG856)
134 Johannes Vermeer, *Young Woman Standing at the Virginal*, c. 1670–72. Oil on canvas 51.7 × 45.2 (20½ × 18). National Gallery, London (NG1383)
135 Hendrick ter Brugghen, *Unequal Lovers*, c. 1623. Oil on canvas, 74.3 × 89.2 (29¼ × 35⅛). Kremer Collection
136 Judith Leyster, *A Man Offering Money to a Woman*, 1631. Oil on panel, 30.8 × 24.2 (12⅛ × 9½). Mauritshuis, The Hague (564)
137 Jacob van Loo, *Amaryllis Crowning Mirtillo*, c. 1648. Oil on canvas, 161 × 192 (63½ × 75½). Rijksmuseum Muiderslot, Muiden (M1998-014)
138 Frans van Mieris, *The Oyster Meal*, 1661. Oil on panel, 27.6 × 20.8 (11 × 8). Mauritshuis, The Hague (819)
139 Eglon van der Neer, *Interior of a Brothel, with a Woman Washing Her Hands*, 1675. Oil on panel, 49.2 × 39.6 (19½ × 15½). Mauritshuis, The Hague (862)
140 Claes Jansz Visscher, Emblem 1 in Roemer Visscher, *Sinnepoppen*, 1614. Letterpress and etching. University Library, Utrecht (LMY 447)
141 Cornelis Jacobsz Delff, *Still Life of Kitchen Utensils*, 1610–45. Oil on panel, 66 × 100 (26 × 39½). Ashmolean Museum, Oxford (WA1940.2.24)

142 Floris van Dijck, *Still Life with Fruits, Nuts and Cheese (A 'Breakfast Piece')*, 1613. Oil on panel, 49.1 × 77.4 (19 × 30½). Frans Hals Museum, Haarlem (os i-76)
143 Pieter Claesz, *Still Life with Herring and Beer*, 1636. Oil on panel, 49 × 36 (19 × 14). Museum Boijmans Van Beuningen, Rotterdam (1122 (OK))/ Photo Studio Tromp
144 Willem Kalf, *Still Life with a Chinese Bowl, Nautilus Cup and Other Objects*, 1662. Oil on canvas, 79.4 × 67.3 (31¼ × 26½). Thyssen-Bornemisza Museum, Madrid (203 (1962.10))
145 Adriaen Coorte, *Asparagus*, 1697. Oil on paper on panel, 25 × 20.5 (10 × 8⅛). Rijksmuseum, Amsterdam (SK-A-2099)
146 Ambrosius Bosschaert, *Vase with Flowers*, 1609. Oil on panel, 51 × 36.5 (20⅛ × 14½). Kunsthistorisches Museum, Vienna (547)
147 Maria van Oosterwijck, *Flowers and Shells*, c. 1685. Oil on canvas, 72 × 56 (28 × 22). Gemäldegalerie Alte Meister, Dresden (1334). akg-images
148 Otto Marseus van Schrieck, *Forest Floor Still Life with Insects and Amphibians*, 1662. Oil on canvas, 50.7 × 68.5 (20 × 27). Herzog Anton Ulrich-Museum, Braunschweig (GG 431)
149 Rachel Ruysch, *Tree Trunk Surrounded by Flowers, Butterflies and Animals*, 1685. Oil on canvas, 99 × 82 (39 × 32). Museum Boijmans Van Beuningen, Rotterdam (1751 (OK)). Photo Studio Tromp
150 Diagram from Sam Segal, *Flowers and Nature: Netherlandish Flower Painting of Four Centuries*, The Hague, 1990. Courtesy RKD Archives
151 Roelant Savery, *Cows in a Stable, with Witches in the Corners*, 1615. Oil on panel, 30.2 × 30.6 (11⅞ × 12). Rijksmuseum, Amsterdam (SK-A-2211)
152 Cornelis Saftleven, *Satire on the Trial of Johan van Oldenbarnevelt*, 1663. Oil on canvas, 63 × 85.7 (25 × 33¾). Rijksmuseum, Amsterdam. Gift of G. de Clercq, Amsterdam (SK-A-1588)
153 Melchior d'Hondecoeter, *A Pelican and other Birds near a Pool, known as 'The Floating Feather'*, c. 1680. Oil on canvas, 159 × 144 (62½ × 56½). Rijksmuseum, Amsterdam (SK-A-175)
154 Johannes Torrentius, *Emblematic Still Life with Flagon, Glass, Jug and Bridle*, 1614. Oil on panel, 51 × 51.5 (20⅛ × 20). Rijksmuseum, Amsterdam (SK-A-2813)
155 David Bailly, *Vanitas Still Life with Portrait of a Young Painter*, 1651. Oil on panel, 89.5 × 122 (35¼ × 48). Museum De Lakenhal, Leiden (S 1351)
156 Gerard Dou, *The Quacksalver*, 1652. Oil on panel, 83.4 × 112.4 (33 × 44¼). Museum Boijmans Van Beuningen, Rotterdam (st4). Loan Stichting Museum Boijmans Van Beuningen. Photo Studio Tromp
157 Carel Fabritius, *View in Delft, with Music Shop*, 1652. Oil on canvas, 15.5 × 31.7 (6⅛ × 12½). National Gallery, London (NG3714)
158 Samuel van Hoogstraten, *A Perspective Box with Views of the Interior of a Dutch House*, c. 1655–60. Oil on wood, 58 × 88 × 60.5 (23 × 34½ × 24). National Gallery, London (NG3832)
159 Samuel van Hoogstraten, *A Perspective Box with Views of the Interior of a Dutch House*, c. 1655–60. National Gallery, London (NG3832)/ Scala, Florence
160 Rembrandt? Ferdinand Bol?, *Portrait of an Old Woman, possibly Elisabeth Bas*, c. 1640–45. Oil on canvas,118 × 91.5 (46½ × 36). Rijksmuseum, Amsterdam (SK-A-714)
161 Melchior d'Hondecoeter, *Trompe l'oeil with Three Dead Thrushes, Currants and Decoy Flutes Hung on a Wooden Plank*, c. 1670. Oil on canvas, 84 × 66 (33⅛ × 26). Suermondt-Ludwig Museum, Aachen (GK 211)/Bridgeman Images

Index

Numbers in italics refer to pages
where a work is illustrated.
Less familiar names are provided with
an indication of who they are. If no
nationality is indicated for a person,
he or she is Dutch.

A

'Abbas the Great, Persian Shah
108
Aelst, Willem van, painter
171–73; *108*
Aertsen, Pieter, painter 182
Afghanistan 171
Africa, Africans 116–20
Agesilaus, king of Sparta 232
Albertus Magnus, German
medieval theologian 68
Alkmaar 113
Altdorfer, Albrecht, German
painter, printmaker 84
Alps 8
Amersfoort 45, 128–29
Ampzing, Samuel, Calvinist
clergyman, historian 209–10
Amstel van Mynden, van,
aristocratic family 126–27
Amsterdam 64, 67–68, 75, 99,
101, 157, 180, 186–87, 214,
236, 246; painters active in
10, 19, 24, 30, 44, 67–68, 70–
77, 84–85, 88, 101, 151, 167,
195, 218, 222, 224, 226, 229,
236; patrons and collectors
in 25, 106, 124, 133, 147, 195,
213–14
Amstel River 72

civic guard 36, 153, 218;
Kloveniers meeting hall 36
Dam Square 72, 122
Damrak 75
Exchange 74
flooded in dike breach 161
guilds 46
house of Andries de Graeff
133
Nieuwe Kerk 72–73, 75
Nieuwezijds Kapel 45
Reformed Diaconate Girls'
Orphanage 62; *41*
Rijksmuseum 105, 195, 214,
244
synagogues 76–77, 183
town government 63, 72, 76,
190–91
town hall (now Royal Palace)
26, 60, 63, 72–73, 75–76
Trippenhuis 113
University of 108
Warmoesstraat 75
weighing hall 71, 75
Zuiderkerk 46, 48–49
Angel, Philips, painter, writer
on art 244
Antwerp 10, 13, 26, 40, 95, 111,
167, 217, 222; chamber of
rhetoric De Violieren 13;
exchange 73; guild of St
Luke 13
Apelles, ancient Greek painter
148–50
Ariosto, Ludovico, Italian poet
148
d'Arpino, Cavaliere (Giuseppe
Cesari), Italian painter 217
Asia 120–22, 229
Avercamp, Hendrick, painter
30–31; *19*

B

Backer, Jacob, painter 85
Baen, Jan de, painter 86
Baer, Ronni, American art
historian 236
Baerle, Suzanne van, married to
Constantijn Huygens 36; *22*
Bailly, David, painter 231–35;
155
Bakker, Boudewijn, art
historian 160
Balen, Sara van, married to
Samuel van Hoogstraten 242

Baltic States 108
Banda Islands 121
Batavia 120
Barberini, House of 19
Bassen, Bartholomeus van,
painter, architect 179; *113*
Becx, Jaspar or Jeronimus,
painters 118–20; *76*
Beeckman, Andries, painter
120–21; *77*
Beecq, Jan van, Dutch painter
in France 167–68; *104*
Beeldemaker, Adriaen, painter
171; *107*
Beelt, Cornelis, painter 190;
122
Beest, Sybrand van, painter
182; *116*
Bega, Cornelis Pietersz, painter
195, 199–200; *130*
Bemba, Diego, African servant
to Sonho envoy 120
Berchem, Nicolaes, painter
217
Berckheyde brothers, painters
45, 77, 80
Berckheyde, Gerrit, 171; *50, 54*
– Job 147
Bergen op Zoom 222
Bergström, Ingvar, Swedish art
historian 235
Beuckelaer, Joachim, Flemish
painter 182
Bie, Cornelis de, Flemish writer
on art 235
Bièvre, Elisabeth de, art
historian 70
Bijlert, Jan van, painter 188–89;
120
Blankert, Albert, art historian
2, 7, 244
Block, Agnes, patron 105–
106
Bloemaert, Abraham, painter
52–53, 91, 126, 147, 164; *33*
Bohemia 55
Bok, Marten Jan, art historian,
economic historian 115
Bol, Ferdinand, painter 60, 71,
244; *16, 160*
– Laurens J., art historian 220
Boogaart, Ernst van den,
historian 117
Bor, Paulus, painter 124,
128–29; *80*

Borch, Gerard ter, father of the
following 105
– Gerard II ter, painter 105,
134–36; *85*
– Gesina ter, painter,
draughtsman 95, 105; *67*
– Moses ter, military man
105; *67*
Borghese popes 19
Borsselen, Philibert van, poet
143
Bosschaert, Ambrosius,
painter 222; *146*
Bourbon, House of 19
Boursse, Esaias, painter 120
Bouts, Dieric, painter 79
Boxer, Charles, British
historian 116
Brabant 26
Bracamonte y Guzmán,
Don Caspar de, Spanish
diplomat 134
Brandenburg, House of 21
Bray, Cornelia de, married to
Jan Lievens 156
– Dirck de, painter 156–57
– Jan de, painter 156–57; *96*
– Joseph de, painter 156
– Salomon de, architect,
painter 156
Brazil (also Dutch Brazil, New
Holland) 106, 116–20, 226
Breda 57, 222
Bredius, Abraham, art
historian 244
Breen, Gillis van, printmaker
184
Brekelenkam, Quiringh van,
painter 193–95; *125*
Brès, Guido de, Flemish
Calvinist theologian
160
Bril, Paul, Flemish painter in
Rome 110–11
Bronckhorst, Pieter van,
painter 59; *38*
Brouwer, Adriaen, Flemish
painter 13; *5*
Bruegel, Pieter 10, 31, 40, 103,
160, 164, 187
Brugghen, Hendrick ter,
painter 89, 91, 115, 126–29,
207–10; *60, 79, 135*
Brun, Charles Le, French
painter, academician 167

Bruyns, Anna Francisca de,
painter 94
Burch, Hendrick van der,
painter 86; *57*
Buytewech, Willem, painter,
printmaker 31; *20*

C
Calvin, John 131, 160
Campen, Jacob van, painter,
architect 36, 60, 63, 72–73,
129; *22*
Canaletto (Giovanni Antonio
Canal), Italian painter 112
Caravaggio, Michelangelo
Merisi da 52–53, 88–90,
110–11, 208
Cardozo, David de Abraham,
Sephardi art owner 182
Castiglione, Baldassare, Italian
writer 147
Castro, Dom Miguel de, African
envoy 120
Cats, Jacob, poet 190; *123*
Cellini, Benvenuto 202
Charles I, King of England 55,
77, 148, 232
Charles II, King of England 24
Chatham, Raid on 137–39
Chigi popes 20
Christian of Braunschweig-
Lüneburg, German military
man 82
Claesz, Pieter, painter 217; *143*
Cleopatra 96, 137, 141
Cock, Cunera van der, married
to Frans van Mieris 211
Codde, Pieter, painter 169, 202
Colenbrander, Herman, art
historian 242
Colijns, David, painter 45–46; *29*
Collier, Edward, painter 114
Cologne 19
Constable, John, British painter
176
Coorte, Adriaen, painter 219–21;
145
Cornelis Cornelisz van
Haarlem, painter 79, 124,
153, 200
Cossiers, Jan, Flemish painter 13
Couwenbergh, Christiaan van,
painter 59–60; *39*
Craesbeeck, Joos van, Flemish
painter 13

Curaçao 106
Cuyp family 71
Cuyp, Albert, painter 114,
175–76, 226; *110*

D
Decker, Cornelis Gerritsz,
painter 193; *124*
– Jeremias de, poet 71
Delen, Dirck van, painter 202; *132*
Delff, Cornelis Jacobsz, painter
215; *142*
– Willem Jacobsz, printmaker 77
Delft 74, 77–79, 173, 236; *157*;
Museum Prinsenhof 77, 168;
Nieuwe Kerk (New Church)
51, 77, 81, 236; *181*; tomb of
William of Orange 51, 77, 79,
179–80; painters active in 9,
19, 45, 51, 70, 74, 180, 195,
222, 243–44; painters' guild
59; patrons and collectors
in 64, 123; Prinsenhof 77;
town hall 79; *52*; town
government 59–60
Den Bosch 52
Denmark, 108, 113, 120
Deshima 122
Diest, Willem van, painter 167
Dijck, Floris van, painter
215–17; *142*
Dordrecht 70–72, 136–37;
Dordrechts Museum 176;
painters active in 57, 174–75,
195; patrons and collectors
in 175; town government
59–60
Dou, Gerard (Gerrit), painter
44, 67, 84, 147, 151, 156, 195,
235; *156*
Drenthe 55
Dudok van Heel, Bas, archivist,
historian 99
Duijn, Mart van, librarian 87
Duquesnoy, François, Flemish
sculptor 17–18
Duyster, Willem Cornelisz,
painter 169; *106*
Dyck, Anthony van 114, 146, 210
– Justina van, painter 95

E
East Indies 121, 218, 229
Eckhout, Albert, painter 116–18,
120; *75*

Edo 122

Eeckhout, Gerbrand van den, painter 130

Egmond, Abbey of St Adelbert 163

Elizabeth I, Queen of England 73

Elizabeth Stuart, consort of Friedrich V 55, 82, 88, 179, 187

Emmens, Jan, art historian 236

Emmerich 106

England (also Britain, Great Britain) 18–20, 26, 40, 55, 57, 77, 108–09, 114–15, 146, 148, 232

Ernst Casimir, Stadholder of Friesland, Groningen and Drenthe 55; *35*

Everdingen, Allart van, painter 113; *72*

– Caesar van, painter 133, 207; *42, 83*

Eyck, Jan and Hubert van 93

– Marguerite van, painter 93

F

Fabritius, Carel, painter 38, 79, 236, 243, 246; *24, 157*

Flinck, Govert, painter 44, 60, 67–68; *40*

Flines, Susanna de, married to David Rutgers 106

Florence 19, 109, 224; Gli Uffizi 67, 147; Netherlands Art History Institute 109; Loggia de' Lanzi 202; Medici court 173, 224

Fraeye, Maria de, married to Willem Thielen 146–47; *90*

France 18–19, 99, 115, 148, 167–68, 179, 210, 222

Francesca, Piero della 84

Frederick III, King of Denmark 120

Frederik Hendrik, Stadholder 26, 30, 55–56, 77, 82, 120, 136, 179, 187, 210; *36*; paintings for 60, 98, 129, 157

Friedländer, Max J., art historian 246

Friedrich V, Elector Palatine of the Rhine, married to Elizabeth Stuart 55, 82, 88, 98, 179, 187

Friesland 55

Frijhoff, Willem, historian 181

Frimmel, Theodor von, Austrian art historian 157

Fuchs, Rudi, art historian 166

G

Gainsborough, Thomas, British painter 176

Gaius Fabricius Luscinus, Roman consul 60

Garcia II, Dom, King of Kongo 120

Geertgen tot Sint Jans, painter 79

Geest, Wybrand de, painter 55; *35*

Gelder, Arent (Aert) de, painter 71, 130

Germany 18, 56, 63, 83, 106, 108, 160, 179, 224

Gerson, Horst, art historian 25, 108

Ghent 167

Gheyn, Jacques de, painter, printmaker 233

Giotto 148, 150

Giustiniani, Vincenzo, Italian aristocrat, patron 110–11

Glarges, Claude de, grandfather of Claude de Jongh 115

Glauber, Diana, painter 94

Godewijk, Margaretha van, painter 94

Gogh, Vincent van 34

Goltzius, Hendrick, painter, printmaker 24, 79, 133–34, 143–44, 161, 231; *84, 88*

Gool, Johan van, writer on art 95

Goos, Abraham, cartographer, *Map of the Seventeen Provinces* 2

Goting, Jan van, painter 157

Gouda 13

Govertsen van der Aar, Jan, art owner, portrait sitter 143–45; *88*

Goyen, Grietje van, daughter of Jan van Goyen, married to Jan Steen 102

– Jan van, painter 142, 173; *109*

Graeff, Andries de, officeholder, patron 133

Graeff, Cornelis de, officeholder 101

– Pieter de, art owner 99

Grebber, Frans Pietersz de, painter 153, 210

– Maria de, painter, daughter of Frans Pietersz de Grebber, 94, 210

– Pieter de, painter 152–53, 210; *94*

Greece 109, 199

Greenwich, Queen's House (National Maritime Museum) 24

Greve, Aleida, painter, patron 94–97; *62*

Groenendijk, Pieter, art historian 95

Groningen 55, 116

Grootenboer, Hanneke, art historian 221

Guarini, Giovanni Battista, Italian playwright 210

Gustav II Adolf, King of Sweden 22

H

Haarlem 19, 52, 74, 79–81, 109, 153, 190, 193, 232; academy 10, 79; Bavokerk (Great Church) 79–81, 156; civic guard 153; *95*; Dominican monastery 81; Frans Hals Museum 34, 81; Grote Markt (Great Market Square) 80–81; *107*; guild of St Luke 156, 190; *96*; lepers' home 152; painters active in 10, 13, 45, 111, 156, 161, 163, 167; patrons and collectors in 99, 143; Prinsenhof 81; Spaarne River 79; town government 153; town hall 81, 156

Haboldt, Bob, art dealer 157

Habsburg, House of, rule over Netherlands 6, 26, 44, 55, 64, 67, 108

Hadrian, Emperor 112

The Hague 82, 91, 179, 229 Buitenhof 55 Great Church 51; *32* House of Constantijn Huygens and Suzanne van Baerle 36 Huis ten Bosch, the Oranjezaal 26, 28, 56, 133, 136; *15*

Haags Gemeentemuseum (until 1998); Gemeentemuseum Den Haag (1998–2019); Kunstmuseum Den Haag (2019–) 6
Mauritshuis (Royal Cabinet of Paintings; town palace of Johann Maurits) 116, 213–14
meat hall (St Nicholas Guesthouse) 182–83; *116*
painters active in 26, 57, 167, 195, 222
residence of Friedrich V and Elizabeth Stuart 55
RKD – Netherlands Institute for Art History 25
Hakvoort, Barend, bookseller 91
Hals, Frans 9, 19, 34, 99, 101, 153, 234; *21*, *64*, *95*
Heem, Jan Davidsz de, painter 13, 199, 222; *129*
Heemskerck, Maarten van, painter 81, 109
Heer, Magaretha de, painter 95
Hegel, Georg Wilhelm Friedrich 6, 184
Hein, Piet, Admiral 116
Helst, Bartholmeus van der, painter 36, 85–86, 148; *23*
Hemessen, Catharina van, painter 93
Henrietta Maria, Queen of England 77
Hillegaert, Paulus van, painter 82; *55*
Hitler, Adolf 214
Hobbema, Meindert, 41–42, 171; *27*
Hofstede de Groot, Cornelis, art historian 41
Hohenzollern electors 21, 157
Holland (province) 70, 91
Holy Roman Empire 148
Hondecoeter, Gillis Claesz de, painter 107
– Melchior d', painter 226, 229–30, 246; *153*, *161*
Honselaersdijk, palace of Frederik Hendrik 129
Honthorst, Gerard van, painter 97–98, 110–12; *36*, *63*, *69*

Hooch, Pieter de, painter 9, 79; *131*
Hooft, Catharina, sitter for childhood portrait 99–100–01; *64*
– Pieter Jansz, father of Catharina Hooft 99
Hooghe, Romeyn de, printmaker 182
Hoogstraten, Samuel van, painter, writer on art 31, 36, 57, 71; 207, 236, 238–40; *159*
Hoop, Adriaan van der, banker, art owner 195
Horace, Roman poet 71
Houbraken, Antonina van, painter 95
– Arnold van, painter, writer on art 64, 71, 75, 93–95, 151, 211, 217, 223–24, 236, 239
Houckgeest, Gerard, painter 45, 51, 74, 77, 180 236; *114*
Huizinga, Johan, historian 168
Huygens, Christiaan, scientist 36
– Constantijn, humanist, auxiliary to House of Orange 36, 63, 73, 157–58, 163, 199, 232

I
India 108, 120
Isaacsz, Pieter, painter 30
Isfahan 108; Capuchin friars 120; Forty Columns Pavilion 108
Italy 45, 52, 68, 70, 84, 89, 99, 109–13, 126, 175, 202, 217; painters active in 8, 18, 53, 109, 112, 129; patrons and collectors in 68, 110

J
Jacobsz, Lambert, painter 85
James I, King of England 55
Jantzen, Hans, German art historian 179
Japan 120–22, 151
Jaucourt, François de, Marquis d'Ausson, art owner 112
Java 121
Jerusalem 46, 59
Jochems, Peter, artist, writer on art 221

Johan Maurits van Nassau-Siegen, Count 116, 120, 189, 226
Johann Wilhelm, Elector Palatine 42, 148, 224
Jonge, Gerard de, cousin of Pieter Saenredam 49
– Pieter de, cousin of Pieter Saenredam 49
Jongh, Claude de, painter 115; *73*
– Eddy de, art historian 102, 184
– Jan de, painter 157
Jonghe, Herman de, father of Claude de Jongh 115
Jonson van Ceulen, Cornelis, painter 144–46, 163; *89*, *90*
Jordaens, Jacques (Jacob), Flemish painter 26; *15*

K
Kalf, Willem, painter, 217–18; *144*
Kaplan, Yosef, Israeli historian 182
Karl VI, Holy Roman Emperor 148
Keyser, Hendrick de, architect, sculptor 49, 73, 77, 179
– Thomas de, painter 46, 49; *30*
Knuijt, Maria Simonsdr van, art owner, patron 64
Knuttel, Gerhardus, art historian 6
Koerten, Johanna, painter 94
Kongo 120
Kraków, Jagiellonian University 116

L
Laer, Pieter van, painter 111–12, 147; *70*
Lairesse, Gerard de, painter, writer on art 133, 136–41, 212, 218; *87*
Lastman, Pieter, painter 46, 48
– Zeger, goldsmith 46
Le Nain brothers, French painters 218
Leeuwarden 45, 55, 85
Leeuwen, Rudie van, art historian 153
Leiden 82–87, 167, 193, 235–36; Blauwpoort 235; Latin school 86; painters active in

70, 84–85, 195, 222, 232–35, 244; patrons and collectors in 236; Serge Hall 84; town government 84; town hall 84; university 67, 83–87, 163, 224

Leopold, Holy Roman Emperor 222

Leopold Wilhelm, Archduke 64–65

Levitt, Ruth, art historian and more 174

Leyster, Judith, painter 94–95, 102, 208–10; *136*

Liebermann, Max, German painter 34

Lievens, Jan, painter 13, 156–58; *97*

Lingelbach, Johannes, German painter in Amsterdam 75–76; *49*

Linz, Führermuseum 214

London 73, 115, 163; Church of Austin Friars 144–45; Old London Bridge 115; *73*; painters active in 57, 109, 114–15, 146, 167, 222; Royal Exchange 73

Loo, Jacob van, painter 210; *137*

Loosdrecht 126

Lorrain, Claude, French painter 110

Louis XIV, King of France 115, 148, 222

Louise Hollandine van de Palts, painter 98, 115

Louvain 83

Lowestoft, Battle of 51

Lucas van Leyden, painter, printmaker 84

Lundens, Gerrit, painter 21; *9, 10*

M

Madrid 25

Maes, Nicolaes, painter 71, 195; *46*

Mander, Karel van, painter, writer on art 10, 13–15, 18, 20, 30, 79, 93, 123, 126, 134, 143, 148, 161, 163–64, 238; *3*

Manet, Edouard 34

Mannheimer, Fritz, German banker in Amsterdam 213–14

Marcgraf, Georg, German naturalist in Brazil 116

Marcus Curius Dentatus, Roman consul 60; *40*

Mark Antony 137

Marle, Eva van, erroneously held to be a painter 91

Martens de Jonge, Jan, painter 168; *105*

Mary Stuart, Queen of England, consort of King William III 55

Mary Stuart, married to Stadholder Willem II 77

Master or Monogrammist I.S., painter 159; *98*

Matham, Jacob, printmaker 60

Matthias, Holy Roman Emperor 229

Maubisson, convent in France 115

Maurits van Nassau, Stadholder 55, 77, 82, 89, 229

Mazo, Juan Bautista del, Spanish painter 25; *14*

Medici, House of 19; Cosimo III de', Grand Duke 67, 222, 224; Ferdinando de', Grand Duke 173; Leopoldo de', Cardinal 147

Meegeren, Han van, painter, art forger 244

Meertman, Evert, painter 92

Mendes de Crasto, Manuel, Sephardi art owner 124

Merian, Maria Sibylla, German artist, naturalist 94, 226

Metsu, Gabriël, painter 25, 184, 195; *13*; *117*

Meulen, Adam Frans van der, Flemish painter in France 168

Michelangelo 110, 217

Middelburg 10, 119–20, 146, 167, 187, 220, 222

Mierevelt, Michiel van, painter 77, 142

Mieris, Frans van, painter 44, 64, 67, 84, 148, 211–12; *44, 138*

Molenaer, Jan Miense, painter 15, 17, 94, 101–102, 210; *7, 65*

Molijn, Pieter, painter 163; *101*

Monte, Isacq del, Sephardi art owner 124

Montias, John Michael, American economist, historian 64, 67, 123, 246

Moreelse, Paulus, painter 88–91; *59*

Moro, Antonio (Anthonis Mor), painter 55

Mundy, Peter, British writer 194

Musscher, Michiel van, painter 148, 151; *93*

mythological personages Aeneas 189; Amor 205; Apollo 17, 207; Bacchus 133; Ceres 133; Cupid 17, 36, 134; Diana 96, 210; Eros 238; Ganymede 207; Hyacinth 207; Hylas 207; Icarus 164; Juno 71; Mars 84, 133; Mercury 36, 84–86; Minerva 84–86; Nais 207; Neptune 217; Pan 210; Phaeton 167; Venus 133

N

Nagasaki 122

Napoleon 136

Nassau-Dietz, House of 55

Neer, Aert van der, painter 178; *112*

– Eglon van der, painter 212–14; *139*

Netherlands, Kingdom 91; Northern (also Republic of the Seven United Netherlands, the Dutch Republic) 6, 10, 18–19, 26, 44, 51, 70, 72, 82, 88, 91, 115, 136, 178, 185, 200, 229; *9*; art of 8, 18–19, 94, 102, 160, 168 Seventeen Provinces (also the Low Countries) 8–13, 70, 87, 108, 222 Southern (also the Spanish Netherlands, Flanders, Belgium) 6, 8–10, 18, 26, 52, 59, 64, 70, 83, 94, 102, 110, 176, 200, 221, 226

Netscher, Caspar, painter 195–97; *1, 126*

Neufville, Agneta, niece of Agneta Block, and daughters 106

Nieulandt, Adriaen van, painter 30; *17*

Nieuwpoort, Battle of 22

Norway 113

Nunes Hendriques, Jacob, Sephardi art owner 182

O

Oever, Hendrick ten, painter 91–92; *61*

Oldenbarnevelt, Grand Pensionary Johan van, 71, 229

Oosterwijck, Maria van, painter 94–95, 142, 222–23; *137*

Oostfries, Catharina, painter 94

Orange-Nassau, House of 21, 26, 30, 36, 55, 77, 82, 88, 109, 136, 157–58, 169, 176, 210; *55*

Oranienbaum, near Dessau 56

Oranienburg, near Berlin 56

Oranjenhof, in the Rhineland 56

Oranienstein, in the Rhineland 56

Orient, orientals 75–76, 137, 148; *97*

Orlers, Jan Jansz, officeholder, writer 84

Ossing, Franz, German meteorologist 164

Ostade, Adriaen van, painter, printmaker 15, 17, 197–98, 200; *6*, *128*

– Isaac van, painter 176; *111*

Ottoman Empire 109

Oudenaarde 13

Ouderkerk aan de Amstel, Portuguese Jewish cemetery 162–63; *100*

Ouwater, Albert van, painter 79

Overlander van Purmerland, Geertruid, mother of Catharina Hooft 99

Ovid 14

P

Pamphili, Camillo, art owner, papal nephew 18

Paris 109, 167, 218; Académie royale de peinture et de sculpture 167

Patinir, Joachim, Flemish painter 160

Pauw, Adriaen, aristocrat, diplomat 134

Peeters, Clara, Flemish painter 95

Persia 108, 120, 151, 218

Petrarch, Italian poet 204

Philip Willem van Oranje, son of William of Orange 82

Pieters, Geertje, painter, housemaid 94, 223

Pigler, Andor, Hungarian art historian 207

Plancius, Petrus, Flemish cartographer 151

Plautus, Roman playwright 207

Pliny the Elder 137, 148

Ploos, Adriaen, patron 126–27

– Adriaen Willemsz, nobleman, donor 126

– Gerrit, son of Adriaen Willemsz Ploos 126

Plutarch, Roman writer 60, 232

Poland 108, 222

Pollmer, Almut, art historian 179

Pool, Jurriaen, painter 224

Porcellis, Jan, painter 167, 244; *103*

Portugal 77, 116, 119, 124

Post, Frans, painter 116; *74*

– Pieter, painter, architect 63, 116, 224; *42*

Potsdam, German Research Centre for Geosciences 164; Sanssouci 157

Protogenes, Greek painter 148, 150

Pseudo-ten Oever, painter of unknown identity 92

Putten, Maria van der, mother of Margaretha Maria de Roodere 97; *63*

Q

Quellinus, Artus, Flemish sculptor 60, 190

R

Raphael 110

Rembrandt (full name Rembrandt Harmensz van Rijn) 9, 30, 70, 84, 157–59, 197, 217, 236; biography 19, 36, 67–68, 71, 86–87, 186; pupils and followers 28, 57, 71, 130, 236; works 129–30, 147–48, 157, 195, 244

Aristotle with a Bust of Homer 68; *45*

Christ Appearing to Mary Magdalene 71

Homer 147

Jan Six 147; *91*

The Jewish Bride 38, 40, 195; *25*

The Mill 30; *18*

Minerva Reading at a Desk 147

The Night Watch 22, 36, 157

Self-portraits 147; *Self-portrait with Two Circles* 148–50; *92*

'Sultan Soliman' 158; *97*

Syndics of the Drapers Guild 157

Renyi, Andras, Hungarian art historian 150

Rhenen, palace of Friedrich V and Elizabeth Stuart 55, 179

Rhodes 148

Riegl, Alois, Austrian art historian 151

Ripa, Cesare, Italian humanist 133

Roman Republic 61–62

Rome 18, 63, 110–11, 114, 180; Accademia di San Luca 110; Castel Sant'Angelo 112; *71*; painters active in 18, 63, 88–89, 109–12, 114, 129, 173, 189, 208, 217, 224; Palazzo Giustiniani 110; St Peter's 112; San Luigi dei Francesi 110; Santa Maria del Popolo 110

Roodenburg, Herman, historian 202

Roodere, Gerard de, father of Margaretha Maria de Roovere 97; *63*

– Margaretha Maria de, painter 97–98; *63*

Rotterdam 151, 167

Rozee, Miss, embroiderer 94

Rubens, Pieter Paul 13, 52, 129

Rudolf II, Holy Roman Emperor 134, 226–27

Ruffo, Don Antonio, Sicilian nobleman, art owner 68

Ruijven, Pieter Claesz van, patron 64

Ruisdael, Jacob van, painter, printmaker 41, 79–80, 113, 162–63; *53*, *100*

Russell, Margarita, American art historian 93

Russia 190

Rutgers, David, Mennonite merchant 106
Ruysch, Frederik, anatomist, botanist 224
– Rachel, painter 94–95, 224, 226; *149*
Ruyter, Michiel de, Admiral 26–28, 137; *12, 16*
Rybczynski, Witold, Canadian historian 199

S

Saenredam, Jan, printmaker 49
– Pieter, painter 21, 49–50, 72–74, 76, 81, 109, 178, 180; *31, 47*
Saftleven, Cornelis, painter 229; *152*
Sandrart, Joachim von, German painter, writer on art 95
Savery, Roelant, Flemish painter in Prague and Northern Netherlands 226; *151*
Savoy, Karel van, painter 130
Scandinavia 113–14
Schalcken, Godfried, painter 56–57, 71, 147; *37*
Schama, Simon, British-American historian 105
Schechem 130
Schellinks, Willem, painter 161–62; *99*
Schooten, Floris van, painter 215
– Franciscus van, mathematician 86
– Joris van, painter 86
Schrieck, Otto Marseus van, painter 224–26, 230; *148*
Schuurman, Anna Maria van, master of all arts, humanist 94
Scotland 55
Segal, Sam, botanist, art historian 221–22, 226–27
Segers, Hercules, painter, printmaker 22, 24; *11*
Serlio, Sebastiano, Italian writer on art 151
Shakespeare 167
Sicily 68
Six, Jan, officeholder, patron 146–48; *91*
Smijters, Anna, miniaturist 93

Smith, John, British art dealer, writer on art 38
Solms, Amalia van, married to Frederik Hendrik 26, 55–56, 187; *36*
Sonho, Count of, African ruler 120
South America 116, 229; *see also* Brazil, Johann Maurits van Nassau
Southern or Spanish Netherlands. *See* Netherlands
Soutman, Pieter, painter, printmaker 153
Spain, 18, 22, 25, 77, 82–83, 99, 116, 134, 168, 188; *105*
Spilberg, Adriana, painter 93–94
Stalpaert, Daniël, architect 62
Steen, Jan 102–104, 140, 197, 204–205, 211–12; *66, 127, 133*
Steenwijck, Hendrick van, painter 114
Steenwijck-Gaspoel, Susanna van, painter 95
Stighelen, Katlijne van der, Belgian art historian 95
Stoter, Cornelis, painter 244
Stuart, House of 109, 210
Suermondt, Barthold, German entrepreneur, art owner 101
Sumowski, Werner, German art historian 130
Sunda, Pedro, African servant of envoy Miguel de Castro 120
Swammerdam, Jan, biologist, microscopist 224
Swanenburg, Agneta van, married to David Bailly 234
Swanenburgh, Isaac Claesz van, officeholder, painter 84; *56*
Sweden, 113–14, 160, 235; *72*
Sweerts, Michael, painter, printmaker 17–18; *8*

T

Talleyrand, French diplomat 136
Taylor, Paul, British art historian 21
Tempel, Abraham van den, painter 84–85; *57*
Terence, Roman playwright 134

Tesselschade Visscher, Maria, poet 95
Theophrastus of Lesbos, Greek philosopher 199
Thielen, Anna van, painter 95
– Francisca Catharina van, painter 95
– Maria Theresia van, painter 95
– Willem, Calvinist clergyman 144–47; *89*
Thoré-Bürger, Théophile, French writer on art 195
Titian 129
Torrentius, Johannes, painter, mystic 231–32; *154*
Trip, Louys and Hendrick, industrialists, art owners 113–14, 189
Tummers, Anna, art historian 21
Turner, William 176

U

Utrecht 52–53, 87–91, 162, 188–89; Centraal Museum 126; chapter of St Mary's 126; painters active in 53, 55, 74, 88–90, 111, 115, 126, 208, 222, 229; patrons and collectors in 87, 126
Uylenburgh, Hendrick, painter, art dealer 67–68

V

Valentiner, Wilhelm, German-American art historian 243
Vasari, Giorgio 14, 148
Vecht River 106
Veen, van, women painters 95
– Otto van, painter, humanist 205
Velazquez, Diego 25
Velde, Adriaen van de, painter 53–54; *34*
– Esaias van de, painter, printmaker 168
– Willem van de, the Elder, painter 24, 40, 53, 114, 167, 175; *12*
– Willem van de, the Younger, painter 24, 40, 53, 114, 167, 175; *26*
Venice 88, 109, 218
Venne, Adriaen van de, painter, writer on art 187–88, 190; *119*

– Jan van de, printer, publisher
187
Verelst, Simon, painter 114
Vermeer, Johannes 9, 19, 53–54,
64, 79, 195, 244; *43, 134*
Victors, Jan, painter 62, 124,
128–30; *41, 81*
Vienna 67, 136, 222;
Kunsthistorisches Museum
67
Vinckboons, David, painter 10,
13; *4, 118*
Virgil 91
Visscher, Anna Roemers, poet,
glass artist 95
– Claes Jansz, printmaker,
publisher 215
– Eva, married to Michiel van
Musscher 151
– Maria Tesselschade Roemers,
poet, glass artist 95
– Roemer, merchant, poet, 214,
219, 232, 235; *140*
Vlieger, Simon de, painter,
printmaker 164; *102*
Vliet, Hendrick van, painter 45,
51, 74, 77; *32*
Vlissingen 120
Vogelaer, Jacob de, city official
190; *121*
– Marcus de, trader 190
Vondel, Joost van den, poet
60, 106
Voorburg 167
Vosmaer, Daniël, painter 79,
236, 243, 246; *51*
– Nicolas, painter 243, 246
Vredeman de Vries, Hans,
architect, painter 45, 59
Vries, Annette de, art historian
189
– Jan de, economic historian 19

W
Walsh, John, American art
historian 164
Wassenaar Obdam, Admiral
Jacob van 51; *32*
Wautier, Michaelina, Flemish
painter 95
Weenix, Jan, painter 106;
68
– Jan Baptist, painter 106
Weller, Dennis, American art
historian 101–102

Werff, Adriaen van der, painter
42, 148; *28*
Wester, Mirjam, museum
curator 95
Weyerman, Jacob Campo,
writer on art 95
Willem I, Count of Holland 70
Willem II, Count of Holland
and Zeeland 42
Willem II, Stadholder 30, 55, 136
Willem III, Stadholder (also
King William III; William
and Mary) 19, 55, 57, 91, 109,
137, 169, 222, 229; *37*
Willem Lodewijk van Nassau-
Dillenburg, Stadholder of
Friesland 82
William of Orange (Willem van
Oranje), Stadholder 51, 55,
77, 82, 179–80, 208; *113, 114*
Withoos, Alida, painter 95
– Maria, painter 95
Witt, Cornelis de, statesman
136–37
– Jan de, statesman 136–37
Witte, Emanuel de, painter 45,
70, 73–74, 77, 182; *48, 115*
Wittel, Caspar van, painter 45,
112; *71*
Wolfsen, Aleida, painter 95, 97
Wolters-van Pee, Henriëtta,
painter 95
Woude, Ad van der, economic
historian 19
Wtenbogaert, Johannes,
Remonstrant clergyman 87
Wtewael, Joachim, painter 89,
124–26; *78*
Wulfraet, Margaretha, painter
95

Z
Zeeland (province) 220
Zeuxis 148
Zoeterwoude 167
Zwiers, Saskia, art historian 91
Zwolle 91–92, 96, 105, 136;
Vrouwenhuis (Women's
House) 97

"This kind of book at this kind of price
is what art publishing should be about"
—*New York Times Book Review*

"An extraordinarily rich and varied series"
—Linda Nochlin

The World of Art series is a comprehensive,
accessible, indispensable companion to the history
of art and its latest developments, covering themes,
artists and movements that span centuries and
the gamut of visual culture around the globe.

You may also like:

William Blake
Kathleen Raine
Introduction by Colin Trodd

Hogarth
David Bindman

Raphael
Paul Joannides

Scottish Art
Murdo Macdonald

Sienese Painting
Timothy Hyman

Velázquez
Richard Verdi

World of Art